An American Strategic Theology

John A. Coleman

PAULIST PRESS   *New York/Ramsey*

Library of Congress
Catalog Card Number: 82-81630

ISBN: 0-8091-2469-6

Published by Paulist Press
545 Island Road, Ramsey, N.J. 07446

Printed and bound in the
United States of America

Acknowledgements
    Chapter 1 was originally written as part of a year-long seminar on "The Church as Mis-
sion," sponsored by The Canon Law Society of America, 1977–1978. It appeared first in *The
Jurist,* Winter 1979. Chapter 2 was initially a paper at a conference on "The Laity in the
Church," at the University of Notre Dame, Spring 1979. It appears as a chapter in Russell
Barta, ed., *Challenge to the Laity* (Huntington, Ind: Sunday Visitor Press, 1980.)Chapter 3
was originally a four-part Lenten series in *The National Catholic Reporter,* Spring 1978.
Chapter 4 was written for the "Theology in the Americas" conference at Detroit, 1975. It
first appeared in *Theological Studies,* March 1976, and is reprinted as a chapter in Leonard
Gilhooley, ed., *No Divided Allegiance: Orestes Brownson and American Thought* (N.Y.: Ford-
ham University Press, 1980). Chapter 5 was also written for the "Theology in the Americas"
conference and appears as a chapter in Sergio Torres and John Eagleson, eds., *Theology in the
Americas* (Maryknoll, N.Y.: Orbis Press, 1976). Chapter 6 was first prepared for a symposium on "The Local Church: The United States Experience," co-sponsored by Perspectives
(Brussels) and Holy Names College, Oakland, California. It appears as a chapter in Irene
Woodward, ed., *The Catholic Church: The United States Experience* (N.Y.: Paulist Press,
1979). Chapter 7 was first given at a symposium on "American Catholicism and the Bicen-
tennial," sponsored by Loyola-Marymount University, Los Angeles. It first appeared in
America, June 26, 1976. Chapter 8 was written for a special edition on American religion of a
French journal, *Revue Francaise d'Etudes Americaines,* Fall 1981. Chapter 9 was developed
for a conference on "Remembering and Reforming: Towards a Constructive Christian Ethics," sponsored by the department of theology, The University of Notre Dame, Spring 1980.
It appears as a chapter in a book by the same name, Stanley Hauwerwas and David Burrell,
eds. (Notre Dame, Indiana: University of Notre Dame Press, 1982). Chapter 10 was originally an address to the National Convention of Catholic Charities, 1976. It appeared as an article in *Charities USA,* November–December 1976. Chapter 11 was first written for Peter
Berger and R. J. Neuhaus' symposium on mediating structures. It appears as a chapter in Jay
Mechling, ed., *Church, State and Public Policy* (Washington, D.C.: American Enterprise Institute, 1979). All of these chapters have been edited and partially rewritten for this volume.
Chapter 12 appears here for the first time. It was originally a Maryknoll lecture at Maryknoll, New York in the winter of 1978. Portions of Chapter 13, which also appears here for

the first time, were originally developed for a conference on "Liberation Theology and North America," sponsored by the department of Latin American Studies, The University of Texas, Austin, Spring 1978. Chapter 14, also new to this volume, owes a debt to a conference on "Political Theology in America," sponsored by the Woodstock Center, Washington, D.C., July 1981. I owe a debt for this book to institutions and persons. Four institutions stand out. The Jesuit School of Theology and the Graduate Theological Union, Berkeley provided forums where I first tested most of the ideas in the book. Chapters 1, 3 and 11 were written during my tenure as a research fellow, The Woodstock Center, Washington, D.C., 1977–78. The introduction and Chapters 8, 12, 13 and 14 as well as the editing and rewriting of each chapter were done during my year as a Woodrow Wilson fellow, The Woodrow Wilson Center for International Scholars at the Smithsonian Institute, Washington, D.C., 1980–81 as part of a larger research project on comparative Catholic Church-society strategies. My yearlong involvement as a member of "The Context of Our Ministries," team for the Jesuit Conference, U.S.A., 1980–1981, informed my writing of Chapters 13 and 14. My intellectual debts to many scholars will be apparent in the footnotes. I want to single out a few whose writings and personal communications have been especially encouraging and helpful: Gregory Baum, Bryan Hehir, Peter Henriot, S.J., Joe Holland, David Hollenbach S.J., David O'Brien and my Jesuit housemate and colleague in Berkeley, Robert J. Egan S.J. I dedicate this volume to two American churchmen who, more than any others, have contributed by their writings, action and example to a distinctively American strategic theology: Msgr. John Egan, Assistant to the President, The University of Notre Dame, and Msgr. George Higgins, emeritus from the United States Catholic Conference.

Contents

Introduction

I want to say something in this introduction about the genesis and genre of this book. Then I will briefly indicate the major themes—theological and sociological—which give it a unity. Finally, I will note how the chapters flow into each other, the structure of the book.

Many of the chapters in this volume were originally written as separate essays. They show the specificity of the contexts and occasions to which they were addressed. Still, over a period of time, I noted how various addresses and essays cohered around certain central themes. I discovered that, after all, unawares I had been writing a book. Friends and editors urged that I collect these essays together both because some of them appeared in less accessible journals or books and because, as an ensemble, they exhibit an argument, a structure and a distinctive approach toward an American strategic theology. Every chapter has been edited and partially rewritten for this volume. The final three appear here for the first time. In the acknowledgements, I purposely indicate the occasion and original date for each chapter. This will permit the reader to note progression in thought over time. It also allows, when the original was a chapter in a collection, comparison with the other contributions.

The genre of this book is practical theology.[1] It is oriented to action, praxis and activation of the Church. Included, as I will note in the themes, are motifs from systematic theology. More particularly, this book is rooted in a long-standing sociological interest in comparative Catholic Church-society relations. The reader will note the prominence accorded to sociological thinkers such as Emile Durkheim, Max Weber, Ernst Troeltsch, Robert N. Bellah and Andrew Greeley. With these giants in the sociology of religion, I am concerned about the sociological pre-conditions for a creative impact of religion on society. As a committed social Catholic, I take seriously the renewed stress in world Catholicism on the Church's mission to justice. In a sense, this book is an attempt at a concrete dialogue between sociology and theology.[2]

1

CENTRAL THEMES

I am going to highlight, briefly, ten central themes or arguments in this book.

1. I assume that, theologically, the Church must exhibit a bi-polar structure. It is simultaneously a *communio* (a community gathered together in response to the revelation about *human* existence in the life, death and resurrection of Jesus) and a *missio,* a sending out to preach the good news to those who have not yet heard it, whether this preaching is through more direct programs of evangelization or through action for justice. While both poles are essential to authentic Church existence, I argue that *missio* takes precedence over *communio.* The Church is gathered precisely for its sending to the world.[3]

I also contend that, characteristically, the Church is always tempted to invert this priority. It pays more attention to inward community and system maintenance than to its primary Gospel mission. Moreover, mission is always to outsiders, to those who have not yet proclaimed Jesus as their and history's Lord. In part, this book is a gentle polemic against the characteristic temptation of religion—and Catholicism in particular—to focus primarily on those already within the fold. The very structure of the Church as *communio* entails, however, an understanding of the Church as a sacrament to the world.[4]

World, in this view, is not simply over against the Church. On one hand, the Church is always in the world, part of a definite sociological context. The Church is always influenced by society. Sometimes it is even determined by it. One needs, therefore—even on theological grounds—to discover the contours of "the world," the context in which the Church actually exists. As the British sociologist of religion, David Martin, notes, "the kingdom language" and the Church which proclaims it—in a comic-tragic dialectic—always *reflects* as well as subverts the world.[5] It mirrors its sociological context even as it stands in judgment on it. On the other hand, world is a theological reality in its own right. For Yahweh, as free Lord and supple spirit, is at work *in the world.* The Church needs, then, to understand its own sociological context, its "world," in order to discern the Lord's "signs of the times."

2. A second theme which unites the chapters of this book is the celebration of a new turn to the "this worldly" and to concern for social structures in international Catholicism. Sacred and profane history are now seen as one history. What humans achieve in history, the structures of justice and community we build, will determine the final contours of the transcendent kingdom of God. Human history is not mere "basket weaving."

I judge that this new turn in international Catholic theology is more faithful to the Scriptures than a simple natural vs. supernatural or time vs. eternity scheme. It is also, potentially, of enormous sociological importance. The pre-conditions for a creative "this-worldly" asceticism, analogous to Max Weber's Protestant ethic, are now available in world

Catholicism and its theology. Already, as studies of the Church in Latin America have shown, this new concern for this-worldly history is having a creative impact on social change, politics and culture.[6]

3. Throughout the book, a dialectic is operative between the need for acculturation and accommodation of the Church to its specific context and the corresponding sense that the Church is transnational in import and serves as a carrier of promises of a messianic future in judgment of every status quo, including the American. The Church, while adapting to context, must also be a locus of alternative visions for society. One of my persistent criticisms in this book of the "Americanizers" in American Catholic history was their failure to provide an alternative vision of America.[7] I applaud their insistence, however, on developing a contextually specific American spirituality and Church order. A perennial danger in all pleas for acculturation—including that of this book—is the loss of a transnational sense or of the conviction that the Church must incarnate alternative visions of community. Chapters 12 and 14 especially address themselves to these two issues.

4. This book represents a dialogue between sociology and theology. I do not think such a dialogue is a luxury. Sociological analysis is a precondition for any reading of the signs of the times or any serious effort at acculturation. It is also an indispensable, integral component—as I argue in Chapter 14—to a "pastoral circle" method of theological reflection in practical theology. Sociology is more than a mere auxiliary discipline for theology. More than presenting "mere data," it includes a conceptual way of looking at the world with which theology must correlate as it does with philosophy. Sociology will help unmask mere ideological rhetoric of the Church. Theology, on its part, can help sociology recognize that it is caught in an inevitable conflict of interpretations.[8] As I have argued elsewhere, the dialogue between theology and sociology is a two-way street.[9]

5. I assume throughout the book that the Church, in any context, is called to embody the universal justice mission of the Gospel. Attention to specific context, while necessary and a decided plea of this book, cannot be allowed to obscure the fact that a contextually specific strategic theology, to be authentic as theology, must intend a strategy for peace and justice. I am wary of attempts to speak of "pluralism" or contextual accommodation which neglect this aspect of a universal mission of the Church to justice. I distrust them as naive celebrations or ideology.[10]

6. Throughout this book, I engage in a dialogue with Latin American liberation theology and political theology in Europe. I do not think that either fits the strategic needs of the American Church, although both are creative in their own contexts and represent one of the most impressive theological achievements in world Catholic theology in the last fifteen years. While I remain critical of both theologies (both in their own context and as export items for North America), I believe that we can also learn from them, not to do precisely the same things in America (often the limits of our context would not allow it even if we wished) but to forge our own

specifically American strategic theology. I fear that attempts at a North American contextual theology which neglect this dialogue run the risk of what Johannes B. Metz calls "tactical provincialism."[11] They also lose the transnational aspect essential to Catholicism in any context. For to be Catholic is to belong to a world Church. As Metz notes, it is by this dialogue between contextually specific theologies that the universal Church will attempt "the reconciliation between the poor and rich churches as a whole, and by so doing make a contribution to our agonizingly riven world."[12] The realities of the third world, its problems of overpopulation, underdevelopment, dependence, are connected to America. We exist as an *imperium,* in consort with Western Europe and Japan and in competition with the Soviet bloc, in an interdependent world. Our actions—not alone, of course—effect outcomes and determine possibilities in the third world. The third world churches are part of the one Church to which American Catholicism remains an integral branch.

8. I assert, in this book, that American Catholics have failed to achieve a "concrete historical ideal" which would address the real social, cultural and political movements of our context. In that sense, we lack a strategic theology. Chapters 13 and 14 represent more a program *toward* an American strategic theology than a deliverance of an achieved result.

9. One of the themes which weaves together these essays is my conviction that the privatization of religion, its relegation to the peripheries of American institutional life, is a genuine American danger.[13] While the public possibilities of religion for both culture and society seem to be greater in America than in Europe (although less than in Latin America), I feel that Americans should be attentive to Johannes B. Metz's protest, on Gospel grounds, to this privatization.[14] In Chapter 9 I argue that privatization of religion is also a danger to the vitality of American culture and its sense of community.

10. Another conviction in this book, perhaps most strongly stated in Chapter 2, is that the entire Church is magistral. Especially in matters of the Church's worldly address and on issues of a theology of culture, the hierarchy has to "consult the laity." Indeed, I argue there that the specific area of practical theology is primarily a lay prerogative.

This book is structured into three main sections. Part I, *Foundations* (Chapters 1 and 2), presents the major theological warrants and sociological conditions for a Church with a worldly mission. Part II, *Dialogue with Political and Liberation Theology,* consists of Chapters 3 through 6. This section, while taking seriously both liberation and political theology, tries to show some of the internal weaknesses of both. It also points out some specifically American resources, both theological (Chapter 4) and wider cultural resources (Chapter 5) for an American Gospel of justice and peace. Since in our context a one-sided Catholic strategy is impossible, Chapter 5 (and, in a different way, Chapter 9) point beyond American Catholicism to wider American religion. Part III, *The American Context,* consists of Chapters 7 through 14. It includes chapters offering a sociological interpretation of American Catholicism (Chapters 7 and 8), chapters on American religious realities (Chapters 9 and 10) and chapters more specifically dealing with strategies for a voluntary Church in the American context (Chapters 13 and 14).

One weakness in this book is that it does not attend enough to American economic and cultural realities. It is perhaps biased by the fact that my specialty in sociology is sociology of religion.[15] These essays are offered as a first step and partial contribution to a debate about an authentically American Catholic strategic theology.

NOTES

1. For the notion "practical theology" and its distinction from and relation to fundamental and systematic theology, cf. David Tracy, *The Analogical Imagination: Christian Theology and the Culture of Pluralism* (New York: Crossroad Books, 1981), pp. 62–79.

2. For a good collection of essays furthering the dialogue between sociology and theology, cf. Gregory Baum, ed., *Sociology and Human Destiny* (New York: Seabury, 1980). Included is my chapter, "The Renewed Covenant: Religion and Society in the Thought of Robert N. Bellah," which broaches the issue of dialogue with theology from the sociological side.

3. Cf. Roger Haight, S.J., "Mission: The Symbol for Understanding the Church Today," *Theological Studies,* 1976, pp. 620–49.

4. For a development of the Church as sacrament to the world, cf. Edward Schillebeeckx, *The Mission of the Church* (New York: Seabury, 1973).

5. David Martin, *The Dilemmas of Contemporary Religion* (Oxford: Basil Blackwells, 1979), p. 17.

6. For two representative social science studies of the Church and politics in Latin America, cf. Daniel Levine, ed., *Churches and Politics in Latin America* (Beverly Hills, Cal.: Russell Sage Publications, 1979), and Daniel Levine, *Religion and Politics in Latin America: Colombia and Venezuela* (Princeton: Princeton University Press, 1981).

7. One treatment of the Americanizers can be found in Gerald Fogarty, S.J., *The Vatican and the Americanist Crisis: Denis J. O'Connell, American Agent in Rome* (Rome: Gregorian University Press, 1974). That the Americanizers lacked a distinctive alternative vision of America is the thesis of Alfred Ede, *A Catholic Quest for a Christian America,* unpublished dissertation, The Graduate Theological Union, Berkeley, 1977.

8. The failure of Latin American liberation theology to assess "the conflict of interpretations" in its use of sociology is one of my criticisms in Chapter 14 of this volume. For this conflict, cf. William Sullivan and Paul Rabinow, eds., *Interpretive Sociology* (Berkeley: University of California Press, 1979).

9. Cf. my "Theology and Sociology," in *The Proceedings of the Catholic Theological Society of America,* 1977, pp. 55–72.

10. This is apparent in the uncritical retrieval of American traditions and the failure to engage in dialogue with other sectors of the world Church in the collec-

tion, focused on pluralism in America, *Towards a North American Theology: Working Papers,* Daniel Flaherty, ed. (Chicago: University of Loyola Press, 1981), limited edition.

11. Cf. Johannes B. Metz, *The Emergent Church* (New York: Crossroad Books, 1981), p. 71.

12. *Ibid.,* p. 11.

13. I treat the issue of the privatization of religion, distinguish this from a "secularization" thesis in sociology and argue that privatization is an apt description of the contemporary situation in my "The Situation for Faith," *Theological Studies,* December 1978, pp. 601–32.

14. Cf. Johannes B. Metz, *Theology of the World* (N.Y.: Herder and Herder, 1969) and *Faith, History and Society: Towards a Practical Fundamental Theology* (New York: Crossroad Books, 1980).

15. For a more ample treatment of economic and cultural themes cf. *The Context of Our Ministries* (Washington, D.C.: Jesuit Conference, 1981) of which I am one of the co-authors.

Part One

FOUNDATIONS

Chapter One

The Church's Mission to Justice

The World Synod of Bishops charted a major new direction in the self-understanding of the mission of the Church in its 1971 document, "Justice in the World," when it proclaimed: "Action on behalf of justice and participation in the transformation of the world fully appear to us as a constitutive dimension of the preaching of the Gospel or, in other words, of the Church's mission for the redemption of the human race and its liberation from every oppressive situation."[1]

This statement flows from several new insights in theology. Among these are the conviction that human history and the definitive reign of God ("the kingdom") converge at critical points such that the kingdom is both a goal *within* and the end *of* history.[2] Moreover, renewed attention to the social consequences of sin—sin's congealment in structures of injustice and oppression—alerted the bishops to the reality of a "social sin" which is not removed by mere personal conversion of heart. As the synod states it, there exists "a network of domination, oppression, and abuses which stifle freedom and which keeps the greater part of humanity from sharing in the building up and enjoyment of a more just and more fraternal world."[3]

Liberation from structures of injustice is increasingly seen as both the pre-condition of evangelization and its effective consequence.[4] For the Church's mission to liberation from structural sin is paramount to the credibility of the Gospel's proclamation of a new creation in Christ. Moreover, the freeing of freedom in human society, while not removing the possibility of sin, is a prerequisite to that freedom which alone can embrace the redemption offered in Christ.[5]

I am mainly concerned with the theological warrants for the Church's mission on behalf of justice and the political purposes and styles congruent with that mission. For reasons of organization, I will take a clue from William Temple's book, *Christianity and the Social Order,* and ask: (1) By what right does the Church intervene in the political/economic social order? (theological warrants for action on behalf of justice) and (2) How should the Church intervene? (purposes and styles of Church action for justice).[6]

9

I. BY WHAT RIGHT DOES THE CHURCH INTERVENE?

I want to consider four theological warrants for the Church's intervention in the social, economic, and political orders.

1. The mission of the Church is grounded in God the Father's moral purposes for creation and the mission of the Son and Spirit to the world. Those purposes and missions intend the creation, sustenance, and eventual eschatological transformation of a this-worldly community of justice.

2. Politics and economics display, at their depths, a religious dimension. The Church is called to discern and proclaim the presence and action of God wherever he is at work. To deny God's presence and action to the political and economic orders is to deny his lordship and sovereign freedom.

3. The unity of love of God and neighbor announced by the Christian Gospel demands attention to issues of economic and political justice.

4. Action on behalf of justice is a constitutive element of evangelization.

As we will see, these four warrants not only ground the right of the Church to intervene in the social order, they also set, to some extent, the style of that intervention.

A. The Church as an Agent of God's Purposes

The Purposes of the Father

The mission of the Church is rooted in the moral purposes of the Father for creation and the mission of the Son and Spirit. The Church, then, is properly understood as "an agent of God's purposes."[7] Its mission is continuous with the mission of Jesus and the Spirit. While the Scriptures do not speak of a mission of the Father—for the Father is not sent—he comes of his own accord into the world. The Father is actively present to his creation both calling and enabling us to share in his purposes. As Saint Paul says, "God was in Christ restoring the world to himself" (2 Corinthians 5:19). Paul also speaks of the Father's active coming into the world, "cheering those who are discouraged" (2 Corinthians 7:6), "raising us up" (2 Corinthians 5:14), "giving us life and freedom" (2 Corinthians 3:16), and "comforting and strengthening us in our hardships and trials" (2 Corinthians 1:4). Indeed, our own mission, just as that of Jesus, comes from the Father. "It is this God who has made you and me into faithful Christians and commissioned us apostles to preach the good news" (2 Corinthians 1:21).

The primary purpose of the Father for creation is the bringing into being, sustenance, restoration when broken, and eschatological completion of a covenant community whose main characteristics are peace (*shalom*) and justice (*sedequah*). Moreover, the community of *shalom* or fidelity and healthy covenant relationship to God and neighbor is rooted in justice.[8]

This covenant community is inaugurated, restored, and transmuted in history, in and through social events such as the mass migration of nomadic workers in the exodus, wars, diplomatic initiatives, and the exile. It is also ushered in through structural institutions of the law, prophecy and priesthood, kingship, and courts. Moreover, both the creation accounts and the Noah story as well as the prophetic announcements of eschatological restoration of the broken covenant community show that God intends a universal this-worldly covenant of justice beyond the ethnic confines of Israel.

It is clear that the primary purpose of God for creation is the sharing of his own justice with a community gathered by him. In intent that community includes all of humanity and every nation. For the Father is himself just and calls all of humanity, through his special call to Israel, to relate to each other after the pattern of his own justice and fidelity. As justice is his primary attribute, so justice is his prime demand. "And I will make justice the line and righteousness the plummet" (Isaiah 28:17). The touchstone of true worship of Yahweh is that justice is done to those who have least resources or position to vindicate their own cause: widows, orphans, the poor, alien migrant workers, foreigners in the land (cf. Amos 5:21–24; Isaiah 58). Role relations in the community are conceived after the pattern of God's justice (king-people; judge-adjudicants; family-tribe; community toward the resident alien and suffering in their midst).

Yahweh reveals his own being as the one who is compassionate toward the oppressed and suffering and, himself, their vindicator (cf. Deuteronomy 10:18; Psalm 82; Exodus 22:21–22). Indeed, in the most central Old Testament revelation of Yahweh's own name and being, Yahweh tells his people that he is the one whose purpose is the vindication of injustice by the creation of a just community. "I have seen the affliction of my people who are in Egypt and have heard their cry because of their taskmasters. I know their suffering and have come down to deliver them out of the hand of the Egyptians" (Exodus 3:7–8). Moreover, it is only by effectively doing justice, especially toward those to whom justice is being systematically denied, that one even knows Yahweh. "Woe to him who builds his house by unrighteousness and his upper rooms by injustice. Did not your father eat and drink and do justice and righteousness? Then it was well with him. He judged the cause of the poor and needy. Then it was well. Is this not to know me? says the Lord" (Jeremiah 22:15–16).

In every strand of the Old Testament tradition, God's action on behalf of justice and his purposes for creating a community of nations through Israel as his instrument, which would model his own justice, appear. History is seen to exhibit a meaning and unity because there is an ultimate *sovereignty* in history, Yahweh, the Lord of the nations (Jeremiah 18:7). Within history an *ultimate norm* for political and economic action is also revealed: equality, inclusion of those who have been excluded, and justice to those who have no voice. Finally, there is an *ultimate hope* for history because Yahweh keeps history open to new possibilities and promise. As James Muilenberg has put it, "We see then that the faith that persists throughout all historical events and records is that God controls and disposes over history, orders and rules it in his ways and calls persons to responsibility in it. . . . History is the word of God actualizing itself in events."[10] As Muilenberg's summation of biblical faith and ethics makes clear, the justice of Yahweh is both gift and call, for God, through a choice of self-limitation which respects human freedom, acts through secondary causes such as prophets, just people, and even non-believers such as "Cyrus, my servant" (Isaiah 41:2). Just people know Yahweh as, reciprocally, Yahweh knows them. For there is a God who lives in justice.

Nor is God's call for justice restricted merely to a conversion of the heart. For he calls for just institutions, the avoidance of class legislation, and impartiality in the administration of justice.[11] As an agent of God's purposes, first Israel and then the Church as the new Israel are called to work for justice in human relationships and structures. If it does not do so it will neither know Yahweh nor worship him in truth. For those who condemn or mistrust active engagement by the Church for justice as a "secular" betrayal of transcendent values, John R. Donohue's remark is apt: "Engagement in the quest for justice is not more 'secular' than the engagement of Yahweh in the history of his people or the incarnation of Jesus into the world of human suffering."[12]

The Mission of the Son

In a New Testament perspective Jesus is sent by the Father into the world as the proclaimer of God's promised messianic kingdom of justice and peace. Jesus is proleptically that kingdom as he is the new Israel, the truly just one who is the parable of God's redeeming justice. He gathers together a community of disciples who are to pattern their life and relationships after him. But Jesus uncompromisingly patterns his own relationships on God's covenant love of mercy (*hesed*) and justice.[13]

In the Synoptic tradition, Jesus is portrayed as the sacrament of God's justice.[14] In the famous last judgment scene of Matthew 25, for example, Jesus rather than Yahweh sits in judgment. But his criterion of judgment is continuous with the Old Testament revelation of Yahweh as the one who identifies himself with a vindicating justice for the poor, the oppressed and marginal members of the community. This episode states that to know Jesus we must do justice and that he, in turn, will know and recognize as his own all—and only—those who do justice. The kingdom that Jesus preaches is to find a home among the poor (Matthew 5:3) and the persecuted (Matthew 5:4). Only with difficulty will the rich enter it (Mark 10:23).

In Luke, Jesus assumes the prophetic mantle of justice in his first sermon in the synagogue (Luke 4:16–21). Throughout he shows conspicuous compassion toward widows (Luke 7:11–15; 18:2–5; 21:1–3) and the stranger in the land (Luke 10:30–37), thus doing Yahweh's justice. Luke avoids any spiritualization of poverty in the Sermon on the Mount. Moreover, he has Jesus praise Zacchaeus because he gives half of his wealth to the poor (Luke 19:8–10). The exorcisms of Jesus show his confrontation with and victory over the powers of evil and are signs that the kingdom has come upon us (Luke 11:20). In Acts, Luke portrays the early Church as continuous with the prophetic mission of Jesus. Its members held all things in common and sold their possessions and distributed them to all, as any had need (Acts 4:32–35).

In his book on the social ethics of Jesus, John Howard Yoder, drawing heavily on Lucan material, argues that Jesus' essentially religious mission had profound political overtones and impact.[15] While Jesus was not himself a member of the party of Zealots, who sought direct political revolution, he drew Zealots to himself as disciples. Indeed, Jesus was crucified, a death usually reserved to political insurrectionists. Clearly some of those who heard his preaching thought that his message pertained to a political kingdom and wished to make him a king (see John 6:15). They understood well the political implications of Jesus' preaching but misunderstood his special religio-political style of non-violent truth-telling and service.

Yoder argues persuasively that Jesus' social ethic was political and economic. Thus, Jesus' preaching contains political allusions—for example, the reference to the tower which fell at Siloam, a tower built by Pilate through stealing of temple funds, parables which thinly veiled allusions to Herod's rash warfare and building projects. Moreover, in announcing the reign of God, Jesus saw himself as inaugurating the jubilee year which called for the remission of all debts (the "forgive us our debts as we forgive our debtors" of the Our Father) as well as the redistribution of capital ("Go and sell all you have and give the money to the poor": Luke 18:22). The political implications of this message did not elude Jesus' hearers, both disciples and enemies.

Jesus did not so much renounce power as demand that power be exercised in the service of justice and the needy. As Yoder sees it, Jesus' strategy of courageous truth-telling, renunciation of violence, and appeal to the vision of justice of the jubilee year had profound political implications for the Palestinian social order such that Jesus was put to death on political charges. Jesus does not abandon the political order to its own devices but seeks to transform politics into an order of truth-telling, justice, and service. His disciples are to expect the cross as their lot since they too will be seen as disturbers of the political-social order if they follow Jesus in non-violent truth-telling.

Three theological themes emerge from the Gospel accounts which pertain to both the warrant and style of the Church's mission on behalf of justice: the kingdom, discipleship and incarnation. The kingdom as the reign of God in the Old Testament closely joined Yahweh's rule and the firm establishment of justice (Psalms 97:1-2; 96:10). In the apocalyptic literature of the inter-testamental period the Messiah was expected to usher in the definitive period of God's justice. There is no question that Jesus subsumed these Old Testament notions of justice in his appeals to the symbol of the kingdom.[16] While the Church is not identical with God's reign of justice, it is a unique agent of God's purposes to establish the kingdom, for the disciples are to preach and do what Jesus did (see John 13:13–15). Moreover, the kingdom intends an ingathering of a community larger than the Church which remains merely a leaven in a larger mass. It is evident that the Gospels, in their horizon of realized eschatology, foresee a kingdom which is to be incarnate in history no less than the proclaimer of the kingdom, Jesus, was incarnate in history.

Immediately after his proclamation of the kingdom, Jesus called disciples to himself. They were to preach, heal, and confront evil just as he did (Mark 3:13). They are called to pattern their relationships after the example of Jesus, eschewing power-seeking to become the servants of all and giving their life for others (Mark 10:35–45). Like Jesus they are called to non-violent truth-telling in the service of God's justice. Their "political" style is to mirror his—respect for truth; care for and bias toward those who have no voice or are marginal in society; the renunciation of manipulative or violent means which undermine freedom. Church politics, then, if exercised in discipleship, are not "politics as usual."

Finally, the principle of the incarnation means that the Church's action for justice must be credibly inserted into the ongoing "secular" struggles for justice. As Jose Miguez Bonino has put it, "there is no such thing as a Christianity outside of or above its concrete temporal incarnations."[17] In some senses, the Church's mission toward justice cannot in fact be simply above culture, politics, or the ongoing struggles for justice. As an institutional actor in the social order, the Church cannot avoid being a political force in the "secular" order, although it may choose to be "political" in a special style befitting its call to discipleship. Clearly, also, as a group called to follow Jesus, the parable of God's justice, the Church cannot avoid its political, economic, and social responsibilities. For the justice it preaches is not its own but Christ's.

The shadow side of this law of concrete temporal incarnation means that Church people are often largely defined by their social location and place in history. Indeed, they are "in need of the protests made by people at other social locations, especially the oppressed, to recognize that their own perspective is limited and even marred by their own privileges. Theologians then discover that not only theology but preaching and piety have a social location; they usually reflect the culture of this location and protect the existing political order. Religion is inevitably political even if religious people are wholly unconscious of this. Unless religion becomes self-critical, it is the bearer of ideological elements."[19] The Church cannot, any less than Jesus, escape history and the concrete political struggles for justice, although it may be wise for the institutional Church usually to choose to be present to these struggles in less than a directly partisan way. Since it is not Yahweh or Jesus, its discernment of God's justice and political horizon will turn it inward in critique of its own ideological cooperation by structures or forces of injustice as well as outward in prophetic telling forth of the truth about injustice in the world and concrete engagement for a more just society.

For Paul, Jesus can be called quite simply "the justice of God" (1 Corinthians 1:30; Romans 1:17). Paul views Jesus as doing battle with "the rulers of this age" (1 Corinthians 2:6–8). He sees this age as held by a captive power, structures of death and injustice. The fight is against "the evil rulers of the unseen world, those mighty satanic beings and great evil princes of darkness who rule this world" (Ephesians 6:12).[20]

We find in Paul a tension between a realized eschatology which proclaims that in Jesus' death and resurrection the new age has begun and an eschatalogical reservation which suggests that Christ's victory over sin and death is not yet complete.[21] This tension between realization of the kingdom and an eschatological reservation is found, among other places, in Romans 8:23: "We ourselves who have the first fruits of the spirit groan inwardly as we wait for adoption as sons, the redemption of our bodies." Paul repeatedly appeals to this tension in his ethics which combines, rhetorically, the indicative and imperative, gift and command. Christians have been gifted with the free grace of God's own justice which makes them free. They are called, then, to preach this justice and do battle, with Christ, against the powers and structures of sin, death, and injustice in the fight to usher in the new age.

John R. Donohue has suggested that this eschatological position of Paul provides both a warrant for Christian action on behalf of justice and a style of Christian realism and critical objectivity for that engagement:

Paul's eschatology suggests a Christian response to being in the world. On the one hand, if the world is still under the reign of sin and death, a prophetic stance of opposition to these powers is demanded. Such a stance demands an accurate diagnosis of what the powers are in contemporary experience. Along with the prophetic stance is an eschatological stance which sees that the quest for realization of God's saving justice is always held in hope and anticipation. Paul sees the world in process of transformation and Christians as co-workers in the process. However, precisely because the world is in process, is "groaning," no one crystallization of God's saving justice will be adequate, nor will any system ever be the final system. To hope to find a total incarnation of God's saving justice at any one time would, in Pauline terms, turn gift into law. The Christian who reflects on Paul's eschatology will realize that the quest for justice always operates between prophecy and vision, between realization and hope.[22]

As Paul's doctrine of the new age parallels the synoptic tradition on the kingdom, so his theology of discipleship is in continuity with the Gospels. The disciple is the one who accepts in faith God's free gift of justice (cf. Romans 3:22; Philippians 3:9; Galatians 2:16). Disciples are "in Christ," putting on Christ and having his mind. That mind is made clear in Paul's famous apostrophe to Christ's attitude of service: ". . . who, though he was God, did not demand and cling to his rights as God, but laid aside his mighty power and glory, taking the disguise of a slave and becoming like men. And he humbled himself even further, going so far as actually to die a criminal's death on the cross" (Philippians 2:5–8). Disciples are to mirror in their lives this self-sacrificing love of Christ. Like Christ disciples bear the burdens of the weak and do not seek to please themselves (Romans 15:2–7).

Paul sees the redeeming purpose of Christ as a reconciliation of conflicting groups in the creation of a new community where membership transcends all race, sex, class, nationality, or social custom. "In this new life one's nationality or race or education or social position is unimportant. Such things mean nothing. Whether a person has Christ is what matters and he is equally available to all" (Colossians 3:11; see Galatians 3:28 and 1 Corinthians 12:13). Indeed, reconciliation is a title of the Pauline Christ, for "Christ himself has been made our reconciliation" (Ephesians 2:14). The disciples are to participate in this unitive and reconciliatory work of Christ by being converted, in faith, to the mind of Christ which is an attitude of self-sacrificing love. Disunity, conflicts, and quarrels among believers are a scandal to the unity of the one body of Christ.

This ideal of unity and peace has been a constant theme of Christian discipleship and preaching through the ages. Sometimes, however, we advocate an ideal of reconciliation in the Christian community that overlooks the differences between people produced by unjust inequalities. But the unity willed by Christ of which Paul speaks is a unity based on conversion to the mind of Christ and the acceptance of God's justice. As Gregory Baum has noted, an ideal of unity, "separated from the demands of justice, is an ideology that protects the dominant groups and their power and makes the people at the bottom submissive. The grave injustices in society cannot be forgiven and forgotten; they must be changed. The only unity that is in accordance with God's will is unity in justice, and in a sinful world this demands a significant shift in power relations. Reconciliation between various parties implies the conversion of all, and this demands on the part of some the restitution of excessive power and undue privilege."[23] As Saint Paul puts it, "God is both kind and severe. He is very hard on those who disobey but very good to you if you continue to love and trust him" (Romans 11:22). The Church can be no less so! Nevertheless, the Christian ideal of reconciliation provides a brake on certain styles of conflict which do not intend an ultimate unity as the goal of conflict or respect the already given unity between parties to the conflict, a unity based on the equal dignity of all humans.

In a profoundly moving and beautiful sermon on justice, Meister Eckhart sums up the way that the mission of the Church on behalf of justice is rooted in the mission of the Son:

A Just man is one who is
conformed and transformed into justice!
The just man lives in God
And God in him! . . .
The Father begets his Son as the just one,
and the just one as his Son.
For all the virtue of the just
is nothing but this:
that the Son
is begotten of the Father.
Therefore the Father
is never at rest
but always hastens
and rushes to the end
that his Son may be born in me. . . .
In the just
nothing shall work but God alone.[24]

To know Christ and Yahweh is to be transformed into justice and never to be at rest but to hasten and rush to the end that God's justice be born in the world.

The Mission of the Spirit

It will not be my purpose in this chapter to develop a full theology of the mission of the Holy Spirit.[25] I am mainly concerned with how the mission of the Spirit throws light on the warrant and style of the Church's mission to justice. The Spirit which is the promised gift of the Father is also called the Spirit of Christ. Indeed, it both searches out and shows us all of God's deepest secrets and purposes (1 Corinthians 2:10), which we have seen in his plan to share life by creating a true community of justice. Again, no one can know Yahweh as Father except in the Spirit (Galatians 4:6). But to know Yahweh is to do justice.

In the Old Testament foreshadowing of the Spirit of God as an external personification of Yahweh, it was mainly understood as the source of prophecy and forthright truth-telling. This same motif is taken up in the New Testament when to the Spirit is attributed bold preaching of the Gospel (see Acts 4:31; 1 Corinthians 2:13). The Spirit is also seen as the source of new missionary strategies. It prompts Philip to approach the Ethiopian eunuch (Acts 8:29), indicates to Peter that the Gentiles are accepted (Acts 10:45), and later moves the whole Church to turn toward mission to the Gentiles and to rescind the Jewish law (Acts 15:8 and 15:27). It was the Spirit who led Paul to go to Seleucia (Acts 13:4). It is, then, no great extension of this motif to see the Spirit in the Church as the source of "reading the signs of the times" in terms of new strategies of combating structural sin and injustice, for, as Paul states it, it is in the power of the life-giving

Spirit that we are finally freed from the vicious circle of sin and death (Romans 8:2).

Moreover, the Spirit who is called "the comforter" is a source of hope in discouragement in struggles for God's justice (see Romans 15:13). In discipleship to Christ in the Spirit the Church is that community on earth which is never allowed to lose hope in the human project or in the possibilities for human society. For the Spirit is the guarantee and first installment of the fundamental Christian hope in the resurrection. But the resurrection is both individual and communal. Indeed, as the eschatological completion of God's promised kingdom, the resurrection is *primarily* communal (see 2 Thessalonians 1:10). In a persuasive analogy, Jose Miguez Bonino has argued that human history is related to the eschatological kingdom of God just as our mortal bodies are related to the "spiritual, heavenly bodies" (see 1 Corinthians 15:46), of the resurrection. There will be both continuities in identity and radical transformation. As Miguez Bonino states it, "The kingdom is not the denial of history but the elimination of its corruptibility, its frustrations, weakness, ambiguity—more deeply its sin—in order to bring to full realization the true meaning of the communal life of man."[26] The Holy Spirit as the foretaste of this transformation of bodily communal history into "the glorious freedom from sin" groans within history and is at work toward that end. Hence, Christians should never lose hope in the struggle for God's justice since the Spirit is the guarantee that justice will ultimately prevail and that, even now, it is breaking through in history.

In Pauline theology, in continuity with Old Testament understandings, the Spirit is seen as the radical source of diverse gifts and charisms. We are told not to despise the variety of gifts or quench the Spirit by trying to reduce them to a uniformity or law. But the varieties of gifts are bestowed toward the end of building up one mutual body (see 1 Corinthians 11, 12, 13). Those who act upon class-based biases or neglect and despise the dignity of the poor in their midst quench the Spirit and bring judgment on themselves. Indeed, they trifle with the death of Christ because they do not recognize the body of the Lord (1 Corinthians 11:27–30) whose source of living unity is the Spirit. Again, Paul asserts that social injustices which break the true sense of community (lying, stealing, etc.) cause sorrow to the Spirit (see Ephesians 4:30). By a profound intuition of Christian piety, the author of the *Veni, Sancte Spiritus* understood this theology well when he hailed the Spirit as "the father of the poor." For the body of Christ in the world—a body which by the universal salvific intent of Christ is ultimately coterminous with the world—can only be built up into a living unity if we bear one another's burdens and, like Christ, show partiality toward the most burdened, the poor and voiceless in our midst.

In Galatians, Paul stresses the aspect of freedom from the law or absolute norms for those who walk in the Spirit. For where the Spirit is, there is freedom (2 Corinthians 3:17). The gifts of the Spirit do not, of course, provide us with a political program for justice. They do, however, supply direction—giving touchstones to judge the style of involvement: love, joy, peace, patience, kindness, goodness, gentleness, and self-control (Galatians 5:22). Moreover, these are contrasted with attitudes which are inimical to the Spirit's prompting: "hatred and fighting, jealousy and anger, constant effort to get the best for yourself, complaints and criticisms, the feeling that everyone else is wrong except those in your own little group" (Galatians 5:20).

In summary, then, the mission of the Spirit grounds the Church's mission toward justice as an indispensable prerequisite to building up the body of Christ in the world and sets directions for the style of the Church's engagement. The ultimate goal of strategies of justice is true reconciliation and the building up of a unity based on justice and truth. However, in the face of sin, an intermediate goal may include conflict, even bold confrontation. The style of ministries of justice must respect the multiple gifts in the Church and freedom of conscience in the Spirit. It will neither lay heavy "guilt trips" nor coerce members of the Church to one concrete strategy of pursuing justice as some "new laws." It biases Christians toward the cause of the weak and defenseless members of the body and to non-violent strategies respectful of freedom. Nevertheless, it exhibits a boldness and tenacity of purpose in the pursuit of justice. For the Spirit provides that "mighty inner strengthening" (Ephesians 3:16) without which we might grow discouraged in the struggles for the kingdom. If the Spirit's mission is to lead us to where the Father and Son are, it will lead us inexorably to the poor. For the Father and Son are pre-eminently to be found and known in the causes and needs of the poor.

The fundamental mission of the Church is that, having accepted a share in the life of the Trinitarian God, it proclaims the new reality that it experiences in this life and invites all of humanity to join in this experience. But the life of the Trinity in this world has a threefold purpose: justice, peace, and the liberation of all those who are oppressed as the means of a community of life with the trinitarian God. The revelation of trinitarian life is the Church's primary warrant for action on behalf of justice as it is the primary warrant for the Church's mission. The non-violent style of the Trinity and its life of unity respectful of differences gives directional clues to the Church for its style of ministry for justice. It does not, however, directly provide a program or concrete strategy.

B. God as the Depth Dimension of the Political, Economic and Social Orders

The Hebraeo-Christian commitment to a radical monotheism ascribes ultimate sovereignty to God over all nations, times, and institutions. No society or institution of society escapes his scrutiny, judgment, active sustaining presence, and care. There are no totally autonomous "lords" or "enclaves" within nature or history, else God ceases to be fully Lord. Of course, God's choice of self-limitation and his transcendent causality, which works in and through secondary causes, i.e., mediations of nature and human freedom, in such a way that he is not one other cause or agent equally ranged with other causes, allow for a relative autonomy of agents and institutions in the order of creation.[27]

Nevertheless, to carve out institutional spheres of life as "sacrally secular" enclaves untouched by God's action and purpose is a species of idolatry. The Church, then, can and must presume that, at its depth, there is a sacral dimension to politics, economics, and the social order. Indeed, it is called today to an especial effort to make this apparent since the systematic exclusion of religion from politics and economics in post-industrial societies and the concomitant taming of the religious by relegating it to the private sphere have eclipsed this truth both for non-believers and Christians alike.

Moreover, as Langdon Gilkey has demonstrated in a recent penetrating phenomenological and ontological analysis of politics, political issues, when pursued to their deepest ground, involve a religious dimension. For the political order is woven out of power, and power, as Tillich argues, is essentially the power to be and the concomitant power to continue secure and expand in being and freedom. Individuals find in their political societies and groups extensions of their own desires to be, to be secure, and to expand in being. Groups vying for power are motivated by the "quest for continuance and expansion of being."[28] The deepest rooted political fears point to a horror of fatedness to permanent exclusion from participation in power on the part of some groups or fears of a waning and extinction of power on the part of others. Political hopes are premised on the as-yet-unrealized possibilities of rearranging power in ways which expand the individual and group's power to be, to be secure in being and expand. Hence, "the deepest question of ordinary political experience has, then, a religious dimension. It is religious because on the one hand it points to the religious fear of fate and to the religious promise of a universal destiny, to a sovereignty that can conquer fate and to the hope for authentic history."[29]

Similarly, every political community is concerned with achieving a "sacred canopy" of legitimation which, by sacralizing its own relative and culture-bound choices and behaviors, wards off threats to its being, continuance, and expansion, and encapsulates serious dissent and critique of existing arrangements of power.[30] From one point of view, political communities are communities of shared meaning and discourse—"plausibility structures" in Peter Berger's phrase—which provide meaning to the processes of everyday political exchanges of power, wealth and status. Political legitimation systems are, of course, sometimes ideologies, i.e., masks for injustice. Even relatively non-ideological legitimation systems, however, come under attack because they are in competition with alternative political world views and discriminate against some groups within society which are excluded from full or equal access to the power centers. Hence, at some point the meaning of political meaning systems and the legitimacy of any given legitimation system for the political order get raised as a question. But at base these are questions which can only be answered by penetrating to "the religious question of a *logos* or system of ultimate meanings in history."[31]

Yet, as Robert Bellah has argued, no society is the final repository or arbiter of its own meaning nor is it its own ultimate norm for community. As he puts it, "Since history reveals the inadequacy of every empirical society, it becomes clear that society no more than the individual is a final repository of transcendence. Rather every society is itself forced to appeal to some higher jurisdiction, to justify itself not entirely on its actual performance but through its commitment to unrealized goals or values. The kind of symbolism that societies develop to indicate their commitment to higher values and define their legitimacy itself varies in historical perspective. But there is no society that can avoid such symbolism."[32] As with the question of ultimate sovereignty and an ultimate meaning, the understanding and grounding of societal normative systems push us to "the quest for an ultimate norm for man and community in history."[33] It was not by chance that the great founders of sociology in the nineteenth century—Weber, Tonnies, Simmel, Durkheim—were all preoccupied with the study of religion as the basis for a stable social order. They knew all too well that questions of ultimate norms lay just below the surface in understanding any empirically-given sovereignty, meaning system and normative structure.[34]

In some respects, politics touches the religious dimension more closely than economics. For, as Joseph Gremillion has noted, "politics is more deeply rooted in human interiority than economics."[35] But even economics calls for a moral and religious interpretation. As Lord Keynes wrote to Archbishop William Temple in response to Temple's manuscript for *Christianity and the Social Order,* in economics "there are practically no issues of policy as distinct from technique which do not involve ethical considerations."[36]

If the Church, then, is to be faithful to its stance of radical monotheism and avoid complicity in the modern idolatry of the isolation of politics and economics from the moral and religious sphere, the Church must be closely present to the "secular" political and economic orders. For the Church cannot accept that these orders are ultimately "secular," unrelated to the lordship of God over all creation. In these spheres, too, God is active, creating, sustaining, judging, renewing, and preparing for the final transformation of creation in Christ. The Church is called to discern and proclaim the action of God wherever he is at work. But God must clearly be at work in those institutional spheres which most affect the lives of people and determine the shape of history: politics and economics. The Church's involvement for political and economic justice is far from a sellout to the horizontally secular. Its failure to be actively engaged in these spheres would be an idolatry, the effective denial of God's ultimate sovereignty.

The Unity of Love of God and Neighbor
and Action for Justice in Economic and Political Systems

Central to the Gospel tradition is the replacement of the complex set of Jewish laws by a single new commandment of love (see John 13:34). In the Synoptics, a teacher of the law approached Jesus with the question about which of the commandments is most important. Jesus replied, "This one that says, 'Hear, O Israel! The Lord our God is the one and only God. And you must love him with all your heart and soul and mind and strength.' The second is: 'You must love others as much as yourself.' No other commandments are greater than these" (Mark 12:29–31). When the teacher agreed that these two are more important than offering all kinds of sacrifices at the temple, Jesus said to him, "You are not far from the kingdom of God" (Mark 12:34).

The love commandment not only embraces both the love of God and neighbor, it unifies the two. In his precision upon the love commandment, the author of the First Epistle of John shows how the love of neighbor is the touchstone for love of God: "For though we have never yet seen God, when we love each other God lives in us and his love within us grows ever stronger" (1 John 4:12). As there is a God who lives in justice, so there is a God who lives in love. Again: "If anyone says 'I love God' but keeps on hating his brother, he is a liar; for if he doesn't love his brother who is right there in front of him, how can he love God whom he has never seen? And God himself has said that one must love not only God, but his brother too" (1 John 4:20).

In the Epistle of James we are reminded that this love must be effective, not a mere sentiment. It is especially directed toward the poor: "The Christian who is pure and without fault, from God the Father's point of view, is the one who takes care of orphans and widows" (James 1:27). James is at pains to show that the love of neighbor is not to be perverted into a class-biased clubbiness. For the love of neighbor does not mean fawning over the rich (James 2:8). "How can you claim that you belong to the Lord Jesus Christ, the Lord of glory, if you show favoritism to rich people and look down on poor people" (James 2:1)?

There is a rich theological and ethical literature on the relation between love and justice.[37] We can sum up much of the discussion of the relation of love and justice in an agreement that "when you translate love into social reality, it becomes justice."[38] In the theological literature, love is seen as the power which heals, corrects, and transmutes justice. To do so, it must be closely involved in issues and struggles for justice. Moreover, while love can transform justice, it never does less than justice requires. It can go beyond justice only by going through the requirements for just relationships and structures. Justice is an absolute prerequisite for love. "For love implies an absolute demand for justice, namely a recognition of the dignity and rights of one's neighbor. Justice attains its inner fullness only in love. Because every man is truly a visible image of the invisible God and a brother of Christ, the Christian finds in every man God himself and God's absolute demand for justice and love."[39] Indeed, in our own time the commandment of love has pushed the Church, more insistently, into the arena of worldwide concern for justice and toward a new stress on structures of injustice.[40]

In moving to this new direction, the Church has expanded narrower parochial concepts of the neighbor which restrict neighbor love to the one close at hand in the family, our small circle of friends, our primary communities and neighborhood. Nor is neighbor love confined to national boundaries. As Paul VI remarked, "The principal fact that we must all recognize is that the social question has become worldwide" (*Populorum Progressio,* no. 3). In spelling out the implications of neighbor love, Pope Paul saw that "there are certainly situations whose injustice cries to heaven" (*Populorum Progressio,* no. 30). He goes on to call for deep structural transformations in the world political and economic order: "We want to be clearly understood: the present situation must be faced with courage and the injustice linked with it must be fought against and overcome. Development demands bold transformations, innovations that go deep. Urgent reforms should be undertaken without delay" (*Populorum Progressio,* no. 32).

In the New Testament there are clear exhortations to an effective love. John urges his listeners to "stop just saying we love people; let us really love them, and show it by our actions" (1 John 3:18). James also calls for an efficacious love (James 2:14). As we begin to see more and more how the neighbor is crippled and oppressed by systematic decisions of governments and large corporations and unions which affect national rates of unemployment and inflation, consumer patterns, availability of housing, health services, transportation, and access to educational opportunities and the professions as well as by international structures which control world money supplies and supply and demand markets or restrict political voice in international decision-making, the love commandment translates, first, into a justice commandment as the pre-condition of love among equals and, second, expands the circle of neighbors whom we love until its scope is nationwide and worldwide. Systematic analysis of national and worldwide structures of injustice leads the Church, finally, to work insistently for "a just and, consequently, necessary transformation of society" (*Populorum Progressio,* no. 51). For as Paul Ramsey has noted, "love passes not directly from man to man but through structures. There is no solution but to look inside the existing structures for cracks where a change might take place."[41] If the Church fails to be present at the birth of a new, more just society and to give voice to systematic oppression of whole classes, races, and nations, it fails no less to be that Church sent by Christ to show forth its discipleship by its strong love (cf. John 13:34). Hence, its warrant to work on behalf of justice is rooted in its very mission.

**D. Justice as the Pre-Condition
and Consequence of Evangelization**

A final warrant for the Church's mission on behalf of justice flows
from the commission of the disciples to preach the Gospel to all nations
(Mark 16:15). For justice is both the pre-condition and the consequence of
evangelization.

Justice is a pre-condition to evangelization, first, because without it
the Christian proclamation of redemption in Christ from structures of sin
and death rings hollow. As the 1971 Synod of Bishops stated it in the document *Justice in the World,* "unless the Christian message of love and justice shows its effectiveness through action in the cause of justice in the
world, it will only with difficulty gain credibility with the men of our
times."[42]

Gustavo Gutiérrez has claimed that there are only two paramount
pastoral problems in our age. The first is the pastoral problem articulated
by Dietrich Bonhoeffer when he asked, "How are we to preach the Gospel
to a generation which has come of age and claimed its rightful autonomy
in history?" This is the major pastoral problem of the developed world,
Europe and North America.[43] The other pastoral problem profoundly
touches two-thirds of the human race and, by structural linkages between
nations, the developed world as well: "How are we to preach the Gospel
with any credibility to that two-thirds of humanity which goes to bed each
night hungry, ill-housed, chronically ill and without hope for the political
and material improvement of their lives? What can the phrase 'God is love'
or 'redemption from the yoke of sin' possibly mean to them?"[44]

It is not, then, a betrayal of the Church's mission to evangelization
but rather a part of its mandate to preach the Gospel to all nations which
has led the Church in developing countries to link programs of catechesis
with a vigorous effort for development and the empowerment of local
communities in their sense of conscious control over their own destiny.
Again, the new sensitivity to and unmasking of ideological misuse of the
Christian symbols to buttress regimes of injustice is part and parcel of pre-
evangelization. For these distortions of the Gospel keep it from being effectively heard and embraced.

Moreover, a certain level of freedom is necessary to accept the Gospels in faith. As the *Declaration on Religious Freedom* of Vatican Council
II puts it, "It is one of the major tenets of Catholic doctrine that man's
response to God in faith must be free."[45] The Church's involvement in liberation from systematic political and economic oppression intends the freeing of freedom in human society so that an appropriate level of freedom
can be achieved which allows a truly human response to God in faith.

Furthermore, as John Courtney Murray forcefully argued in his book
The Problem of Religious Freedom, the only suasive secular agruments for
that freedom of the Church which the Church has always claimed for itself
as the pre-condition of effective preaching of the Gospel are of a piece with

arguments for the freedom of other voluntary associations in society: universities, labor unions, political groups, and the press.[46] The effective societal freedom of the Church stands and falls with the genuine freedom of other groups. In espousing the justice and rights of persecuted and suppressed organizations, minorities, and ethnic groups, the Church is championing its own cause. Since society as such is incompetent to adjudicate the claims of competing religious groups, the only secular ground for an effective freedom of the Church to preach the Gospel is a societal consensus and commitment to justice and the dignity and rights of human persons and their groups. In pursuing this form of justice, then, the Church is both seeking that human freedom which is the pre-condition for the acceptance of the Gospel and strengthening the consensual basis on which its own freedom to preach the Gospel depends.

But the Church's mission to justice is much more than a phase or pre-evangelization. With the collapse of earlier dualistic notions which sharply divided history and the kingdom of God, the very proclamation of the Gospel entails even now within history the real breakthrough of God's just kingdom and his new creation.[47] This is especially so on Catholic theological premises where God's action to destroy the cycle of sin and death is not seen as merely "forensic," as mere imputation of justice, but rather as an effective transformation of the creation by the justice of God. As Saint Paul put it, "the kingdom of God is not just talking, it is living by God's power" (1 Corinthians 4:20). We can claim, then, on Catholic theological premises, that God's power to break the cycle of sin and death involves effective transformations which we can and should experience in our lives as a new set of personal and societal possibilities, a new creation. The experience within history of such transformations is the ultimate experiential base, for both believers and non-believers alike, of the credibility of the Gospel message of redemption in Christ. Action on behalf of social transformation toward justice, therefore, is a constitutive part of the preaching of God's kingdom which has already come, is coming in history, and ultimately will come definitively as both the goal and end of history.

II. HOW SHOULD THE CHURCH INTERVENE?

Having established several theological warrants for the Church's intervention in the political and economic orders as a constitutive part of its mission, the next question which arises is how should the Church intervene in its quest for justice. The importance of the question stems from the fact that there have been enormous abuses and serious damage to the social order or to the Church in the past because of hasty or ill-planned and wrong-headed intervention by the Church. We need only recall how in the period before World War I in France, for example, the Church condemned Marc Sangnier's Christian Democratic movement, allegedly because it involved the Church in politics, while at the same time the Church openly flirted with the right-wing royalist and integral nationalist movement, Action Francaise.[48] This caused considerable scandal to sections of the Church and wider society.

There are limitations as well as warrants for Church action on behalf of justice. The limitations apply more to the style or manner in which the Church exercises its moral and religious witness in the political arena rather than some call for cautionary prudence. For the purpose of clarity in the following discussion, I want to distinguish three levels of the Church: (a) the corporate dimension—the Church as institution; (b) the communal dimension—para-ecclesial groups in the Church; (c) the personal dimension—Christians as citizens.[49]

In a widely discussed book *Who Speaks for the Church?* Paul Ramsey raised the question of limitations on the institutional Church speaking out on issues of justice.[50] Ramsey scored the over-specificity of the World Council of Churches' documents, especially those stemming from the 1966 Geneva Conference on Church and Society. He argued for the rightful autonomy of secular spheres in determining technical questions and concrete policy in politics and economics. There is no specially Christian political prudence which allows Christians to claim greater political wisdom in concrete strategies and choices. Moreover, Ramsey deplored the abuse of liberty of conscience of individual Christians in their capacity as citizens by the irresponsible specificity of Church documents on political issues which pretend to speak for the Church. Instead of specific condemnations of political actions or highly concrete programs for a new social order, Ramsey pleaded for middle-axioms which would provide a "shaping, discriminating and nourishing address to the environing culture."[51]

These middle-axioms are to be more than vague ethical generalities but less than concrete directives for policy. Ramsey foresaw a set of action-oriented and decision-oriented principles which would set a tone to political discussion without infringing upon the rightful autonomy of the political sector or of individual Christian conscience. As Ramsey saw it, "Christian political ethics cannot say what should or must be done but only what may be done. . . . In politics the Church is only a theoretician. The religious communities, as such, should be concerned with perspectives upon politics, with political doctrines, with the direction and structures of the common life, not with specific directives."[52] This is all the more urgent because Church people show little consensus on the norms for action. They are more likely to agree on specific policies than on their theological grounding. Finally, in order to protect Christian liberty of conscience, Ramsey asked that no social position be taken in the name of the whole Church without a specific theological warrant: "No more [should] be said in addressing the urgent political problems of the present day than can be clearly said on the basis of Christian truth and insights."[53]

I want to build upon Ramsey's arguments to suggest limitations and appropriate styles of the institutional Church's action on behalf of justice. Ramsey's strictures, of course, betray his own political viewpoints and his assumption—by no means always or, even, usually valid—that the Church will mainly play a corrective role in basically just societies. His position also rests on a peculiarly Calvinist doctrine of the role of the magistrates in society, foreign to Catholic social teaching. Moreover, he overstates the case against the possibility of a Christian discernment of the signs of the times which might contain very specific options in the political order.[54] Ramsey does not handle the case where the Church is faced with a massively unjust society or is the last resort for humane protest against very specific abuses against human rights.[55] Moreover, his caution against the Church's becoming too specific is better read as a caution against partisanship. For when there are specific abuses of justice—torture, unjust imprisonment, gross inequalities which refuse the majority the basic needs for human survival and dignity—the Church can and must be very specific in its prophetic denunciations.[56] While the Church may lack the expertise to present specific policies in the economic and political orders, it sometimes has Gospel warrant to proclaim in very specific language which abuses may no longer be tolerated. In the final section, I will discuss action for justice which is more appropriately undertaken by communal, para-ecclesial groups or personal action for justice.

Appropriate Style for Action for Justice by the Institutional Church

A first norm regulating the style of the Church's engagement for justice stems from the nature of the Church as a free community of believers and its relationship to other groups in accord with the freedom of the Gospel. As the document of Vatican II, the *Declaration on Religious Liberty,* puts it, "the truth cannot impose itself except by virtue of its own truth and it makes its entrance into the mind at once quietly and with power."[57] The Church as an agency of God's truth partakes of the very power of the truth. Moreover, it seeks those means which make the power of truth effective. Such means, however, must be consonant with the truth. In a real sense, the Church does not and cannot renounce all power. It must, however, renounce all dominative and manipulative power and, perhaps for the most part, competitive forms of power. It embraces non-coercive power, nutrient and mutual forms of empowerment in its relations toward others.[58] Unless it is clear about what forms of power are or are not consonant with its own nature and mission, the Church runs the risk that *its* truth will not appear.

A second norm for the institutional Church's interventions for justice is rooted in the rightful autonomy of secular spheres in areas of their own expertise and technical competence. Like God, the Church must respect the integrity of the orders of creation and society. The Church has neither exclusive knowledge nor, however great its sincerity, privileged knowledge about economics and politics. It has, as Church, no special technical expertise. Too often Church people fail to recognize the complexity of political prudence. There is no science of the contingent and concrete. While it must fight a cynical divorce between morality and the political and economic orders, the Church also needs to remember that politics is the art of the possible. Moreover, while the Gospels suggest perspectives on political and economic questions, they do not provide concrete programs or policies. The Church has a duty to try to be in dialogue about the major political and economic issues. It has neither the duty nor the right to control the outcome of these issues. Its own historical experience has taught the Church the wisdom of avoiding directly partisan insertions into the political realm. An overly partisan stance by the Church has never led to anything but harm to the Church as well as political order. As Jose Miguez Bonino puts it, "Christians neither have nor want to have a political road of their own."[59]

Some caution is needed, however, when dealing with this stricture. Faithfulness to the Gospel will sometimes lead the Church to prophetic denunciation of specific abuses and injustices. As we have seen, the Gospel also biases the Church toward the poor. If the Church preaches the Gospel with fidelity, it will be accused by many in society of being partisan. Its protection against the charge is threefold. First, it will always present the Gospel warrant for its prophetic denunciation. Second, it will attempt to be universal in condemning abuses across the political spectrum when they occur. Finally, it will leave to those with direct political expertise the manner and method of correcting abuses of justice.

Ramsey argues that binding Church teaching on social issues should aim mainly at middle-axioms, principles, and directives—what John Courtney Murray called "norms of discernment"—rather than overly concrete programs.[60] As Charles Curran has stated it, "such directives would not involve judgments of facts or judgments involving other competencies (e.g., the validity of the domino theory in international relations), for these lie outside of the competency of the Church as such."[61] Such middle-axioms are directives, inviting toward decision and action. They are more concrete than general principles. Paul VI seemed to have something like them in mind when he stated in his apostolic letter Octogesima adveniens, "If it [the Church] does not intervene to authenticate a given structure or to propose a ready-made model, it does not thereby limit itself to recalling general principles. It develops through reflection applied to the changing situations of this world, under the driving force of the Gospel as the source of renewal. . . . It also develops with the sensitivity proper to the Church which is characterized by a disinterested will to serve and by attention to the poorest."[62] The Church's norms for discernment are grounded in more than rational principles. They also rely on experience and enlightenment through the Spirit.

A third norm for corporate Church teaching and action in social issues lies in the Church's need to respect the liberty of conscience of individual believers and of those outside the Church. This means that the Church is obliged to speak and act only on the basis of specifically Christian warrants. Otherwise it runs the risk of appealing to Scripture or the action of God to justify social positions already taken on non-theological grounds. The stricture that the corporate Church only teach and act on the basis of Christian warrants should protect the Church, on the one hand, from many ideological distortions of its social teaching and, on the other, from creating false crises of conscience among sincere believers who disagree with concrete political options.

The social teaching of the Church is an instance of authoritative but non-infallible teaching. As such it can only enjoy presumptive truth. The historical and contingent nature of a theology of culture and society means that much of social teaching is, in principle, reformable. The faithful are called to respond to the Church's social teaching with seriousness and assent as to its presumptive truth unless they have strong and urgent reasons to doubt its wisdom. For it is always possible, under definite conditions, to dissent from the Church's social teaching on specific issues and remain a Catholic in good standing. Such dissent would depend on both the careful study of the issue and prayerful discernment of the Gospel, the thrust of Catholic social teaching, and the community of those most faithful and sensitive to justice issues in the Church. Such dissent *in* the Church will be *for* the Church when it is rooted in the mission toward justice which is the Church's own.[63]

Again, the Catholic emphasis on appealing to all persons of good will, rooted historically in its stress on natural law, means that the Church must respect both the consciences and experience of those outside the Church. On some occasions it will judge, as it has in the past, that the good of social order and cooperation in a pluralist society will be overriding when compared to some injustices. For the Church's social ethic looks to both an ethic of authentic witness to Gospel values and to the real possibilities to transform social orders to a greater state of justice. To achieve effectively this latter objective, the Church's mission to justice means that it must cooperate with men and women outside the Church.

A fourth norm is rooted in the variety and pluralism of social settings and structures within the international Church. Reflecting upon this pluralism, Joseph Gremillion has suggested that in the future "one uniquely social teaching universally applicable to all economic systems should not be expected from the universal Church."[64] Paul VI seemed to recognize this limitation when he remarked in *Octogesima adveniens* that "the universal Church now realized that there is, of course, a wide diversity among the situations in which Christians—willingly or unwillingly—find themselves according to regions, socio-political systems and cultures. . . . It is up to the Christian communities [local, regional, national] . . . to discern the options and commitments which are called for in order to bring about the social, political, and economic changes seen in many cases to be urgently needed."[65] While this limitation applies especially to pronouncements of the universal Church, it will also be relevant to the teaching voice of national and regional conferences of bishops.

Moreover, a fifth norm stems from the fact that the corporate Church as an international or national institution has limited resources in terms of money and personnel. It cannot take on all good causes or pursue every strategy of justice. If it wishes to be responsible it will try to set priorities and devise strategies about the most important issues of justice. It will not try to duplicate what other private or public agencies are already doing well. It will not undertake tasks for which it does not have the resources to see through to the end. Moreover, it will respect the diversity of charismatic gifts in the Church by leaving to the initiative of para-ecclesial groups or individuals many works of justice. As Charles Curran puts it, "not every involvement of members of the Church in striving for social justice, human development, or the liberation of the oppressed should be the work of the whole Church as such."[66] When even governments are unable to meet all claims of justice because of limited resources, the Church must learn to operate within those modest goals which it can effectively implement. Anything else would be irresponsible and a serious risk of the limited but real moral authority the Church enjoys in the public arena.

A final norm asserts that while action on behalf of justice is a constitutive dimension of preaching of the Gospel, it is not the only dimension of the mission of the Church. For "the heart of the Gospel message includes the preaching of the good news, and the celebration of God's loving gift to man and not just the new life that the Christian should lead in the service of his fellow man."[67]

The appropriate stance of the corporate Church in its interventions for justice has been suggested by Ramsey as "a shaping, discriminating, and nourishing address to the environing culture."[68] Mindful of creation and the reality of God's sustaining providence, the Church will nourish as well as condemn, support as well as oppose. For not every structure of society is evil and unjust. Some societal structures bear the weight of sustaining the common life. Mindful of the reality of sin, the Church will sometimes denounce in prophetic style the current structures of injustice. But critical negativity of those aspects of the status quo which cannot be allowed to stand is not enough. Besides a forceful social teaching based on middle-axioms as a shaping address to the environing culture, the Church can go beyond directives and principles to sketch ideal visions and imaginative hopes of a healthy communal society in what Paul VI refers to as the rebirth of utopias. Imaginative projection of utopias seems consonant with the Church's hope in an eschatological transformation of the structures of history. As Paul VI remarks, these utopias provoke "the forward-looking imagination both to perceive in the present the disregarded possibility hidden within it, and to direct itself toward a fresh future; it thus sustains social dynamism by the confidence it gives to the inventive powers of the human mind and heart."[69]

The Church has been called a bearer of moral tradition. Out of this tradition the Church will teach. It is also a shaper of Christian moral identity. As such the corporate Church will use its limited resources to give priority to education and motivation to its members for commitment to justice. This education will, besides explicit programs and resources for education to justice, need to touch catechesis, liturgy, and the Catholic media. Education for justice should include more than an immediate response to the latest crisis. For "if basic biblical understandings are not incorporated by Christians before a moral and ethical crisis arises, then biblical resources are unlikely to play any significant role."[70]

Finally the Church ought to and can be a community of moral deliberation by which Christians, nourished by the Gospel, find a forum to discuss major political and economic issues and to discern the signs of the times in the light of the Gospel. Hence, the corporate Church should and can use its resources to enable groups of Christians in community to engage in moral deliberation. Normally, it will not prejudice that deliberation by an overly directive teaching of its own. Church-sponsored platforms for moral deliberation—whether congresses, consultations at the diocesan and national level, newspapers, and Catholic media or congregational forums—will normally look to broadening and deepening the public debate on urgent questions and seeing that Gospel principles are included as one essential horizon in the debates about policy rather than binding the consciences of Church members to one specific course of action.[71]

The Communal Dimension—Para-Ecclesial Groups

Action on behalf of justice by the *institutional* Church, because of the Church's competency and limitations already seen, will not be sufficient to fulfill the Gospel mandate for justice. For as Jose Miguez Bonino notes, "a prophetic denunciation on the part of the institutional Church of the conditions of oppression . . . usually fails at the critical point of assuming the concrete struggle of the people."[72] It would seem that in the fullest sense the Church could not assume the concrete struggle of the people without becoming a partisan political actor in society or an alternative state. Were the institutional Church to do that, it would lose its credibility as an ethical authority and forego certain mediatory political roles it can play precisely because it eschews direct partisan choices. On the other hand, the Church can identify with the concrete struggles of its people by providing moral support and teaching toward a just society and by training the people to a sense of leadership, responsibility and community empowerment.

Besides the institutional Church, there is always the dynamic, charismatic element in the Church. The two can never be either fully identified or fully divorced from one another. The whole Church is magistral. Within that whole Church there is a ministry of the magisterium, of the Pope and bishops, and of the theologians as teachers. There is also the indispensable non-institutionalized *sensus fidelium* carried by charismatic elements in the Church, what I call here para-ecclesial groups.[73] The nomenclature is meant to stress that they do not represent the institutional Church. Nevertheless, they are a full part of the ecclesial reality and mission of the Church. For the Church has never failed to engender in its midst voluntary associations of committed Christians and community groups who are moved to join directly the concrete struggle of people at the neighborhood, urban, regional, national, and international level.

Such para-ecclesial groups—I think in the current American Church of the Catholic Committee on Urban Ministry, the Catholic Worker movement, the Catholic anti-war and human rights forces, Right to Life groups, American Christians for Socialism, community organizers, the various justice movements among the Hispanic speaking, etc.—are *of* the Church since their inspiration comes from the Gospel. Moreover, their concrete action for justice is rooted in the Church's mission to incarnate justice. Without such groups the Church cannot be Church and fulfill its mission to justice. They also speak *to* the whole Church of a concrete option for justice which flows out of a Christian life and discernment. They claim that in conscience and through the guidance of the Spirit they cannot do other than they do in the concrete choices which they make.

Their concreteness challenges other Christians who might use social justice principles as an ideological mask to protect them from a real conversion to justice or real involvement. For in the order of history and a fallen world, not all possible choices are really compatible. Some real options need to be made in the political order. On the other hand, these groups do not pretend to speak *for* the whole Church nor can they since, as we have seen, most of the time concrete programs demand prudential judgments beyond the scope of the Gospel. Ordinarily, in both their constitution and financial base, these groups make clear that they do not claim to represent the entire Church. Their freedom from direct organizational connection with the hierarchy or institutional Church is to their own advantage as well as to that of the corporate Church. This freedom allows them to be much more specific and partisan in their concrete struggles for justice than it would be usually wise for the institutional Church to be, to lobby directly for particular legislation and candidates, to be more direct in their espousal of policies and programs than the institutional Church can be.

Because of the need, as Jose Miguez Bonino claims, to move to the level of assuming or, at least, joining in the concrete struggles for justice, the whole Church very much needs these para-ecclesial groups. On some occasions, the whole Church will learn from them and even adopt their choices as part of a Church-world strategy. The institutional Church, it is hoped, especially the hierarchy, will keep in good relation to these groups, encourage them in their concrete, often partisan, struggles without endorsing them as such, and recognize that such groups are indispensable to the life and vigor of the Church. The corporate Church must leave them free to follow the dictates of their Christian conscience, as *e contra* they will not try to force the whole Church into identification with their movements of Christian inspiration.

Although the specifics of the Catholic Action movement of the 1930's and 1940's cannot and should not be revived in our current situation, since such movements were often too clerically dominated and too specifically confessional in their orientation, the wisdom of the Catholic Action strategy for justice was that it was two things simultaneously.[74] One was that the institutional Church usually needed a buffer, intermediate groups of Christians who did not officially represent the institutional Church, to make the move from middle-axioms of ethical wisdom to concrete, even partisan, options. The other was that there is a need for para-ecclesial *groups* to bear witness to the Church's mission to justice. Such groups form Christians in expertise on issues and in ways of discerning the sign of the times. They provide support for individuals. They also give corporate witness. Individuals left to their own resources will usually not give effective corporate witness to the Church's commitment to justice.

The proliferation of many such para-ecclesial groups, struggling concretely for justice in housing, income, education, job opportunities, civil rights, and international restructuring of the economic order, etc., as well as large numbers of Christians personally involved in action for justice, will be the indispensable and ultimate test for the corporate Church that its teaching as a bearer of moral tradition has been heard, that its task as a shaper of moral identities has been fulfilled and that its opportunity and mission to be a community of moral deliberation has been seized. When the number and variety of initiatives toward justice by individuals as citizens and para-ecclesial groups so multiply that it becomes difficult to keep a careful account of them then "hopefully the Church might once again be known as

> a center of the spirit
> a place where poetry dares to speak,
> —where the song reigns unchallenged,
> —where art flourishes
> —where nature is welcome
> —where little people and little needs come first,
> —where justice speaks loudly
> —where in a wilderness of idolatrous destruction the great voice
> of God still cries out for life."[75]

NOTES

1. *Justice in the World,* no. 6 in Joseph Gremillion, ed., *The Gospel of Justice and Peace* (Maryknoll: Orbis, 1976), p. 514. See also the Medellín documents in *ibid.,* pp. 445–76.

2. See Avery Dulles, "The Meaning of Faith Considered in Relation to Justice," in John C. Haughey, ed., *The Faith That Does Justice* (New York: Paulist, 1977), p. 13.

3. *Justice in the World,* no. 3 in Gremillion, *op. cit.,* p. 514.

4. See the 1974 Synod document on evangelization with its reaffirmation of

"the intimate connection between evangelization and liberation" in *Evangelization of the Modern World* in Gremillion, *op. cit.,* p. 597.

5. For a profound reflection on "social sin" as the binding of freedom and "social liberation" as the freeing of freedom in human society, rather than the removal of the possibility of sin—a reflection which clearly does justice to both personal sin and social factors and which sees social sin in the classic category of *sequelae* or congealed consequences of personal sin—see Langdon Gilkey, *Reaping the Whirlwind* (New York: Seabury, 1976), 236ff. where Gilkey remarks, "The freeing of freedom, liberation, achieves the conquest of the consequences of human sin in history . . . and so . . . is an essential aspect of Christian concern and action. Nevertheless, it does not represent the conquest of the sin itself out of which fate and fatedness continually arise. Only a new relation of mankind to God, to self and to the neighbor can achieve that goal, an achievement far beyond the range of political activity."

6. See William Temple, *Christianity and the Social Order* (New York: Seabury, 1977).

7. See, for this phase, Temple, *op. cit.,* p. 38.

8. See Isaiah 32:16: "Then justice will rule through all the land and out of justice, peace."

9. See Genesis 1–2, Genesis 8, and Isaiah 56 and 60.

10. James Muilenberg. *The Way of Israel, Biblical Faith and Ethics* (New York: Harper and Row, 1961), p. 46.

11. For these egalitarian norms in political life as an Old Testament motif see Exodus and Deut 1:16–18.

12. John R. Donohue, S.J., "Biblical Perspectives on Justice," in John C. Haughey, ed., *The Faith That Does Justice,* p. 109. For another treatment of Old Testament themes of justice, see Porfirio Miranda, *Marx and the Bible* (Maryknoll: Orbis, 1974).

13. The biblical notion of justice includes more than the modern idea. It is a unity of love and justice where love, however, never does less than what justice demands. See E. Berkovits, "The Biblical Meaning of Justice," *Judaism* 18 (1969), pp. 188–209.

14. See John C. Haughey, S.J., "Jesus as the Justice of God," in John C. Haughey, ed., *The Faith That Does Justice,* pp. 264–89.

15. John H. Yoder, *The Politics of Jesus* (Grand Rapids: Eerdmans, 1972).

16. See Norman Perrin, *Jesus and the Language of the Kingdom* (Philadelphia: Fortress, 1976), pp. 29–32.

17. Jose Miguez Bonino, *Doing Theology in a Revolutionary Situation* (Philadelphia: Fortress, 1976), pp. 29–32.

18. My position here betrays a bias toward H. R. Niebuhr's fifth type of Church-world strategy, the "Christ, transformer of culture." See H. R. Niebuhr, *Christ and Culture* (New York: Harper and Row, 1971), p. 6.

19. See Gregory Baum, "Political Theology in Canada," in *The Ecumenist,* Vol. 15, No. 3 (March–April 1977), p. 38.

20. Amos Wilder suggests that Paul's allusion to the principalities and powers of this world refers to social structures in *Eschatology and Ethics in the Teaching of Jesus* (New York: Harper, 1950).

21. See Victor Furnish, *Theology and Ethics in Paul* (Nashville: Abingdon, 1968).

22. John R. Donohue, S.J., *op. cit.,* pp. 91–92.

23. Gregory Baum, *op. cit.,* p. 39.

24. James M. Clark and John V. Skinner, eds., *Meister Eckhart: Selected Treatises and Sermons* (New York: Harper, 1958), pp. 53–54.

25. For a recent effort at a theology of the mission of the Spirit, see Piet Schoonenberg, "God Geest als Gave," a paper prepared for the Dutch episcopacy in 1977. Available upon request from the Secretariat of the Roman Catholic Church in The Netherlands, Maliebaan 13, Utrecht.

26. Jose Miguez Bonino, *op. cit.,* p. 142.

27. For the nature of transcendent causality as opposed to finite causality see Piet Schoonenberg, *God's World in the Making* (Pittsburgh: Duquesne University Press, 1964).

28. Gilkey, *op. cit.,* p. 119.

29. *Ibid.,* p. 56. For an expansion of Gilkey's evidence and reasoning see pp. 36–39.

30. See Peter Berger, *Sacred Canopy* (Garden City: Doubleday, 1967).

31. Gilkey, *op. cit.,* p. 119.

32. Robert N. Bellah, *Beyond Belief* (New York: Harper and Row, 1970), p. 201.

33. Gilkey, *op. cit.,* p. 119.

34. See Robert Nisbet, *The Sociological Tradition* (New York: Basic Books, 1966).

35. Joseph Gremillion, *The Gospel of Justice and Peace,* p. 37. For a sociological argument that religion has closer affinities to politics than to economics, see Hans J. Mol, *Identity and the Sacred* (New York: The Free Press, 1977), pp. 109–128.

36. Cited in the introduction to Temple, *op. cit.,* p. 9. For another view of the moral and religious foundations of economic decisions, see E. F. Schumacher, *A Guide for the Perplexed* (New York: Harper and Row, 1977).

37. Much of this literature is summarized in Gene Outka, *Agape* (New Haven: Yale University Press, 1972). See also John P. Langan, S.J., "What Jerusalem Says to Athens," in John C. Haughey, ed., *The Faith That Does Justice,* pp. 152–180.

38. John Shea, "Spiritual Empowerment and Social Ministry," in The Proceedings of the 1976 Catholic Committee on Urban Ministries' Conference, p. 1.

39. *Justice in the World* in David O'Brien and Thomas A. Shannon, eds., *Renewing the Earth* (Garden City: Doubleday, 1977), p. 398.

40. See the documents *Populorum Progressio, Octogesima Adveniens,* and *Justice in the World,* in O'Brien and Shannon, *op. cit.,* pp. 307–411.

41. Paul Ramsey, *Who Speaks for the Church?* (Nashville: Abingdon Press 1967), p. 116.

42. O'Brien and Shannon, *op. cit.,* p. 399.

43. Since the goal of liberation envisions adult autonomy in participation in setting collective goals, presumably this pastoral problem is linked to the liberation themes of the third world.

44. Oral remarks at the convocation on liberation theology held in Detroit (August 1975).

45. "Declaration on Religious Freedom," no. 10, in O'Brien and Shannon, *op. cit.,* p. 299.

46. See John Courtney Murray, *The Problem of Religious Freedom* (Westminster: Newman Press, 1965).

47. For the collapse of dualism in Church understandings of the kingdom and history, see William Dych, S.J., "The Dualism in the Faith of the Church," in John C. Haughey, ed., *The Faith That Does Justice,* pp. 47–65.

48. For the condemnation of Sangnier's group and the support of Action Francaise see Eugen Weber, *Action Francaise, Royalism and Reaction in Twentieth Century France* (Stanford: Stanford University Press, 1962), pp. 65–67.

49. I leave the personal dimension undeveloped in this chapter.

50. Paul Ramsey, *Who Speaks for the Church?* (Nashville: Abingdon, 1967).

51. *Ibid.,* p. 91.

52. *Ibid.,* p. 152.

53. *Ibid.,* p. 30.

54. For a positive understanding of the possibilities of concrete options on Christian warrant, appealing to the discernment of the signs of the times, see Edward Schillebeeckx, "Church, Magisterium and Politics," in *God the Future of Man,* trans. N. D. Smith (New York: Sheed and Ward, 1968), pp. 141–166.

55. Thomas Bruneau argues that this is the case in Brazil in his *The Political Transformation of the Brazilian Church* (New York: Oxford University Press, 1974).

56. For examples of specific denunciations of unjust practices which appeal to Gospel warrants but avoid partisan choices, see the Statement of Guatemalan Bishops' Conference, "The Presence of the Church in National Reconstruction," July 1976, L P Documentation, Latin America Press, August 9, 1976, pp. 3ff; statement of the Paraguayan Bishops' Conference, "Between the Persecutions of the World and the Consolation of God," June 12, 1976, L P Documentation, Latin America Press, July 15, 1976, pp. 6ff and other recent documents from national hierarchies in Latin America and the Philippines.

57. "Declaration on Religious Liberty," no. 1, in O'Brien and Shannon, *op. cit.,* p. 292.

58. For these distinctions between forms of power, see Rollo May, *Power and Innocence* (New York: Norton, 1972), pp. 105–13, where May distinguishes five kinds of power—two immoral: dominative and manipulative; one neutral: competitive; two positive: nutrient and integrative.

59. Bonino, *op. cit.,* p. 41.

60. John Courtney Murray, "Key Themes in the Encyclical," appended to the encyclical *Pacem in Terris* (New York: America Press, 1963), p. 57.

61. Charles Curran, "Theological Reflections on the Social Mission and Teaching of the Church," in *New Perspectives in Moral Theology* (Notre Dame: University of Notre Dame Press, 1976), p. 150.

62. *Octogesima Adveniens,* no. 42, in O'Brien and Shannon, *op. cit.,* p. 375.

63. For the ecclesial authority of Church social teaching and the possibility and norms of dissent *in* the Church *for* the Church, see Charles Curran and Robert E. Hunt, *Dissent in and for the Church* (New York: Sheed and Ward, 1969). An earlier, basically conservative dissent from John XXIII's *Mater et Magistra* is found in Garry Wills, *Politics and Catholic Freedom* (Chicago: Henry Regnery Co., 1964). I treat of the historical limitations in Church social teaching in my "What Is an Encyclical?" *Origins,* Vol. 11, No. 3 (June 4, 1981), pp. 34–41.

64. Gremillion, *op. cit.,* p. 37.

65. *Octogesima Adveniens,* no. 3–4, in O'Brien and Shannon, *op. cit.,* pp. 353–54.

66. Curran, *op. cit.,* p. 143.

67. Curran, *op. cit.,* p. 141.

68. Ramsey, *op. cit.,* p. 91.

69. *Octogesima Adveniens,* no. 37, in O'Brien and Shannon, *op. cit.*, p. 371. For a very stirring example of Church social teaching which includes a clear search for imaginative utopian elements, see The Appalachia Pastoral, "This Land Is Home to Me," in O'Brien and Shannon, *op. cit.,* pp. 472–515.

70. Bruce Birch and Larry Rasmussen, *Bible and Ethics in Christian Life* (Minneapolis: Augsburg Publishing House, 1976), p. 200.

71. Cf. Ramsey, *op. cit.,* p. 119 and chapter 13 of this volume.

72. Bonino, *op. cit.,* p. 158.

73. For the indispensable character of the charismatic element in the Church as an opposite pole to the institutional element, see Karl Rahner, "Dynamic Element in the Church," *Quaestiones Disputatae,* 12 (New York: Herder, 1964).

74. For a treatment of the Catholic Action strategy, see William Bosworth, *Catholicism and Christ in Modern France* (Princeton: Princeton University Press, 1962), pp. 97–182. This point is developed further in Chapter 2.

75. "This Land Is Home to Me," in O'Brien and Shannon, *op. cit.,* p. 515.

Chapter Two

A Church with a Worldly Vocation

I want to begin this chapter by coopting language congenial to the transcendental Thomists when they speak about the "conditions for the possibility" of something's being or happening. My topic will be the conditions for the possibility of a Church with a worldly vocation. Much of what I am going to say is merely an extended application of the thought of Max Weber. In particular, I want to reflect upon an insight of his found in *The Sociology of Religion* where Weber asserts that there is an elective affinity between the kind of prophetic religion which undertakes a world-transforming mission and organizational modes of the Church which center on the laity. Weber's thesis, in brief, argues that prophecy, world-transformation and the laity belong together.[1] Throughout I will make some comments about what factors or conditions I see missing in the contemporary American Church which impede its possibility for an effective worldly vocation.

As I see it, there are three main conditions for a Church with a worldly vocation: (1) a tension between a compelling vision of a social order based on mutuality, respect for persons, community and justice, on the one hand, and the thrust, on the other, to accommodate that vision to the world of everyday life; (2) a consistent pastoral strategy aimed at eliciting solid motivational commitments among the laity such that they see the world and their life of work as an arena of meaningful *religious* action; (3) the mobilization of committed lay energies around concrete choices for influencing the social order by infusing religious values into the "secular" realm.[2]

This last condition envisions what Jacques Maritain once called "a concrete historical ideal," i.e., an ideal which, while it transcends the present social arrangements, is, in principle, within the realm of societal possibility within a generation or so.

Maritain contrasts a concrete historical ideal with a utopia, without scouting the social relevance of the latter. "What is meant by a 'concrete historical idea' is that *prospective type,* that particular and specific [ideal] image of itself toward which a given concrete historical epoch tends."[3] You will note in this description by Maritain a certain determinism and contextual fixity. Concrete historical ideals are forged out of a careful weighing of the *limits* as well as the *possibilities* of any given epoch or social system.[4] Alexis de Tocqueville's work on the prospect for democracy in nineteenth century America and France represents, perhaps, the classic sociological delineation of a concrete historical ideal, although Maritain's use of the term suggests a programmatic thrust beyond mere social analysis.

Maritain continues his contrasting elucidation of the concrete historical ideal and utopias. "A *concrete historical ideal* is not an *ens rationis* (like a utopia) but an ideal *essence* which is realizable (with more or less difficulty, more or less imperfectly . . . not as a finished thing, but as a thing in process), an essence able to exist (unlike a utopia) and called to exist in a given historical atmosphere, and as a result corresponding to a *relative maximum* (relative to that historical state) of social and political perfection."[5]

By the nature of the case, every theology of culture, acculturation and societal change, every model for Church-society relations, is historically specific. Each is tailored to the limits and possibilities of a particular epoch, culture, economic or political system.[6] Christian social teaching, then, is an evolving, shifting corpus. Its changing emphases react to, reflect and—hopefully—inform and shape evolving social process. It is not by chance that there are no defined dogmas about the social order. As I will argue later, it is by sheer chance that the bulk of Catholic social teaching has been articulated by the hierarchy: Popes and bishops. It is, to be sure, a happy chance and a treasured legacy that this hierarchical social teaching has been, by and large, so wise and helpfully directive.

Nevertheless, the appropriate voice for enunciating a theology of culture and Maritain's concrete historical ideal is not hierarchical but lay. The laity uniquely have experience in the shifting realities of the cultural worlds of marriage, family, neighborhood, secular work and politics. A compelling concrete historical ideal can only grow out of such lived experience and prudential discerning choices of the appropriately Christian response to definite contexts. Thus, in the area of Church social teaching, I would go beyond John Henry Newman's plea for *consulting* the faithful. I would argue for the necessity of Church forums and platforms for addressing social issues and enunciating social Christianity where the lay voice is the predominant, although not necessarily only, ingredient.[7] I will return to this point at the end of this chapter when I suggest some pastoral strategies that would seem necessary if we in America are going to be serious about a Church with a worldly vocation.

VISION AND WORLDLY ADDRESS IN TENSION

Perhaps no one has seen as keenly as Max Weber *the inherent* and *perennial* tensions between transcendent religion and the worldly arena. Weber delineates the latter by dividing it into economics, politics, art and the erotic and intellectual spheres.[8] He postulates a *permanent* tension between any religion based on a personalist vision of "brotherly love" and the economic sphere governed, in large part, by rational, impersonal calculations.[9] Similarly, every religion in its ideal formulations exists in sharp strain with *every* political order's preoccupation with external and internal distribution of power and its ultimate reliance upon the weapon and sanction of force.

Art and religion, especially the mystical element in religion, exhibit close psychological affinities. Nevertheless, the aesthetic realm is never easily tractable in the face of religion's moral evaluation. Moreover, art can function at times—at least for the cultured classes as it did for Matthew Arnold—as a substitute religion of this-worldly ecstasy and meaning. The erotic is also not easily pliant to religious moral norms. It is rooted in a profoundly non-rational thrust toward unitive mutuality. Even though eros and agape may not be in simple opposition, they exist, at least, in some sort of strained tension. As regards the intellectual sphere, Weber contends that "there is absolutely no 'unbroken' religion working as a vital force which is not compelled at *some* point to demand . . . the sacrifice of the intellect."[10] The faith that searches for appropriate correlative understanding and grounding in the realms of reason always transcends reason's reach and grasp. If I am reading Weber correctly, he is arguing that there could never be, in H. Richard Niebuhr's terms, "a Christ *of* culture," without serious and compromising concessions by Christianity.[11]

The historical genius of phenomenological Christianity among the world religions, in Weber's view, was its ability to sustain, at certain key periods of its history, the tension between a compelling vision of an ideal social order—the kingdom of God as symbol of transcendent justice and mutuality and as transhistorical utopia standing in judgment on the imperfect justice of *every* social order—and, simultaneously, the accommodation of this vision to the relativities of history and social particularity. The radical source of the Christian refusal either to accommodate too closely with the given structures of society or, conversely, to flee, in world rejection, engagement in historical society lies in its doctrine of the incarnation. As Howard Butt has finely phrased it in his book on Christian lay witness, *At the Edge of Hope,* Christians believe that the transcendent, in Jesus, "took on legs." Thus, Christians find themselves, paradoxically, "bending toward the 'other world' of God's kingdom and 'this world' at the same time."[12]

Sociologist Roland Robertson captures much the same flavor in a remark which expresses the social vision implicit in the choice for incarnation rather than radical eschatology: "Social and terrestrial reality constitutes some God-given testing ground to be lived through, confronted and not eschewed."[13] More recent theology expresses this same theme forcefully when it asserts that the kingdom of God is not only the transcendent goal toward which history tends but, equally, "a reality at work within history" itself.[14]

In an early work, writing at a time when he was preoccupied primarily by Weberian questions in looking for an analogue to the Protestant ethic in other world religions, sociologist Robert Bellah caught the point I am making here:

> Two conditions seem especially unfavorable for the religious encouragement of progress: too close a fusion between religious symbolism and the actual world and too great a disjunction between them. . . . The situation in which progress is most likely to be advanced seems to be that in which transcendent ideals, in tension with empirical reality, have a central place in the religious symbol system, while empirical reality, itself, is taken very seriously as at least potentially meaningful, valuable and a valid sphere for religious action.[15]

Of course, the transformative capacities of religion for influencing a social order redound back upon religion by transforming it in turn. Every strategy for Church-society relations involves, in Ernst Troeltsch's sense, "a compromise." That is why a theology of culture is always in process. For every compromise is brittle and unstable. Bellah expresses this point well in his book on Japanese religion:

> Every religion seeks to proclaim a truth which transcends the world, but is enmeshed in the very world it desires to transcend. Every religion seeks to remake the world in its own image, but is always to some extent remade in the image of the world. This is the tragedy of religion. It seeks to transcend the human but it is human, all too human. And yet tragedy is not the last word about religion. As long as religion maintains its commitment to the source of ultimate value, which is to say as long as it remains religion, the confrontation of religion, and society remains. Holding to that commitment, religion turns every human defeat into victory.[16]

Both poles in this paradox are important. Both the tension of religion with and its thrust to accommodate to and appropriately address the world are necessary conditions for a Church with a worldly *vocation*. As Weber remarks in his classic study of *The Protestant Ethic and the Spirit of Capitalism,* there is a profound difference in a social ethic such as the classic Lutheran two kingdoms ethic which sought God "in vocatione" but without a compelling sense of any transformative possibilities for the world and the Calvinistic totalistic impulse to seek God "per vocationem" by transforming societal structures to fit a pattern worthy of the glory of God.[17]

From the tension with the world comes religion's prophetic leverage to criticize the anti-communitarian and anti-personalist elements in any economic or political system. From the tension stem religion's powerfully collective utopian symbols of an order based on justice and non-dominative mutuality, in order transcending racism, narrow tribal loyalties, sexism and nationality. Transcendent religion projects and incarnates a transnational community of free persons governed by interactive love. On the other hand, from the thrust toward relevance and appropriate address—a vector rooted deeply in Christianity's claim to universal validity and its foundational mission to preach the Gospel to all epochs, peoples and situations—flows, for each generation, renewed energy to make relevant "an impossible ideal," to humanize and civilize social orders always less than just, to transform the world of everyday life and work such that it has *religious* meaning by its approaching and embodying, even if always asymptotically, the vision of the kingdom.

It is not necessary or usual that both poles in this paradox of tension and accommodation be borne by the same social carrier groups within the Church. There is in the Church as in the social order a variety of gifts. But both those with prophetic visions and those who work to implement the vision, so that it takes on sturdy legs and formed flesh in their world of neighborhoods, family, political wards and nine-to-five, year-in, year-out, jobs and careers, need to be in constant contact and dialogue with each other. If I may appeal to Weber's precise sociological meaning of the term, whatever may be said of prophets in the history of the human spirit, there are no prophets worth remembering in *social* history without followers. There is no genuinely prophetic Church with world-transforming sociological consequences without constituencies.[18]

There is, to be sure, from the standpoint of ethics, the possibility of prophecy which does not succeed. Indeed, every genuinely religious ethics shies away from purely utilitarian calculations of consequences. But from the sociological perspective I would underscore Weber's contention of an affinity between a world-transforming mission and organizational and pastoral strategies centered on the laity. The laity are *the key* social action agents of the Church in the world and the critical point of insertion of transforming Christian action in the arenas of economics, politics, the erotic, aesthetic and intellectual spheres.

It is possible, of course, for a Church that is not lay-centered and lay-mobilized to bring some moral voice of protest in a witness ethic. Such a witness ethic has been the mainstay of sectarian modes for organizing the Church. The Catholic bias, however, in social ethics has always contained transformative pretensions toward culture and society. Catholics have not yet, it seems to me, found an appropriate organizational form to focus Church-society strategies on predominantly lay-centered and *lay-con-*

trolled—this latter has been, historically, the sticking point—movements and forums for social actions.

It is also possible for the clergy and hierarchy, as a status-class in the Church, to contribute to the transformation of social orders. They can, at times, inject a commanding articulation of moral values into the worldly societal realm by enunciating middle-axioms or direction-orienting principles. They can also denounce concrete violations of justice and human rights in an exercise of "critical negativity." Indeed, this exercise of moral leadership by bishops and clergy is a crucial input into secular life. I would argue, however, that this element of a worldly and world-transforming vocation on the part of the clergy and hierarchy is a secondary or derivative, even though essential, task for them. It is not their unique specialization. Moreover, it is a task of secondary importance, when compared to the mobilization of lay vocations, to the essential world-transforming mission of the Church.

Since this is a delicate and controversial distinction, I want to make my intentions here clear. I am not arguing for a rigid cleavage between all clergy and laity. That would be a pastorally disastrous situation. Obviously, too, more and more laity are engaging in intra-Church ministry. Nor am I denying that it may be ministerially useful to the Church to have clergy—even fairly large numbers, although I think by the nature of the case they will always constitute a minority of their status-class—who are hyphenated clergy in the sense that they also labor at a "worldly" vocation as a politician, taxi driver, novelist, painter or economist. I am simply asserting what seems to me to be an obvious sociological fact, namely that the bulk of the clergy and religious, as a status-class, will lack enough tutored expertise in the worldly realm to be the carrier class for a world-transforming mission in and through the arena of work, politics, economics and aesthetic, erotic and intellectual spheres. Again, by the nature of the case, the clergy and religious will be a small, elite minority without sufficient cadres and bodies to penetrate the world. Finally, as always in some sense "official" agents of the corporate Church, the clergy and religious will forever be less than free and autonomous in essaying bold, particular and embodied concrete historical ideals. For in so doing, they would risk jeopardizing a stance of non-partisanship and the eschewal of claims to "technical" competence. This stance is essential if the Church, as an institutional actor in the social realm, is to gain credibility and audience as an articulator of moral values and as a moral authority in the secular world. The institutional Church, as one corporate actor in the social arena, plays an important and indispensable *political* role as the authentic articulator of moral values such as justice and human rights precisely by eschewing any special competence in the "technical" worldly questions whose rightful autonomy the Church respects. As a consequence, only those less officially tied by ordination or religious profession to the apparatus of the institutional Church—although by reason of baptism they are full and equal members

of the Church as a community of faith and discipleship—can be the primary agents of the prophetic mission of Christianity in Weber's sense. Only a
lay-centered strategy of Christian insertion in the world creates the possibility of a Church with an effective worldly vocation. The laity alone can
essay a concrete historical embodiment of social action for which they neither claim nor seek "official" Church sanction. Instead, they rely simply
on their own gift of "Christian inspiration" coupled with that technical
competence necessary for a prudential concretion of Christian action and
the discernment and delineation of the concrete historical ideal.

Before moving on to discuss my second condition for the possibility of
a Church with a worldly vocation, I want to make a number of assertions
which I will not have time to argue, though I think each, when weighed,
will stand the test of evidence. My first assertion is that the Catholic
Church has never successfully achieved a truly lay-centered Church. To be
sure, the laity have always, in fact, had more access and input into hierarchical decision-making than would appear from an organizational chart of
Church decision-making. Moreover, lay initiative has been important, at
crucial times, for the articulation of hierarchical social doctrine. Lay pil-
grimages to Leo XIII, culminating in the drafting of *Rerum Novarum,* is
the classic, if somewhat isolated, instance of such lay input. Certainly, as
Jay Dolan and David O'Brien have shown, strong lay initiative was both
respected and encouraged by the American Church in the nineteenth century.[19]

To dispel possible misunderstandings about my point, I want to make
clear that I am restricting my remarks here about a lay-centered Church to
the precise and defined area of Church-society relations. I am in no way
calling in question the rightness of ordained ministry (although not all the
ordained, it seems, minister and not all ministers are ordained) or the hierarchical principle as the legitimate Catholic source of dogmatic teaching
and pastoral discernment. I want to focus narrowly on the mistaken usur-
pation—a long, residual legacy of medieval Christendom which, of course,
I do not assume as normative—by the hierarchy and clergy of the focused
area of Church mission to the world. By Church-society relations I am referring to a missionary thrust, generated from out of the body of the
Church, which intends a theology for genuine inculturation and the ongoing formulation of the concrete historical ideal.

I am, obviously, not imputing any motives or dominative intentions to
the clergy and hierarchy in their usurping this essentially lay realm. But
one of the reasons Catholicism has failed to achieve Maritain's concrete
historical ideal—both articulating and embodying it—has been Catholicism's failure to distinguish properly between an ethics of the institutional
Church consisting mainly in middle-level principles for morality—an ethics where the hierarchy and clergy also have an appropriate task—and the
more concrete ethical struggle to translate these principles into programmatic action and strategy dependent on a prudential discernment of the
"give" points and concrete possibilities in the economic, political, aesthetic

and cultural spheres. It is obvious to anyone who knows the corpus that Catholic social teaching, combining concerns for both personalism and the common good, represents a decided "third way" between Marxist, socialist visions of the social order and Western, utilitarian, individualist versions of capitalism.[20] It is also notoriously obvious that this "third way" has always represented an arcane deposit of social wisdom with only minimal impact on the Church, let alone social orders. For there can be no effective "third way" without a genuine "third force" of energy mobilized in opposition to the anti-communitarian thrust of historic capitalism and the anti-personalist dynamic inherent in historic forms of collectivist socialism. Such a third force, to be politically effective, demands a programmatic concretion beyond the technical competence of the "official" Church to provide. God forbid that it should ever again pretend to be equal to that task, even if in the name of progress!

The proper status-class in the Church to essay this concretion of "the third way"—obviously, in pluralistic societies this will entail coalitions with other Christians and men and women of good will in voluntary social movements and associations—is the laity.[21] It is their *religious* province by reason of their missionary commission in baptism. It is their *appropriate* religious task because only they have the lived experience to maintain a creative strain between tension with and accommodation to the world. Whatever the situation of individual clergy and religious, the laity are the only carrier group—as a status-class—within the Church with steady access to and immersion in the world in Weber's sense.

The one sustained attempt by Catholics heretofore to build a lay Church with a worldly vocation was the historic thrust of the Catholic Action and Christian Democratic movements mainly in France, Germany and the Lowlands. Catholic Action and Christian Democracy were, notably, not effective in Italy and Latin America.[22] The rightful autonomy of the Christian Democratic Party, labor unions, and professional associations as the platforms for articulating a theology of culture and the concrete historical ideal were almost always compromised by the hierarchical, institutional Church. This was due, in part, to an imperfect differentiation, in theory and practice, of the Christian Democratic Parties, etc.—as voluntary associations "of Christian inspiration" but in no way organs of the institutional Church—from the Church as a corporate institution. Nor was the fault for this "contamination" of institutional spheres entirely due to hierarchical interference, although this latter played a strong role. The laity, too, often felt uneasy about their autonomy and thus sought improperly official religious sanction for their concrete programs by appealing to hierarchical intervention.

Some have contended, perhaps correctly, that the Catholic Action and Christian Democratic strategies lacked any compelling alternative visions to what Emmanuel Mounier trenchantly labeled "the established disorders" of modern, capitalistic, Western societies. To the extent that this is true, they were unable to sustain the creative strain between tension and accommodation to the world. They thus became vehicles for an, at best, slightly differently flavored status quo. This may account for the fact that these movements all collapsed in the 1960's. Nevertheless, I share Michael Fogarty's considered judgment of this European-based movement when he asserts that it deserves to rank with Ernst Troeltsch's two candidates—medieval Christendom and Anglo-Saxon Puritanism in England and the United States—as unique moments of genuine world-transforming Christianity.[23]

As I argue in Chapter 6, the Catholic Action strategy never fit the strategic needs of Catholicism in the United States and Latin America.[24] It never really took hold in these contexts. Moreover, as David O'Brien has contended, American Catholics, focusing so uniquely on a program of upward mobility and "Americanization," certainly lacked a compelling alternative vision for the American social order.[25] Catholic Action has, in any event, spent its creative force even in Europe. The only new Church-society models in the post-Vatican Church, supplied by liberation theology, so stress the aspect of tension between Church and world—properly so, it seems to me, in the Latin American context—that they provide little linkage with ordinary work roles in current structures. With the collapse of the Catholic Action strategy in the post-Vatican II Church, there is, at present, no viable European or North American model for Church-society relations, no sustained pastoral mobilization of lay energies toward world transformation, no compelling sense of the world of work as, genuinely, a *religious* vocation, no appropriate vision with powerful leverage to criticize the imperfections and rank injustices of the social order. The absence of these creates a situation of pastoral tragedy and represents a serious dereliction of duty on the part of the Church. For their absence means the effective abdication of the Church's vocation to transform the world.

There is a paradox in the post-Vatican Church's social teaching. In some senses, Catholic social teaching since John XXIII has become more prophetic, clearer about the established disorder of world society, stronger in its emphasis on the worldwide dimensions of the social question, more ringing in its stress on structural sin and the need for profound, deep-reaching, structural change.[26] There is little danger that this corpus of social teaching could be mistaken for an endorsement of a mere superficial, cosmetic transformation of the status quo. There is also little risk that this authentic social teaching will lose the precarious balance between tension and accommodation to the world by sacrificing the transcendent dimension. These developments in Catholic social teaching represented by the superb social encyclicals of Pope Paul VI and the 1971 World Synod of Bishops seem to me sheer gain.

Still this new turn in Catholic social teaching, influenced no doubt by the new emphases on political and liberation theology, has not yet descended to the level of Maritain's concrete historical ideal. It remains in the realm of middle-level axioms and direction-orienting principles and visions. Moreover, as some commentators have noted about the papal presence at Puebla, the Church still has difficulties distinguishing between the proper province of social and political activity appropriate to the institutional Church, as such, as a moral voice in society and the concrete embodiment of this moral thrust growing out of the Church as a community of faith but worked out in the voluntary sector and *in* the world. The Church still finds it hard to recognize the distinction between the laity as members, *parts* and participants of the Church and the laity as an independent *element* and vital Christian force with its own mission and initiative to translate middle-level axioms into concrete programs, struggles and movements for political and social change.[27]

The compelling new vision for social orders contained within the hierarchical teaching in the post-Vatican Church lacks any specific junction with those ordinary social roles through which the laity serve and act upon the world. In the absence of such linkages, mediated through a sustained ministry in contact with the laity precisely in their location in the worlds of work, neighborhoods, politics and culture rather than in the sanctuary, school or expressive devotional group (whether the ministers involved in this ministry are lay or clergy seems a matter of indifference once the issue of institutional *control* vs. lay *autonomy* in the worldly mission is squarely faced), the new prophetic social voice in the post-Vatican II Church is not truly prophetic in Weber's sense of the term. It lacks significant followers. It is not articulated in a way that is directed toward mobilizing lay energy. It lacks the constituency uniquely capable of acting as a carrier group of genuine world-transformation. The danger could be that this post-Vatican II vision for the social order will so stress the tension with the world in the precarious balance between tension and accommodation that it will be difficult to translate the vision in America into appropriate address and a concrete historical ideal.

LAY MOTIVATIONAL COMMITMENTS

I want to move now to the second condition for the possibility of a worldly Church, i.e. a consistent and sustained pastoral strategy aimed at eliciting solid motivational commitments among the laity such that they see the world and their life work as an arena of meaningful *religious* action. We have sufficient evidence from both journalism and the social sciences which points to the fact that most Americans have difficulty enough seeing work as meaningful even in this-worldly profane terms, let alone in religious categories.[28] For most, the world of work evokes a sense of powerlessness in the face of bureaucratic controls, of walking a treadmill on careers without inner criteria for evaluation and meaning. Work is seen increasingly in purely instrumental terms as a means of livelihood which provides material sustenance to engage in the real and meaningful tasks of life which lie, if anywhere, elsewhere. While most Americans spend the bulk of their waking hours in their jobs, their real preoccupations, satisfactions, fantasies and desires lie elsewhere—in family, leisure activity and interpersonal satisfactions. Sociological studies show that even in the world of work it is the quality of these latter rather than any sense of intrinsic meaning that creates the greatest job satisfaction. There is, moreover, little sense of a deep inner testing of strengths and possibilities as the necessary pre-condition for choosing a career as a vocation or of the slow transformation of body and spirit as "the trade enters into the man," in Simone Weil's fine phrase, in the course of a work career.[29] Weber caught this sense of the denuding of meaning to work when he referred to the world of modern work as an iron cage.

Part of this lack of inner meaning to work stems from a sense of futility about controlling the conditions of work or the final distribution and substantive quality of the product. Part flows from a division of labor which makes it difficult for workers to see how their contribution fits as a unique element into a whole process of satisfying production. But part of the sense of a lack of intrinsic meaning to work comes from the erosion of over-all societal purpose and destiny which might provide a strong sense of meaning for an historical existence that consists largely of Hesiod's duality of work and days. As Paul Goodman has remarked about American society: "If we turn to the deeper human and religious answers to the question 'Why should I work?'—for example, work as fulfillment of one's potentialities, work as the vocation that gives justification—our present economy has little to offer."[30]

I recently directed a graduate student in Berkeley who has specialized in the sociology and theology of work. Through the extensive bibliographical material she has brought to my attention I have been forced to conclude that one could become an expert on the theology of work and command the corpus of its literature in a few weeks' time. Among Catholics, little has been written on a theology of work since the brief pastoral effervescence connected with the priest-worker movement in France in the post-World War II period. The writings of Simone Weil represent a rare, if precious, flower in this desert of reflection on work. Among Americans, nothing of substance has appeared to address the sense of work as a vocation since Robert Calhoun's neglected but penetrating theological analysis of a world-vocation in his 1935 book, *God and the Common Life.*[31]

This paucity of theological literature on work reflects clearly an absence of Church concern and focus upon the properly lay vocation. Another reflection of the abandonment of serious attention to the world-transforming mission of the Church is the fact that most of the experiments with industrial apostolates and lay professional sodalities which marked an earlier era of American Catholicism have all withered away. They were always, at best, rarities. At present, they have become an extinct species. In this context, the Chicago Declaration of Concern sadly notes "the demise of those organizations and networks of the recent past whose task it was to inspire and support the laity in their vocation to the world through their professional and occupational lives."[32] Of course, as some have noted in commenting on the Declaration, it would be a misplaced hope to wait upon the clergy, especially in its diminished numbers, to take the initiative in devising functional alternatives to these earlier networks and organizations.

I have no doubt that we need some functional alternative to these earlier associations and networks. Sustaining a sense of a worldly vocation has never been an easy task. As Weber notes, there are several alternatives to an asceticism directed at world-transformation: an inner-worldly asceticism too comfortable with the world, as in classic Chinese Confucianism, extreme world-rejecting asceticism, world-rejecting mysticisms, and forms of inner-worldly mysticism which lack concern for any outer world which transcends interior states of blissful consciousness and personal fulfillment. The difficulty in trying to maintain the dialogue between the Bible and the daily newspaper—to use Karl Barth's somewhat simplistic formula for worldly address—is that an inevitable tension will always exist between the two worlds. The temptation is to move toward the reduction of that tension either by opting for only one of the poles in the dialogue or by compartmentalizing the two worlds by moving between them without any serious exercise in translation. Simone Weil caught this temptation in her remarks about French Christians. Does anyone doubt that her remarks apply with equal force to contemporary American Christianity? "They . . . resign themselves to being irreligious . . . in all that appertains to the secular side of their own lives, which is what usually happens today to a far greater extent than those concerned realize themselves. In any case, they set aside the proper function of religion, which is to suffuse with its light all secular life, public or private, without ever in any way dominating it."[33]

The precarious balance which makes for an effective worldly vocation has always necessitated a very definite kind of pastoral strategy. Once again, Weber is a helpful guide. Every significant impact which Christianity has made upon the social order in modern times—from the Puritans' transforming vision of a democratic polity based on virtue and the common weal and the proliferation of voluntary associations concerned with the public welfare in nineteenth century American Protestantism, to the influence of the social gospel on the progressive movement, the Catholic Action strategy in Europe and the new attempt to build "base communities" in Latin America—has been built upon the pious lay conventicle, the *ecclesiola in ecclesia,* the small group of pious formation which strenuously combines religious socialization and deepening in Christian self-identity with a steadfast insistence on worldly service and action. I know of no instances of extraordinary Christian impact on society which have not grown out of a matrix dependent on this corporate, cell model.

The parish congregation, so important for other purposes, is too diffuse and unspecialized to serve as the organizational core for mobilizing the worldly vocation. Expressive devotional movements such as marriage encounter and the charismatic movement, so useful in deepening religious identity in other contexts, lack any specific focus on the world of work. Ad

hoc voluntary networks searching for social justice such as the Right to
Life Movement or the community organizing model in parishes tend to
minimize or overlook the sustaining community of piety necessary to guarantee that the input into the social order will maintain a strong Christian
ingredient. Thus, we see the recurrent phenomenon of the burnt-out case
in social justice activism. Such ad hoc groups are also usually and, probably properly, so focused on one issue or set of agenda that they do not
generate over-arching commitments to the world of work as, throughout,
an area of meaningful religious action. No one, I suppose, presumes that
scattered individual lay inspiration and initiative, in the absence of the sustaining context of small group support for a worldly vocation, will achieve
any focused influence on the social order.

The genius of the Catholic Action model in Europe and the base community model in Latin America—with all their imperfections, drawbacks,
and failures and, in the case of the Catholic Action model, its historical
irretrievability since it has spent its creative force—is that they recognize
the need for the organizational form of the pious lay conventicle which *simultaneously* maintains *religious* identity and spurs on *secular* mission.[34]
Some such organizational form has always, it seems to me, been a pre-condition for arousing, sustaining and channeling lay commitments to transform the world of politics, neighborhood and work as a religious task. As I
read Weber's remarks about the Puritan ethic I see him asserting that this
kind of organization is a pre-condition for an effective transformation of
cultures through a this-worldly asceticism. This achievement of the simultaneous balance and tension of religious identity and secular mission is,
however, inherently precarious and unstable as a sociological form. There
is always the temptation to neglect the cell of religious socialization to
press forward with the urgent secular task. Efficiency and "effective" political or economic action take precedence over religious vision and identity. In the process, the "secular movement of religious inspiration"
becomes almost, without remainder, "secular" and thin, as tended to occur
in the European Christian Democratic movement. The balance between
tension and accommodation becomes tilted. As the statistics about those
formed in Catholic Action movements in France make clear, individuals
forsake the group of Christian socialization for a totally integrated role in
a "secular" political party, labor union and profession, in the process losing contact with an indispensable source of on-going religious sustenance
of the worldly task.[35] I am arguing here that there is no guarantee that the
inherently precarious simultaneous address to both religious socialization
and secular task will be maintained over time, even with the adoption of
the lay conventicle form. This is a matter which calls for constant scrutiny
and discernment. I do not, however, see it as even a remote possibility that
there will be sustained and concerted Christian action in the world
through organizational forms which neglect "the pious lay conventicle or-
dered to work and service in the secular order." As I read Max Weber, at

any rate, I think he had something like this in mind when he insisted that religion and the world exist in inherent and permanent tension.

Of course, there is no necessity that the pious lay conventicles or prayer and reflection cells all exist under one organizational umbrella. A loosely coordinated network could achieve the same purpose. Moreover, in America, there is no possibility of an effective mission toward transforming the social order that would restrict itself uniquely to Catholic energies. Pastoral strategies to implement the world-transforming mission of the Church must be, properly, inter-denominational. They should respect, as well, the pluralistic nature of American society. But, in calling our attention to the fact that almost *nothing* like this pastoral strategy is currently available in the American Catholic Church, the drafters of the Chicago Declaration of Concern are making a telling observation. In effect, they assert that one of the necessary conditions for the possibility of a Church with a worldly vocation is absent in the American Catholic scene. Nor do the other American churches present a strikingly different picture. One hopeful sign represented both by the Chicago Declaration and the Congress of the Laity, held, under largely evangelical auspices but with wide representation from all the churches, in Los Angeles in 1978, is that at least some forces in the Church recognize the lacuna and are signaling the need for serious discourse and action to redress the problem.

Taking this challenge of the Chicago Declaration seriously would entail a thoroughgoing assessment of the inner-Church reward structures for lay involvement, the creation of predominantly lay forums for sustained analysis and address to societal issues, and initiating practical programs for pastoral care of the laity precisely in their secular tasks. When I speak of reward structures I am not, of course, mainly concerned with monetary rewards. By the nature of the case, the laity will receive monetary reward from their secular occupations. I am merely asserting a sociological truism that every group, the Church included, largely gets the behaviors and activities which it encourages and rewards through its reward structure of either money, esteem, power or participatory access. In a profound sense, the American Catholic laity in its worldly vocation is, at present, in the situation of a group which Ivan Vallier called "a disenfranchised religious proletariat." It is really impossible, over the long pull, to expect sustained lay energies for a religious task which lacks *all* reward—I am referring here to inner-worldly and intra-group rewards and not merit accrued in heaven! Effective mobilization of the laity as a status-group with a special religious task in the world presupposes a concomitant upgrading of the laity as a status group *within* the Church. Thus, concern for a worldly mission must go hand in hand with intra-Church reforms that will increase collegiality and participatory access to decision-making, formal voice and concomitant esteem for the laity in the Church.

By lay forums I have in mind a modern equivalent of the lay congresses in Europe and the United States in the nineteenth century and the vision of the American Federation of Catholic Societies before World War I.[36] These movements obscurely saw what I have earlier contended, namely that the articulation of Church-society relationships is an appropriately lay task. By and large, they skirted all direct pretensions to supplant the proper hierarchical task of defining doctrine, determining what constitutes "official" teaching and discerning pastoral strategies for the over-all Church.[37] They studiously avoided any direct confrontations with the prerogatives of the hierarchy by claiming to restrict their activity to concrete questions of Church-world strategy. Nevertheless, as history attests, the American hierarchy was deeply uneasy both about the lay congresses and the American Federation of Catholic Societies as, much later, it was about the Detroit Call to Action. This latter type of convocation represents what I have in mind when I speak of predominantly lay forums to address the social question. Other examples would include the Pastoral Council in The Netherlands and its successor, the National Pastoral Consultation, which both in The Netherlands and Belgium meet biennially. Perhaps, as the Chicago Declaration asserts, the Call to Action tended to focus too much on internal Church questions or to draw its constituency too much from full-time Church professionals rather than the ordinary laity, although these seem to me more an accident of history than something inherent in the process of holding such convocations on a regular basis.

In regard to practical pastoral care directed to the laity in their unique and proper vocation (as opposed to pastoral care directed to private woes, the family or interior spirituality), Weber stresses the point that the genius of Christianity, when compared to other world religions, in gaining transformative leverage on the social order derived from the fact that it alone maintained a truly lay-centered program of pastoral care.[38]

CONCRETE CHOICES IMPACTING THE SOCIAL ORDER

I have already addressed the final condition for a Church with a worldly vocation in my earlier remarks about the concrete historical ideal. You will recall that this third condition postulated the mobilization of committed lay energies around concrete choices for influencing the social order by infusing religious values into the "secular" realm. It is not enough to maintain the balance between tension with and accommodation to the world in *theoretical* visions for transforming the social order. These visions become *a social force* only when they become a compelling and concretized vision for a significant lay constituency socialized, in and through the pious lay conventicle, to both Christian identity and the secular task as of *religious* meaning. By the nature of the case, only a minority of the laity will ever be mobilized through the pious conventicles. They will represent a leaven in the mass. What is unfortunate, in the American case, is that there is currently no pastoral strategy to facilitate the emergence of such a committed lay cadre. Thus, splendid lay energies remain random, dissipated and dormant.

Finally, the visions become "appropriate vision" only when they are translated into a concrete historical ideal. At this point, the appropriate arena for action is not *within* the Church. The concrete historical ideal can only be forged in very particular programs, struggles, options and prudential decisions in the economic, political, erotic, aesthetic and intellectual spheres. The institutional Church will have failed in its task as Church and its essential mission to the world unless it gives birth, in each generation, to a large cohort of laity actively articulating, envisioning and embodying an appropriate concrete historical ideal. Once it gives birth to them through its sustaining community of tradition, sacraments and social vision, the institutional Church and the hierarchy, clergy and religious professionals lack authority, except that which derives from a special charism, not office, to control, shape or direct this properly lay ministry.

The institutional Church knows of hierarchical distinctions and status grading. The Church as community of faith knows only of equality among Christians and a diversity based on charisms, not office, orders or ecclesiastical power. Everyone who is baptized belongs to both the Church as institution and the Church as community of faith. These are two inseparable, although analytically distinct, faces of the one Church. I am arguing here for two changes in our self-understanding of the Church. The first is an institutional change which would provide a serious platform for the laity to address social questions. The second is an assumption that the laity are the key action agents of the community of faith in its mission to transform societal structures. It is the face of the Church as a community of faith where all members are equal in their call to discipleship which makes it impossible to maintain rigid status distinctions between clergy and laity. Nevertheless, I argue that world-transformation, as a functional task of the Church, is properly a lay charism.

The Church as institution is constantly to be judged by how well it nurtures and serves the Church as community of faith because the institution, while indispensable, is always of merely instrumental value, a necessary minimal ingredient of order as the pre-condition for the deeper reality of freedom, variety and dynamic interaction with the world. The proper arena for forging the concrete historical ideal, then, is not within the Church but in the world. The appropriate organizational mode to express this concrete historical ideal is the autonomous voluntary association of the laity, whether in the form of pious conventicle, lobby group, social movement, lay congress, lay-controlled newspapers and magazines, ad hoc political association, pressure or ginger groups in the secular order. These voluntary associations are in no way directly subject to hierarchical control, surveillance or governance. They fall outside the hierarchy's or clergy's sphere of competence. They can never be more, nor should they ever be less, lest they lose the vision of transforming the world as a religious vocation, than "of Christian inspiration."

These lay groups cannot, in consequence, compel the assent of the institutional Church as such whose worldly vocation is restricted to the guardianship of orienting principles and a non-partisan, usually middle-level and non-programmatic, moral leadership role.[39] The institutional Church should provide sufficient money and personnel to grant some priority to the kind of sustained pastoral care which would facilitate the conditions for the possibility of the emergence of a Church with a worldly vocation out of whose matrix the autonomous voluntary groups are constantly being born, subsequently to live their own life "in the world." If it does not, it will be hard to sustain the judgment that the institutional Church takes the worldly vocation very seriously.

In the absence of such a turnabout of pastoral priorities, the future of social Catholicism may look much the same as the past. The splendid corporate wisdom of the "third way" of Catholic social teaching will never make much of a dent outside the pale world of "interesting ideas" and bookish intellectuals because it lacks genuine embodiments in "a third force" at work in the secular world.[40] Or, to paraphrase Chesterton, the failures of social Christianity will not stem from the fact that it was tried and found wanting. The failure will lie in the fact that it will "never have been really tried," because no one cared all that much about thinking through the sociological conditions for the possibility of a Church with a worldly vocation.

NOTES

1. Max Weber, *The Sociology of Religion*, trans. Ephraim Fischoff (Boston: Beacon Press, 1963), p. 79.

2. I am aware of the snares in defining the secular in opposition to the sacred in sociology. Cf. my "Situation for Modern Faith," *Theological Studies,* Vol. 39, No. 4 (December 1978) pp. 601–632. Hence, I have put "secular" in quotes.

3. Jacques Maritain, *True Humanism* (New York: Charles Scribner's Sons, 1938), p. 121.

4. I treat the issue of the limits and possibilities of American Catholicism for devising Church-society models in Chapter 6.

5. Maritain, *True Humanism,* p. 122.

6. Cf. the remarks of Paul VI to the effect that there can be no one Church-society model applying across cultures in his encyclical, *Octogesima Adveniens,* no. 4 in David O'Brien and Thomas Shannon, eds., *Renewing the Earth* (Garden City: Doubleday, 1977).

7. The appropriate form for such lay address to social issues might be a national synod or a national pastoral consultation such as those held regularly in Belgium and The Netherlands. For a description of the National Pastoral Council and the National Pastoral Consultation in Dutch Catholicism cf. my *The Evolution of Dutch Catholicism* (Berkeley: University of California Press, 1978), pp. 159–82.

8. Cf. "The Relationship of Religion to Politics, Economics, Sexuality and Art," in Max Weber, *The Sociology of Religion,* pp. 223–245 and "Religious Rejec-

tions of the World and Their Directions," in Hans Gerth and C. Wright Mills, eds., *From Max Weber* (New York: Oxford University Press, 1958), pp. 323–59.

9. Since Weber was writing in a period before the rise of feminist consciousness, he could still use the fine, economic phrase, "brotherly love." In our day we would need, less eloquently, to speak of fraternal and sororal love.

10. "Religious Rejections of the World and Their Directions," p. 352.

11. Cf. H. Richard Niebuhr, *Christ and Culture* (New York: Harper and Brothers, pp. 83–116.

12. Howard Butt, *At the Edge of Hope* (New York: Seabury Press, 1978), p. 205.

13. Roland Robertson, *The Sociological Interpretation of Religion* (New York: Schocken, 1970), p. 93.

14. Cf. Avery Dulles, "The Meaning of Faith Considered in Relationship to Justice," in John C. Haughey, ed., *The Faith That Does Justice* (New York: Paulist Press, 1977), p. 13.

15. Robert N. Bellah, *Religion and Progress in Modern Asia* (New York: The Free Press, 1965), pp. 193–94.

16. Robert N. Bellah, *Tokugawa Religion* (Boston: Beacon Press, 1957), p. 196.

17. Max Weber, *The Protestant Ethic and the Spirit of Capitalism* (New York: Charles Scribner's Sons, 1958), p. 215.

18. Max Weber, "The Prophet," in *The Sociology of Religion,* pp. 46–60.

19. Cf. Jay Dolan, *Immigrant Church* (Baltimore: The Johns Hopkins Press, 1975) and David O'Brien, "The Organizational Revolution in Nineteenth Century Catholicism," in Irene Woodward, ed., *The United States Catholic Experience.*

20. For an articulation of this third way of social Catholicism cf. Emmanuel Mounier, "De la propriété capitaliste à la propriété humaine" and "Révolution personnaliste et communautaire," in *Oeuvres de Mounier,* Vol. 1 (Paris: Editions du Seuil, 1961), pp. 129–46.

21. For a non-Catholic social program directed at "mediating structures" which seems congenial to Catholic social thought of cf. Peter Berger and Richard J. Neuhaus, *To Empower People* (Washington, D.C.: The American Enterprise Institute), 1977.

22. For the Catholic Action strategy cf. William Bosworth, *Catholicism and Crisis in Modern France* (Princeton: Princeton University Press, 1962) and Michael Fogarty, *Christian Democracy in Europe* (Notre Dame: University of Notre Dame Press, 1957). For Italy cf. Gianfranco Poggi, *Catholic Action in Italy: The Sociology of a Sponsored Organization* (Palo Alto: Stanford University Press, 1967).

23. Fogarty, *op. cit.,* p. 82.

24. Cf. Chapter 6, "American Catholicism and Strategic Theology."

25. David O'Brien, *The Renewal of American Catholicism* (New York: Oxford University Press, 1972), pp. 80–162.

26. For a compendium of Catholic social teaching since the pontificate of John XXIII, cf. David O'Brien and Thomas Shannon, eds., *Renewing the Earth* (Garden City: Doubleday, 1977).

27. For the distinction between part and element in social organizations cf. Guy E. Swanson, "To Live in Concord with Society," in *Cooley and Sociological Analysis,* Albert J. Reiss, ed. (Ann Arbor: University of Michigan Press, 1968) and my application of these categories in *The Evolution of Dutch Catholicism,* pp. 103–07 and *passim.*

28. Cf. Studs Terkel, *Working* (New York: Avon, 1972), and Robert Blauner, *Alienation and Freedom: The Factory Worker and His Industry* (Chicago: University of Chicago Press, 1964).

29. For an excellent brief theological treatment of discerning one's call to a career, cf. "Finding and Doing One's Job," in Robert Calhoun, *God and the Common Life* (New York: Charles Scribner's Sons, 1935), pp. 207–37.

30. Paul Goodman, *Compulsory Mis-Education and the Community of Scholars* (New York: Random House, 1962), p. 109.

31. Calhoun, *God and the Common Life.* As Calhoun's book makes clear a theology of work needs to retrieve a sense of the "day's work as divine calling" by facing both "ideals and actualities in the working world." It also needs to relate these issues to the working of God in creation and human cooperation in God's creation. I am indebted to conversations with Clare Denton Fisher for many of my insights into a theology of work.

32. The text and various responses, including mine, to the Chicago Declaration of Concern appears in *Commonweal,* Vol. CV, No. 4 (February 17, 1978), pp. 108–16.

33. Simone Weil, *The Need for Roots* (New York: Harper Colophon Books, 1971), p. 119.

34. Thomas Bruneau of McGill University has recently completed a manuscript reporting his research into base communities in Brazil. Since I am not yet in possession of this manuscript, I am relying on his chapter, "Notes Toward the Study of Popular Religiosity and Strategies of Change in the Church: Evidence from Eight Brazilian Dioceses," in Daniel Levine, ed., *The Church and Politics in Latin America* (Beverly Hills: Sage, 1979).

35. For the evidence of defections from the religious socialization groups, cf. Bosworth, *Catholicism and Crisis in Modern France,* and comparative material on Christian democracy in Chile and France in Brian Smith, *Religion and Social Change in Chile,* unpublished dissertation, Department of Political Science, Yale University, 1979.

36. For the vision of the American Federation of Catholic Societies as a lay-controlled forum for articulating Church-society relations cf. Alfred Ede, *A Catholic Quest for A Christian America,* unpublished dissertation, The Graduate Theological Union, Berkeley 1977.

37. In my own theological vision, the laity need to be consulted even on doctrinal and pastoral issues. On social issues, the direction is reversed. Social teaching constitutes a lay prerogative, although, naturally, the laity would also "consult" the hierarchy.

38. Cf. "Religious Congregation, Preaching, Pastoral Care," in Weber, *The Sociology of Religion,* pp. 60–79.

39. For a strong case for restricting the social teaching role of the institutional Church to middle-level axioms or only those conclusions which can be grounded on clear Christian warrant, cf. Paul Ramsey, *Who Speaks for the Church?* (Nashville: Abingdon Press, 1967).

40. It is worth noting that Weber asserts that the religion of intellectuals is, typically, a world-rejecting mysticism. Intellectuals are unlikely candidates for the carrier class of a worldly social ethic with the contours of a concrete historical ideal. Cf. Weber, "Religious Rejections of the World and Their Directions," pp. 350–57.

Part Two

DIALOGUE WITH POLITICAL
& LIBERATION THEOLOGY

Chapter Three

On Political and
Liberation Theology

I am by training both a sociologist, with special interest in the sociology of religion, and a theologian concerned with social ethics. In both capacities, I have been fascinated and delighted, if sometimes critical, over the past decade as I watched the strong emergence of a new, explicitly political theology and charted its moves from Europe to Latin America to North America.

Much of theology in the past decade has followed the vagaries of fashion. But political theology is no passing fad. It answers to a critical need in society which seeks for deeper norms and meanings in history than can be supplied by the reigning "technical reason" with its preoccupation with what "works" in the short run.

Political theology also addresses the crisis in traditional ways of relating the Church to society. It is grounded in a renewed theology of Church and culture. It will not go away with next spring's best sellers. One also finds an unusual convergence between official Church teaching, the writings of political theologians and new strategies by social activists.

Two key sociological problems for the churches lie behind this emergence of political theology. The first is the privatization of religion. The second is the breakdown, for both Protestants and Catholics, of earlier models of Church-world engagement and the fragmentation of concerted Church action in the political order.

I am impressed by the sociological arguments of Peter Berger, Bryan Wilson and Charles Glock that religion has become, increasingly, a private matter.[1] This is something quite different than wholesale secularization. Modern people live no less by myths than their ancestors. As Robert Bellah, David Martin and Andrew Greeley have persuasively argued, modern humanity is almost certainly no less religious than earlier generations. Questions of ultimate concern are still being asked insistently.[2] Indeed, Church membership—at least in America—seems once more on the increase.

But the sociological question to press about privatization is not about the absolute numbers of Church adherents or individual attitudes toward religious values. These can remain favorable for the churches while the systematic linkage between religion and economics, politics, education and the public media shows dramatic slippage. Even if religion holds steady in its influence on individuals, if it declines in institutional impact it decreases as a "public" concern. As Roland Robertson has remarked, Great Britain and the Soviet Union have roughly equal per capita members of the churches.[3] But in England religion has greater public relevance. Questions of ultimate meaning can continue to be asked across a wide spectrum of interpersonal interactions without touching issues of public policy, distributive justice and international peace and order.

Religion became "guaranteed" to the private sphere for many reasons. There is the necessity for public consensus in pluralistic societies and the need to quell sectarian conflicts. The churches often meddled in the rightful affairs of society or imposed their will on others. Legal separation of Church and state restrains Church access to public issues. Modern philosophies of the person and legal rights are excessively individualistic. There is the assumption that everything public belongs to the domain of the state. One result of this privatization—even if unintended—is a cynical divorce of the moral and political. Society has suffered because it lacks language, a forum and reflective tradition to address questions of substantive social goals, ideals, values.

The Church also acquiesced in its own privatization. Most of its energies are expended on individual morality and spirituality, the family, sexuality, private charity and interpersonal counseling. Even today most Church members identify public morality with the private ethical standards of public officials. Do they cheat, lie, appropriate public funds for private gain, etc.?

Sociological studies show that few sermons touch on public issues. Salvation is preached as an individual achievement. Theology in the past was more personalist and existential than social. It often neglected any careful analysis of the analogical differences between personal and civic morality. It tried naively to apply the Sermon on the Mount to complex economic and diplomatic issues. It stressed grace and human freedom without attending to the socially structured determinants which limit freedom.

The second problem is the breakdown of earlier models of Church-world engagement. Neither Christendom nor culture Christianity remains viable. Naked power politics are unworthy of the Church. The earlier Catholic strategy of affecting public issues through explicitly Catholic organizations is gone. Protestant hopes for influence by individuals acting alone did not materialize. The sellout of the churches to Nazism remains fresh to European memories. In the United States, key slogans refer to the "suburban captivity of the churches" or Martin Marty's epithet for culture religion, "American Shinto."

Vatican II began to address these two problems in its *Pastoral Constitution on the Church in the Modern World.* This was the first time in history that a Church council issued a social document. At Vatican II, the

Church was seen as a sacrament for the unity, justice and love which God intends for the whole world. No more the ordinary means of salvation for most people, the Church was no longer viewed as the only locus of God's activity. It is now a "servant Church," called to read carefully the signs of the times and to discern in worldly action what God is asking and enabling it to do. A new emphasis on the public concerns of the Church for nuclear disarmament, peace, the right to development and human rights emerged at the council. A new stance of seeking cooperation and coalition-building with all persons of good will became apparent. The *Pastoral Constitution on the Church in the Modern World* became the charter document for a new political theology.[4] It was now clear, as Jose Miguez Bonino puts it, that "the Church neither has nor wants a political road of its own."[5]

POLITICAL THEOLOGY IN EUROPE

Some theologians found the *Pastoral Constitution on the Church in the Modern World* overly optimistic in its assessment of modern liberal society and too willing to adopt a cooperative rather than a critical prophetic stance. They feared that cooperation might mean, once again, cooptation. While accepting much of the council's new emphases, a new political theology reversed some of its trends. Jürgen Moltmann and Johannes B. Metz are the giants of this new theology. Edward Schillebeeckx has contributed to it.[6]

These theologians shifted classic emphases in theology away from faith toward hope and from the eternity of God as a timeless omnipresence toward God's future which was seen as the only ground for hope that history itself has an open future. God acts from the future which is his to pull us forward toward it and a greater realization of his kingdom. Metz, especially, is explicit about his desire to combat the privatization of religion.

The political theologians rediscovered the communal aspects of eschatology. They also saw its relevance to history. The kingdom which is yet to come will be a community of justice and peace. God's will for universal salvation means that all must be touched by the kingdom, not just believers. Christian engagement in social action makes a difference for the shape of the final kingdom. There are not two histories, one sacred, one profane. The kingdom is not a denial of history but the elimination of its corruptibility, its ambiguity and frustrations, its sin, in order to bring to full realization the true meaning of communal life. As Langdon Gilkey puts it, "If the final purposes of God have little or no relation to the betterment of the social order, it is difficult to know why God is at work in social history, or what he might be about if he is, and it is even more difficult to say why Christians should have a concern which apparently God does not."[7]

The kingdom stands in judgment over every political and economic system which exploits and oppresses poor people. The Church as the proclaimer of this kingdom is called to a stance of "critical negativity" toward every form of exploitation and injustice. It raises its voice to say: "This must go on no longer!" In recent years, political theologians have stressed the cross as a symbol of the Church's suffering service toward the poor.[8]

In close dialogue with leftist neo-Marxist philosophers and students, these theologians are sensitive to the Marxist criticism that religion often serves to sacralize the forms of society and so is an enemy of social change toward justice. The Church is also tempted to sell out the Gospel for state protection or secular prestige in the name of "effectiveness." Political theology calls the Church to unmask and denounce the ways it gets used to bless unjust social orders. It studies not only theology but the social consequences of Church piety, preaching and popular devotion. The church of the *Sacre Coeur,* for example, in Paris was dedicated to the Sacred Heart, in gratitude for deliverance, on the very ground where the Paris commune of 1870 was brought to its knees. This was a political statement of conservatism.

These theologians also adopt the Marxist concept of praxis, i.e., a theory for action and strategic implementation of what the Church teaches. They hold that theological assertions are distorted into a conservative ideology if their symbols do not have critical and transformative meaning for future action. Against criticisms that they are overly optimistic in their hopes, the political theologians maintain that theirs is less a belief in a perfect, sinless society on earth than a conviction of the non-necessity of the present imperfect order.

Political theology has been rightly criticized for its vague eschatological impatience with every status quo, its occasional apocalyptic posturing, its neglect of the doctrines of creation, sin and providence. Some find the idea of a God who only *exists* in the future metaphysical nonsense. Others object to a too slavish adherence to Marxism. Some of the earlier criticisms of political theology as a utopian optimism have been tempered by a recent turn of this theology to the doctrine of the cross and essays on suffering.

There is little concrete in this theology in the way of direct political policy, few specific directives for Church or society. The political theologians also pass rather cavalierly from theology to politics without touching base in social ethics. They lack a developed theory of justice, human rights or the state. Moltmann has written on a theological base for human rights. With the exception of Dorothee Sölle's political prayer meetings in Cologne and a few "critical communities" in The Netherlands, there is little translation of the new theology into popular liturgy, preaching and catechesis.[9] Perhaps it is not surprising that a basically German theology of politics should sound at times abstract and utopian. As Johannes B. Metz once remarked, "We Germans, and especially we German Catholics, have had so little sustained or practical experience in politics."[10]

But criticism should not lose sight of the permanent gains for theology in this new public turn. Eschatology undercuts conservative notions of a static order of creation, natural law and providence. New attention is given to the social forms of theology and the social consequence of belief.

A steady assault has been mounted on the privatization of religion. The political theologians have provided fresh theological warrants to explain why the Church's big questions are now the same as the world's and why this is not a secular copout. Again, the Catholics among them have begun to transform traditional Church social teaching, largely if not entirely philosophical, into a genuine theology based on the Bible. As Langdon Gilkey has noted in commenting on this theology, "To have recentered our theological concentration on history and the future, and on the divine participation in the task of liberation from the oppression and the bondages of the present—in effect, to have sounded once again the call of the social gospel—has been of the greatest significance for theology and the Church, and for this we are all in debt."[11]

LIBERATION THEOLOGY

Political theology moved naturally to Latin America when students of Metz, Pannenberg and Moltmann went home. Soon the European version came under attack as too abstract, too tied to a European political economy. New names appeared on the international theological roster: Gutiérrez, Miranda, Sobrino, Segundo, Dussel, Bonino, Alves and Beatrice Couch. Political theology, in the sea change, became Latin American liberation theology. For the first time, serious ecumenical theology occurred in Latin America.

The Latin Americans are clearer than the Europeans about the need for specific sociopolitical and economic analysis of their situation of internal poverty and external dependence. They are, perhaps, rather narrow in always adopting a Marxist perspective for this analysis. Unlike the Europeans, many Latin Americans do their theology in non-university settings in collaboration with social scientists and pastoral planners. The thrust of their theology finds echoes in episcopal teaching such as the Medellín and Puebla documents and the letters of episcopal conferences in Brazil, Peru, Chile and Paraguay.[12] This theology rejects Western models of development and historic capitalism as we know it.

Liberation theology is also inventive in its reinterpretation of classic doctrines of sin so as to include the category of social sin. Social sin is the structural congealment of past personal choices for injustice into systematic institutions of economic oppression and political deprivation. Conversion from social sin calls for more than a change of heart. It demands, as well, society's transformation. Liberation theologians accuse the present worldwide economic structures of tending, systematically, toward an unjust maldistribution of wealth, of producing a growing chasm between rich and poor nations and of relegating power to a small minority.

Liberation theology also takes history seriously. History is the locus of God's saving action. Liberation from oppression is an experiential ground of credibility for believing the good news of redemption from sin.

The unmasking of historical distortions of the Gospel which serve as ideologies to bolster dictatorial, paternalistic, corporist states is a phase in pre-evangelization. Without it, the real Gospel message may stand no chance of being heard.

As Jose Miguez Bonino puts it, "there is no such thing as a Christianity outside or above its concrete temporal incarnations."[13] Liberation theology's main quarrel with European political theology is over the concrete role of the Church in struggles for justice. The Latin Americans are not content with mere "critical negativity." As Miguez Bonino says, "prophetic denunciation on the part of the institutional Church of the conditions of oppression . . . usually fails at the critical point of assuming the concrete struggle of the people."[14]

The Latin Americans claim that religion is inevitably political whether religious people are conscious of it or not. They demand that the Church take sides, as God does, with the poor, underprivileged and oppressed. In doing a class analysis of theology they discover that theology, like all forms of thought, is very particular to its social location. Our perspective is largely defined by the place we hold in history, our class structure, groups. Theology, like other forms of thought, needs correction by people in other social locations, especially the oppressed who can show us how our attachment to privilege distorts our thought.

Liberation theology is not only political but revolutionary inasmuch as it sees that situations of injustice in Latin America cry out to heaven. Some theologians advocate violent revolution, appealing to classic Catholic criteria for a just war. They argue that armed violence is justified by the "institutional violence" of oppressive societies. Others opt for non-violent revolution, either because it is more consonant with the Gospel or for tactical reasons. None is naive about the reality of conflict. They know that the unmistakable lesson of history is that no significant human group, class or nation has voluntarily yielded power and that no changes take place except by pressure from those below or outside the system.

This theology has also reflected upon the traditional Christian doctrine of reconciliation and unity. It does not reject these as goals nor the respect due another, even an enemy, because of his or her human dignity. Nevertheless, it knows, as Gregory Baum has put it, that "the only unity that is in accordance with God's will is unity in justice, and in a sinful world this demands a significant shift in power relations. Reconciliation between various parties implies the conversion of all, and this demands on the part of some the restitution of excessive power and undue privilege."[15]

Three behavioral changes are demanded of the institutional Church by the liberationists: (1) The social base of the Church should show a pastoral identification with the poor. (2) The hierarchy is called upon to denounce violations of human rights and dignity by governments. The Latin American hierarchy has been conspicuous in responding to this call. They have exercised their prophetic function on Gospel warrants rather than narrow political choices. (3) The Church should *lead* in the struggle of the poor.[16]

This last desire is the most debatable since it seems to call for a direct insertion of the Church in the political realm. Perhaps, as Thomas Bruneau has argued in his study of the Brazilian Church, this is justified because the Church is the last and only resort in issues of justice.[17] Such conditions do not apply in all other national settings.

Latin American liberation theology has inspired similar theologies in the Philippines, Sri Lanka, South Africa and South Korea. The Latin Americans have been in dialogue with North American black theologians, feminist theology and other theologians of the third world. The center of revolutionary thought in theology has moved, in the last three years, from the southern cone of Latin America northward to central America. A significant meeting of North American and Latin American theologians took place in Detroit in 1975.[18] An even more important discussion occurred in Dar Es Salaam, Tanzania in the summer of 1976 when the Latin Americans met African and Asian theologians. Africa suffers less than Latin America from interference by multi-national corporations or an entrenched class system. The basic African plea for liberation is cultural, looking toward the indigenization of the faith in African soil. Charles Nyamiti of Tanzania is a major voice of this new African theology. It agrees with Latin American theology on the need of the Church to form local, small communities and the importance to the Gospel of the question of a right to development.

To the extent that its themes and method are continuous with European political theology, liberation theology falls under the same strictures. More particular criticisms have been leveled at the vagueness of some of its key terms. Who, exactly, are the oppressed? Some feel that the Latin Americans are too ready to endorse a particular system of government or political platform, thus betraying the historic conjunction of Church and state in that continent. Still others accuse the liberationists of a shallow view of sin as if social freedom from oppression precludes the possibility of further domination by a "new class." Again, some argue that the Latin Americans focus too much on factors of external dependence and not enough on internal economic and political factors impeding development. Finally, some feel that while the Latin American theology "fits" the Latin American context, it is not exportable to less oppressive economic and political regimes. In effect, they remind the liberationists of their own discovery about the social location of every theology.

As one who has joined at times in the criticism of some aspects of Latin American liberation theology I want here, partially, to correct the record. Clearly this theology has contributed to the world Church. Both *Populorum Progressio* and *Octogesima Adveniens* of Paul VI, while partially corrective of the liberationists' themes, endorse the general thrust of this theology. The 1971 World Synod of Bishops' document, *Justice in the*

World, was clearly under its influence. On their part, Medellín and Puebla are of more than mere regional significance. They speak to the world Church. In that sense, the liberation themes now belong to all of Catholic theology.

Criticism and internal correction of liberation theology will continue precisely because so many of its basic intuitions are correct. At points, its analysis or conceptual thinking is still vague and faulty. Its choice of a pastoral problem as a source for theology is not. Liberation theology has forcefully reminded all theologians and Christians that "there are certain situations whose injustice cries to heaven." Moreover, it states a call to action to all to work for "bold transformations, innovations that go deep. Urgent reforms [in the world economic and political order] should be undertaken without delay."[19] Constructive criticism of the liberationists should flow from basic agreement on the preceding premises.

POLITICAL THEOLOGY IN NORTH AMERICA

It was not surprising that the European political theology and liberation theology found an audience in North America. This continent cannot remain a cultural enclave in an increasingly interdependent world. Besides, the category of dependency in liberation theology pointed a finger of accusation for responsibility northward.

North America has a different history to its theology and very different institutional structures than Europe and Latin America. For one thing, North America has a long indigenous history of social theology which weds theology to careful social ethical thinking. Here the churches have undergone an apprenticeship of dealing with specific issues on the basis of political analysis and moral evaluation. Theology on this continent has been closely involved in policy ethics and the analysis of specific political and social reforms. From Rauschenbusch and the social gospel through Reinhold Niebuhr to John C. Bennett, and James Luther Adams,[20] American Protestantism has not lacked its own tradition of political theology. On its side, American Catholicism gave us Edward McGlynn, John Ryan, John Courtney Murray, Virgil Michel and Paul Hanley Furfey as a legacy for an American political theology. In that sense, political theology in America long antedates the council.

Our institutions have also been unique. Here, Church and state are legally separated. Religious pluralism and the tradition of denominational voluntarism create a special climate for the Church's strategy to influence the social world. We have a long history of Church involvement in social reform movements, from the abolition movement in the nineteenth century to the rise of the labor movement and the civil rights and anti-Vietnam movements.[21] I was impressed as a participant at a Conference on Inter-Mediate Technology and Ecology celebrating the work of the late E. F.

Schumacher held at the University of California, Davis by how many Church groups were in the forefront of this movement. Moreover, our "secular" political style has never been rabidly anti-clerical. We knew neither radical liberalism nor radical socialism. Populism, the Progressive movement, the New Deal and early American socialism—especially in Canada—included vague Christian elements in their core.

But political and liberation theology have revitalized the North American thinking on political issues. Both John C. Bennett and Robert McAfee Brown have been deeply influenced in recent years by these theologies.[22] In their own way, the New Evangelicals about whom Richard Quebedeaux has written are also under their spell.[23] It is noticeable how many systematic theologians have explicitly turned their attention to the ethical and political as necessary ingredients in a valid hermeneutic of biblical and doctrinal symbols. Avery Dulles, David Tracy, Langdon Gilkey and Gregory Baum are the most notable among them. I would argue that this new turn in systematic theology with its unmistakable attention to the ethical and political consequences of doctrinal statements as a necessary feature of theology is a response to the challenge of the new political and liberation theologies.

Two widely noticed pronouncements in recent years on theology and social issues have been the Hartford statement and the rejoinder by a group of Boston theologians.[24] Both were responses to a climate created by political and liberation theology. Whatever their doctrinal differences, both statements attest to the political dimensions of theology. As John R. Donohue has put it, "Engagement in the quest for justice is no more 'secular' than the engagement of Yahweh in the history of his people or the incarnation of Jesus into the world of human suffering."[25]

Political and liberation theology have found a ready climate of interest and acceptance among social activists in the American Church. The Hispanic-speaking Catholic communities find in it a ready chord of recognition. The themes of liberation theology are dominant on seminary campuses. At my own theological setting, Berkeley's Graduate Theological Union, liberation theology constitutes almost a "school." Both before and after the 1975 and 1980 Detroit "Theology in the Americas" meetings on liberation theology, groups of interested social activists and theologians have pursued further its themes. Probably no other "school" in theology has gained such a wide following and dedication to developing its major thought. It is no fad.

Probably the most rounded and profound American theological assessment and advancement of political theology to date appeared with the publication of Langdon Gilkey's *Reaping the Whirlwind: A Christian Interpretation of History.*[26] The book is too rich in themes and "thick" in its texture of argument to summarize here.

Building on the work of Reinhold Niebuhr and Paul Tillich, Gilkey corrects some of the imbalance in political and liberation theology. He ties together eschatology with the doctrines of creation, sin and providence. He notes that God creates and sustains as well as judges social structures. His book will be remembered, if for nothing else, for the way it brings back providence as a key theological concern for understanding political life. He undercuts static conservative, ideological uses of providence by linking it with eschatology as well as creation.

Gilkey's treatment of social sin is especially good. He sees it as the structural closing of history's open possibilities, the fall of human destiny into fate. For him liberation is the freeing of freedom in human society— something other than the elimination of the possibility of sin. There is a unity between the inner and outer faces of history, between the determining factors of social structures and personal freedom. But political and social liberation are not identical with the salvation promised in the Gospel. Liberation frees us from the consequences of past human sin in history. "It does not represent the conquest of the sin itself out of which fate and fatedness continually arise. Only a new relation of mankind to God, to self and to the neighbor can achieve that goal, an achievement far beyond the range of political activity."[27]

In a penetrating analysis of the nature of politics and its key concerns of power and freedom, Gilkey shows how the issues of politics, when probed deeply, reveal religious questions about the ultimate sovereignty, norm and meaning in history. The role of religion in politics is both constitutive and critical. It is meant to keep the possibilities of history open toward a new future closer to the kingdom of God. As he puts it, "A Christian understanding of history is different from a secular one not only because of its affirmation that God supports the historical process of liberation; even more it is unique in its affirmation of the grace of forgiveness, reconciliation and of new possibility that God gives to the continuing waywardness of liberated humans."

While work abounds on the theological warrants justifying the churches' involvement in the political order, explicit work on the models and strategies for that involvement are few. But we can expect further work on the political dimensions in theology. Gregory Baum has written on Catholics and Canadian socialism and is working now on a political theology for North America.[28] Joe Holland of the Center of Concern has dealt with the various historical strategies of the Church for political involvement. David Hollenbach, S.J. of Boston's Weston School of Theology has written an excellent book on the theological bases for human rights.[29]

There has occurred a shift, with the emergence of political theology, from an excessive emphasis on philosophy as a tool for analyzing social justice to explicit theological motifs such as the kingdom, social sin, and salvation as liberation. In the process, however, while much has been gained, something has been lost. For theology alone is not enough to produce a social ethics. There is a need now to show specific links between these theological motifs and philosophical theories of justice, human rights, development and society. These, in turn, must be translated into policy directives with the help of political science and economics. By forging these links, the American vision of a Christian social ethics which would be truly a rounded political theology will be fulfilled.

NOTES

1. Cf. Peter Berger, *The Sacred Canopy* (Garden City: Doubleday, 1967) and Bryan Wilson, *Religion in a Secular Society* (Baltimore: Penguin Books, 1969).

2. Cf. Robert Bellah, *Beyond Belief* (New York: Harper and Row, 1970) and Andrew Greeley, *Unsecular Man: The Persistence of Religion* (New York: Schocken Books, 1972).

3. Roland Robertson, *The Sociological Interpretation of Religion* (Oxford: Basil Blackwell, 1970), p. 183.

4. "The Church in the Modern World," in David O'Brien and Thomas A. Shannon, eds., *Renewing the Earth* (Garden City: Image Books, 1977).

5. Jose Miguez Bonino, *Doing Theology in a Revolutionary Situation* (Philadelphia: Fortress, 1976), p. 30.

6. Jürgen Moltmann, *The Experiment Hope,* M. Douglas Meeks, ed. (Philadelphia: Fortress Press, 1975); Johannes B. Metz, *Faith in History and Society* (New York: Seabury Press, 1980) and *The Emergent Church* (New York: Crossroad Books, 1981); Edward Schillebeeckx, *God, The Future of Man* trans. N. D. Smith (New York: Sheed and Ward, 1968).

7. Langdon Gilkey, *Reaping the Whirlwind* (New York: Seabury, 1976), p. 215.

8. Cf. Jürgen Moltmann, *The Crucified God* (New York: Harper and Row, 1974).

9. Cf. Dorothee Sölle, *Political Theology* (Philadelphia: Fortress Press, 1974).

10. Oral communication, University of Notre Dame conference, "Toward Vatican III," 1977.

11. Gilkey, *op. cit.,* p. 313.

12. For the Medellín documents cf. O'Brien and Shannon, *op. cit.,* pp. 541–579, and for Puebla documents cf. John Eagleson and Philip Scharper, eds., *Puebla and Beyond* (Maryknoll: Orbis, 1979).

13. Miguez Bonino, *Doing Theology in a Revolutionary Situation,* p. 98.

14. *Ibid.,* p. 103.

15. Gregory Baum, "Political Theology in Canada," in *The Ecumenist,* Vol. 15, No. 3 (March–April 1977), p. 39.

16. T. Howland Sanks and Brian Smith, "Liberation Ecclesiology," in *Theological Studies,* Vol. 38, No. 1 (March 1977), pp. 3–39.

17. Thomas Bruneau, *The Political Transformation of the Brazilian Church* (New York: Cambridge University Press, 1974).

18. The Detroit meeting is reported in Sergio Torres and John Eagleson, eds., *Theology in the Americas* (Maryknoll: Orbis, 1976).

19. For *Populorum Progressio* cf. O'Brien and Shannon, *op. cit.,* pp. 307ff.

20. Cf. James Luther Adams, *On Being Human Religiously* (Boston: Beacon Press, 1976); John C. Bennett, *The Radical Imperative* (Philadelphia: Westminster,

1975); Reinhold Niebuhr, *Moral Man and Immoral Society* (New York: Charles Scribner's, 1960); Walter Rauschenbusch, *Christianity and the Social Crisis* (New York: Macmillan, 1907).

21. The story of this involvement is told in W. Carey McWilliams, *The Idea of Fraternity in Society* (Berkeley: University of California Press, 1973).

22. Cf. Robert McAfee Brown, *Theology in a New Key* (Philadelphia: Westminster, 1978) and *Gustavo Gutiérrez* (Atlanta: John Knox, 1980).

23. Cf. Richard Quebedeaux, *The Worldly Evangelicals* (New York: Harper and Row, 1977).

24. Cf. Peter Berger and Richard J. Neuhaus, *Against the World for the World: The Hartford Appeal* (New York: Seabury Press, 1976) and the Boston Declaration in "The Boston Affirmations," *WorldView* (March 1976).

25. John R. Donohue S.J., "Biblical Perspectives on Justice," in John C. Haughey, ed., *The Faith That Does Justice* (New York: Paulist Press, 1977), p. 109.

26. Langdon Gilkey, *Reaping the Whirlwind* (New York: Seabury Press, 1976).

27. *Ibid.,* p. 181.

28. Cf. Gregory Baum, *Catholics and Canadian Socialism* (New York: Paulist Press, 1981).

29. David Hollenbach, *Claims in Conflict* (New York: Paulist Press, 1979).

Chapter Four

Vision and Praxis in American Catholic Theology

I am going to argue that there are only three deceased American Catholic theologians still worth reading today for more than historic interest.[1] If the proposed population-universe is small, however, it is my contention that these three are giants who rank with any comparable European theologians of their day.[2] While most of American or European Roman Catholic theology in the nineteenth and the first half of the twentieth century was posing what seem like peripheral Scholastic questions, such as whether there are one or two *esse*'s in the Christ of the hypostatic union, these three men were addressing the key unresolved issues in post-Tridentine Catholic theology: the relation of nature to grace and the corollary questions about the relation of the contingent and temporal order to the order of salvation and the responsibilities and stance of the Church to the temporal order.[3] The three provide us with rich, often fresh insights to answer our own contemporary questions about the relation of human history as the one locus of truly human liberation to the saving power of God in Christ. The three men are Orestes Brownson, John A. Ryan, and John Courtney Murray.

I propose to extract three central themes, one from each man, which seem to me essential mediating concepts between eschatology and political praxis for a developed liberation theology. In Brownson I will focus mainly on the theme of providence as a mediating religious concept—intermediate between eschatology and praxis—which puts faith and political praxis together in ways which make clear the contributions each makes to the other. From Ryan I will draw upon the developed ethical theory of justice as applied to the economic order. From Murray I will extract the Catholic understanding of a pluralism in social authority in the doctrine of state and society. My treatment of each man is concerned with what each might contribute as a resource for doing liberation theology in North America. My master thesis is that one cannot move from eschatology to politics without the mediation of a developed theology, respectively, of providence, social ethics, and the nature of the state. In effect, I am arguing that we need theological tools of the middle range to take up the yawning gap between eschatology and politics.

Brownson, Ryan, and Murray were theologians in the strict or technical sense of the term. Hence they demanded of their work that it be tested, on the one hand, by a "criterion of appropriateness" to the received revelation of God in Christ as that is mediated through Scripture and tradition. On the other hand, they subjected their thought to the "criterion of adequacy" to human experience.[4]

Theology always involves a faith proclamation. It can never be reduced simply to philosophy, phenomenology of religion, social analysis, or social praxis, although it needs all these as necessary methodological tools for critical reflection on lived faith. Indeed, strictly speaking theology has no method of its own. It needs to rely on "secular" disciplines such as history, philosophy, the social sciences, and literary and linguistic analysis. Theology is a sustained critical analysis of and reflection upon the *human* meaning and challenge of "the Christian fact." As such, its method of investigation always entails serious hermeneutical analysis of those classical Christian texts, Scripture especially, and experiences which embody the Christian fact. Theology can never restrict itself exclusively to reflection upon contemporary experience or the reading of the signs of the current times. A reasonable faith in the promise of the present guidance of the Spirit is necessarily premised upon appropriated past experiences of the Spirit's presence and guidance. There has never been a time since creation when God has been absent from human history. Nor is God's action in history ever simply discontinuous.

A critical appropriation of the Christian fact avoids, in John Courtney Murray's terms, both archaism, i.e., the belief that the tradition ceased to develop at some fixed point in the historic past, and anachronism, i.e., the belief that later developments can be found, in any explicit way, in earlier texts and experiences.[5] It also avoids an exaggerated contemporaneity. The criterion of appropriateness to the Christian fact follows from the Christian belief in the gratuity of revelation and the belief that revelation involves the self-disclosure of the presence and activity within our history of the mysterious God, a self-disclosure not totally accessible to ungraced reason.

Murray is referring explicitly to American society. His remarks, however, seem universally applicable as a pre-condition for the fulfillment of the criterion of appropriateness:

> The Catholic may not, as others do, merge his religious and his patriotic faith, or submerge one in the other. The simplest solution is not for him. He must reckon with his own tradition of thought which is wider and deeper than any that America has elaborated. He must also reckon with his own history which is longer than the brief centuries that America has lived.[6]

Human experience is mediated through both vision (symbols and ideals) and praxis. Human experience can never truly ground revelation, either in the sense of proving the truth of the symbols of faith or showing that they are the only adequate human symbols to express human, even religious, experience. Nevertheless, human experience remains, almost tautologically, the necessary and only testing ground of the *human* meaning and adequacy of the symbols of faith. The necessity of a correlation between the Christian fact and human experience flows from the universal claims in Christianity. On the other hand, correlation is not the same as equation. The criterion of adequacy to human experience is a point-of-contact test for the Christian symbols. Logic or philosophy can demonstrate that they are not unreasonable. Praxis can show that they are not unworkable. In the end, as David Tracy puts it, "the theologian cannot resolve the religious and theistic claims of theology by any ordinary criteria of verification or falsification" either by logic or praxis.[7]

Neither logic nor praxis exhaustively tests the Christian symbols. Christianity remains a faith and a vision. Christian theology retains its conviction that truth is ultimately one, if not univocal. In this conviction it finds the condition for the possibility of a correlation between the Christian fact and human experience. Christian theology maintains, moreover, a piety toward the real. The recalcitrance of even one stubborn contrary human fact provides it with the testing ground for its claims to be universally valid for all of humanity. The criterion of adequacy uncovers the conditions for the possibility of a *reasonable* faith.

But how is the method of correlation related to praxis? The truth of the symbols of the Christian faith is more than mere conceptual truth. Their truth lies in their power to make true. Christian symbols, in Durkheim's words, "transfigure the realities to which they relate."[8] All of the Christian symbols are, in some sense, sacramental symbols. They are all directed to the primary sacraments of Christ and the Church, the centers of Christian life. They not only signify or mediate another reality but embody that reality and transfigure the realities to which they relate.

Consequently, praxis, i.e., the making true of the truth of the Christian symbols in human experience and history, is as fundamental to the method of correlation between the Christian fact and human experience as it is to the very truth-claim of the Christian symbols themselves. The Christian symbols exist less to help us to understand the world than to transform it. For example, the very credibility of the Christian claim to adhere to an eschatological vision of the kingdom of God, a kingdom of absolute justice and peace, depends upon the breakthrough, at points, of partial realizations of transforming justice and peace within history. The eschatological vision implies a task, and the task is sincerely accepted in a concrete praxis. If it is dangerous to identify the City of God and the City of Man, it is not less disastrous to deny them all points of contact within history. The liberation theologians, then, are absolutely correct and absolutely traditional in insisting that praxis lies at the heart of the theological enterprise. They are simply summoning theology to pay heed to its own criterion of adequacy to human experience.

Theology, like human experience generally, is mediated through both vision and praxis. Some caution is needed if we are to understand properly the dialectic between vision and praxis. No vision is totally derived from or fully tested in the forge of praxis. The very nature of symbolic vision is that it becomes a reality *sui generis* related, but not totally reducible, to the activities or events which give rise to it. Put in other terms, culture is always partially autonomous from structure. It is almost never merely ideology or merely superstructure.[9]

A vision unrelated to praxis, to be sure, remains simply visionary, utopian. Through vision and symbol we shape and inform our praxis, as in turn vision is refined by, reformulated and tested in, praxis. On the other hand, there is no praxis which is not informed by some vision, however implicit. Nor is the informing vision really derived from praxis. It is either a hypothesis, an imaginative projection, or a faith. Indeed, to collapse vision into praxis is to lose the negative, critical quality inherent in vision. It is to lose a transcendent reference which gives to praxis its aim and future orientation. A refusal to see the dialectical co-partnership between vision and praxis in asserting the utter priority of praxis leads either to (1) a reification of the status quo or (2) the informing of praxis by some pre-given, unreflective vision.[10]

If it is a deep mistake to exclude praxis from the theological enterprise, it is no less misleading to claim that one really *starts* theology with an unmediated reflection upon human praxis. The Christian vision is already given as a starting point in Christian praxis. Praxis is a crucial test of that vision. Here, too, some caution is needed to avoid the pitfalls of vulgar pragmatism. As John Courtney Murray once put it, "it is false to say that what works is true. But it is an altogether sound proposition that what is not true will somehow fail to work."[11] The two criteria of appropriateness and adequacy maintain a dialectical tension between vision and praxis in Christian theology. The criterion of appropriateness guarantees that the vision is truly Christian. The criterion of adequacy impels us to participate in projects of human liberation to test the credibility of our holding that vision. It is only by avoiding a fetishism of either vision or praxis and by eschewing every form of reductionism that we can construct a Christian theology of liberation in the strict sense of the word.

Brownson, Ryan, and Murray were each steeped in the full tradition of Christian theology. Each, however, moved beyond theology to correlate his thought with a secular discipline: philosophy, economics, and political science respectively. All three were significantly involved in discerning the signs of their own times. Indeed, Brownson and Ryan were political activists in contact with the key political figures and movements of their day. The three were, in Martin Marty's phrase, "public theologians" who drew upon their Catholic tradition to address issues and audiences in the wider American or international context. Brownson is the only leading American Catholic theological thinker to have ever developed a Roman Catholic theology out of indigenous American philosophical resources. Ryan and

Murray left a significant impact on the episcopal or conciliar magisterium of the Church.

Each was unmistakably the leading American Catholic intellectual spokesman of his day. All three were mainly interested in the political and public character of their faith. Each combined Catholic vision with political praxis. In a sense, Murray captured the understanding that all three had of the task of theology in a way which combines the criterion of appropriateness to tradition with that of adequacy to human experience. For Murray, the task of theology is "to discern the 'growing end' of the tradition; it is normally given by the new question that is taking shape under the impact of the historical movement of events and ideas. There remains the problem of synthesis—of a synthesis that will be at once new and traditional."[12]

LEGACY OF BROWNSON: A THEOLOGY OF PROVIDENCE

It is customary to view the life and thought of Orestes Brownson as a kind of pilgrim's progress.[13] There are, admittedly, apparent discontinuities in Brownson's life and work.[14] Born an unchurched American in Stockbridge, Vermont, on September 16, 1803, Brownson became in his teenage years a strict Calvinist Presbyterian. In the process of shedding, in early manhood, that lightly-worn identity, Brownson discovered two lifelong convictions. In rejecting strict predestination, he asserted his belief in the correlative freedom of God and the freedom of humanity. In his spiritual autobiography *The Convert,* written in 1857, thirteen years after he became a convert to Catholicism, Brownson wrote lyrically on the topic of the freedom of God. He asserted, on the one hand, that "while God binds nature, nature can not bind him"; on the other, "in God's freedom, I had a sure pledge of my own."[15] The correlative freedom of God and human freedom forms one cornerstone of Brownson's doctrine of providence.

The second lifelong conviction which Brownson made his own in rejecting Presbyterianism was the impossibility of postulating a radical break between nature and grace or between reason and revelation. Convinced of the unity of life and truth, he joined the Universalists in 1824 and became a preacher. In reflecting upon this choice for the "reasonable faith" of Universalism, Brownson asserts: "If I understood reason better, I should perceive no discrepancy, because God can never teach us one thing in his word and a contradictory thing through our natural reason. What he tells us in his word may be above reason, but cannot be against it."[16]

Doctrine of Life in Communion: Nature and Grace

Throughout his life Brownson wrestled with the ontological and epistemological implications of his assertion of a unifying correlation between nature and grace, between God and the world. He was always looking for unities. Part of his mind showed a strong philosophical bent. Indeed, on two different occasions he almost accepted offers to assume an academic position as professor of philosophy, once at Harvard University, on the advice of Benjamin Constant, and once at Newman's Irish University, on the strong urging of Lord Acton. Brownson is perhaps the finest (albeit self-taught) philosophical mind of the American nineteenth century, certainly within his Catholic America. In his mature years Brownson struggled with a careful study of Kant and Plato and drew upon the unlikely philosophic resources of the French eclectics Benjamin Constant, Victor Cousin, and Pierre LeRoux, as well as on the thought of his circle of transcendentalist friends, Channing, Emerson, Parker, and Thoreau, before coming to his settled position of the doctrine of all life in communion.

From his years as a transcendentalist Brownson retained a lifelong belief in the importance of sentiment, intuition, and personal experience in the life of the mind and religion. His focus on sentiment provided him with a philosophy which bridged the gap between subjective intuition and objective evidence, between existences and Being. One of his strictures against the Scholasticism to which he was forced by his bishop, John Fitzpatrick, to mold his thought and writings in his early years as a Catholic, was its sterile objectivism. Brownson also agreed with the transcendentalists that there was something divine in humanity. With them he sought a God who was immanent in human history. He shared, as well, their romantic nature mysticism. His break with the transcendentalists came over their identification of God and man. As he once put it, in commenting on the work of William Ellery Channing, "Dr. Channing makes man a great god, but God a little man."[17]

Brownson opposed Theodore Parker's assertion that religion was natural because it originated in human sentiment. He viewed religion as natural because he saw

> thought and life as the joint product of the inter-communication of subject and object. . . . While admitting still the religious sentiment as in some sense natural to man and therefore proving that man may be religious without violence to his nature, indeed in harmony with it, I now explicitly rejected that sentiment as the origin and ground of religion and denied that religion is simply the result of its development.[18]

In his search for unities Brownson was looking for a way to bridge the dichotomy between subject and object. He found the key in the thought of the French Saint-Simonian Pierre LeRoux, especially in his insistence that human life and thought is a joint product of subject and object. All of life and all of truth exists in relation. The transcendentalists had been correct in asserting a universal inspiration in humanity, though wrong in their premises. Man was divine because there had taken place "a real infusion of a

Divine element into human life, by which that life should be supernatural-
ly elevated, and rendered progressive."[19] Hence "man lives and can live
only by communion with what is not himself."[20] Man lives by immediate
communion with God as his object and, therefore, the objective element of
his life is Divine, and through this objective element his life is the life of
God. Man thus *in his natural life even* partakes of God and this partaking
of God I called inspiration."[21]

Brownson's quest for a correlation between the order of nature and
the order of grace, between God and the world, led him, long before the
nouvelle théologie in postwar France, to reject the hypothesis of a *natura
pura*. From the beginning there was but one order of reality: the world under the economy of grace and the incarnation:

> It is necessary to show, not merely assert, that the two orders are
> not mutually antagonistic; that one and the same principle of life
> runs through them both; that they correspond one to the other,
> and really constitute but two parts of one comprehensive whole,
> and are equally embraced in the original plan and purpose of
> God in creating. God could have created man, had he chosen, in
> a state of pure nature; but in point of fact, he did not, and nature
> has never for a single instant existed as pure nature. It has from
> the first moment of its existence been under a supernatural provi-
> dence; and even if man had not sinned there would still have
> been a sufficient reason for the incarnation to raise human nature
> to union with God, to make it the nature of God, and to enable
> us, through its elevation, to enjoy endless beatitude in heaven.
> The doctrine that all dependent life is life by communion of the
> subject with the object shows that this is possible, shows the
> common principle of the two orders.[22]

> Communion between God and man is possible, although
> only like communes with like, because man has in his nature a
> likeness to God. Human reason is the likeness in man of the Di-
> vine reason, and hence, nothing hinders the intercommunion be-
> tween the reason of God and the reason of man. . . . By this
> communion the subject partakes of the object, the human reason
> of the Divine reason, which is infinite, absolute truth. The Divine
> Being, in this communion established by himself, communicates
> the life of his own reason to the life of the subject, so that our
> reason lives in and by his reason. This is the origin and ground of
> the truth of natural reason; and this natural reason, thus in com-
> munion with the Divine, is the source and ground of the unity of
> the human race in the natural order and the formative principle
> of natural society. . . .

The infinite and the finite, then, are correlative. Brownson caps the above
citation with a reaffirmation of the freedom of God over against nature

and human history. "God does not exhaust his light in natural reason, any more than he does his creative power in natural creation."[23]

Doctrine of Life in Communion: Reason and Revelation

If the order of being was somehow one, it followed that the orders of knowledge and action must be as well. Brownson developed the epistemological and political implications of the correlation of nature and grace. Much of his life he was hounded by accusations of ontologism, the assertion that human knowledge could achieve a direct intuition of God, largely because of his sympathetic reading of the Piedmontese philosopher-theologian Vincenzo Gioberti. Brownson seems, however, to have held a moderate realism, closer to Bonaventure than to Aquinas, which granted a large role to intuition, emotion, and sentiment in human knowing. God was immanent in human knowing not as the knowing subject or the object of knowledge but as the light in which we see all existence.

> The Divine reason, indistinguishable from the Divine Essence or Being, at once creates human reason and presents itself as its light and its immediate object. We see all things in God, as we see visible objects in the light which illuminates them, though not simply as ideas in the Divine Mind, as Malebranche appears to have held; for we see existences themselves in their concreteness and reality, not merely their ideas, or possibility of being created.[24]

Perhaps he never stated so clearly his position on the epistemological consequences of his organic view of ontology, which held that divine life really flows into our life, as in this passage from *The Convert:* "It is not God who knows and loves in us, but God in us who creates in us our power to know and love. The Divine reason is not our reason, but, so to speak, the reason of our reason. It creates our reason, and is its immediate light and object."[25]

Just as all life exists in relation or communion, so all truth exists in relation. Brownson would never allow a radical break between reason and revelation or between science and religion. In an essay on "Science and the Sciences" he pleaded for the freedom of inquiry in the sciences, since there could be no real contradiction between the findings of science and those of the faith. He also argued for the need to correlate the findings of the sciences with the "science" of faith. Thus, "in the field of science, as distinguished from that of faith, revelation is adjutative rather than imperative. Its light and that of reason coalesce and shine as one light."[26] In a similar way he rejected Bossuet's position that God's providence could be restricted to Israel and the Christian Church. For Brownson, there is something hideous about the restriction of providence to a special religious empire. "It would be unjust to leave all the rest of mankind to the mere law of nature, and untrue to say that no rays of Divine light had penetrated to them but through the inherent and necessary laws of nature and humanity."[27]

Doctrine of Life in Communion: Eternity and the Temporal Order

Brownson's temperamental quest for unities would never have allowed him to read the relation between eternity and the temporal order as a tale of two cities. He continued, throughout his life, to believe that religion and politics were virtually inseparable, although he never wavered in his support of the institutional separation of Church and state. His pilgrim's progress entailed a twofold quest: (1) an earnest wrestling for religious certainty, for the truth of his personal relation to God and the Church; (2) a lifelong quest for justice between person and person, political liberty and order, the good of the earthly city. For Brownson, the two quests could never be separated.

A journalist and political activist all his life, Brownson was always concerned about the relation of religion to temporal and contingent realities. Neither dualistic nor reductionist, Brownson knew that "the world has its place in the Christian economy, and is God's world, not Satan's. The earth according to the Copernican system is one of the celestial bodies. *Natural society is not our end, but it is as necessary to it* as the cosmos is to palingenesia. Civilization is initial religion."[28] Thus the "religion that neglects civilization is in principle as un-Catholic as the civilization that neglects religion."[29] These assertions flowed from his doctrine of communion. Human well-being and progress depended on communion with nature, humanity, the generations across history and God.

In his mid-twenties Brownson drifted away from Universalism and came, for a spell, under the sway of the early feminist and humanitarian reformer Fanny Wright, an atheist. He fell under the influence of Robert Owen, William Godwin, Robert Jennings, and George Evans. In his own terms, he became a world-reformer; in ours, a socialist. In 1828 he was instrumental in founding the first Workingmen's Party in modern history in Philadelphia. By adding American political thinkers such as Jefferson and Tom Paine to the thought of European socialists, Brownson sought to achieve social as well as political equality. He also sensed that an American socialism could only grow out of some indigenous American seeds. He realized that the American ideal of political democracy was unworkable without a concomitant social equality: "Political equality may be a blessed thing; but to be real, anything more than a delusion, it must rest for its basis on social equality: equality in wealth, position, education, ability, influence. Man against man and money is not an equal match."[30]

From 1828 until 1840 Brownson was the intellectual spokesman for a radical new economic order in America. In the words of his biographer, Arthur Schlesinger, Jr., he was "the nearest forerunner of Marx in America," and in those of his friend and disciple Isaac Hecker, "the American

Proudhon." By 1831 Brownson took up again his personal search for religion and became, under the influence of Channing, a Unitarian. In so doing, he tried to join in a unity the Universalist's concern for external nature with the Unitarian's focus on the inner man. Both needed to be fed into the struggle for institutional social reform.

In 1836 he organized the Society of Christian Union and Progress in Boston, to reach the laboring masses untouched by the mainline churches. He was active as a pamphleteer, lecturer, and journalist. In the latter part of the 1830's he began to be deeply influenced by the work of the French socialist Henri Comte de Saint-Simon. He also became an active Jacksonian Democrat. Indeed, his social pamphlet "The Laboring Classes" fell like a bombshell in the midst of the 1840 presidential campaign. It is sometimes credited with scaring off the voters in that election from casting their lot with the "radical" Democrats.

The failure of the 1840 campaign to usher in the new religion of social democracy convinced Brownson of "the inadequacy of an individual-oriented approach to social reform."[31] It also provided him with both a growing bias against New Pelagianism and a deeper sense of the powerful reality of sin. These two biases, as well as his conviction of the fundamental necessity of *institutional* reform, led him to maintain a polite distance from the utopian commune experiment at Brook Farm, an experiment he otherwise viewed benignly. Through the thought of Saint-Simon, Brownson, in his search for social justice, tended to focus on objective institutions or Church substitutes in the form of the Workingmen's Party, his own "church of the future," and the Democratic Party. Saint-Simon also convinced him that institutional reform of the political or social order, while necessary, was not enough. A genuine moral regeneration and spiritual renewal in the form of a new religion of humanity was called for, if the institutional reforms were not to ring hollow. Moral and spiritual regeneration must go hand in hand with social reform. Always Bronson sought for the unities.

Brownson never lost his predilection for the cause of the workingman or his animus against disproportionate wealth. In switching from the narrowly class-based Workingmen's Party to the wider-based Democratic Party, he seemed to sense that in America, with its multiple and interlayered class system (at least through the middle class), an organization anchored in one class base alone was insufficient to generate substantive social change. In the United States the major motor for reform and social change has never been an economic class but the social movement—partly religious, partly political, and based on a constituency which joins lower-class rights and demands in a coalition which includes several classes. Brownson expresses his change of mind on this question:

> I wished sincerely and earnestly to benefit the working-men but I
> saw as soon as I directed my attention to the point that I could
> effect nothing by appealing to them as a separate class. My policy

must be, not a workingmen's party, but to induce all classes of society to cooperate in efforts for the workingmen's cause.[32]

In his Catholic period (1844–76) Brownson always insisted that property and inheritance was a "municipal" or conventional right, not a natural right based on some metaphysical property. Even in his late and only systematic work *The American Republic: Its Constitution, Tendencies and Destiny* (1866), written in a period when Brownson's political thought, under the impact of the work of Joseph de Maistre, became more organicistic and conservative, many of the older themes break through.[33] Thus, his abiding concern for social democracy remains apparent in such reminders as "property is not entitled to govern. . . . The rich have in their riches advantages enough over the poor, without receiving from the state any additional advantage."[34] Let government take care of the weak; the strong can take care of themselves. Universal suffrage is better than restricted suffrage, but even universal suffrage is too weak to prevent private property from having an undue political influence."[35] *The American Republic* also attests to Brownson's newfound theological liberalism in its rejection of an established church. Greatly influenced by Lacordaire and the *L'Avenir* group in France, Brownson was unequivocal on the point. "Faith cannot be forced."[36] "Since her kingdom is moral and spiritual [the Church] has and can only have moral or spiritual power. She can resort neither directly nor indirectly to physical force, for that would make her a secular kingdom—a kingdom of this world—and belie her own spiritual nature."[37]

Brownson even went so far as to attack the temporal power of the papacy. On one point of then current Catholic political theology he was absolutely clear. "It is impossible, even if it were desirable, to restore the mixture of civil and ecclesiastical governments which obtained in the Middle Ages."[38] Brownson was no believer in the ideals of a Christendom. Long before John Courtney Murray, Brownson argued that state and Church should agree on the institutional freedom of the Church and religious freedom. If the Church had a right to proclaim its institutional freedom from the interference of the state, the state was to be no less free from Church meddling: "Though derived from God only through the people, civil authority still holds from God and derives its right from him through another channel than the Church or spiritual society, and therefore has a right, a sacredness, which the Church herself gives not, and must recognize and respect."[39]

Although he was relatively late in taking up the cause of the anti-slavery movement, largely because of his support of the Federalist principle of states' rights (he agreed with Calhoun) and some personal antipathies toward some of the leaders of the abolitionist movement, by 1860 he threw in his lot with the anti-slavery unionists. He resumed vigorous political activity as an active patriot, traveling across the land giving lectures. He actively lobbied, and directed political appeals through his friend Charles Sumner. He toyed with the idea of running for Congress. As early as 1861 he urged Lincoln, who had attended his lectures, to issue the Emancipation Proclamation. Especially when weighed against the ominous silence of the official Catholic Church on the greatest moral issue of the day and the irritation of Archbishop Hughes and the leading members of the hierarchy at Brownson's pro-unionist sentiments and activity, it is no exaggeration to assert, as Brownson's biographer Theodore Maynard does, that "on the central question of slavery he was one of the few Catholics who had something of importance to say."[40] It is perhaps typical of Brownson's sense for unities that in *The American Republic* he proceeds from a carefully argued case that the southern states had no constitutional right to secede from the Union to a plea against sentiments of rancor or severity in the post-war task of reconstruction.

Providence and Politics

In a peculiar sense the relation between providence and politics was Brownson's most central intellectual concern. On the one hand, Brownson saw the temporal common good of man as directed toward his ultimate good. On the other, he was reluctant to identify the religious qualities inherent in the achievement of historical forms of justice with the eschatological City of God. Providence provided him with an intermediate concept. Providence had about it the same smell of contingency and the humble acknowledgment of imperfect knowledge as had those "Providential Men" Brownson wrote about in his Unitarian period, whose function was to mediate for individuals some objectivity and direction in the quest for religious truth and action without themselves being totally identical with the divine.

In his important essay "The Philosophy of History," Brownson scores the transcendentalists for their ahistorical political stance. A doctrine of providence would alert them to the changing moods and circumstances of history, the possibilities inherent in one epoch or culture which are absent in another. Against them he asserts the continuous operation of God's providence in human history. Nor will it do to hold for "the non-intervention of Providence save through the fixed and permanent laws of human nature," as Victor Cousin did. This restricts too much the freedom of God. Also, "it will not suffice to explain and account for the facts of human history." Next, Brownson objects to Bossuet's philosophy of history, which, while good on the subject of the freedom of God, is too narrow in restricting the activity of God's providence to the explicitly religious realm: "We are not willing to regard the effects of this providential interference as shut up within the limits of this empire or as confined exclusively to the peculiar people of God."[41] The Church exists for all humankind. Moreover, Bossuet does not do justice to the freedom of humanity.

Brownson sees three agencies active in human history: nature, humanity, and providence. Nature sets some fixed limits to the flexibility of human history. Brownson maintains a modified version of natural-law theory as the norm of just law. God's freedom respects, but is not totally restricted to, nature and the freedom of humanity. Thus "Providence is God intervening through the laws he, by his creative act, gives to creatures, not their suspension or abrogation."[42] Human freedom makes a difference to the direction and ultimate meaning of history. Hence "the course of human history depends in no slight degree on the voluntary activity of individuals. . . . All humanity shall fare worse, if we do not act."[43] Human history was not for Brownson, in John Courtney Murray's telling phrase, merely basket weaving.

The eschatological kingdom of God is primarily God's activity. It is a grace, a judgment, and a gift. It is a kingdom of absolute justice and peace. It will never be fully realized in history. Within history, God is restricted in his activity. He desires the kingdom of God and invites toward it, but only as that is possible within the limits of providence by which God uses human freedom and circumstances as his instruments. In Ernst Troeltsch's poignant phrase, within history "history can only be overcome by more history."

The doctrine of providence alerts us to the "distinction between the purpose inherent in a free human act and the further purpose to which God can direct this same act."[44] The freedom and providence of God directs us to the deeper possibilities in human praxis and achievements. It may lead us to acknowledge the flaws and failures in what seems, at first glance, triumphs, and the grounds for hope in what seems a humanly hopeless praxis. Even a prolonged total failure to achieve human liberation may have its purposes in the providence of God, although we are continuously called upon to work for justice, since we know that this is the will of God. Providence reminds us that there is more to human history than praxis. Providence, to be sure, has often been used in the history of theology as a conservative doctrine, especially when it is exclusively related to creation and the good of order. Brownson, however, insisted that providence entailed a providential task, a mission. It was as much directed to eschatology as to creation, as much to the good of societal transformation as to order.[45]

In *The American Republic* Brownson again deals with the central concept of providence. He asserts that "every living nation has an idea given it by providence to realize, and whose realization is its special work, mission or destiny."[46] He thought the mission of the United States "is to bring out in its life the dialectic union of authority and liberty, of the natural rights of man and those of society."[47] In another place he asserts that its mission is to find a middle way between individualism and socialism, a mission which had been Brownson's own since the days when, under the influence of Saint-Simon, he sought a socialism with a human face in the union between political democracy and social equality.

Throughout *The American Republic* Brownson attacks the ideas of Hobbes and Locke, who maintained that the common good was simply the result of the conciliation of private interests. Nor is it the case that the government, as Augustine held, is merely *propter peccatum*. Government constitutes a kind of social providence:

> Government would have been necessary if man had not sinned, and it is needed for the good as well as the bad. . . . Its office is not merely repressive, to restrain violence, to redress wrongs and to punish the transgressor. It has something more to do than to restrict our natural liberty, curb our passions and maintain justice between man and man. Its office is positive as well as negative. It is needed to render effective the solidarity of the individuals of a nation and to render the nation an organism and not a mere organization—to combine men in one living body and to strengthen all with the strength of each and each with the strength of all—to develop, strengthen, and sustain individual liberty and to utilize and direct it to the promotion of the commonweal—*to be a social providence,* imitating in its order and degree the action of the divine providence itself and while it provides for the common good of all, to protect each, the lowest and meanest, with the whole force and majesty of society.[48]

Brownson directed political thinkers to take cognizance of the priority of social conditions and circumstances over political forms. Thus he distinguished between the state or nation, what he called "the providential constitution," and government. No reform or change in the political constitution of a government would be successful if the social pre-conditions were lacking. As he put it, "there must be for every state or nation a constitution anterior to the constitution which the nation gives itself and from which the one it gives itself derives all its vitality and legal force."[49]

In a homely simile, he likened forms of government to shoes. If a form of government fitted the social conditions and circumstances, it was part of the providential design for the nation. "No one form of government is Catholic in its nature or of universal obligation."[50] The necessity of uncovering the providential constitution of a nation—what we would call the economic and structural conditions and the limits and possibilities of a national ethos—was the work of prudential discernment. Brownson stood with the classical assertion that there could be no *science* of the contingent aspects of politics, no science of praxis. Praxis was governed by prudence and not science. As such, his doctrine of a providential constitution and providence as a mission reminds us that uncertainty and ambiguity remain permanent elements of the political order. Brownson's own preferences remained firmly fixed on democracy and a limited form of government; he opposed all totalitarianism; for "man does not depend exclusively on society, for it is not his only medium of communion with God, and therefore its right to him is neither absolute or unlimited."[51]

Sydney Ahlstrom has said of Brownson: "Perhaps no American before the Civil War testified more strenuously to the significant relationship between religion and social problems."[52] I have argued that he provides us with a doctrine of providence to serve as a necessary mediating concept between eschatology and politics in doing a liberation theology. The problem with eschatological symbols in politics is that they yield "little of positive and constructive significance in making practical and material moral judgments about particular conditions."[53] In the end, unmediated use of eschatological symbols in political thought either functions as a kind of vague "eschatological impatience" with the status quo but with an appalling paucity of content, or, more disastrous, lends itself to an identification of some particular social movement, class, or institutional restructuring of society with the ushering in of the kingdom of God in history. Providence as task is, in Tillich's term, a kind of *kairos,* an opportunity which may not come again. Providence directs us to read the signs of the times in the light of the eschatological vision of the kingdom. It reminds us, however, that the signs of the kingdom are not the same as the kingdom itself. When related to eschatology, providence is a way of saying that the temporal order makes a real difference to the shape of the kingdom of God and that nothing of justice, truth, or liberty in human achievement will ever be lost in eternity. Providence moves us to a concrete praxis. The kingdom remains eschatology, a faith and vision from whose transcendent reference we have continuous critical leverage on every human achievement.

Providence is more likely than directly eschatological symbols to keep us realistic in our expectations and religiously motivated, enthusiastic, and persistent in our commitments to social justice and a liberating transformation of societal structures. Brownson's life illustrates for us that a steady passion for justice need not be premised on Joachimite illusions about the millennium. Arthur Schlesinger sums up the reasons why Brownson might still be considered a resource for doing liberation theology in America: "His life still touches contemporary nerves—from the antagonisms of capital and labor to the place of the Catholics in American society, from the nature of American culture to the death of God."[54]

LEGACY OF JOHN A. RYAN: A DEVELOPED ECONOMIC ETHICS

The best way to capture the flavor of the life and work of the "Right Reverend New Dealer" Msgr. John A. Ryan is in the phrase he chose for his autobiography, *Social Doctrine in Action.*[55] Born in the latter part of the nineteenth century in Vermillion, Minnesota, Ryan came early under the spell of the Populist movement. He inherited a distaste for monopolies from his father, whom he frequently accompanied to the meetings of the National Farmers' Alliance. The Populist orator-agitator Ignatius Donnelly, who later founded the Anti-Monopoly Party, was one of John Ryan's boyhood heroes. The son of Irish immigrants, Ryan read each week the copy of the *Irish World* which came to his home. Under the editorship of

Patrick Ford, the *Irish World* was constantly attacking the abusive power of the corporate trusts. Through Ford, who espoused George's New York mayoral campaign, Ryan also came to read, with sympathy, Henry George's program for a single tax on the land, *Progress and Poverty.*

When Ryan went down to St. Paul to attend John Ireland's seminary, he imbibed that indefatigable prelate's Americanist enthusiasms. He recalls especially being stirred by Ireland's words: "These are days of action, days of warfare. . . . Into the arena, priest and layman! Seek out social evils, and lead in movements that tend to rectify them. Speak of vested rights, for this is necessary; but speak, too, of vested wrongs, and strive, by word and example, by the enactment and enforcement of good laws to correct them."[56]

In the seminary Ryan read Leo XIII's encyclical *Rerum Novarum* for the first time in 1894. From Leo he derived an abiding belief in natural law and the absolute right of every citizen to a living wage. Ryan also began to nourish his single passion—one might almost call it the substance of his interiority—for social and economic justice.[57] While in the seminary, he commenced his lifelong serious reading and study of economics. From the British economic historian William Lilly Ryan derived what would remain a cornerstone of his mature thought, his convictions about the inherent limitations upon the right of private property and the social responsibilities of property. As he was later to write in his most important theoretical work *Distributive Justice,* "It is the exigencies of reasonable distribution that constitutes the fundamental justification of every title to ownership. . . . *All titles of property, productivity included, are conventional institutions which reason and experience have shown to be conducive to human welfare.* None of them possesses intrinsic or metaphysical validity."[58] Again, he asserts, in arguing for a legal limitation of large fortunes: "There is nothing in the nature of things nor in the purpose of property to indicate that the right of ownership is unlimited in quantity any more than it is in quality. The final and only justification of individual rights of property is human welfare, that is, the welfare of all individuals, severally and collectively."[59]

In the same work he appeals to the social nature of capital property to ground his conclusion that the employer is bound to distributive as well as commutative justice:

> The employer has obligations of justice, not merely as the receiver of a valuable thing through an onerous contract, but as the distributor of the common heritage of nature. His duty is not merely contractual, but social. He fulfills not only an individual contract but a social function. Unless he performs this social and distributive function in accordance with justice, he does not adequately discharge the obligation of the wage contract. For the product out of which he pays wages is not his in the same sense as the personal income out of which he repays a loan. . . . How

futile, then, to endeavor to describe his employer's obligation in terms of mere equivalence and contractual justice. It is governed by distributive justice also.[60]

After ordination, Ryan enrolled at The Catholic University of America for a graduate degree in moral theology. His two most influential teachers were the sociologist William Kerby, a champion of the cause of labor unions and consumers' cooperatives, and the Belgian moral theologian Thomas Bouquillon. From Bouquillon, the director of his dissertation, Ryan learned his method in theological ethics. Bouquillon

> tried first to understand the sociology and economics of a problem before passing on to its morality. He complained that existing theological manuals were out of touch with contemporary life, and he warned that moral theology would not regain its position of true distinction until theologians would intelligently apply Judaeo-Christian principles to the social, religious and civil problems of the modern individual.[61]

In preparation for his dissertation *The Living Wage,* Ryan immersed himself in a study of the medieval Scholastic doctrine of the just price and the social teaching of Catholicism on the ownership, use, and responsibility of property. He also read widely in economics: the Webbs, Hobson, Richard Ely, and William Ashley's *Introduction to English Economic History and Theory.* With Ely, the founder of the American Economic Association and an influential figure in the American social gospel movement, he was in constant correspondence.

After four years in Washington, Ryan returned to St. Paul to teaching duties at Saint Thomas' Seminary. In 1905 his completed dissertation was published by The Macmillan Company with a preface by Ely. Ely claimed that Ryan was the only man in America who combined a thorough competence in ethical theory with an equal proficiency in economics. The book was received with favorable notices in the United States, England, and Ireland. In his years of teaching in St. Paul, Ryan began to gain a national reputation. He worked actively for the passage of minimum-wage laws across the country, authoring the first such bill for the Minnesota legislature in 1913. He also pressed for legislation outlawing child labor. He became active in Minnesota civic organizations. Born into the Populist era, he joined organizations connected to the "progressive movement" for economic, social, and political reform, and he urged his fellow Catholics to follow suit. Meanwhile, scholarly articles poured from his pen, most notably a careful moral study of monopoly and an ethical analysis of the practice of stock watering. He urged reforms in the practice of stock speculation.

In 1914 Ryan was catapulted into national prominence when he was invited to join Morris Hillquit, the leading theoretician of the American

Socialist Party, in a debate on the question "Socialism: Promise or Menace?" in the pages of *Everybody's Magazine.*[62] Ryan's main objections to socialism, at that period, rested on its theory of economic determinism and its anti-religious and anti-moral (e.g., free love, divorce) tenets. He thought socialism economically impractical and feared its centralizing tendencies. Nevertheless, Ryan was no defender of the status quo. His option was for "the existing system, greatly, even radically, amended."[63]

Ryan pointed to three major evils in the present system: (1) insufficient wages, (2) excessive income, (3) the concentration of capital ownership. The third was crucial. "The narrow distribution of capital ownership is more fundamental than the other two evils because it threatens the stability of the whole system."[64] Because he feared a totalitarian tendency in socialism, Ryan preferred in its stead a widespread people's capitalism embracing industrial democracy and consumer and productive cooperatives. His program was a far cry from *laissez faire.* He exhorted to a vigorous governmental intervention through anti-trust legislation and the regulation of prices and interest rates by government agencies. If necessary, the government should inaugurate state-financed and state-run competitive corporations to bring about true competition. "The state should compete with some of the obstinate and intractable trusts by manufacturing and selling their own kinds of products."[65] Nor was Ryan totally unsympathetic to socialism. He would not give the time of day to routine or doctrinaire denunciations of socialism. In an extended review of the European moralist Victor Cathrein's widely-read book *Socialism and Christianity,* Ryan commented that Cathrein failed to do justice to the truth in Marx's insight about the predominant role of economic factors in history.

In 1916 Ryan returned to Washington, D.C. to become a professor of moral theology at The Catholic University of America, where he also offered courses in the department of economics. Washington became a congenial home base for this intensely political animal. In his years in Washington, Ryan began to join his voice to that of progressives such as Brooks Adams and John R. Commons. He became active in the National Catholic Welfare Conference and was appointed in 1920 the first chairman of the Social Action Department of that Conference, where his was an influential voice in national Catholic social pronouncements. He kept a busy pace lecturing, lobbying for social legislation, and writing on topics of social justice.

In 1919 the American hierarchy published a paper, which Ryan had originally written for delivery before a Knights of Columbus audience in Louisville, as their national pastoral letter on "Social Reconstruction." In this pastoral—originally intended as Ryan's response to the program of the Fabian socialists in England—he argued his welfare program: minimum-wage legislation; social insurance for unemployment, old age, and sickness; a national employment agency to guarantee full employment to returning veterans; public-housing projects to insure low-cost housing; the legal right of labor to organize; the regulation of public utility rates in the consumers' interest; government competition to regulate monopolies; labor's participation in the decisions of management; the establishment of consumers' and productive cooperatives. The bishops' pastoral letter of 1919 caused a storm. The president of the National Association of Manufacturers, himself a Catholic, was stirred up to brand Ryan a socialist. The socialist Upton Sinclair was provoked to proclaim it as a "Catholic miracle."

The 1920's were very difficult years for Ryan. He saw the post-war return to normalcy in the presidencies of Harding, Coolidge, and Hoover as a triumph of graft, greed, and self-interest over the common good. A conservative Supreme Court overturned the most minimal social-welfare legislation. The American hierarchy opposed legislation abolishing child labor for fear that such laws would set a precedent of state control over the family and impinge upon the freedom of the parochial schools. Ryan became, against his will, embroiled in the Smith campaign because of his defense of the classic Catholic thesis-hypothesis position on separation of Church and state in his book *The State and the Church.* He became sick at heart at the bigotry that re-emerged, even from liberals, during the Smith-Hoover election.

During that same decade Ryan became an active civil libertarian. He reacted sharply to the anti-Bolshevik scares of Attorney General A. Mitchell Palmer. He wrote to Morris Hillquit, in a public telegram featured in the national press, congratulating him for his legal defense of the socialist assemblymen who were barred from taking office in New York State. He wrote and spoke against the antisedition laws and joined the American Civil Liberties Union (he was, for a time, a vice president). He pleaded for amnesty for the political prisoners who had refused to serve in the armed services in World War I. During the same period, the warm and mutual friendship between Ryan and another civil libertarian, Louis Brandeis, began.

At first Ryan was a reserved, if reluctant, defender of the moral and obliging character of the Volstead Act. By the mid-1920's, however, he began increasingly to attack prohibition. He noted the class-based Toryism of the Anti-Saloon League. By the end of the decade he was urging, in carefully argued moral analysis, not only the right but the necessity of civil disobedience to national prohibition. The Volstead Act was bad law. It attempted to use prohibition instead of control of liquor as a means of curtailing the abuse of something whose normal and temperate use was morally good. It did not properly distinguish between private manufacture and use of liquor and profiteering manufacture and export. The law had done grave harm to the common good, giving rise to criminal extortion and government graft in bootlegging. Civil disobedience was called for, since the law was a constitutional amendment. Ordinary legislative redress was not available. In response to Ryan's writings, President Hoover was prompted in a speech on national radio to attack professors of ethics who asserted that individuals had the right in conscience to decide whether a law was binding or not.

In the 1920's Ryan's thought also turned to problems of the international order. He worked actively for disarmament and strongly supported the League of Nations. Largely influenced by John Maynard Keynes, Ryan fought for the cancellation of the crippling German war debt. In 1927 he attended the first International Catholic Conference on disarmament and peace held in The Hague.

Distributive Justice

Ryan's first interests and efforts remained directed to the ethics of the economic order. In 1927 he published his abiding theoretical work *Distributive Justice*. It is a masterpiece of cogent style, closely-reasoned argument, and practical wisdom. Probably no work on economic ethics has ever, before or since, combined Ryan's magisterial command over both disciplines. In his book Ryan deals systematically with the rights and duties, titles and limitations to land ownership, taxation, interest, profits, a fair wage and prices. He dissects the defects in the then existing American land, corporate, wage, price, and interest systems and proposes a specific program of reforms. He is always careful to qualify the degree of certitude with which he asserts any proposition and to cite the evidence on which his conclusions are based. He presents a canon of diverse criteria for determining distributive justice and specifies the priorities in case of conflict. The book must be read in all the entirety of its tight argumentation to be really appreciated. I cannot here do more than give a sample of its flavor.

Land Ownership

Ryan commences his book with a discussion of the right of private property in land ownership. He asserts that such private ownership has been widespread in history and *seems* more conducive to a sense of individual well-being, responsibility, and incentive than state ownership. He is careful to nuance his claim. "Private land ownership is a natural right because *in present conditions* the institution is necessary for individual and social welfare."[66] The criterion of social welfare is the only claim on which a right of private property can be based. It is never an inherent or metaphysical right. Moreover, it is a restricted right, "strictly limited in the interest of non-owners and of the community as a whole."[67]

The right to ownership of land for one's own use is not the same as to ownership of land as a source of income through rent or speculation. Landowners have a right to a fair rent based on their sacrifice of alternative uses of the land. Their right to rent, however, is inferior to the fundamental right of their tenants to a decent livelihood. In a case of conflict, the latter takes priority. "The landowner has not a right to the full economic or competitive rent. His right thereto is morally inferior to the tenants' right to a decent livelihood, just as the capitalist employer's right to the prevailing rate of interest is morally inferior to the laborer's right to a living wage."[68] Ryan saw three defects in the existing land system in America: (1) monopoly; (2) excessive gains: it enables some men to take a larger share of the national product than is consistent with the welfare of their neighbors and of society as a whole;[69] (3) exclusion from the land: owners of the large estates refuse to break up their holdings by sale; many proprietors are unwilling to let the use of their land on reasonable terms, and a great deal of land is held at speculative prices instead of at economic prices.[70]

As specific reforms, Ryan urged that the government lease instead of sell any government-owned land. He also advocated municipal ownership of *all* city land to abolish urban land speculation. In the absence of that, he proposed a confiscatory tax which would take away the entirety of increment values of land derived from speculation. "Investments in land which have as their main object a rise in value are an injury rather than a benefit to the community; for they do not increase the products of the land, while they do advance its price, thereby keeping it out of use."[71]

Capital and Interest

In his treatment of the morality of private capital and interest, Ryan discounts the labor theory of value. He argues: (1) labor produces some things which have no value; (2) some things have value—exchange value—which is not due to labor; (3) utility, scarcity, and demand have some moral claim to contribution to value. Nevertheless, he shows sympathy toward the "ethical intuition which connects reward with effort and which inclines to regard income from any other source as not quite, in the same sense, moral."[72]

Ryan concedes to the capitalist a right to interest and a fair profit: "In a general way we may say that they have a strict right to interest on the intrinsic ground of sacrifice. Inasmuch as the community benefits by the savings, it may quite as fairly be required to pay for the antecedent sacrifices of savers, for the inconvenience undergone by the performer of any useful labor or service."[73]

In an important caveat Ryan distinguishes between small businesses and the large trusts. If it is true that interest possesses the same moral claim as rent, the same moral argument for breaking up large and excessive holdings in land applies to corporate capital. He notes that this distinction "is too often overlooked in technical treatises."[74]

Moreover, any right to interest or profit is inherently limited by the laborer's opposing right to a fair, living wage. The latter takes priority in a conflict of rights. "Perhaps the most important difference between the moral claims of the capitalist and laborer is the fact that for the latter labor is the sole means of livelihood."[75] Again, he writes: "The right to any interest at all, except as a return for genuine sacrifices in saving, is not certain, but only presumptive. Consequently, it has no such firm and definite basis as the right to a living wage."[76] Like a refrain running through the entire book is Ryan's reminder that "no industrial right is absolute."[77]

Ryan saw glaring inequities in the modern industrial system's protection of the right of interest and profits. As his solution, he prescribed remedies which would reduce the sum total of interest and profit. He argued for redistribution of the national wealth by a system of progressive taxation. Because he saw first occupancy rather than labor, scarcity, or contribution to productivity as the *original* title to ownership, he could argue that "the future increases of land value may be regarded as a sort of no man's property, which the state appropriates for the benefit of the community."[78] Similarly, collective bargaining through unions had its fair claim to whatever share it could get from an increase in profits or interest within the industrial systems. "The interest share of the produce is morally debatable as to its ownership. It is a sort of no man's property . . . which properly goes to the first occupant as determined by the processes of bargaining between employers and employees."[79]

Ryan looked to institutional reforms such as producers' and consumers' cooperatives, credit unions and co-partnership between capital and labor in owning and operating business, as the means of more widely distributing incomes derived from interest and profits. His ideal was a sort of people's capitalism based on cooperatives.

Ryan is especially stringent in his judgment of monopolies. Monopolies are unjust institutional arrangements which use unfair methods (discriminatory underselling, exclusive-selling contracts, advantages in transportation) to perpetrate injustice against competitors and consumers. The state is obliged to intervene for the common good. Prevention and dissolution of the trusts through government intervention rather than permission or a compromising regulation is the only way to break the stranglehold of the large trusts. If necessary, the government should go into competition to tame a monopoly. Ryan did not think that a legal limitation on inheritance or large fortunes constitutes an infringement of the social good which flows from a limited right to private property. He could also argue that "the receivers of exceptionally large profits are bound in equity to share them with those persons who have cooperated in producing and providing them, namely wage earners and consumers."[80]

Principal Canons of Distributive Justice

In what is perhaps his most original contribution to ethical theory, Ryan devised a five-item canon of distributive justice. He argued for a pluralism of claims to the distributive share of the wealth of a nation. An exclusive appeal to any one item in the canon would not yield justice.

1. *The Canon of Equality.* All persons are equal as moral entities. As human persons, however, they are unequal in desires, capacities, and pow-

ers. It would be unfair, then, to restrict distributive justice to an appeal to the fundamental equality among persons. "Justice in industrial distribution must be measured with reference to welfare rather than with reference to incomes. . . . Any scheme of distribution which provided equal incomes to all persons would be radically unjust."[81] ·

2. *The Canon of Needs.* Proportional need is a genuine factor in determining distribution. Indeed, human needs constitute the primary title or claim to material wealth. They are not the only title. "Justice would seem to require that in each case compensation should be proportionate to exertion rather than needs. At any rate, the claims of needs should be modified to some extent in favor of the claims of exertion."[82]

3. *The Canon of Efforts and Sacrifice* (Labor Theory). Efforts and sacrifice have a just claim upon wealth. They must be balanced against the claims based on need and contribution to productivity.

4. *The Canon of Productivity.* The industrialist has some claim to have contributed to the productivity of output on the basis of which interest and profit is justified.

5. *The Canon of Scarcity.* The claim to a share of the wealth on the basis of the scarcity value of one's goods and services is, according to Ryan, reductively based on reward for sacrifice and the contribution of this sacrifice to productivity. Sheer speculation on the basis of falsely-created scarcity, in his opinion, should be outlawed. "It is increase of utility and not either actual or virtual increase to which men attribute a moral claim."[83]

Ryan sums up these five items in his own inclusive canon of human welfare for determining distributive justice:

> The canon of human welfare includes and summarizes all that is implied in the five other canons. This is its individual aspect. It requires that all human beings be treated as persons, as possessed of natural rights. This is equality. It demands that all industrial persons receive at least that amount of income which is necessary for decent living and reasonable self-development. This is a recognition of needs. The canon of human welfare declares that some consideration must be accorded to manifestations of good will by those who take part in the processes of industry. This is a recognition of efforts and sacrifices. And it gives reasonable recognition to the canons of productivity and scarcity.[84]

Ryan also provides priority rules. Needs have first priority to reward. Next, "efforts and sacrifices are superior to productivity as claims to reward."[85] Finally, productivity has priority of moral claim over scarcity. By stressing the first priority of needs, long before John Rawls, Ryan was arguing that the industrial system's scheme of distributive justice must be so arranged that it is to the advantage of the least advantaged.

Duty of Distributing Superfluous Wealth

Ryan turned to the theological tradition to ground his assertion of a doctrine of ownership as a kind of stewardship of resources which are, in some original sense, common. He distinguishes three separate levels of wealth:

1. *Wealth sufficient to provide the necessities of life.* This is the definition of a minimum living wage. Appealing to the medieval criterion which used a *communis aestimatio* for the determination of a just price, Ryan defines the minimum living wage as "that quantity of goods and opportunities which fair-minded men would regard as indispensable to humane, efficient and reasonable life."[86] Ryan attempted, in constantly revised forms, to determine the dollar value of an annual minimum living wage to meet these standards.

2. *Wealth sufficient to provide the conventional necessities and comforts of one's own social plane or station in life.* Ryan conceded the justice of some inequalities of wealth and position within society, although he would keep the disparities to a reasonable limit. He seemed to regard upper-middle-class wealth (or the lower reaches of it) as the utmost moral limit to material possessions. Anything beyond that constituted superfluous luxury. Ryan also tried to determine this level of wealth in absolute dollar values. He estimated, for example, that any income (1927 values) in excess of $20,000 a year would be superfluous.

3. *Wealth that is superfluous to maintain the standards of a decent livelihood or one's station in life.* Once again Ryan provides priority rules in cases of conflict. Thus, no one who is at level one is obliged in justice to forego any portion of his or her minimum living standard to meet the needs of others below that minimum. In case of relatively equal need, self-interest can prevail over other-interest. At level two, the claims of any who have fallen below level one take priority over one's own claims to a standard of living consonant with one's own social plane or station in life. Level one has absolute priority over level two. On the other hand, one's own right to wealth sufficient to provide the conventional necessities and comforts to one's own social plane or station in life need not yield to others who fall below level two but are at least at level one. In this case, also, self-interest can prevail over other-interest. While Ryan allows, correctly I think, some role to self-interest as a moral motive, he is most careful to circumscribe its limits. He is no utilitarian in morals, let alone an egoist.

Finally, no one has a right to retain or use wealth at level three. To make this point, Ryan draws on the long history of moral theory to conclude:

> In other words, *the entire mass* of superfluous wealth is morally subject to the call of grave need. This seems to be the unanimous teaching of the moral theologians. It is also in harmony with the general principle of the moral law that the goods of the earth

should be enjoyed by the inhabitants of the earth in proportion to their essential needs.[87]

To those who argued that the distribution of superfluous wealth would entail deleterious economic results, since it would rob the market of necessary large sums of capital for investment purposes, Ryan's rejoinder was curt. The money could be transferred to the investment portfolios of charitable institutions that could live off its interest while investing the capital. No sums of capital need be siphoned off the market.

Ryan ends his book with a treatment of theories of wage justice. He rejects prevailing-rate theories because they wrongly assume that "the dominant thing is always the right thing. Justice is determined by the preponderance of economic force."[88] No more than in politics does might make right in economics. He finds exchange-equivalence theories of wage justice faulty because they leave wages to the whims of an impersonal market where wage contracts are usually not really free. An appeal to common class needs is also insufficient: "For it makes no provision for those laborers who deserve a wage in excess of the cost of living of their class; nor does it furnish a principle by which a whole class of workers can justify their advance to a higher standard of livng. It is not sufficiently elastic and dynamic."[89]

Moreover, the labor theory of value, i.e., the theory that labor has the right to the whole product, is not very helpful. It gives us "no rule for determining distributive justice as between different classes of labor."[90] It also neglects to honor the just claims of needs, sacrifices, and contribution to productivity. Finally, Ryan proposes his own solution: (1) a living wage as the minimum of justice and (2) eventual complete wage justice through labor organization and legislation. A decade before the emergence of the C.I.O., Ryan argued for industrial unions as superior to craft unions in giving to labor an organizational power relatively equal to capital.

Toward the end of the book Ryan betrays a growing pessimism about the modern industrial system as compared to his hopes for reform in the debate with Hillquit. "Our industrial system as now constituted is well-nigh bankrupt."[91] He agrees with Brownson's earlier contention that social reform and spiritual renewal must go hand in hand:

> Neither just distribution, nor increased production, nor both combined, will insure a stable and satisfactory social order without a considerable change in human hearts and ideals. . . . The only life worth living is that in which one's cherished wants are few, simple and noble. For the adoption and pursuit of these ideals the most necessary requisite is a revival of genuine religion.[92]

Ryan's pessimism turned again to a qualified hope in the 1930's with the election of Roosevelt and the issuance of *Quadragesimo Anno* by Pius

XI. His colleagues at Catholic University greeted the encyclical as a vindication of Ryan's life's work. Ryan became an enthusiastic New Dealer. He served for a time on the appeals board of the National Recovery Act, which he saw as an embodiment of Pius XI's occupational-groups system. He was bitterly disappointed at the Supreme Court which ruled it unconstitutional. Ryan helped deflect the attacks on Roosevelt in the 1936 campaign by the demagogue radio priest Charles Coughlin, who bestowed on Ryan the soubriquet "The Right Reverend New Dealer." In return, Roosevelt invited him to give the benediction at his second and fourth inaugurations.

In 1940 Ryan authored a second landmark social pastoral of the American bishops on the "Church and the Social Order," which pleaded, among other things, for an industrial democracy and workers' councils as part of management. In the 1940's, now an old man, Ryan moved to a concern for race relations and problems of post-war reconstruction. In 1944, in a talk to the Catholic Economic Association, he made his first concerted attempt to apply his principles of social justice to the international economic order: "Just as the common right of property is morally superior to the private right, just as the social element in ownership takes precedence, in some situations, over the individual elements, so the common right of mankind to the natural resources of a particular country is sometimes superior to the right of that country's inhabitants."[93]

Ethics and Politics

I have turned to the life and thought of John Ryan as a resource within American Catholic theology for doing liberation theology in North America. Ryan's developed economic ethics, or something much like it, seems to me a necessary intervening variable for the move from eschatology to politics. The vision of eschatology is too broad to provide concrete norms for political action. The praxis of politics is too restricted to contingent situations to yield ethical norms. Ethics, like providence, provides eschatology with a theory of the middle range to effect its translation into political praxis.

It is apparent, in making this point, that I agree with James Gustafson's strictures about attempts "to move from theology to history or politics without going through a stage of more careful *ethical* reflection—both about why certain things are judged to be bad and about what concrete proposals are necesary to make them better."[94] I am suggesting, then, that liberation theology must become much more a social ethics than it has so far, if it is going to be an effective instrument in suggesting concrete political praxis. The peculiar genius of the social-ethical tradition in America has been its ability to make particular moral judgments about particular social proposals and to suggest, among optional courses of moral action, those which might be judged morally approvable. There has generally also been a tendency in America to pay careful attention to the historical character of ethical issues. Gustafson notes that while this approach to social ethics has sometimes led to an uncritical acceptance of the institutional framework in which certain problems are posed, this need not be the case. John Ryan stands squarely in this tradition of social ethics.

There are historical limits, of course, to Ryan's vision. He was perhaps not sufficiently aware, in his New Deal enthusiasm, of the dangers of government centralization. His thought shows a certain rationalistic bias. It deals inadequately with the reality of power. He did not push his work enough into the context of international economic justice, although much of his ethical analysis seems translatable to the international arena. Ryan was too sanguine about the possibilities inherent in legislative action, although in his more sober moments he knew that there is "an inherent contradiction between the spirit [of] political democracy and industrial autocracy."[95] Living and writing as he did in the first generation after the rise of the large trusts in America, he still thought their progress could be halted and a people's capitalism of small enterprises instituted. His vision of a successful cooperative movement never materialized. For some, his conviction that underconsumption and oversaving are the main causes of industrial slumps and depressions smacks of a dated Keynsian view in economics. Like almost every other economist of his generation, Ryan was unable to conceptualize inherent natural limits to ever-increasing industrial production. For others, he remains too much the Scholastic Thomist.

Ryan always refused to accept socialism as a solution, although this seems to have been conditioned much more by the historic anti-religious stance of the socialism that he knew than by its economic doctrine. Perhaps he was also smitten by the time-conditioned allergy toward socialism implicit in historic social Catholicism.[96] And yet, as one historian of American socialism has commented, "Ryan's ideas were more radical than the program of a good many moderate dues-paying socialists."[97] In the conclusion of his last book, written as the New Deal was entering its third term, Ryan wrote: "Historical capitalism cannot and ought not to survive."[98] It is only by turning to careful ethical and economic analysis—*both* together, since it is simply not true that good economics makes good ethics—similar to his that we, who perhaps know better than he the justice of his remark, can both ground that conclusion and begin to construct, piece by piece, an alternative ethical program and vision of what should take capitalism's place.

LEGACY OF JOHN COURTNEY MURRAY: A DOCTRINE OF SOCIAL PLURALISM

My treatment of the work of John Courtney Murray will be both more brief than that of Brownson and Ryan and less biographical. Murray's life and work stand closer to our own time. It is easily accessible in his own major works, *We Hold These Truths* and *The Problem of Religious*

Freedom. Murray was more of an intellectual than an activist. Still, his eager participation in the early ecumenical movement, his involvement in public-policy discussions at the Fund for the Republic and the Center for Democratic Institutions in Santa Barbara, and his years as a *peritus* at Vatican Council II, where he engineered the writing and passage of the document on religious liberty, gave to his intellectual vision the taste of praxis. What lends a peculiar stamp to his theological work is its combination of careful hermeneutic of the classic documents of social Catholicism with a wide knowledge of constitutional law and history.

With Maritain, whose work, especially *Man and the State,* Murray influenced, Murray stands as the major reinterpreter of the Thomist position on politics and the state in the post-war period. From Aquinas, Murray derived the cornerstones of his political thought. He held firmly to "the idea that government has a moral basis; that the universal moral law is the foundation of society; that the legal order of society—that is, the state—is subject to judgment by a law that is not statistical but inherent in the nature of man; that the eternal reason of God is the ultimate origin of all law."[99] Murray held also to the doctrine of a natural law: "that man is intelligent; that reality is intelligible; and that reality, as grasped by intelligence, imposes on the will the obligation that it be obeyed in its demands for action and/or abstention."[100] He adds to the tradition of the natural law, however, a keen sense of that "historical consciousness that ought to preside over all argument about human rights." Thus he can speak of "a demand of the natural law in the present moment of history."[101]

From Aquinas, Murray also extracted the conclusion that reality exhibits an analogical structure. This led him to make three crucial distinctions:

1. *The distinction between the secular and the sacred.* For Murray, it is not possible to collapse the two orders of authority within society, the temporal and the spiritual. The world is ruled "by a dyarchy of authorities within which the temporal is subordinate to the spiritual, not instrumentally, but in dignity."[102] The Catholic may not submerge his religious faith into his patriotic allegiance. Murray was a realist. Religious pluralism is against the will of God. Nevertheless, "religious pluralism is theologically the human condition."[103] Since the state has no province in the *cura animarum,* "the public powers are not competent to judge whether conscience be erroneous or not."[104] The public powers may not make windows into men's souls. Hence, in the temporal order, the public care of religion is limited to the public care for religious freedom. The First Amendment establishment of religious freedom is the only establishment consonant with the Catholic doctrine of a limited character of state authority.

2. *The distinction between society and the state.* Murray was a firm advocate of limited, constitutional government. Government is not co-extensive with man's existence, because "the whole of man's existence is not absorbed in his temporal and terrestrial existence."[105] There is a distinction between the order of politics and the order of culture which grounds the

right of freedom of inquiry and academic freedom. The institutions of the *imperium* and those of the *studium* are not to be merged. Moreover, "the purposes of the state are not co-extensive with the purposes of society. The state is only one order within society, the order of public law and political administration."[106]

As an advocate of social pluralism in societal authority, Murray held that the authority of the Church as an institution and of the family are not derivative from the state. The rights to assembly and organization into voluntary associations are also inherent natural rights in society. Intermediate organizations within society do not exist at the whim of the state. Murray appeals both to the Catholic principle of subsidiarity and to the limited character of the state to ground the general right of voluntary association: "This latter right is based on the social nature of man, whose sociality is not exhausted by his citizenship in the body politic. It is likewise based on the principle of subsidiary function as a principle of social organization."[107]

3. *The distinction between the common good and public order.* Social justice depends upon the achievement of the common good of all individuals within society. Public order—the order of jurisprudence and law—stands under the judgment of the common good. Murray would not countenance a cynical divorce between law and morality, although he was careful to distinguish, in accord with his position that reality exhibits an analogical structure, between individual and public morality. There should not be a law for every vice. The goods of the public order, freedom, and the common good may lead legislators to leave to the private sphere those vices which involve no real "victims." Murray was no Puritan.

Murray asserted, on the other hand, the service character of the state. It exists as an instrument to promote justice and liberty. The ends of the public order are fourfold: public peace, public morality, justice, and the freedom of the people. "The democratic state serves both the ends of the human person (in itself and its natural forms of social life) and also the ends of justice. As the servant of these ends, it has only a relative value."[108]

If the state is both subject to and the servant of the common good, it "is not the sole judge of what is or is not the common good." Moreover, "in consequence of the distinction between society and state, not every element of the common good is instantly committed to the state to be protected and promoted."[109] There are inalienable civil liberties. Furthermore, the people must be consulted, both through constitutional consent and through the channels of public opinion, about the nature of the common good. Murray assumes that the authority of any government, derived from God and not from the Church, devolves upon it through the consensus of the people. Murray is an ethical democrat. "There is a sense of justice inherent in the people, in virtue of which they are empowered, as the medieval phrase had it, to 'judge, direct, and correct' the process of government."[110] Nevertheless, he is careful to respect the evidence of diversity. There can be no ideal instance of constitutional law. Any attempt to canonize one constitutional arrangement involves a contradiction in terms.

If justice was the predominant passion of Brownson and Ryan, liberty was Murray's. He could say that "ideally, I suppose, there should be only one passion in the city, the passion for justice."[111] Liberty, however, is a demand of justice itself. Murray is best known as the theologian who demolished the classic Catholic position of a thesis-hypothesis on the question of religious establishment. By a painstaking historical reconstruction, he charted the "growing end" of the tradition on religious liberty from Pius IX and Leo XIII through Pius XII and John XXIII, to show the appropriate linkages of a doctrine of religious freedom to the corpus of Catholic social thought. Murray's argument for religious freedom was of a piece with his case for civil liberty in general. His was a single complex insight: the free person under a government of limited powers.

> The personal or corporate free exercise of religion as a human and civil right is evidently cognate with other more general human and civil rights—with the freedom of corporate bodies and institutions within society, based on the principle of subsidiary function; with the general freedom of association for peaceful purposes, based on the social nature of man; with the general freedom of speech and of the press, based on the nature of political society.[112]

Murray would not allow himself to claim a freedom for the Church and deny similar liberty to other religious or human intermediate associations: "Constitutional government, limited in its powers, dedicated to the defense of the rights of man and to the promotion of the freedom of the people, is the correlate of religious freedom as a juridical notion, a civil and human right, personal and corporate."[113]

In his reading of the signs of his time, Murray saw that the demand of natural law in the present moment of history was a demand of freedom in regard to the goods of the human spirit: "the search for truth, the free expression and dissemination of opinion, the cultivation of the arts and sciences, free access to information about public events, adequate opportunities for the development of personal talents and for progress in knowledge and culture."[114] He grounded his case for civil freedoms, in his arguments about the service character of limited, constitutional government, in his assertion that "the freedom of the people is also the higher purpose of the juridical order, which is not an end in itself. Furthermore, freedom is the political method *per excellentiam.*"[115]

For Murray, the basic rule of jurisprudence remains freedom under the law. Its dictate runs: let there be as much freedom, personal and social, as is possible; let there be only as much restraint and constraint, personal and social, as may be necessary for the public order. Indeed, in his treatment of the ethical justification of coercion, he boldly affirms that coercion can only be morally tolerable if it is exercised in the name and for the sake of freedom. Thus, in treating of possible governmental restraint of the freedom of religion, he is careful to circumscribe state power:

> In what concerns religious freedom, the requirement is fourfold: that the violation of the public order be really serious; that legal or police intervention be really necessary; that regard be had for the privileged character of religious freedom, which is not simply to be equated with other civil rights; that the rule of jurisprudence of the free society be strictly observed, scl., as much freedom as possible, as much coercion as necessary.[116]

Murray laid to rest, with the publication of *We Hold These Truths* in the year John Kennedy was elected president, non-Catholic fears of Catholic authoritarianism. Throughout the nineteenth century, Catholic social thought had failed to come to grips with two central movements of the modern era: socialism and the quest for the freedom of the individual. In the thought of Brownson and Ryan lie perhaps the seeds of a rapprochement between Catholicism and socialism; in that of Murray, the definitive Catholic position on the free individual. Let Murray make the case for himself:

> The spiritual order of society is founded on truth—on the true virtue of man, his dignity, his duties and rights, his freedoms and obligations. This order must be brought into being under fidelity to the precepts of justice, whose vindication is the primary function of the public power as well as the primary civic duty of the citizenry. This order needs to be animated and perfected by love; for civic unity cannot be achieved by justice and law alone; love is the ultimate force that sustains all humans living together. Finally, this order is to achieve increasingly more human conditions of social equality, without any impairment of freedom.
>
> Truth, justice, and love assure the stability of society; but freedom is the dynamism of social progress toward fuller humanity in communal living. The freedom of the people ranks as a political end, along with justice; it is a demand of justice itself. Freedom is also the political method whereby the people achieve their highest good, which is their own unity as a people. A society of men achieves its unity (*coalescit*) by freedom, that is, by methods that are in keeping with the dignity of its citizens, who are by nature men of reason and who therefore assume responsibility for their own actions. Society is bound to the usages or methods of freedom (*libertatis consuetudinem teneat*) in its constant effort to base itself on truth, govern itself with justice, and permeate itself with civic friendship. When the freedom of the

people is unjustly limited, the social order itself, which is an order of freedom, is overthrown.[117]

Civil Liberty and Liberation Theology

The thought of John Courtney Murray puts us in contact with what
seems to me to be the permanent legacy of social Catholicism: the theory
of societal pluralism in authority and a doctrine of social and civil rights of
the human person within society. Parts of social Catholicism need to be
outgrown, e.g., Leo XIII's almost metaphysical insistence on the right of
private property and a false distinction of planes between the Church and
the temporal order. The doctrines of subsidiarity and a pluralism in social
authority, however, form a bedrock legacy of social Catholicism to which
Murray both attests and contributes.

I take it that the fundamental task for a liberation theology in North
America is to achieve a species of socialism with a human face; to find a
viable alternative to the false dichotomies of individualism and monistic
socialism of the nineteenth century; to combine the goods of justice and
liberty in a new synthesis. There are dangers, of course, in overemphasizing the doctrines of subsidiary functions and civil liberties. By appealing to
a one-sided political analysis—as Murray sometimes does—and scouting
the economic order of welfare and material justice, one can run the risk of
an abuse of a putative order of civil liberties in order to protect special
privilege and institutionalize injustice. The language of the civil libertarian
tradition is not without its ideological social uses.[118] Nevertheless, in a
modern world where the realities of a smothering bureaucratic centralism
seem the mark of all currently competing economic and political systems,
the language of pluralism and subsidiarity gains an added luster.

I find it rather surprising that the treatment of social Catholicism by
the Latin American theologians of liberation mainly focuses on the out-
moded, and justly discarded, doctrine of a distinction of planes between
the natural and supernatural and a false Church-world strategy which assumes that the Church stands as an arbiter of temporal reality and culture.
The Latin American theologians are correct in rejecting, as archaic, the
concept of Christendom. They urge us to adopt a new strategy to relate the
Church to the world. They say almost nothing about the doctrine of the
state.[119] They are curiously silent about the whole question of social pluralism, subsidiarity, and civil liberties, perhaps because of a justifiable fear
that libertarian language in their context will undergird a *laissez faire* economic liberalism.[120] The two doctrines need not coincide.[121]

To be perfectly honest, we have never yet seen a socialism with a civil
libertarian base. Nor was politics and the doctrine of the state the strong
point of Marx, the master unmasker of the economic factor in history. Neither has it been the long suit of those who work in his tradition of thought,
certainly not of those who have already assumed the reigns of power, but
also not of those who now seek political power, perhaps because, as outsid-

ers to the seats of political power, they have been justifiably more concerned with the politics of gaining power than with the visions of its political uses—and the need for its limit—once they reach the seat of power.[122]

I think it would be a grave mistake for liberation theology to enter the dialogue with Marxist social analysis, as it certainly should, while forgetting its own major contribution in such a dialogue, its tradition of social pluralism, political liberty, the nature of politics and the state. An unmediated passage from eschatology to political praxis without the intervening variable of a social ethics of the state and the ends and limits of political society could mean a descent into hell. It seems clear enough that in the North American context the tradition of civil liberties, due process, and common law continues to constitute in the present, as it has in our past, a key weapon in the fight for social justice. As Ivan Illich remarks:

> It could even be used to preserve the continuous development of a set of laws that fit an inverted society. There is nothing in most constitutions that prevents the passage of laws setting upper limits to productivity, privilege, professional monopoly, or efficiency. In principle, the existing process of legislatures and courts can, with a reversal of its focus, make and apply such a law.[123]

There are those, in our own time, who are predicting anyway a descent into hell and the inevitable emergence of totalitarian regimes in the West.[124] It is neither a pleasant nor a necessary prospect. It seems to me that in this climate of easy acquiescence in the default of the rule of limited, fair, and constitutional law in the furtherance of justice, Catholic theology will represent a force for liberation by recalling with pride, as a *cri du coeur,* the legacy of Murray. As Murray put it trenchantly, "in the present moment of history, the freedom of the people of God is inseparably linked with the freedom of the peoples of the world."[125]

NOTES

1. Because of the difficulty in judging the work-in-process of still living American theologians, I have restricted myself to a population which is already decreased. For a rather dismal record of the state of American Catholic theology—indeed, melancholy reading—cf. John L. Murphy, "Seventy-Five Years of Fundamental Theology in America, Part I." *American Ecclesiastical Review* 150 (1964) 384–404, and "Part II," *ibid.,* 151 (1964), pp. 21–41; George W. Shea, "Seventy-Five Years of Special Dogmatic Theology in America," *ibid.,* 151 (1964), pp. 145–65.

2. For an overview of the state of European theology 1800–1970, cf. T. M. Schoof, *A Survey of Catholic Theology: 1800–1970* (New York, 1970). Schoof does not include any Americans in his survey.

3. I am persuaded of the importance of rethinking the relation of nature

and grace for the possibility of a liberation theology by a paper by my colleague Joseph M. Powers, S.J., "Some Roots of Gutiérrez' Liberation Theology in Recent Roman Catholic Theology," delivered at the Pacific Coast Theological Meetings, April 10, 1974.

4. In the section that follows I am following closely David Tracy, "The Task of Fundamental Theology," *Journal of Religion* 54 (1974), pp. 13–35. The terms "criterion of appropriateness," "criterion of adequacy," and "the Christian fact" are derived from Tracy.

5. John Courtney Murray, *The Problem of Religious Freedom* (Westminster, Md., 1965), p. 101.

6. John Courtney Murray, *We Hold These Truths* (New York, 1960), p. 11.

7. Tracy, *art. cit.,* p. 33.

8. Emile Durkheim, *Sociology and Philosophy* (New York, 1974), p. 95.

9. For an expansion of this point, cf. "Between Religion and Social Science," in Robert N. Bellah, *Beyond Belief* (New York, 1970), pp. 237–60.

10. I am informed, in my contention of the non-reducibility of vision to praxis, by the discussion of the work of the Frankfurt School in Martin Jay, *The Dialectical Imagination* (Boston, 1973), pp. 108ff., and by the extraordinary book on vision and praxis in politics by Sheldon Wolin, *Politics and Vision* (Boston, 1960).

11. *We Hold These Truths,* p. 92.

12. *The Problem of Religious Freedom,* p. 102.

13. Cf. Arthur Schlesinger, Jr., *Orestes Brownson: A Pilgrim's Progress* (Boston, 1939).

14. I am prepared to argue that the two major periods of discontinuity in Brownson's thought, 1844–56 and 1868–76, are due to the interference of Church authorities in his work. In an earlier period he wrote under the censoring eye of his bishop, John Fitzpatrick. In the later period he was under the spell of Pius IX's *Quanta Cura* and its Syllabus of Errors. I think it much more productive to stress the continuities in Brownson's work. For a good example of this, cf. Richard M. Leliaert, *Orestes Brownson: Theological Perspectives on His Search for the Meaning of God, Christology and the Development of Doctrine* (unpublished doctoral dissertation, Graduate Theological Union, Berkeley, 1974).

15. Orestes Brownson, *The Convert* (New York, 1886), p. 238.

16. *Ibid.,* p. 51.

17. *Ibid.,* p. 126.

18. *Ibid.,* p. 263.

19. *Ibid.,* p. 254.

20. *Ibid.,* p. 214.

21. *Ibid.,* p. 234.

22. *Ibid.,* pp. 296–97.

23. *Ibid.,* pp. 307–08.

24. *Ibid.,* p. 214.

25. *Ibid.,* p. 235.

26. Cf. Alvan S. Ryan, ed., *The Brownson Reader* (New York, 1955), p. 253.

27. "The Philosophy of History," in *The Brownson Reader,* p. 197.

28. "The Dignity of Human Reason," in *The Brownson Reader,* p. 248. This essay should be read as Brownson's definitive defense against the charge of ontologism. In it he compares his position to that of Aquinas.

29. "Essay on Lacordaire," in *The Brownson Reader,* p. 347.

30. *The Convert*, p. 169.

31. Leliaert, p. 201.

32. *The Convert*, p. 104.

33. Orestes Brownson, *The American Republic* (New York, 1866).

34. *Ibid.*, p. 136.

35. *Ibid.*, p. 383.

36. "Freedom" (1864), in *The Brownson Reader*, p. 353.

37. *Ibid.*, p. 352.

38. *The American Republic*, p. 415.

39. *Ibid.*, p. 121.

40. Theodore Maynard, *Orestes Brownson: Yankee, Radical, Catholic* (New York, 1943), p. 320.

41. For the above citations, cf. "The Philosophy of History," in *The Brownson Reader*, pp. 189–205.

42. *The American Republic*, p. 173.

43. *The Brownson Reader*, p. 205.

44. Stanley J. Parry, "The Premises of Brownson's Political Theory," *Review of Politics* 16 (1954) 196. Parry's article contains a substantive treatment of providence and politics in Brownson's political writings.

45. I was first led to reflect upon the need for a doctrine of providence for a developed liberation theology and the importance of relating providence to eschatology in a course conducted by Langdon Gilkey, "History, Politics, and Providence," offered at the Divinity School of the University of Chicago in the spring of 1974.

46. *The American Republic*, p. 3.

47. *Ibid.*, p. 5.

48. *Ibid.*, p. 57.

49. *Ibid.*, p. 144.

50. *Ibid.*, p. 173.

51. *Ibid.*, p. 57.

52. Sydney E. Ahlstrom, *A Religious History of the American People* (New Haven, 1972), p. 640.

53. For this criticism of an unmediated move from eschatology to politics, cf. James M. Gustafson, *Theology and Christian Ethics* (Philadelphia, 1974), p. 187.

54. Schlesinger, *Orestes Brownson*, pp. xi–xii.

55. John Ryan, *Social Doctrine in Action* (New York, 1941); cf. also Francis L. Broderick, *Right Reverend New Dealer: John A. Ryan* (New York, 1963).

56. John Ireland, *The Church and Modern Society* 1 (Chicago, 1896), p. 78.

57. Ryan was accused of a lack of concern for interiority by the Benedictine liturgist and social reformer Virgil Michel; cf. David J. O'Brien, *American Catholics and Social Reform* (New York, 1968), p. 147.

58. John Ryan, *Distributive Justice* (New York, 1927), p. 130. Hereafter cited as *DJ*.

59. *Ibid.*, p. 260.

60. *Ibid.*, p. 328.

61. *Right Reverend New Dealer*, p. 34.

62. Morris Hillquit and John A. Ryan, *Socialism: Promise or Menace?* (New York, 1914). Hereafter cited as *Socialism*.

63. *Ibid.*, p. 13.

64. *Ibid.*, p. 41.

65. *Social Doctrine in Action*, p. 190.

66. *DJ*, p. 66.

67. *Ibid.*, p. 21.

68. *Ibid.*, p. 69.

69. *Ibid.*, p. 78.

70. *Ibid.*, p. 83.

71. *Ibid.*, p. 94.

72. *Ibid.*, p. 181.

73. *Ibid.*, p. 164.

74. *Ibid.*, p. 179.

75. *Ibid.*, p. 158.

76. *Ibid.*, p. 324.

77. *Ibid.*, p. 227.

78. *Ibid.*, p. 99.

79. *Ibid.*, p. 348.

80. *Ibid.*, p. 225.

81. *Ibid.*, p. 213.

82. *Ibid.*, p. 214.

83. *Ibid.*, p. 47.

84. *Ibid.*, pp. 220–21.

85. *Ibid.*, p. 307. It is instructive to contrast Ryan's concrete lexical ordering in his canon of distributive justice, based on economic as well as ethical analysis, with that of John Rawls, *A Theory of Justice* (Cambridge, Mass., 1971).

86. *DJ*, p. 322.

87. *Ibid.*, p. 274.

88. *Ibid.*, p. 287.

89. *Ibid.*, p. 297.

90. *Ibid.*, p. 307.

91. *Ibid.*, p. 389.

92. *Ibid.*, p. 397. Simplicity of life was a constant theme in Ryan's writings; cf. his 1907 *Catholic World* article "The Fallacy of Bettering One's Position," in *Social Doctrine in Action*, p. 100.

93. Cited in *Right Reverend New Dealer*, pp. 273–74.

94. James M. Gustafson, *Theology and Christian Ethics* (Philadelphia, 1974) p. 188.

95. *Social Doctrine in Action*, p. 18.

96. Historically, the thought of social Catholicism sought a middle way between individualism and socialism. Its emphasis on the priority of the common good and its model of a kind of guild society made it closer to socialism in its economic doctrine than to individualism. My own intuition is that social Catholicism objected more to nineteenth century socialism's monistic doctrine of social authority than to its economics. It also rejected its anti-religious bias. Unfortunately, social Catholicism in practice often turned out to look more like economic individualism. For a history of social Catholicism, cf. J. B. Duroselle, *Les débuts du catholicisme social en France* (Paris, 1951), and Alec R. Vidler, *A Century of Social Catholicism 1820–1920* (London, 1964).

97. Ira Kipnis, *The American Socialist Movement 1897–1912* (New York, 1952), p. 428.

98. *Social Doctrine in Action*, p. 280.

99. John Courtney Murray, *We Hold These Truths* (New York, 1960), p. 53. Hereafter cited as *WHTT.*

100. John Courtney Murray, *The Problem of Religious Freedom* (Westminster, Md., 1965), p. 19. Hereafter cited as *PRF.*

101. *WHTT,* p. 113.

102. *Ibid.,* p. 32.

103. *PRF,* p. 109.

104. *Ibid.,* p. 22.

105. *Ibid.,* p. 28.

106. *Ibid.,* p. 29.

107. *Ibid.,* p. 36.

108. *WHTT,* p. 308.

109. *PRF,* p. 42.

110. *WHTT,* p. 45.

111. *Ibid.,* p. 20.

112. *PRF,* p. 26.

113. *Ibid.,* p. 67.

114. *Ibid.,* p. 19.

115. *Ibid.,* p. 31.

116. *Ibid.,* p. 43.

117. *Ibid.,* p. 82.

118. Yet, cf. Ivan Illich, *Tools for Conviviality* (New York, 1973), pp. 104–05, where he remarks that "the abuse of the formal structure of common law does not corrupt the structure itself" and "people can defend language and law as inherently theirs."

119. For relevant passages cf. Gustavo Gutiérrez, *A Theology of Liberation* (Maryknoll, N.Y., 1973), pp. 53–58, and Juan Luis Segundo, *The Community Called Church* (Maryknoll, N.Y., 1973), pp. 128–32. Neither Gutiérrez nor Segundo even mentions the doctrine of societal pluralism or subsidiarity in their brief treatments of social Catholicism, which they tend to repudiate.

120. In a sympathetic personal communication, Peru's Ricardo Antonsich informed me that in Peru civil libertarian language has such a history of ideological use that it is difficult to retrieve its liberation meaning.

121. For a good attempt at putting together the civil libertarian language with a case for socialism, cf. Stephen Lukes, *Individualism* (Oxford, 1973).

122. For a treatment of the antipolitical elements in the thought of Marx and his lack of a developed doctrine for the state, cf. Sheldon Wolin, *Politics and Vision,* pp. 416–17.

123. *Tools for Conviviality,* p. 103.

124. Cf. Robert Heilbroner, *An Inquiry Into the Human Prospect* (New York, 1974).

125. *PRF,* p. 70.

Chapter Five

Civil Religion and Liberation Theology in North America

I once took part in a conversation with a Latin American theologian of liberation about the possibility of creating a liberation theology in the North American context. When the discussion turned to the topic of civil religion as a resource for projects of liberation in the United States, he smiled disarmingly and said, "Of course, I do not have a clue what this civil religion of yours is all about. We do not speak of such things."

Anyone conversant with the literature on civil religion that has grown up since Robert Bellah's celebrated essay on the topic of "Civil Religion in America" knows that to speak of civil religion is to raise a hornet's nest of unresolved problems of definition and evaluation.[1] In debates and colloquies devoted to the subject, questions range from "Does it exist anywhere except in the minds of intellectuals?" or "Is it a purely American phenomenon?" to "Is it anything more than mindless or idolatrous patriotism?" Martin Marty has suggested somewhat flippantly that "civil religion at least existed once in a speech or two of Abraham Lincoln."[2] He also suggests that it is a sociologist's social construction of reality.

It is clear that civil religion is, nonetheless, one of the things we do speak about, if not under that rubric, then in terms of patriotism, the civil heritage, national destiny or purpose, or political and public theology. I will attempt in the following pages to address myself to civil religion under three topics:

1. What is civil religion? Problems of definition and evaluation.
2. America's civil religion.
3. The relevance of liberation theology for civil religion and of civil religion for understanding liberation theology.

The limits of both my competence and my time will not allow me more than a brief suggestive analysis of each of these topics. The controversial nature of the term "civil religion" demands that I give, first, some special attention to questions of definition and evaluation.

108

CIVIL RELIGION:
PROBLEMS OF DEFINITION AND EVALUATION

Probably the best place to begin a discussion of civil religion is to define it simply as the religious dimension of the national political experience. Civil religion is a functional universal. Every nation has one. Each nation has to make some sense of its continuity and meaning in world history and its collective identity and vocation vis-à-vis other nations and its own citizens. What does it mean—in terms of ultimate vocation and moral identity—to be an Israeli, an American, or a Frenchman? To ask a deeply probing question about collective identity and purpose is to skirt on religious ground. In this, the religious dynamic is not unlike that operative in personal identity questions. To define the "soul" of a nation is to see it, in some sense, as before a more ultimate bar of judgment since no nation is the final repository of its own meaning. Nevertheless, questions about ultimate national identity and purpose transcend the peculiar provinces or exclusive competencies of either the state or particular world religions and churches.

If you like, civil religion is the mystic chord of communal memory (always being summoned to reinterpretation in the face of new historic tasks) which ties together both a nation's citizenry and the episodes of its history into a meaningful identity by using significant national beliefs, events, persons, places, or documents to serve as symbolic repositories of the special vocational significance of the nation-state in the light of a more ultimate or transcendent bar of judgment: ethical ideals, humanity, world history, being, the universe, or God.[3]

Presumably, ultimate values are involved as the depth dimension of all significant human behavior. If marriage and the family have nowhere been totally secularized, one would hardly expect that something as potent as the nation-state would be. The claims of one's nation upon the conscience are strong, compelling, and complex. William Butler Yeats caught this sense of the functional universality of civil religion when he stated, "One can only reach out to the universe with a gloved hand—that glove is one's nation; the only thing one knows even a little of." When national existence and history becomes a place where one has contact with more transcendent values, the nation becomes a moral and significantly religious identity.

Let us return, for a moment, to our simple starting definition: Civil religion is the religious dimension in the national political experience. I should like to underscore that word "dimension" as a way of safeguarding us from reifying the civil religion. It is not a "thing." It is an aspect of a seemingly permanent dimension in politics. Civil religion does not exhaust all religious functions. It leaves relatively untouched the contemplative, theological, and inner spiritual dimensions usually associated with the churches. Conversely, civil religion reminds us that the churches do not, also, exhaust all religious functions, nor, seemingly, can they.

Secondly, civil religion is only one of several aspects of the political realm. Of course, there is room for a non-religious analysis of the polity. The term "civil religion" merely suggests that political analysis which restricts itself to questions of "Who gets what from whom and under what form of coercion" is blinded to an essential factor in all political life: the presence of shared restraining moral norms and collective religious ideals.

It may help us to understand civil religion if we ask whether the political or national realm has a religious dimension *only* when it is judged in the light of some separate world religious tradition or some separately institutionalized religious organization in society. Is the religious dimension in the political realm always borrowed or usurped from some other institutional context, e.g., the Church, where it rightfully belongs? I think the clear answer is no.

Every authority system, as Max Weber reminds us, feels the need for symbols of legitimacy. It needs, in Peter Berger's terms, a "sacred canopy" of justification, grounding not only external obedience to its particular demands but inner assent to its rightful existence. Indeed, even tyrants must try to shore up their sheerly coercive authority with moral and religious trappings as the Nazi religious system shows us. They spin out ideologies. Unless we are radical anarchists who view all present or potential political authority as illegitimate, we will need to avoid a cynical view which sees every legitimacy system for political realms as, in all respects, a false ideology.

But, to continue the argument, systems of legitimacy are never purely rational. Nor are they grounded simply on utilitarian empirical calculation of consequences. Political authority systems are not legitimate just because they work. Every authority system relies upon non-rational symbolic "charisma." Because authority systems touch potent and ambiguous realities such as power, position, force, contingency, personal and collective destinies, it is impossible that the political realm lack—in however attenuated or disguised a form—a religious and mythic dimension. If the churches will not provide society with the "charisma" that it needs, it will either create its own or seek for it elsewhere.

Note that I am arguing that a religious dimension is intrinsic to the political or societal realm as such. If the experience of personal contingency, limit, and death leads individuals to ask ultimately religious questions even in the absence of any sustained contact with explicitly religious groups, national experiences of threat, contingency, breakdown, and possible decline and death bring collectivities to a similar religious threshold. There are collective situations which provide analogues to the "limit situations" or "peak experiences" which phenomenologists of religion point to as the locus for personal religious experience. Revolutionary beginnings, periods when national history hangs in the balance, moments of collective ferment, redefinition of national purpose, or acceptance of humiliation and defeat—these are the collective "signals of transcendence," again borrowing Peter Berger's language, which indicate the concrete points of contact between national political experience and experiences of transcendence. They are the places where we would expect political language to have a religious tinge. They are also, interestingly enough, the situations to which political theologians must point if their claims about the public character of religious language such as "the judgment of God over the nation," "providence," or "liberation theology" are to have any concrete reference and public significance.

The religious dimension of the political realm is, then, neither a borrowing from nor a usurping of the rightful domain of another institutional sector of society, i.e., organized religion. Most nations, to be sure, will probably employ the religious symbols which are culturally at hand to ground and interpret their political authority and national identity. It is worth remembering, however, that even when the symbols for understanding national destiny are largely borrowed from the great world religions, these borrowings usually involve creative and ad hoc applications of that symbolism to religious problems which arise not from within the religious tradition itself but from critical historical events within the national political experience. No knowledge of Islam, for example, as a world religion can help us to deduce a priori the way it will be used to ground the particular meaning and destiny of Egypt. Similarly, nothing in Catholicism understood as a world religion would lead us to understand the way it functions as a *civil* grounding for the experience of the Republic of Ireland where, as Conor Cruise O'Brien put it, "To be an Irishman is to be at least an 'honorary' Catholic."

It was precisely this understanding of an *intrinsically* religious aspect to the political or social realm which led Emile Durkheim to insist that every society in some profound sense is a moral and religious reality to its members. He also saw that every society, "in all its aspects and in every period of its history, is made possible only by a vast symbolism" of moral ideals which are never perfectly realized by given empirical states of the society.[4] This insight of Durkheim and, indeed, some analysis according to the mode of Durkheimian sociology would seem a necessary background for determining our answer to these questions: "Is there such a thing as a civil religion?" and "If there is, how should we evaluate it as a religious reality?" I have been arguing that even when a great world religion such as Christianity provides the main symbols for interpreting national purpose and destiny, civil religion remains, in Durkheim's terms, a dimension *sui generis,* irreducible to the constitutive properties of the tradition of that world religion. It is, at any rate, a dimension whose religious significance addresses itself properly to *all* those who participate in the national political realm, not merely to members of the churches.

It would be a mistake, therefore, to follow Martin Marty when he suggests that the only reason civil religions exist is because "the nation, state or society is one of the most potent repositories of symbols in the modern world and can often replace religious institutions in the minds of people."[5] Civil religion does not derive exclusively from the arrogance and potencies of nation states. Neither does it arise because of the failures of organized religions sufficiently to apply their more universal symbols to the concrete contingencies of national histories or because of the complacency of the churches in idolatrous patriotism. Neither civil religion nor patriotism is inherently idolatrous. Civil religions exist because of the empirical impossibility of a purely "secular" state. As W.H. Auden once put it, "Without a cement of blood (it must be human, it must be innocent) no secular wall will safely stand."[6]

If civil religion is a functional universal, the actual empirical state of civil religion in any given nation varies according to social or cultural context. The quality of the civil religion, its intensity or extensiveness, its relative importance to national self-identity and its primary institutional locations all vary from context to context. In some cases, the civil religion is mainly sponsored by the state as in Japanese Shinto. In other cases, such as traditional Catholicism in Latin America, the civil religion is derived from the Church. Religious pluralism—either as intense conflict or in accommodation—as opposed to religious monism is an important factor to explain cases where "there actually exists alongside of and rather clearly differentiated from the churches an elaborate and well-institutionalized civil religion" with its own set of national feast days, shrines, sacred founding experiences, documents, saints, etc., as opposed to cases where Church religion and civil religious functions are fused.[7] In cases of religious pluralism, the symbols of the civil religion, if they are to function as a powerful moral reference, must be both concrete enough to provide some meaningful content and direction to national identity and general enough so that civil religion does not become a serious alternative rival to particular religious groups within the nation.

The absence, in some cases, of a clear differentiation of the civil religion from the state or particular world religious traditions has blinded some observers entirely to the phenomenon of civil religion. Some, for instance, find the historic coalescence of Christianity and national identity as natural. They fail to see this coalescence for what it is: an historical accident involving a creative synthesis between Christianity and national culture where *both* elements contribute to the synthesis in a sort of creative compromise.[8] The symbolism, for example, involved in the creation of a Saint Louis or a Joan of Arc was neither purely Christian nor purely French. It was as much a symbolism of French national identity as of world Catholicism. It was as much a civil as—if I may be permitted the misleading barbarism—a religious religion.

The civil religious dimension does not seem to differ, at least as a phenomenological system of beliefs, rituals, and moral codes, from other religions, although civil religions may be less intense and personal. Emile Durkheim once put this point bluntly by asking, "What essential difference is there between an assembly of Christians celebrating the principal dates of the life of Christ or of Jews remembering the exodus from Egypt or the promulgation of the decalogue, and a reunion of citizens commemorating the promulgation of a new moral or legal system or some great event in the national life?"[9]

Civil religions display the dialectical tensions inherent in all religious systems. I can merely cite some of the most important of these to illustrate the main paradoxes inherent in the institutionalization of *any* religious system.

Transcendence vs. immanence: Civil religion is confronted by the paradox of transcendent reference and immanent embodiment, a tension deriving from the universal religious need to incarnate the transcendent "in symbolic forms which are themselves empirical and profane and which with repetition become prosaic and everyday in character."[10] The perennial danger is that the empirical national group becomes itself a deity instead of a carrier medium of transcendent reference "where politics operates within a set of moral norms, and both politics and morality are open to transcendent judgment."[11]

Routinization of ritual: Of course, emblems like the flag, special political institutions, national shrines, and ritual days such as Memorial Day, the Fourth of July, etc., may become mere lifeless symbols devoid of any capacity to evoke significant commitments to national faith and purpose. They become prosaic and everyday, as cold and lifeless as the Christian ritual of Sunday vespers portrayed so vividly in Ingmar Bergman's film *Winter Light.* For civil religions too the dictum holds good that they must be *semper reformanda.*

Priestly vs. prophetic functions: Again, civil religions embody the perennial tension between the priestly and prophetic functions of religion. They must find the right balance between the holiness of the is and the holiness of what ought yet to be. Like the other religions, civil religions are called upon both to comfort and to challenge, to celebrate and to call to action. At its best, however, a nation's "ideals and aspirations stand in constant judgment over the passing shenanigans of the people, reminding them of the standards by which their current practices and those of their nation are ever being judged and found wanting."[12]

Inclusion-exclusion: Civil religions face the temptation of overemphasizing the exclusive election of their own group by refusing to open up national symbol systems and reality reference points to participation in and judgment by the wider body of humanity. Of course, civil religions are not the only religious systems mistakenly to think that outside their little church there is no salvation. There are also distinctions to be made between the general high priestly civil religion of the state and the various sub-species of the civil religion: the folk tradition of the people and the public theologies of the denominations whereby "the particular communities—be they religious, ethnic, or oriented around interest groups—can creatively refract generalized civil religion through specific prisms."[13] As these distinctions make clear some analysis of conflicting interests of subgroups in a society and of competing "civil religions" as well as analysis of the articulation or conflict between the civil religion and what Clifford

Geertz has referred to as "primordial loyalties" toward intermediate groups in the society would be necessary for understanding and evaluating civil religions.

Moreover, like other religious systems, a civil religion "does not make any decision for us. It does not remove us from moral ambiguity."[14] Neither past successes nor failures are totally determinative. Americans are no more saved by Lincoln's faith than the Jewish audiences addressed by Jesus were by Abraham's. Whatever a nation's achievements and already attained ideals, it is still called upon to know "that here on earth God's work must truly be our own."[15]

Evaluation

It is impossible in advance of careful study of each case to give any straightforward answer to the evaluative question about the religious worth of civil religions. Nevertheless, the relevant criteria for discerning authentic from inauthentic civil religions would seem somewhat clear:

1. The nature and pervasiveness of the transcendent reference of judgment over the nation's acts.

2. The capability of national symbols and ritual to engender commitments to the deepest spirit and highest ideals of the nation. In this context, Emile Durkheim once suggested that "what we must above all cherish in society—that to which above all we must give ourselves—is not society in its physical aspects, but its spirit."[16] Indeed, he argued that we should be more willing to see our empirical society disappear than to betray the principles and spirit on which it was founded.

3. The presence or absence and relative strength of a prophetic strain in the civil religion.

4. The capability of civil religions to open up the symbols of national patriotism to include references to the wider human family. National patriotism, like world religions, has a profound vocation toward universalism. Somehow true patriotism must be wedded to cosmopolitanism so that our meaning as citizens of the nation is related to our vocation as citizens of the world. This is all the more incumbent in the modern world where projects of national self-sufficiency fly in the face of the growing interdependence of our world.

I would add to the above list a fifth and crucial factor for evaluating civil religions: justice. I have earlier claimed that a Durkheimian perspective in sociology seems necessary for an appreciative understanding of the concept of civil religion. Such a perspective, while realistic, forbids mere cynicism or negativity in the face of national moral and religious ideals. Although not unaware of the extent to which consensus could mask coercive injustices under the cloak of patriotic ideology, Durkheim was sensitive to the authentic consensus on moral ideals which often underlay and regulated conflicts, just as Karl Marx, in another context, uncovered the genuine conflicts masked by consensus ideologies.[17] Both Durkheim and

Marx need to be read together in a creative dialogue if one wishes to evaluate a civil religion. Durkheim, correctly I think, once asserted that a commitment to justice could be the only national ideal capable of generating an *authentic* consensus in the modern world. "Just as ancient peoples needed above all a common faith to live by, so we need justice."[18] I do not hesitate to suggest, then, that a commitment to justice at home and in the nation's dealings with other countries be used as the touchstone for evaluating a nation's patriotic identity. Civil religions which *celebrate* constitutional arrangements that perpetrate national and international injustice are *merely* civil.[19] They are, in no authentic sense, religious. Such civil religions are functioning, in Marx's sense of the term, as ideologies. If we follow Durkheim's suggestion, in the modern world "this is true civil religion: to love justice and do the right."

How should a believing adherent of one of the world's religious traditions evaluate a civil religion in his midst, even an authentic one? Much will depend on the way in which he sees the civil religion. Is it an alternative rival to the Church? Some religion above the other religions? Is it consonant with his own religious tradition? If his own religious tradition is open to wider human—even religious—values, simultaneous participation in his own religious tradition and his nation's civil religion will seem no more incongruent to him than ecumenism. If he can join with even non-religious people in common enterprises, presumably he could also become a partner in a shared national identity which includes religious symbols not entirely his own. No one, I think, would suggest that the civil religious dimension exhausts all, or even the most relevant, aspects of religion. Nor do the churches exist mainly to lend institutional support to the civil religion. A division of religious functions need not imply conflict between the churches and civil religion or the eclipse of the churches.

Robert Bellah has also suggested a fairness rule for judging civil religions: one should not compare the worst strains in the civil religion to the best ones in his own. He also appeals to a principle of responsibility: "I am convinced that every nation and every people come to some form of religious self-understanding whether the critics like it or not. Rather than simply denounce what seems in any case inevitable, it seems more responsible to seek within the civil religious tradition for those critical principles which undercut the ever-present danger of national self-idolization."[20]

AMERICA'S CIVIL RELIGION

To seek within the civil religious tradition those critical principles which undercut the ever-present danger of national self-idolization and to find therein the symbols which promote national and international justice—we have here the essential program for a creative use of America's civil religion for doing liberation theology in North America.

In the aftermath of Vietnam, Watergate, CIA and ITT interference (to use a cold, neutral term for the reality of subversion of justice) in Chile, it is difficult for many Americans to find much solace in their national heritage. David O'Brien captures the mood of many when he assesses the legacy of the 1960's. If John Kennedy in his inaugural address could still speak glowingly of "those human rights to which this nation has always been committed and to which we are committed today at home and around the world," in the 1980's the phrase rings hollow in our ears.

> It is hard to sustain devotion to democracy as blacks are denied it, and whites adopt it as a slogan to justify the murder of Asians. Liberty ceases to have meaning for people who hear it from the lips of men who assist in its destruction. The people seem to know democratic responsibility only as a part of a preorganizational past, and their vague sense of loss is smothered in the pillow of affluence. Unable to understand how the crisis came about, given little leadership in solving their problems, many Americans seem certain only of failure, explicitly the failure of their leadership, secretly the failure of themselves. The American dream of shaping the course of history, leading the world to material sufficiency, personal liberty, and popular government, gives way to apathy and despair, to a sense of impotence and frustration before the rush of events over which men appear to have no control.[21]

I caught this mood of nostalgia for a dream gone sour when I heard Patty Andrews of the Andrews Sisters sing "Where have all the good times gone?" in a Broadway musical. One sensed in the audience an anxious question: Just yesterday all seemed so right, so where did we stray and go wrong? Part of the answer lies in the often yawning chasm between high American ideals and actual moral performance. Part of it is to be found in the imperfection of the dream itself.

It seems that we *all* know now that the dream was somehow flawed from the beginning.[22] John Winthrop's fellow Pilgrims may have seen themselves as a "city upon a hill" but there was no room in that spacious mansion for America's native Indians. The Pilgrims' errand in the wilderness projected their own fears of the demons within their hearts upon the wilderness whose sheltering spaces their descendants callously destroyed and whose inhabitants they largely cheated, emasculated, or slaughtered. Long after the Pilgrims' Calvinist doctrine of predestination had lost theological relevance in the Church, it continued to operate as a social model for many Americans' self-understanding. An "elect" nation seemed to need to have some in their midst who were not quite saved.

Jefferson's much-praised proclamation of inalienable rights of life, liberty, and pursuit of happiness did not, until the Fourteenth Amendment, remove the scandal of chattel slavery from the land. By the 1840's de Tocqueville feared the shadow side of Jacksonian democracy and the cult of the common man when he wondered whether mediocrity and slavish conformity might smother America's institutional liberty and virtuous voluntarism. We know now also that too much of the American dream was shaped during America's gilded age in the post-Civil War period when the bitch goddess success replaced Thoreau's ideal of simplicity and Samuel Adams's insistence that solid virtue was the only lasting basis of a free republic. Too much of that dream was premised on false, energetic individualism, a secular legacy of the Arminian pietistic revivalist strain in American Church religion. America's greatest failure, however, has been its ineffectual struggle with the moral dilemmas of industrialism and the riotous growth and unchecked independence of American corporate power. The older American doctrine of individualism has become, in large part, a liability for all but the industrial and banking interests whose disproportionate privileges it protects.

Arthur Schlesinger has termed the post-Civil War decades as "the critical period in American religion."[23] In that crucial turning point for American religion—denominational or civil—the robber barons went largely unchecked. Speaking of that period, David Wells says:

> As the network of relations affecting men's lives each year became more tangled and more distended, Americans in a basic sense no longer knew who or where they were. The setting had altered beyond their power to understand it, and within an alien context they had lost themselves. In a democratic society who was master and who was servant? In the land of opportunity what was success? In a Christian nation what were the rules and who kept them? The apparent leaders were as much adrift as the followers.[24]

These questions still exercise our moral imaginations and judgments today.

In the period between the Civil War and the end of World War I, the famed "melting pot" image was tried and found seriously wanting as immigrant groups, largely Catholic and Jewish, were forced to worship at WASP cultural altars and where prolonged racism, anti-Catholicism, and anti-Semitism showed that, in America, some groups melted more easily than others. The failure of American religion—denominational and civil— in the post-Civil War epoch is tragically conspicuous in the way religious symbols were trotted out to glorify America's first non-continental imperialistic expansion in the McKinley-Roosevelt era. Sydney Ahlstrom has characterized that period by remarking:

> Kipling's words on "the white man's burden" became for a season the battle hymn of the republic. Never has patriotism, imperialism, and the religion of American Protestants stood in such fervent coalescence as during the McKinley-Roosevelt era.[25]

In reading the evidence for this period of American history we should be careful not to let the debunking spirit run riot. Through the nineteenth century and up to World War II, the American myth exercised a powerful attraction upon the minds of Europeans as well as Americans. Indeed, British conservatives such as Walter Bagehot needed to argue to the "special circumstances of the American continent" to fend off claims by Englishmen, inspired by the American example, for an extended franchise and the incorporation of the working classes into the national political life.[26]

The fusion of religion with shallow and exclusionary patriotism is a constant thread which runs through America's history from the Know-Nothings in the 1840's through the Protestant nativists at the turn of the century, Attorney General A. Mitchell Palmer's anti-red hysteria in the aftermath of World War I, and the revival of the Ku Klux Klan in the 1920's, down to McCarthyism and the Dulles cold-war rhetoric in the 1950's and the hard-hat stickers during the Vietnam War: "America, love it or leave it."

America—the righteous empire with a manifest destiny to conquer the vast continental expanses; the redeemer nation called to leave the tired Babylon of Old Europe and receive the teeming masses to its bosom; the bold adventure in freedom, as Oscar Handlin has called it, that was dynamic, optimistic, pragmatic, individualistic, moralistic, and egalitarian: perhaps it's for the best that the good times have gone!

My own mood in the face of the awful puncturing of the American dream and the painful confrontation with the often surrealistic nightmare of a multiplier-effect in national breakdown and failure is, somehow, something far less than despair about our national heritage. National failures have left some healthy scars. They have planted some seeds of hope. If no generation of Americans has lacked its prophets, ours seems not stingily blessed with those who wear the mantle of the best American spirit: Ralph Nader, Sam Ervin, John Sirica, and Justice Douglas to name but four who stand in the mainstream, not to mention Daniel Ellsberg and the brothers Berrigan. Has any generation of Americans shown as much passion for justice and distrust of the arrogancies of power without having the staff of presumed national self-righteousness to lean upon?

After Vietnam, fewer Americans believe that they have a mission to make the world safe for pseudo-democracies. We have become, again, distrustful of foreign entanglements in the face of exposés of CIA activities in Latin America. We have probably buried forever the symbol of manifest destiny. After Watergate, many citizens have the same salutary distrust of those who hold inordinate power that inspired James Madison at his best in *The Federalist Papers.* Mass defections by the young who turned in the 1960's to a counterculture, environmental pollution, and an energy crisis have deeply undermined the seemingly invulnerable American myths of capitalistic expansion, the salvific consumer society, and so-called free enterprise. Indeed, Michael Harrington can persuasively assert that there is in America today an "invisible mass movement" in support of the goals of a democratic socialism.[27]

No religion is healthy which never confronts the reality of sinful failure. No religion is safe which does not include a healthy dose of doubt in its heart. In that sense, American civil religion is not dead, as some have concluded, but is healthier than ever before. However weak or imperfect the response, it is comforting that thousands of Americans refused to serve in Vietnam; that an incumbent president has been removed from office for criminal and moral failure; that serious efforts have been undertaken to end racial or sexist discrimination in our institutions; that some, at least, are prepared to celebrate national days of humiliation proclaimed by Congress. The body politic still includes pockets of health.

National failures have, further, placed us all in a period of collective choice where America's history over the next few decades hangs in a balance. In such a period of challenge and threat, we are summoned to remember (both in the sense of recall and reconstruct) our past in terms of what we collectively will to prevail in the future. We need to find today a "usable past" in order to forge a "usable future."[28] These choices of national identity and projected purpose are ultimately serious not only for the soul of America in completing the task of justice at home but for the future of most of the world as it struggles for liberation from economic neo-colonialism. I fail to see how such choices can be denominated as anything less serious than religious, whatever the symbolism used to interpret them.

The future direction of America's civil religion and the reconstruction of a usable past are not merely *a* resource for doing liberation theology in North America. I would argue that they constitute the key arena of "conscientization"—to use the technical term of liberation theology—in the struggle. It should be obvious that it would be a national disaster if, at such a time, we left the civil heritage and patriotism to the yahoos.

It would be a disaster for strategic reasons. For, as Susan Sontag reminds us, "probably no serious radical movement has any future in America unless it can revalidate the tarnished idea of patriotism."[29] In a similar vein, Robert Bellah criticizes the new left movements of the 1960's for failing to make a "strong link to that deep religious and moral tradition in America that had itself never wholly surrendered to capitalist utilitarian society with its systemic evils of competitive meritocracy, privatism, consumerism and arrogant bureaucracy." Nor did the leaders of the new left grasp the fact that without making that link their efforts were doomed to failure. An alliance of outraged college youth and elements of the most oppressed ethnic minorities could not permanently change the direction of American society. Something much closer to the mainstream of the cultural tradition and with a potential appeal to a much larger constituency would be needed for basic change to be affected, if it can be effected at all.[30]

If the new left has failed to create a new consensus for justice, no religious denomination in America alone nor even the whole of them in consort contains symbolic resources powerful and general enough to build, unaided, a national religious ideal capable of mobilizing common American consent. This, of course, has been true from the beginning of our history. America has never had a church culture. Radical and seemingly irreducible religious pluralism at the institutional level has meant, as John Smylie puts it, that in America, "only the nation bears universal purpose and has continuing historic meaning."[31] Thus, America came to be, in Sidney Mead's terms, "a nation with a soul of a church." If the best spirit of that soul has now departed, it seems unlikely that the churches will be able to achieve what eluded them in their heyday of public influence: a common faith for Americans to live by. It would be well for Church critics of the very idea of a civil religion to remember the salutary challenge of liberation theology. The churches are called today to participate in a reality both larger and, in some respects, more important than they. For both Latin and North America this means that what is needed is the forging of new links at the cultural level between the churches and larger movements for social justice. The task at hand is the creation of a new, revitalized civil religion.

The genius and peculiar nature of America's civil religion has been that it is not essentially an idolatry. Americans have always understood the nation as under God. Its authentic spokesmen have always somehow known that, in President Lyndon Johnson's words, "God will not favor everything that we do."[32] Moreover, the civil heritage has not been antithetical to particular, denominational religions. America has been spared anti-clericalism and the churches have been bulwarks of the authentic American ethos.

The peculiarly American doctrine of separation of Church and state largely explains the absence of serious or sustained conflicts between the churches and the civil heritage in America. Toward the end of his *American Commonwealth,* Lord Bryce admits that in discussing the national and state governments of the United States, he

> never once had occasion to advert to any ecclesiastical body or question, because with such matters government has in the United States absolutely nothing to do. Half of the wars of Europe, half the internal troubles that have vexed European states, from the monophysite controversies in the Roman Empire in the fifth century down to the Kulturkampf in the German Empire in the nineteenth, have arisen from theological differences or from the rival claims of Church and state. This whole vast chapter of debate and strife has remained virtually unopened in the United States.[33]

It is the combination of the institutional arrangement of separation of Church and state and the cooperation of Church and state in the religious definition of America which explains the peculiar nature of America's civil religion. For, "the fact that we have no established religion does not mean that our public life does not have a religious dimension nor that fundamental questions of our national existence are not religious questions."[34]

For those who would argue, like Sydney Ahlstrom, that our patriotic heritage is dead or at least bankrupt, I would suggest a warning reminder and a test. The reminder is that the American civil heritage, however flawed, is, in Ernst Troeltsch's sense, our fate. It is, of course, impossible to devise a phenomenological or historical test which would prove the superior place of America's among the world's civil religions. It is probably not necessary to add that no phenomenological or historical test would show a superiority of American Church religious performance over the civil heritage on issues of collective justice. Our national heritage remains the most potent, if not the only, glove we have to reach out to the universe.

Out of the resources of that heritage Americans have always understood the religious significance of their vocation in world history. America, to put it bluntly, is our fate. When that fate is freely chosen and critically restructured, it can be changed from fate to destiny. The challenge of liberation theology to America's civil religion is to call it to retrieve (recall, remember, and reconstruct) its best heritage, to create a usable past for a hopeful future not only for ourselves but for the world. Bellah has suggested three tasks for the work of intellectual praxis involved in retrieving our past:

> 1. that we search the whole tradition from its earliest beginnings on and in its heretical byways as well as its mainstream;
> 2. that we subject everything we find to the most searing criticism, something that goes far beyond simply distinguishing the good tradition from the bad tradition, but a criticism that sees the seeds of the bad in the good and vice versa; and
> 3. that we open our search entirely beyond the ambit of our own tradition to see what we can learn from radically different traditions that may supplement blind spots in even the noblest strands of our tradition.[35]

The test I would suggest to those who argue that the civil religion is simply bankrupt is that they search the tradition themselves to find if there are any symbols, documents, persons, or episodes of history which embody principles that undercut the ever present danger of national self-idolization and promote national and international justice.

I tried this test myself recently on a Catholic friend who has been deeply involved in the praxis of social justice as a community organizer in Chicago slums and, later, as a director of Catholic social action programs. He had little difficulty citing numerous examples of Americans he would place in the national pantheon: John Winthrop, William Penn, Roger Williams, Jonathan Edwards, Samuel and John Adams, Thomas Jefferson, Andrew Jackson, William Lloyd Garrison, the normative figure of Lincoln, Eugene Debs, Susan Anthony, Justice Holmes, Clarence Darrow,

Jane Addams of Hull House, Justice Brandeis, Norman Thomas, the early F.D.R., Walter Reuther, Reinhold Niebuhr, Martin Luther King, Justice Warren, and Walter Lippmann. His choices led me to reflect upon the criteria upon which individual Americans are admitted by the general culture to the pantheon of the civil heritage. It became apparent to me that the sacred heroes we choose to remember and celebrate tend to be men and women somehow associated with historic deeds of liberation either for the whole country or oppressed subgroups within the nation. We are more likely to remember today the names of Sacco-Vanzetti and to call them to mind as symbols of the miscarriage of justice than we are to celebrate Calvin Coolidge. In a similar way, fifty years from now Martin Luther King will still be remembered and his words and deeds celebrated when those of Eisenhower and Ford will be dim memories. Even those who constantly try to tame the American "gospel" of equality and justice and respect for the common person of its more radical implications cannot remove the revolutionary potential in the roster of those already in the pantheon. To call upon their names in a ritual litany of American celebration is to raise up specters who sit in mighty judgment on the passing shenanigans of the people.

My friend thought that Emerson, Hawthorne, Melville, and John Dewey from our national literature still had much to teach us. Walt Whitman was singled out for his egalitarian depiction of the inherent strength of the people and his trust in the common person. Mark Twain and Will Rogers belonged in his canon of American scriptures for the way their humor punctured the pretensions of power. Unlike Bagehot's England, the American republic was not, historically, premised on Americans being a deferential people. He suggested, further, that the photos of Dorothea Lange and the art of Winslow Homer and Edward Hopper deserved a special prominence in the temples of American politics as did, at another level, the poster art of Norman Rockwell.

My friend saw no need to rewrite the Declaration of Independence or the Bill of Rights, although he thought the Constitution should be rewritten so that it more clearly reflected the priority of the rights of people over the rights of property. In his view, the Constitution should take public cognizance of the special social power and corporate responsibilities of American corporate wealth. As a disguised "fourth" branch of government, corporate power needed to be unmasked and subjected to the checks and balances guaranteed in the constitution to the other three branches.

These reflections led him to consider the periods of American history which were somehow paradigmatic for him in approaching our own historical point in time and for giving a sense of identity to the whole of the American experience. They became his usable past. He suggested America's revolution and the early republic; the abolitionist movement; the populist movement of Senator Carl Schurz and William Jennings Bryan; the early labor movement at the turn of the century; the progressive movement, especially in its attack on the corporate trusts and its attempt at cooperatives; the early years of the New Deal; the movement for civil rights in the 1960's.

I cite these paradigms of my friend merely to illustrate how America's civil heritage might be re-examined as a resouce for doing liberation theology in America. For alongside the mindless and idolatrous patriotism of the yahoos, there exists a patriotism, whose authentic credentials cannot be denied, which represents the best and most potent conscience of America. This high tradition of civil religion does not obviate the need to do realistic social, political, and economic analysis or to devise a politico-economic program for a more just America. Besides keeping our best ideals alive, we need to fight for structural reforms—most would call them in this context revolutions—that will reduce the great chasm between America's ideals and the realities of its institutional life. Not to do so would be to reduce the ideals to an ideology. A retrieval of America's best conscience would seem, however, the logical place to begin a program of conscientization as part of a liberation theology for North America. We need to learn how to make most Americans again believe in returning power to the people. To practice that heritage as liberation theology one must be willing to stand within the civil religion as a committed adherent and engage in the public arena's discourse and action, if not totally on its own terms, at least to challenge it to rise to the best of its tradition and fault it when that heritage is misrepresented to serve as a cloak over the interests of corporate power or imperialistic design. One must take part in our public rituals such as the bicentennial so that their rhetoric is less characterized by Stephen Decatur's mindless "My country right or wrong" than that which the American Catholic bishops suggested for the bicentennial: "Liberty and justice for all."

THE RELEVANCE OF LIBERATION THEOLOGY FOR CIVIL RELIGION AND OF CIVIL RELIGION FOR LIBERATION THEOLOGY

I am prepared to argue that, in a paradoxical way, the best strands of America's civil religion is a liberation theology and the Latin American liberation theology is an attempt to create a civil religion. The convergence of themes between America's civil religion and Latin America's liberation theology is striking. Both are political theologies addressed to the religious significance of the political realm. Both stress the relevance of the historical experience of the community as the locus for critical religious reflection—in the one case the community is the nation, in the other it is the Church and a continent. Both are future oriented, premised on a pervasive hope for a more just, this-worldly future. In America's case that future has been, historically, both a *futurum* (a hope that the future will be as gracious as the past) and an *adventus* (a hope for a future that will include the breakthrough, at points, of the eschatological vision of an ideally just society). America's self-image has always included large doses of messianic expectation. While Latin America's liberation theology stresses the future mainly as revolutionary *adventus,* in the precise hope that the future will not resemble the past, one could argue that the new situation in America of awareness of national moral failure has diminished the relevance of the *futurum* and, like Latin America, led us to place a new stress on the emergence of a dramatically different future.

Each of the liberation theologies stresses praxis, the testing of any theoretical position in the crucible of historical experiment. Each includes an energetic voluntarism which insists that God's work of justice here on earth must truly be our own. Each theology has strong egalitarian strains, a distrust of elitism and aristocracy and the cult of the common person. Each has a jaundiced eye ready to greet the pretensions of power. Both insist that the particular theologies of the Church must be seen as interpretive schemes for larger historical tasks in which the Church participates but which the Church does not control.

Finally, for both theologies experiences of liberation are paradigmatic for participating in and interpreting not only our own period of history but the whole of the historical process. For in America we care to remember and celebrate only those episodes of our national history which are related to exodus experiences of liberation from some historic bondage: the Pilgrims' fleeing England as a release from religious discrimination; the American Revolution as a casting off of the unjust British yoke of dominion; the victory of Jefferson and, later, Jackson over the aristocratic party of Hamilton; Lincoln's emancipation of the slaves as a completion of the initial American intent of freedom and justice for all, the assimilation of Europe's teeming peasant masses as full citizens of the land; the extension of the franchise and the full incorporation of women and the working class into the American task; the movement for full civil rights for America's blacks. At least at the mythic level, America celebrates liberation and justice as of the essence of its own deepest meaning.

This convergence of themes between America's civil religion of conscience and Latin America's liberation theology is not surprising when we recall how the historical experience of Israel's exodus in the Old Testament serves as a paradigm for both. Somehow both see themselves as in the situation of a new Israel. In America's case, however, there is a strong need to recall Israel as the redeem*ed* rather than the redeem*ing* nation. As Rubem Alves reminds us, "No nation will ever fly the flag of freedom and equality for all."[36] Nor should any nation again pretend to. America needs to retrieve, as well, the moral motivation operative in Israel when its prophets reminded the people that they must do justice to the alien because "you, too, were once in bondage and an alien in a strange land." America should be reminded often of the possible ideological uses of the civil model of God in the Old Testament. As Herbert Richardson puts it, often "when America analogizes from the Old Testament—with its paradigm of the entire universe as an emerging *civitas* under the sovereignty of

God—she 'discovers' a divine ratification of her own aspiration to establish a holy nation-state: one people, one government, one faith, one God. Such analogizing from the Old Testament involves America in an ideology that gives a religious sanction to the most destructive aspects of modern nationalism."[37]

The ironic, if not tragic, results of American foreign policy since World War II both for America and other lands make it abundantly clear that this danger of ideology is very close at hand. Graham Greene's quiet American in Vietnam playing god or the representative of the messiah nation is the very opposite of liberation theology. America was a gracious land to generations who went before because its inhabitants found here a new freedom which, in principle, belonged to all. It will continue to be gracious only on the same terms. Only on the condition that the civil religion be practiced as a liberation theology can we accept, unhesitatingly, America's civil heritage—our fate, in any case—as our destiny.

If America's civil religion must become a liberation theology, I would argue that America's experience forging that civil religion might be of some use to Latin American theologians in their efforts to construct a liberation theology. As I see it, their strategies for a liberation theology involve, at one level, an attempt to create a new Latin American civil religion for a just society.

As a social scientist, I have often been puzzled, if not irritated, by the almost religious importance many Latin American theologians of liberation give to the writings and analysis of Karl Marx. At times, Marxist thought (albeit with a revisionary attempt to extrapolate a "scientific" Marx from Marx the materialist, atheistic philosopher) is identified *tout court* with social scientific analysis.[38] Such an approach does not accord with the anti-dogmatic stance of a social science. The insistence by some Latin American liberation theologians on the use of Marxist social science as *the* essential and indispensable tool for doing critical reflection on historical experiences of oppression and liberation becomes less mystifying, however, if we view liberation theology as a civil religion in the process of coming to be.

The Roman Catholic Church in Latin American countries has witnessed, in this century, a new kind of religious competition and pluralism. Predominantly Catholic in population, Latin American countries now contain significant numbers of Protestants and, especially, the non-churched Marxist left. The Church itself can be divided into those who use Catholic symbols as an ideology to support conservative or repressive political regimes or at least take no political stance, and those who are attempting a new Catholic liberation theology related to political action for revolutionary changes in social structure. At least among Catholic theologians and leaders, a third group, mainly priests of European and North American origin, represents an as yet uncommitted middle group. Protestants in Latin America reflect somewhat similar divisions.

It is necessary, in the Latin American context, to find ways to forge symbolic links to build a viable community among the liberationists, those who are as yet neutral and, most importantly, the other large religious group of the continent: committed Marxists whose passion for justice and desire for revolutionary restructuring of society around ideal pictures of the just society is nothing short of religious. In this context, Gustavo Gutiérrez's attempt at creating a common platform around a shared Marxist-Christian utopian vision and program for a just society and his insistence on the use of Marxist social scientific analysis is a creative—if not, indeed, necessary—step in bringing about a "spirit or self-understanding of a community which gives it specific social substance."[39] Liberation theology in Latin America is a project which looks toward the emergence of a shared *religious* self-understanding of a political community (now in opposition) which hopes that its ideals will eventually become the national and, indeed, continental self-understanding. It intends to represent already in germ the authentic political—or civil—religious position on which to base a consensual agreement about the contours and principles of a future just society. In this situation for Latin America, Marxist thought functions not merely as a social scientific symbol system but equally as a religious point of reference. It must be taken with *religious* seriousness as one component of an emerging national community of revolution.

Ivan Vallier, one of the most astute North American sociological analysts of Latin America, has described the new theological leadership roles he sees emerging in the Latin American Church. In speaking of a new kind of bishop or theologian he says:

> Instead of using their office and prestige as bases for promoting confessional goals and mobilizing commitments to sacramental participation, the stress has been on the problems of the poor, the importance of human freedom and dignity, and the sacredness of the value of social justice. In these allocations, the "Catholic" elements of religious meaning are subordinated to values and goals that are universally sacred. Political issues are implied in these endorsements, of course. [Nevertheless] ... these values hold a charisma and legitimation on many bases other than Christian beliefs or Catholic theology. The important point is the Church as a religious system articulates them in conjunction with other sponsors. ... The solidification of symbolic linkages between religious leadership and human welfare enhances the charisma of both, helping to bring sacred meaning to the latter and secular legitimacy to the former.[40]

As the Church allies itself with the vigorous Marxist movement in Latin America, Catholicism gains new political relevance for the masses and Marxism inherits some of the sacred charisma of the church. For Gutiérrez, the Marxist-Christian dialogue is mutually corrective. Christian faith informs Marxist thought with a deeper ethical concern for personalism. Marxist analysis alerts Christians to the ideological uses of their faith in practice. For a sociologist, however, the problem Vallier refers to as central to the task of creating a liberation community in Latin America seems clearly a problematic at the level of what Bellah has called the civil religion.

If we in North America keep in mind this special religious situation of Latin America with its civil religious imperative to forge symbolic linkages between Christianity and Marxism, we can be freer than those in the Latin American context in "demythologizing" or "secularizing" Marxist analysis when using the Latin American liberation theology as a resource for doing liberation theology on our own continent. Just as the structures and even meaning of Christianity differ in both continents, so also does Marxism as a living political movement. In North America Marxist movements have never generated widespread religious resonance. Indeed, most explicitly Marxist groupings in America have almost always degenerated into what religious sociologists would refer to as dogmatic, sectarian groups with little impact on mainstream American life and few resources to link up with wider constituencies. The difference in the meaning of Marxism in both contexts should not be overlooked. Marx's impact on German, French, Italian, or Latin American social and sociological thought extends far beyond the explicitly socialist organizations: however, both in the social gospel movement as well as in the American labor movement as in American thought generally, Marxian influence has been slight and heavily filtered, even among the Christian socialists on the social gospel's left wing.

The above remarks are not meant as either polemical or disparaging of Marx's rightful place alongside Max Weber, Emile Durkheim, Alexis de Tocqueville, and Sigmund Freud as one of the giants of modern sociological theory and analysis. It is simply a cautionary note that for North American liberation theology Marxist analysis needs to be judged entirely in terms of the adequacy of its conceptual tools to filter and illuminate social reality and not also, as in Latin America, as an essential religious pillar to support the overarching sacred canopy of an emerging national civil religion and conscience for justice.

I should like to end this chapter with a quotation from one of America's authentic spokesmen of the civil religion, Ralph Waldo Emerson. I choose it because of its appeal to the wider community of humanity as a criterion for judging our civil religion. I choose it also because it makes clear my contention that America's civil religion at its best has always seen itself as a kind of liberation theology. Emerson was addressing himself in 1854 to Daniel Webster in the great pre-Civil War political debate about the future of slavery in America. In his speech on the "Fugitive Slave Law," Emerson appeals beyond the mundane rhetoric of partisan political strife to the conscience of America. His words, and especially his criteria for choice, have relevance to North Americans today as they seek to find ways to unite their experience of America to the historic and larger struggle of the twentieth century of the oppressed peoples of the third world:

> Who doubts the power of any fluent debater to defend either of our political parties or any client in our courts? But the question which history will ask is broader. In the final hour, when he was forced by the peremptory necessity of the closing armies to take a side—did he take the part of great principles, the side of humanity and justice, or the side of abuse and oppression and chaos?[41]

NOTES

1. This chapter is largely an extended, derivative footnote on Robert Bellah. Cf., besides his original essay found in *Beyond Belief* (New York: Harper & Row, 1970), pp. 168–93, the discussions of this essay in Donald R. Cutler, ed., *The Religious Situation: 1968* (Boston: Beacon, 1968), and Russell E. Richey and Donald G. Jones, eds., *American Civil Religion* (New York: Harper & Row, 1974). Bellah's most extended analysis of American civil religion is his *Broken Covenant* (New York: Seabury, 1975). Other helpful sources for analyzing America's civil religious heritage are Sydney Ahlstrom, *A Religious History of the American People* (New Haven: Yale University Press, 1973); Robert Benne and Philip Hefner, *Defining America* (Philadelphia: Fortress, 1974); Sidney Mead, *The Lively Experiment* (New York: Harper & Row, 1963). David O'Brien, *The Renewal of American Catholicism* (New York: Oxford University Press, 1973), ch. 3, "American Catholicism and American Religion," has some helpful remarks about Catholicism and the civil religion.
2. Martin E. Marty, "Two Kinds of Civil Religion," in *American Civil Religion*, p. 142.
3. Most of these summary symbols, when probed deeply, function as God-terms.
4. Emile Durkheim, *The Elementary Forms of Religious Life* (New York: Free Press, 1965), p. 264.
5. Marty, *American Civil Religion*, p. 140.
6. W. H. Auden, "Vespers," *Shield of Achilles* (New York: Random House, 1955), p. 80.
7. The citation is from Bellah, *Beyond Belief*, p. 168. I have treated some problems on viewing civil religions in a comparative perspective in "Civil Religion," *Sociological Analysis* 31 (Summer 1970).
8. For this point of non-Christian elements in Christian national cultures, cf. Ernst Troeltsch's classic, *The Social Teachings of the Christian Churches*, 2 vols. (New York: Macmillan, 1960).
9. Emile Durkheim, *Elementary Forms of Religious Life*, p. 475.
10. Thomas O'Dea, *The Sociology of Religion* (Englewood Cliffs: Prentice-Hall, 1966), p. 92.
11. Robert Bellah, "American Civil Religion in the 1970's," in *American Civil Religion*, p. 271.

12. Sidney E. Mead, "The Nation with the Soul of a Church," in *American Civil Religion,* p. 60.

13. Marty, *American Civil Religion,* p. 156.

14. Bellah, *Beyond Belief,* p. 186.

15. John F. Kennedy, Inaugural Address.

16. Emile Durkheim, *Sociology and Philosophy* (Glencoe: Free Press, 1953), p. 93.

17. For Durkheim on repression and false consensus, cf. *The Division of Labor in Society* (New York: Free Press, 1933), bk. 3, ch. 2, "The Forced Division of Labor."

18. *Ibid.,* p. 388.

19. I have found a paper delivered October 27, 1974, at the annual meeting of the Society for the Scientific Study of Religion, Washington, D.C., by Sister Marie Augusta Neal of Harvard Divinity School, "Rationalization or Religion: When Is Civil Religion Not Religion But Merely Civil?" helpful in formulating some of these points. Neal supplies some tools for uncovering ideological uses of the civil religion.

20. Bellah, *Beyond Belief,* p. 168.

21. O'Brien, *Renewal of American Catholicism,* p. 6.

22. In his *Broken Covenant* Bellah traces the split between an emphasis on community vs. self-interest which has divided America's national soul from the beginning.

23. Arthur Schlesinger, "The Critical Period in American Religion: 1875–1900," *Proceedings of the Massachusetts Historical Society* 64 (1932–33), pp. 523–47.

24. David A. Wells, "Recent Economic Changes," in *The Nation Transformed: The Creation of Industrial Society,* ed. Sigmund Diamond (New York: Braziller, 1963), p. 41.

25. Ahlstrom, *Religious History,* p. 880.

26. Cf. Walter Bagehot, *The Collected Works of Walter Bagehot,* Vol. 5, Norman St. John-Stevas, ed. (London, 1974), p. 410.

27. Michael Harrington, *Socialism* (New York: Saturday Review Press, 1972), pp. 305–31.

28. Cf. Henry Steele Commager, *The Search for a Usable Past* (New York: Knopf, 1967) and Martin E. Marty, *The Search for a Usable Future* (New York: Harper & Row, 1969).

29. Susan Sontag, *Trip to Hanoi* (New York: Farrar, Straus and Giroux, 1968), p. 82.

30. Robert Bellah, "Reflections on Reality in America," *Radical Religion,* Vol. 1, Nos. 3–4 (Fall 1974), p. 35.

31. John E. Smylie, "National Ethos and the Church," *Theology Today* 20 (October 1963), p. 316.

32. Lyndon B. Johnson in *U.S. Congressional Record,* House (March 15, 1965), p. 4926.

33. James Bryce, *The American Commonwealth,* Vol. 2 (London: Macmillan, 1888), p. 554.

34. Bellah, "Reflections on America," p. 41.

35. Bellah, in *American Civil Religion,* p. 266.

36. Rubem A. Alves, "The Hermeneutics of the Symbol," *Theology Today* 29 (April 1972), p. 50.

37. Herbert Richardson, "Civil Religion in Theological Perspective," in *American Civil Religion*, p. 174.

38. In a personal communication, Chile's Arturo Gaete told me that he did not feel that liberation theology was necessarily tied to one kind of social analysis.

39. Alves, "The Hermeneutics of the Symbol," p. 46. It is interesting that Alves quotes Durkheim extensively in this article, which gave me the idea that Latin American theologies of liberation are concerned with civil religions coming to be. For Gutiérrez, cf. *A Theology of Liberation* (Maryknoll: Orbis, 1973).

40. Ivan Vallier, *Catholicism, Social Control and Modernization in Latin America* (Englewood Cliffs: Prentice-Hall, 1970), pp. 85–86.

41. R.W. Emerson, "The Fugitive Slave Law," in *Speeches and Documents in American History*, ed. Robert Birley (London, n.d.), 2:867.

Chapter Six

American Catholicism and Strategic Social Theology

At least since the 1950's there has been an increasing number of voices in the American Church calling for a distinctively *American* Catholic theology. Since Vatican Council II, these voices have risen to a crescendo.[1] David Hollenbach and Andrew Greeley have been only the latest in a long line of those pleading for an American Catholic theology rooted in the unique experience of Catholic America.[2] Often these pleas fail to pay sufficient attention to the structural limitations and possibilities of the American Church as the conditioning context for an American Catholic theology.

I want to focus on these structural limits and possibilities for action in American Catholicism as they relate to public or social theology. My concern is more narrowly with theologies of Church-society relationships. I will argue that American Catholicism has not been well served by international Catholic models for understanding the Church-society nexus or mobilizing Catholic energies for influencing the direction of their host societies. In order to mount this argument I am borrowing the term "strategic theology" from John C. Bennett who notes that "all theologies are to some extent strategic theologies. They give emphasis to the questions of a particular time and place and they seek to counteract what are believed to be the errors that are most tempting at the time."[3] My main interest will be in uncovering a model for public theology that promises to have a strategic fit to the structural limits and possibilities of American Catholicism.

THE PRIORITY OF MEANING OR CONTEXT OVER TRUTH

There is no genuine theology without human interpretation of the Christian symbols, application of these symbols to contemporary contexts and personal and collective decision. Theology as a living enterprise demands interpretive reconstruction of the received symbols of the tradition to contextual questions arising from very particular places, times and problems.[4] Theology is enmeshed in history. It is always implicated in strategic pastoral choice. It is only by obfuscation that theology can be called, in any simple sense, a-historical or a-cultural. Even a-historical orthodoxy, to use Michael Novak's descriptive phrase for post-Tridentine Catholic theology, contains implicit strategic decisions for Church-society relationships. Every theology is a strategic theology.

The difficulty arises when strategic theology is done a-historically without a careful hermeneutic of the immediate structural and cultural contexts to which the theology is a response. It is not sufficient, for example, as Avery Dulles has attempted in an otherwise brilliant recent book, for theologians simply to range in a typology the various logically possible or scripturally given models for a Christology or ecclesiology, as if they were all equally viable options for a Church in its particular context.[5] In his book, Dulles claims to have been inspired by H. Richard Niebuhr's typology building in *Christ and Culture*.[6] Niebuhr also neglects to pay sufficient attention to the specific organizational prerequisites for the various models of relating Christ to culture. They are not, in context, equally available strategies for the Church. In this, Niebuhr fails to follow his great master, Ernst Troeltsch.[7]

Troeltsch, relying upon Dilthey and Weber, saw his models as symbolic constructions derived from unique and unrepeatable historical experiences and configurations. They were Weberian ideal-types which drew upon thematic constellations abstracted from a very particular historical epoch. For Troeltsch, model-building did not provide an avenue of escape from the problem of historical hermeneutics.[8] For ideal-types illuminate the meaning of what Troeltsch calls "individual totalities." They are not formal but substantive, rooted in history. As James Luther Adams has remarked, Troeltsch "wished primarily to discern 'from case to case' the uniqueness of milieu within which the mutual interplay between idea and institution, between idea and social forces takes place."[9]

Ideas or typologies for Troeltsch do not live a life entirely or primarily of their own. Foundational social or religious symbols contain varied, even potentially contradictory, latent potentialities. We can usually discover these latent potentialities only by following the vagaries of the idea through history, a history that is neither rationally necessary nor primarily controlled by what structuralists might call the stable content of the idea. As Adams states it, "In general, then, a religious idea in its impact and exfoliation has to be understood by means of a sociological analysis of its influence upon the organizations and institutions emanating from it, and of the influence of these institutions upon it. These ideas and institutions in turn should be seen in mutual relation to other social forces, institutions and their value systems. Moreover, even 'in the idea,' i.e., the Christian idea, there reside different possibilities of organizational development."[10] Troeltsch agreed with Hegel that there is a cunning to history, although, against Hegel, he assumed that this cunning was contingent, not necessary.

Troeltsch also saw that creative syntheses or correlations between Christianity and culture—what he called "compromises"—are inherently unstable. Models of Church-society relationship are culturally and contextually pre-conditioned by the structural limits and possibilities inherent in a Church and societal structure. Because of its minority sectarian organization, early Christianity could not have the same impact on its host society that the medieval Church had on Christendom. After secularization, modern forms of Church organization are restricted in the kind of authority they can exercise in modern, differentiated societies. As Adams notes in his essay on Troeltsch, "compromise is always a process of give and take and different compromises exhibit various relative proportions of this give and take."[11]

I assume that Troeltsch remains, even today, the master of those who aim to do strategic social theology. There is no escaping history or the problem of social hermeneutics and choice. Theologians need to ponder more than they have Troeltsch's sociological insight that some models for the Church and the Church-society relationship presuppose rather definite organizational and contextual conditions for their viability.

The invocation of the name of Troeltsch raises two questions for theology. The first is related to the problem of relativism and the claims of truth, a question which haunted Troeltsch in the last years of his life when he was writing *Der Historismus und Seine Probleme*.[12] Without necessarily espousing Troeltsch's solution to the problem of truth-claims, I am assuming that he is correct in asserting a priority-rule by which the question of truth-claims (the judgment of the truth or falsity of propositions) can only be legitimately asked after the question of meaning has been posed. Hermeneutics—to use Lonergan's phraseology—logically precedes dialectics.[13] It has become usual in current theology to distinguish between the *meaning* (internal coherence), *meaningfulness* (power to disclose actual experience) and *truth* (cognitive claim about adequacy to experience) of any symbol or proposition.[14]

I am here maintaining that the question of truth presupposes prior attention to the question of meaning and meaningfulness. These latter are the function of both a limited range of logically coherent potentialities inherent in the structure of any symbol and the historical context which determines the impact and exfoliation of the symbol. Hence, in terms of its meaning or meaningfulness, any theological symbol is contextually specific. That specific meaning is uncovered by what I have called "strategic theology."

The second question from Troeltsch deals with determinism and freedom. Because human freedom is always situated or limited freedom, strategic social theology must attempt "rigorous ethical analyses of the possibilities and limitations of the various infra-structural and suprastructural components of our social reality."[15] These analyses will largely condition, although not completely determine, the critical retrievals or inventions of various symbol systems for a strategic social theology. It will, in particular, greatly condition our strategic choice of a model for Church-society relations. Political theology, like politics itself, is the art of the possible. Or, as Troeltsch put it, history (limited, situational freedom) can only be overcome by more history.

By stressing the contextual specificity of theological symbols, I am not denying that there can be and has been fruitful borrowing of models and symbols across national and cultural boundaries. In arguing for a specifically American Catholic strategic social theology, I am not, then, closing off dialogue with other Catholic theologies. The problem lies in exporting one strategic theology from the locale of its origin to other churches which do not share the same context and strategic definition of the problem without a very careful hermeneutics of the institutional prerequisites or correlates of that theology.

Presumably, there is some more universal directionality to the shaping symbols of the Bible and tradition which transcends the contextual particularism of a definite time and place. Symbols have their own logical coherence, structural content and possibilities which partially direct their interaction with cultures, organizations and institutions as these, in turn, shape them. Fundamental theological symbols, however, are relatively abstract forms in terms of which experience is to be thematized. As Langdon Gilkey has noted, "They are, not unlike Kant's categories, 'empty' unless they receive content from our experience."[16] Gilkey further states that "a religious symbol . . . is a notion which, as Paul Ricoeur has said, invites conceptuality and factual content, but does not itself contain them. It does not in itself entail or assert, though it may refer to, any factual propositions."[17]

Foundational religious symbols take on flesh as they are forged into strategic theology. Their content, however, tends to be culturally specific. Thus, in a very perceptive essay, Garry Wills has shown how the strategic theology of France in the post-war period never penetrated much more than to an isolated Catholic liberal elite in America for whom the "real" Church was elsewhere, namely in France. France's theology did not suit the historic needs and structural possibilities of the American Church.[18]

Similarly, Dom Virgil Michel was greatly inspired, in launching the liturgical movement in America, by the concepts and vision of the Belgian pioneer liturgist, Dom Lambert Beauduin. It was through his contact with Beauduin that Michel came to introduce the concept of the mystical body of Christ to the American liturgical movement.[19] Michel, however, gave to that concept a special American nuance by the way he combined his liturgical thought with an emphasis on radical social reform. This combination and Michel's unique stress on the social implications of the liturgy was rooted in a number of contingent historical circumstances such as Michel's close contacts with the social vision of the German-American Catholic *Central Verein* as well as with the early circle of *Commonweal* editors and associates who eagerly sought a Catholic contribution to American society.[20] Michel from the first consciously sought to make the liturgical movement specifically American.

In the late 1920's and 1930's when Michel took a commanding role in the American liturgical movement, American Catholics began to be concerned in a heightened way about a uniquely Catholic contribution to the American social order.[21] This was partially a function of Catholic mobility in American social structure with the closure of immigration and partially a response to the trauma of Al Smith's massive defeat. Nowhere in Europe did the liturgical revival stress the social implications of the liturgy since the social question had been long since posed there and—it was assumed—solved. The meaning of the term "mystical body" had, then, very different connotations in the European and American contexts. As H. A. Reinhold observed:

> We had no Virgil Michel in Germany. The close interconnection of the liturgical revival with social reform ... was never expressed in that forceful way in which you see it in the writings of the late Dom Virgil and *Orate Fratres*. ... Maria Laach, Guardini, Pinsk and Klosterneuberg only occasionally pointed out the necessary social consequences of a true liturgical revival among our German people. ... America is in an enviable position. ... While in Germany the leaders of the liturgical and the social revival, both strong and powerful movements, never really met and sometimes antagonized and criticized each other, here you have a close cooperation of the two, a unity of both, right from the start.[22]

As the example of Michel and the American liturgical movement makes clear, even when some borrowing takes place of models and symbols from some other locale, they usually undergo a profound sea-change in the process. No one should be more sensitive to these strategic alterations of theological symbols than American Catholics. The American Church suffered an immense setback and took on a new, unhappily hierarchical and clerical, direction in the wake of Leo XIII's papal letter *Testem Benevolentiae,* issued on January 22, 1899, in which "Americanism" was condemned as a heresy.[23] It is very clear that this condemnation was directed toward various groups in France who espoused the democratic doctrines of Isaac Hecker, John Ireland and John Lancaster Spalding in a political, cultural and social situation absolutely different from America's. The American Church paid a high price for the failure to attend to these contextual differences between France and the United States. Somewhere between the 1890's and 1920 bold, innovative American Catholic experiments with lay national congresses, lay control of the Catholic press and charities' movement, interfaith cooperation and a nascent national organization of lay-controlled Catholic societies became the stuff of past history.[24]

In turning to the Holy See for adjudication of essentially French disputes, the French episcopacy foreclosed an open debate and discussion

about the distortions in the Americanist propositions. It would be a
strange irony if the American bishops today too quickly turn to Rome for
pronouncements binding on the universal Church on issues such as steril-
ization or the ordination of women before sufficient debate and research
on these issues takes place either in America or elsewhere. Sensitivity to
strategic theology would keep them from doing so.

FIVE STRATEGIES OF CHURCH-SOCIETY RELATIONSHIP

American Catholicism in the Counter-Reformation through the modern period never developed according to international Catholic models of
the Church-society relationship, either the Christendom model or models
of Catholic Action. So-called Catholic Action movements in the United
States such as the Young Christian Workers and the Young Christian Students always restricted mobilization tactics along socio-expressive lines.
These movements, unlike their counterparts in Europe and Latin America,
lacked significant secular political impact. To uncover the structural significance of this point it will be necessary to treat, even if briefly, the evolution, within international Catholicism, of alternative strategies related to
Church influence upon its host societies. There have been basically five
since the Counter-Reformation. It will be important to bear in mind that
these five strategies as I develop them are conceived as Weberian ideal-
types which have been successively available in history. I make no claims,
beyond historical description, for these types. Nor do I claim that their
succession or "evolution" was either necessary or "logically" entailed in
some idea of Christianity. Moreover, the latest in chronological order is
not necessarily superior to earlier models. I will further argue that only
one of these five strategies has a strategic fit with the structural possibilities and limits of American Catholicism. Finally, I will explore the creative
potentialities of that strategy for the ways Catholics might exert some influence upon the direction of American society.

(A) Strategy I—The Christendom Model

A carry-over from the Middle Ages, the Christendom model was the
operative self-understanding of the international Church from the
Counter-Reformation until almost the turn of the century. The Church,
viewing itself as a *societas perfecta* ranged as an equal partner to the state,
looked to the secular power for both patronage and political enforcement
of Catholic ideals. In turn, the Church lent a religious canopy of legitimacy to the authority of the regime. The Church aimed at a position of religious monopoly for itself and pursued an inclusive pastoral strategy: full
coverage territorially, across class distinctions and during the life-cycle
from cradle to grave. Through the springboard of the papal states, the key

weapon of Church influence was the diplomacy of the concordat and the chief targets for influence were the secular rulers and cultural elites. Mobilization efforts were largely restricted to the clergy, especially the religious clergy. By preaching, charitable works and schools these latter restricted any mobilization of the laity to socio-expressive revivals in movements of pietism.

The loss of the papal states, severe checks to Catholic freedom in France, Italy, Germany and Brazil and significant losses among the working classes in France, Belgium and Germany led the Church to respond to crises in several creative accommodations such as the ralliement in France, social Catholicism and the first seeds of Catholic Action in France through Marc Sagnier and his *Le Sillon* movement, and in Italy through Dom Liugi Sturzo.

The Christendom model never fit the needs of the American Church. As John Courtney Murray remarks in commenting upon a meeting which took place in 1783 between the papal nuncio at Paris and Benjamin Franklin concerning the appointment of an American bishop: "Not for centuries had the Holy See been free to erect a bishopric and appoint a bishop without the prior consent of government, without the prior exercise of the governmental right of presentation, without all the legal formalities with which Catholic states had fettered the freedom of the Church."[25] Nevertheless, the American Church was saddled with the embarrassment of the Catholic theology concerning religious liberty and separation of Church and state, rooted in this Christendom model, until even as late as 1960. Even so astute an American as John A. Ryan in the 1920's was incapable of perceiving the historical specificity of this Catholic doctrine which grew out of what I have called strategic theology.[26]

As late as the 1950's this Christendom model was being espoused by Joseph Clifford Fenton and Francis J. Connell as the official version of authentic Catholic Church-society relationship. If we are strongly in debt to John Courtney Murray for demolishing the official status of this model, it is also worth noting four things about Murray's brilliant championing of religious liberty and the doctrine of Church-state separation.[27] First, Murray achieved his aim precisely by engaging in strategic theology. Murray combined close analysis of the American and American Catholic experience to an historical and political hermeneutic of the contextual specificity and, hence, relativity, of international papal documents. It would be no exaggeration to state that Murray stands *alone* among American Catholic theologians of this century—even to this day—in doing strategic theology.

Second, Murray did not expect the American situation to become paradigmatic for the entire Church. He limited his claims modestly, eschewing the earlier Americanists' overstatement of the American Catholic experience as *the* international Catholic model. Third, Murray implicitly rejected the notion that there could be *one* international model for Church-society relationships which would fit, simultaneously, the needs of missionary churches in Africa and Asia and the European and North American contexts. Finally, he was extraordinarily restrained, if not ironic, in his realistic appraisal of Vatican II's *Declaration on Religious Liberty:*

> Its achievement was simply to bring the Church abreast of the developments that have occurred in the secular world. The fact is the right to religious freedom has already been accepted and affirmed by the common consciousness of mankind.[28]

(B) Strategy II—The Catholic Action Model (1920–1939)

As a response to the rise of unfriendly secular governments and vigorous secular competition to the Catholic religious identity, the international Church turned to programs of mobilization of the laity who were, in any event, with the advent of the Kulturkampf in Bismarck's Germany and "the lay laws" in the Third Republic in France, the only nexus between the hierarchy and the secular world. Two different models for Catholic Action evolved in Europe. The Italian or conservative model mobilized the Catholic laity according to groups segregated by age and sex. The Italian hierarchy strictly forbade any direct Catholic involvement in the political order and suppressed Luigi Sturzo's nascent Christian Democratic Party. The laity was called to be piously obedient auxiliaries of the hierarchy. Italian Catholic Action also tended to be diffuse since it became segmented along diocesan lines. This Italian Catholic Action model, wherever followed, remained highly traditional, merely expressive and in the main ineffective.[29]

In France and Belgium, largely under the impetus of Cardinal Cardijn, Catholic Action took a new turn. Sexual segregation did not form a basis of mobilization. Moreover, activation of the laity took place along functional occupational lines as groups were formed for university students, workingmen, the rural small farmer, the white collar workers, professionals, etc. Each group had its corps of priest chaplains whose specialization was ministry to a definite milieu. Each had its set of episcopal sponsors. Moreover, Catholic Action groups were national in scope. Their lay leaders had direct access to the hierarchy and represented a definite constituency which crossed parochial, even diocesan, lines. As a result of its choice for milieu Catholicism, the French Church (and other churches which followed its pattern) was really several denominations within one Church as competing groups vied for episcopal favor and attention. Not the parish but the organized Catholic Action group represented the "real" Church. There is considerably greater lay leverage for influence in national churches organized along the French Catholic Action model than in those, such as America, which have not known this Catholic Action syndrome. Influential French laity had greater access to the hierarchy in France than did their counterparts in America.

As a result of following a very different pattern of evolution, the

American Church is less internally differentiated than, for example, the French or Chilean Catholic systems and substantially less specialized in the task sector for influencing the wider society. In fact, the American Church has been extraordinarily decentralized and parish-centric. The American Church has been unable to overcome parish-centricity even to the extent of pursuing its own interest by developing a diocesan-wide parochial school *system*. There have been almost no renewal movements among the American laity where the lay sector constituted a diocesan or nationally based constituency with some autonomy or leverage vis-à-vis the hierarchy.

Even today, there is an assumption in America that the parish is the "real" Church. Renewal movements of the laity are somehow not really Catholic until they feed into the revitalization of the parish. As David O'Brien has noted, in America "the pattern of lay initiative [has] remained confined to the congregational level."[30] The story of lay renewal movements in the United States has exhibited a repetitive pattern of fragmentation, loss of vigor and deep ambiguity about whether to focus on an agenda directed toward inner renewal of the Church or outer influence on the wider society. This has been true in recent years of both the Cursillo movement and the underground church.[31] A rapid mobilization of the laity along socio-expressive lines has, time and again, foundered on the shoals of the intransigent parish with the result of a sapping sense of the absence of any greater purpose vis-à-vis diocesan or national Church goals.[32]

One of the exciting *structural* developments in the current Catholic pentecostal movement—I will prescind from any evaluation of the movement in terms of its expressive, religious purposes—is that the movement has, thus far, been able to develop its own semi-autonomous national, regional and diocesan-wide structures under lay leadership and has avoided the trap of being sucked into the fragmenting vortex of parish organization. Several such structurally autonomous lay movements would seem necessary if the American laity is to exert any leverage upon the Church in its present situation of crisis. The Detroit *Call to Action* by the American bishops is a hopeful sign in this regard.

(C) The Catholic Action Model (1939–1960)

With all of its brilliant innovative characteristics for mobilizing a mass Catholic movement, the initial French Catholic Action model had several built-in contradictions. Realizing that neither monopoly nor total pastoral coverage was any longer possible, the Church focused its pastoral energies within a specialized strategic concentration upon key target populations. It is no secret that the French Catholic Action syndrome favored the workers and the university students. The hierarchy bartered away some of its power by granting new autonomy to the lay-sector. In return, the laity was organized into active cadres to influence its milieu. On the other hand, the Church never developed a commensurate new reward system to compensate the laity for the new responsibilities asked of them in the worldly sphere. They remained excluded from inner Church decision-making or rewards.

Again, there were many vestiges of the Christendom model in the early Catholic Action ideal since the hierarchy directly forbade explicit involvement by Catholic Action groups in controversial political conflicts within the secular order. In a sense, the groups were mobilized right up to the point of action, without any clear vehicle for direct action. The hierarchy still controlled the moves of the Church in the political order. The prohibition against direct political activity by Catholic Action groups was more than a control mechanism. The hierarchy had learned well the bitter lesson of the heavy costs to Church authority and autonomy of direct insertion of the Church as an institution in the political order. On the other hand, mobilization without political outlet led to frustration and the loss of the most active elites to secular movements.

In the period between the wars, the seeds were sown for a way out of this initial Catholic Action impasse in the incipient move toward the creation of the Christian Democratic Parties, a movement which only came to full fruition in France, Italy, The Netherlands and Belgium in the immediate post-war period and in Latin America, especially Venezuela and Chile, in the 1950's and early 1960's.[33] The Christian Democratic parties provided the Church with what Ivan Vallier has called a "buffer" between the Church as a religious institution—a universal ethico-religious body "above party politics"—and the hurly-burly of concrete and, therefore, highly debatable political programs.[34] Direct movement of the institutional Church from the level of ethico-cultural leadership (which need not be *so* abstract that it lacks any political relevance as a shaping or orienting vision) to concrete political activity without such a buffer has never been anything but disastrous for the Church.

The political programs of the Christian Democratic parties, although of Catholic inspiration, made no pretense to represent some official Church position although, in some countries, especially Italy, there was a rather direct sponsorship and, sometimes, interference by the hierarchy. With the adoption of the Christian Democratic strategy, there was a relatively direct linkage between Catholic Action movements and the party. Most of the leadership in the Christian Democratic parties had received their formative training in Catholic Action groups. The party provided an outlet for action for the most radical elites. To the extent that the party was a centrist or governing party intent on winning elections and bound to compromise, these more radical elites became restive under the new strategy of influence through the Christian Democratic party. In the post-war period these radical elites moved directly to alliances with the secular left.

The dominant theology in the international Church during this period was written mainly in France by theological philosophers such as Maritain, Emmanuel Mounier and, in the 1950's, Congar, de Lubac, Daniélou and Chenu. It has not been recognized, I think, to what an extent this

French *nouvelle théologie* was "strategic theology" contextually specific to the dilemmas inherent in the Catholic Action syndrome. Congar's ground-breaking work in theology, *Lay People in the Church,* for instance, is really a book on the nature of Catholic Action and its place in the total frame-work of the Church's European adaptations to modernity.[35] Similarly, de Lubac's *Surnaturel* which revolutionized traditional Catholic conceptions about the relation between nature and supernature was as much an essay which wrestled with the theological rationale for the Church's Christen-dom strategy as a speculative metaphysical treatise on nature and grace. In this context, it is perhaps worth noting that almost all of the innovative theologians in the *nouvelle théologie* had, somewhere in their backgrounds, close contacts with Catholic Action movements.

Meanwhile, the American Church remained oblivious to the fact that it had from the beginning evolved according to a different pattern than the Catholic Action syndrome, for America had more successfully than France differentiated between the Church and what Robert Bellah has called "the civil religion."[37] In the American case at least, there is a reli-gious dimension to the national experience and the national state which, although partially dependent upon the symbols of the churches and on Church support for its maintenance, is, institutionally, semi-autonomous, although not competitive with the churches. This has meant that the American Catholic Church, like other American denominations, is located corporately or systemically much more in the specialized *religious* sector than in the political sector of the total institutional structure of society. It does not need to provide the national religious legitimacy.

Nor does one's Catholic status in America carry any *directly* political overtones. Despite a proliferation of special Catholic organizations in the immigrant subculture, the American Church has never maintained any di-rectly political or economic organization such as a political party or labor union. Hence, if the absence of the Catholic Action syndrome meant that the American Church was less internally differentiated and pastorally spe-cialized than the French Church, it also meant that American Catholics could be in society as members of a religious body rather than as a politi-co-religious type. In the period of the Catholic Action model in Europe, on the other hand, Catholicity entailed a political as well as a religious status in the wider society. One could predict rather accurately from a respon-dent's political preferences whether he or she was a practicing Catholic or not and vice versa. It has never, except by the accident of class position, been as possible to do so in America.

It would be my further contention that the Catholic Action syndrome and the strategic theology which underpinned it still retained vestiges of the neo-Christendom ideal inasmuch as it fostered inordinate expectations for Catholicism's *directly political* impact upon its host society. Moreover, it generally assumed that Catholics would be inserted into the political or economic order through the necessary intermediate buffer of an explicitly Catholic, even if not official Church, organization or party, instead, as in the American case, as citizens who directly insert themselves into the political order through secular political and economic organizations.

(D) The Cultural-Pastoral or Voluntary Association Model (1960+)

At Vatican Council II a new Church-society model emerged which promised, at last, to bear an elective affinity to the strategic needs of the American Church. In this Vatican II model, which I will call a cultural-pastoral or voluntary association model, the Church sees itself as a voluntary association within a wider non-Catholic or not explicitly Catholic host society whose autonomous competencies the Church respects. Moreoever, the Council acknowleged the kind of religious pluralism that characterizes a denominational society such as the United States.[38] The council provided theological underpinning for a host of American values as these are captured in the conciliar code-word, collegiality: democracy, pluralism, tolerance, civil and religious liberties, the rightful autonomy of the secular, the voluntary principle of organizations and participant co-responsibility for the direction of organizations and accountability by management.

It was not by chance, I think, that the schema on religious liberty, largely authored by John Courtney Murray, was a key document for debate at the council. It was the linchpin for much of the new theological thinking the council mandated. This schema, along with the schema on the Church's relations with the Jews, represented the specifically American agenda in Rome.[39] There was a wider American agenda, however, in what seemed, at first glance, to be the European agenda. In the post-war European countries, industry and even politics have been enormously influenced by American organizational techniques and philosophies. The human relations movement so widely applied in American management has taken on distinctive European roots. By a kind of osmosis from the complex organizational society post-war Europe has become, functional views of authority in management by objectives and expectations of participatory democracy have also penetrated into the Church.[40]

In the cultural-pastoral model for the Church great stress is placed upon the communal dimension. The central locus for Church experience becomes the supportive small group. It is here that one celebrates experiences of transcendence and probes ultimate questions of the meaning of life and human activity. On the other hand, as Ivan Vallier has noted in his explanation of the cultural-pastoral strategy, these smaller communal units need to be integrated into larger bureaucratic units:

> The growth of bureaucracy carries at least two consequences, other than the strengthening of the Church's autonomy in society: (1) it provides a structural basis for developing collective strength at the episcopal level, thus increasing the bishops' capacity to function as socio-ethical leaders; (2) it provides an organizational framework within which local movements and

experimental programs can be given flexibility and freedom. This latter point bears special emphasis since I hold that the development of local community patterns, e.g., around the parish, depends on the existence of a wider system of coordination and leadership. Otherwise dispersion rather than development occurs. This is important in light of the fact that *one of the basic problems of the traditional Church stemmed from its centrifugal tendencies.*[41]

The human-relations model is pervasive throughout American corporate, political and educational life. Indeed, America rather than Europe is the primary host society for it. Until Vatican II, Catholic understandings of authority, obedience, personal autonomy, etc., were widely divergent from the prevailing American human relations or voluntarist models. Since the council, however, the Church perceives itself, more and more, in human relations terms. The failure to implement collegiality, a functional view of management by objectives, management responsibility and participatory democracy within the structures of the American Church has led to widespread American Catholic dissatisfaction with Church authority and power arrangements *within* the Church.

In my recent research on lay dissatisfactions in Chile, France and the United States, the coding of interview materials from the American laity has uncovered a specially American constellation of dissatisfactions and a specifically American model of the Church. First, in both frequency and salience, the American laity have focused dissatisfaction more than the other national samples on the internal power structures of the Church. Whereas, in France and Chile, dissatisfactions of the laity tended to cluster around themes related to the Church-society nexus, the Catholic Action syndrome and the need for lay autonomy in the secular sphere, the American laity directed its complaints primarily to demands for rearrangement of power *within* the Church. For the Americans, the wider society, political, social and religious was seen as generally benign. If I could choose code words to describe the differences between national samples, I would describe the implicit French ideal model for the Church as "professionally expert" and "efficiently mobilized to produce a maximum missionary impact upon the wider French society." The American code words were "radical democracy" and "radical community" and the desired stance for the Church vis-à-vis the wider society was that of the "good neighbor," a clear indication, it seems to me, of the greater dominance of the human relations paradigm among American Catholics.[42]

It would seem, then, that the most promising strategy to ease lay dissatisfactions within the American Church is to attempt truly to implement the human relations model by, for example, mandating smaller congregational units which represent real communities to replace the large, unwieldy and often impersonal parishes. Secondly, the Church must see through the task of instituting conciliar or synodal structures which per-

mit greater member participation in the key decisions of the parochial, diocesan and national Church.

This cultural-pastoral model is also aptly called a voluntary-associ-
ation model for the Church. It would have been strange if the largely congregational or voluntary pattern of American Protestant and Jewish
polities did not exert a strong influence upon American Catholicism. It
was not possible, perhaps, to fathom the full implications of the essentially
voluntary understanding of Catholicism in America until a generation of
descendants of immigrants began to vote with their feet vis-à-vis Catholicism.[43] There are very few compulsory sanctions available to the Church in
America. It cannot force either membership or fidelity. The voluntary
Church must rely upon its own moral attractiveness and powerful ability
to provide a sense of meaning and belonging in a pluralistic society. It is in
competition with other Christian, and increasingly non-Christian, bodies
for providing meaning, identity and belonging.

There are both special possibilities and liabilities in the voluntary
Church understanding.[44] The first strong point of the voluntary Church is
that it depends upon the free, adult responses of members of the Church to
mandate legitimate action in the name of the Church in the social arena.
The voluntary Church has no captive constituencies on moral or political
issues. The voluntary Church depends, like the wider American society, on
building coalitions toward moral consensus on specific social policies and
issues. When successful, the voluntary Church, by engaging the free, adult
responses of Christians, is superior to culture Christianity and established
religion in engaging genuine commitments of its members to action. Motivation is stronger when it is freely chosen rather than coerced. Moreover,
voluntarism in a pluralistic society can force executive officers of the
Church to adopt a ministerial rather than a magisterial attitude toward the
world and their Church constituency. In the voluntary Church, genuine
authority rests on consensus.

The liabilities in this voluntary model of the Church lie in what has
been called the suburban captivity of the Church wherein the Church loses
any leverage for a prophetic critical edge in society. Members of the
Church fall too easily into a class-based moral consensus in their homogeneous parish and lose a sense of the wider unity of the Church and humanity. I do not think it will be feasible, in the post-Vatican Council II period,
to mobilize the American Church around unitary prophetic strategies in
ways which may still be possible for churches organized around the Catholic Action syndrome or, as in the Latin Church, where strong vestiges of
the neo-Christendom model may still inform what seem to be, from some
points of view, new, radical turns. I am pointing in particular to assumptions that the Church as institution has some direct political program or
agency role in the secular order as the organizing catalyst for the socialist
revolution or that the Catholic citizen will move toward the political order
through the mediation of a specifically Catholic buffer organization, either
the party or the "party within the party" among the socialist left, such as

"Christians for Socialism." Nor is the unity of the immigrant Church any longer available to us.

A strategy based upon the tacit assumption of an inheritance of the Catholic Action syndrome in the American Church would be doomed to failure. The cultural-pastoral or voluntary model need not, however, entail the suburban captivity of the Church or the death of a critical social ethic. The critical problem in the voluntary model is the issue of authority—who speaks and acts *for* the Church. Whatever one's theology, it is clear that there are sociologically inevitable restrictions on the freedom of the Church to speak and act when action depends upon consensus for its authority. Again, whatever one's theology of episcopal authority or lay voice, the authority and credibility of the Church vis-à-vis the wider society—its measure of influence—depends in America on Church-wide consensus. If the bishops in unison speak out on issues of societal morality such as abortion or a guaranteed annual wage, their pronouncements will have little societal impact unless they can bring their constituency with them. Similarly, small coteries of priests and laity with little contact with grass-roots support will be a socially ineffective voice.

Thus, we need to be more imaginative than we have been so far to find many and diverse forms for speaking and acting for the Church, for there are multiple options for the American Church to keep ethical prophecy alive within the Church and the wider society. One has been suggested by John Bennett who calls for serious platforms within the Church that would provide "a variety of forms of speaking *in* the Church which would also in many situations be speaking *to* the Church."[45]

What forms might these platforms take? James Gustafson has suggested that we look upon the local communal units of the Church as places where serious moral discussion and collective ethical discernment take place about those key personal and social issues which impinge upon the Christian conscience.[46] The Quakers and Protestant congregations, in meeting, provide one model of such local platforms. The movement of Catholic parishes into sponsoring community organizers is another example. Ad hoc parish social action groups around specific issues such as housing or community health or police services is a third.

Nor do these forms need to be restricted to local congregations. Diocesan-wide groupings such as the now defunct Catholic Inter-Racial Councils or cluster groupings such as the Oakland Diocese's Flatland Concerned Citizens are other possibilities. Church sponsored or affiliated lobby groups in state capitals or Washington, D.C. can provide still another voice of Church influence on American society. I find it strange, in fact, that so many American Catholics look to episcopal pronouncements as the single or even most effective way to make the Church's voice heard in society. They overlook, thereby, the proliferation within American Catholicism in the post-Vatican II period of innumerable voluntary associations concerned with the public interest such as Right to Life groups, Network, Center of Concern, groups working to reform American prisons, etc. As the long history of religious groups in America shows, the "buffer" between the institutional Church and the world of politics has not been the political party but the voluntary association organized to address the public interest. Such voluntary groups in American Protestantism learned, already in the 1830's, that they were most effective when organized along interdenominational lines. These groups represented concerned Christian citizens engaged in political action. The institutional Church, as such, remained above the partisan fights.

I would urge the splendid histories of the American Friends and the effective lobbying of the various American Jewish agencies as proof that the voluntary principle need not entail ineffective voice for the Church in American society. It does restrict, however, unitary strategies which bypass consultation, coalition-building and the forging of consensus. More dedicated or avant-garde groups are bound to that consensus no less than the bishops. As the history of the Church and other voluntary associations prove, such groups can serve as *ecclesiola in ecclesia,* reforming ginger groups, speaking *in* the Church, *to* the Church and *out of* the Church about key social issues. Unfortunately, short of consensus, no one in a voluntary society can speak *for* the Church to the wider society, not even the bishops.

This is not to say that the episcopal voice is unimportant for the voluntary Church. Bishops as the first pastors, teachers and spokesmen of the voluntary Church can provide a special type of platform or voice for the Church in society. Ivan Vallier has described this voice as an "ethico-cultural leadership" whereby the bishops address themselves mainly to religious or moral-value questions in a style which carries, indeed, political implications, but avoids, in the main, the direct insertion of the institutional Church into partisan political battles.[47] Indeed, following the example of John XXIII, the bishops can speak to all persons of good will, beyond their Catholic constituency, in the name of the Gospel values of human dignity, rights and freedom. Perhaps the most creative American Catholic social document to have appeared in recent years embodies this style of "ethico-cultural leadership": the Appalachian bishops' regional pastoral letter calling for an America of social justice, decentralized control and cultural pluralism.[48] The document avoids directly partisan stands to stress new dreams, new sensibilities, new values and new authorities. The serious lacunae in moral leadership in American society may suggest that this episcopal strategy—if it avoids sectarian particularism—could prove to have an extraordinarily receptive audience.

What seems abundantly clear is that the American Catholic Church cannot have its cake and eat it too. It cannot hunger after unitary prophetic strategies which presuppose authoritarian patterns within a largely hierarchical Church or a restricted lay autonomy and, simultaneously, foster a human relations and voluntary model premised on pluralism and personal freedom. The old tactic of resort to power politics will no longer, in any event, be able to deliver the votes in America. The Church, then, must learn to respect the autonomous conscience of the laity, both its own and non-Catholic laity, in the political order. It cannot accept the game of pluralism and still expect to impose its unique agenda on the societal outcome. What I have argued here is the need to explore all of the creative possibilities of this human relations and voluntary model, despite its liabilities. With the collapse of the immigrant Church and the increasing education and mobility of American Catholics, the Church is fated to that model in America.

(E) The Liberation Model (1970+)

There are many in the American Church who are looking closely to the Latin American Church for directional clues for a strategy for American Catholicism. They presume to find a program in the new liberation theology which has burst upon the theological scene since 1970. Liberation theology is much too complicated to treat adequately here. Its agenda is various: (1) a constructive dialogue with Marxism; (2) a criticism of the ways in which the Latin American Church has been used as an ideological legitimating agency for an unjust political and social order; (3) a pastoral reorientation of theology such that theology becomes critical reflection on pastoral experience; (4) a definite pastoral option to do theology in the name of and with the oppressed poor.[49] No one familiar with the corpus of liberation theology could dismiss it out of hand. Most who have studied the Latin American Church see its move toward liberation theology as an absolutely essential option for the survival, with credibility, of the Latin American Church. Moreover, I have no doubts that some of the methodology and content of this liberation theology may be exportable for reformulation in North American terms. I do not think that North or South American theologians, however, have done enough of their sociological homework to penetrate the extent to which liberation theology is what I have called a contextually specific strategic theology.

The evolution of the Catholic Church in countries such as Argentina, Brazil, and Chile is very different from that in the United States. In cursory terms, their evolution has been from the Christendom model through Catholic Action according to the Italian syndrome to the French Catholic Action syndrome which was only adopted in the 1950's or early 1960's. Importantly, in most cases the move toward the Christian Democratic Party as a "buffer" was never effectively taken.[50] In his excellent book on the Church in Brazil, *The Political Transformation of the Brazilian Catholic Church,* Thomas Bruneau has argued that because of the harsh political dictatorship in Brazil the Church is the one agency in the national society with enough maneuverability to speak out for human rights, against torture, for the restoration of democracy and for justice. Bruneau charts the progress of the Brazilian Church in the 1960's from an adoption of developmental programs for the promotion of social change within the structures of society through both legitimation and programs to further the adoption of a revolutionary mission of the Church. He sums up the current external environment which serves as the context for the Brazilian Church in the succinct judgment: "The social situation is horrible and injustice seems to rule."[51] He points out that because the Brazilian laity had never really been formed or mobilized into autonomous cadres, the burden of prophetic protest against the cruelly unjust society rests entirely with the hierarchy—one thinks of such international Catholic heroes as Cardinal Arns, Dom Helder Camara, Dom Fragoso—and the lower clergy. Bruneau makes what seems to me an astute comment about the structural specificity of the situation which has produced the strategy of liberation theology in Brazil:

> If the society was unconstrained, if channels of social mobility were open, politics democratic and the situation of the masses improving, it is not likely that the prophetic mission would be assumed. . . . If, on the other hand, the regime changes its policies, prophecy will either diminish or turn into straightforward ethical criticism with little [directly] political content.[52]

I have very few doubts about the wisdom of the Latin American Church in its situation choosing the path of liberation theology. Nor do I doubt the extraordinary courage of the churchmen who have suffered exile, imprisonment and death for their tenacious witness to human dignity and justice. I have enormous doubts whether the unitary prophetic strategy many Latin American liberation theologians envision would be possible in other than a hierarchically dominated Church with strong vestiges of the neo-Christendom or Catholic Action ideal in its recent history and where there has not yet occurred a full differentiation between one's Catholic role as a member of the Church and one's role as a Christian citizen who autonomously chooses the concrete political strategies and parties which seem best to fit a Christian vocation in society. I suspect Langdon Gilkey has something like this caution in mind when he says, "Perhaps wrongly, I believe the question of secularity, as opposed to that of oppressive domination, has not yet appeared in South America as pointedly as it has here."[53]

I conclude with the proposal that the American Church in facing its contemporary crisis do its theology explicitly in ways which promise a strategic fit with its own genetic history and development. On the proviso that it does not mean that we tend our own garden or neglect the larger questions of global justice implicit in being an American today, I would make my own Geno Baroni's proposal:

> We must begin to develop our own American theology of pluralism based upon our own Catholic experience as individuals and collectively as an American Church. We can no longer import German or Dutch or even third world liberation theology. Later

when we understand our own American experience we can dialogue with them.[54]

American Catholic theology will be creative only if it stays in close
touch with its full Catholic heritage and engages in multi-directional dialogue. Perhaps under these conditions the American Church might finally
achieve a role as ethico-cultural leader in American society. It can do so by
making its own the advice of Ivan Vallier when he defines what he means
by ethico-cultural leadership in the church vis-à-vis society:

> The long range vocation of the Church is not to make "the so-
> cialist revolution" a first step, but the cultural revolution which
> will lay the basis for new dreams, new sensibilities and, in Michel
> de Certeau's words, "new authorities."[55]

NOTES

1. Daniel Callahan, ed., *The Generation of the Third Eye* (New York, 1963).

2. From among many loci in Greeley's writings, cf. Andrew M. Greeley, *The Catholic Experience* (Garden City, 1967). Cf. David Hollenbach, "Public Theology in America: Some Questions for Catholicism After John Courtney Murray," in *Theological Studies,* Vol 37, No. 2 (June, 1976).

3. John C. Bennett, *The Radical Imperative* (Philadelphia, 1975), p. 127.

4. I am here adopting David Tracy's paradigm for theology which he presents in *Blessed Rage for Order* (New York, 1975) in which Tracy argues that theology is essentially tied to a method of correlation between the Christian texts and human experience and language.

5. Cf. Avery Dulles, *Models of the Church* (Garden City, 1974).

6. H. Richard Niebuhr, *Christ and Culture* (New York, 1951).

7. Cf. Ernst Troeltsch, *The Social Teaching of the Christian Churches,* 2 vols., Olive Wyon, trans. (New York, 1960).

8. Thomas Kuhn in *The Structures of Scientific Revolution* (2nd ed., enlarged; Chicago, 1970) argues that even abstract scientific models are historically specific. Paradigm shifts in science are explained more by attention to the sociology of knowledge than to the inner logic of ideas.

9. James Luther Adams, "Human Relativity and Religious Validity: Ernst Troeltsch," in *Being Human Religiously* (Boston, 1976), p. 214.

10. *Ibid.,* p. 216.

11. *Ibid.,* p. 218.

12. Ernst Troeltsch, *Gesammelte Schriften,* Vol. III (Tübingen, 1922).

13. For Lonergan's distinction between hermeneutics and dialectics cf. Bernard Lonergan, *Method in Theology* (New York, 1972).

14. For these distinctions cf. David Tracy, *Blessed Rage for Order,* p. 8.

15. Tracy, *op. cit.,* p. 246.

16. Langdon Gilkey, *Catholicism Confronts Modernity* (New York, 1975), p. 101.

17. Gilkey, *op. cit.,* p. 100.

18. Cf. Garry Wills, *Bare Ruined Choirs* (Garden City, 1972), pp. 56–57.

19. Cf. Paul B. Marx, O.S.B., *Virgil Michel and the Liturgical Movement* (Collegeville, 1947), pp. 298ff.

20. For Michel's contacts with the early *Commonweal* circle cf. Rodger van Allen, *The Commonweal and American Catholicism* (Philadelphia, 1974), pp. 80–82; for the thought of the German-Catholic *Central Verein,* cf. Philip Gleeson, *The Conservative Reformers* (Notre Dame, 1968).

21. David O'Brien details this new Catholic concern for the social order in his *American Catholics and Social Reform* (New York, 1968).

22. Marx, *op. cit.,* p. 180.

23. For the issues in the Americanist controversy cf. Thomas T. McAvoy, *The Great Crisis in American Catholic History 1895–1900* (Chicago, 1957).

24. To the best of my knowledge, no one has written the history of the loss of autonomy of the bulk of the American Catholic diocesan press and its change into house organs controlled by the bishops. The shift from lay to clerical domination of the Catholic Charities movement occurred in the 1920's; cf. Donald Gavin, *The National Conference of Catholic Charities 1910–1960* (Milwaukee, 1962), p. 38. Alfred Ede of Berkeley's Graduate Theological Union argues that the American Federation of Catholic Societies (1900–1917) remained under lay control. The bishops, significantly, were advisors rather than leaders or moderators of the group. Cf. *A Catholic Quest for a Christian America,* unpublished dissertation, Graduate Theological Union, Berkeley, 1977.

25. John Courtney Murray, *We Hold These Truths* (New York, 1960), p. 79.

26. Cf. John A. Ryan and Moorhouse F. Millar, eds., *The State and the Church* (New York, 1922).

27. Murray's method in theology and the controversies with Fenton and Connell are related in Donald E. Pelotte, S.S.S., *John Courtney Murray, Theologian in Conflict* (New York, 1976).

28. Cited in Pelotte, *op. cit.,* p. 100.

29. For a sociological analysis of the Italian Catholic Action model, cf. Gianfranco Poggi, *Catholic Action in Italy: The Sociology of a Sponsored Organization* (Stanford, 1967). The Latin American Church seems to have followed the Italian Catholic Action model until the 1950's when it switched to the French model.

30. David O'Brien, *The Renewal of American Catholicism* (New York, 1972), p. 97. As early as 1925 Mark O. Shriver was arguing the same case against "the exaggerated spirit of parochialism so widely prevailing—the determination not to have within a parish any organization or activity coincident with parish lines and associated with the parish and with the Church, over which the pastor would not have at all times absolute dominion and control." Cf. Mark O. Shriver, "Catholic Lay Organization," *Commonweal* (Nov. 4, 1925), pp. 642–43.

31. For a study of the underground church, cf. Theodore M. Steeman, "The Underground Church: The Forms and Dynamics of Change in Contemporary Catholicism" in Donald R. Butler, ed., *The Religious Situation: 1969* (Boston, 1969), pp. 713–49. The story of the Cursillo movement in the United States is told in Al Blatnik, *Your Fourth Day: For the New Cursillista* (Dallas, 1973).

32. I have done some preliminary comparative research on the Cursillo movement in the United States in different U.S. dioceses. It is instructive to compare the sustained vigor of the movement, for example, in the diocese of Worcester, Massachusetts, where the bishop mandated the cursillistas to pursue wider diocesan pur-

poses, with Seattle where the movement, after a rapid mobilization period, became fragmented and aimless.

33. For the relation between French Catholic Action and the rise of the Christian Democratic movement, cf. William Bosworth, *Catholicism and Crisis in Modern France* (Princeton, 1962) and Michael Fogarty, *Christian Democracy in Europe* (Notre Dame, 1957).

34. Ivan Vallier, *Catholicism, Social Control and Modernization in Latin America* (Englewood Cliffs, 1970), pp. 92–93.

35. Cf. Yves Congar, *Lay People in the Church*, rev. ed., trans. Donald Attwater (Glen Rock, 1965), esp. pp. 349–99.

36. Henri de Lubac, *The Mystery of the Supernatural,* Rosemary Sheed, trans. (New York, 1967). It is not by chance that de Lubac entitled his great work on Catholicism "a study of dogma in relation to the corporate destiny of mankind." Cf. *Catholicism* (New York, 1964). Of course, the Catholic Action paradigm was only *one* way of relating the Church to the corporate destiny of mankind.

37. Cf. Robert Bellah, *Beyond Belief* (New York, 1970), pp. 168–93.

38. For the special characteristics of a denominational society, cf. Andrew Greeley, *The Denominational Society* (Glencoe, 1972).

39. Cf. Walter M. Abbott, ed., *The Documents of Vatican II* (New York, 1966).

40. For a development from a Durkheimian perspective of the vision of authority and identity under the human relations model, cf. Guy Swanson, "The Basis of Authority and Identity in Post-Industrial Society," in Roland Robertson and Burkart Holzner, *Authority and Identity* (New York, 1977).

41. Vallier, *Catholicism, Social Control and Modernization in Latin America,* p. 90, italics mine; cf. p. 72 for a chart presentation of the cultural-pastoral model.

42. An earlier version of this research is reported in Ivan Vallier and Rocco Caporale, "The Roman Catholic Laity in France, Chile and the United States: Cleavages and Developments," *IDOC,* no. 68, 7–8, Feb. 18 and Feb. 25, 1968, published looseleaf. Also, Ivan Vallier and Jean Guy Vaillencourt, "Catholicism, Laity and Industrial Society: A Cross National Study of Religious Change," in *Archives de Sociologie des Religions,* Vol. 75, No. 3 (Summer 1968), pp. 99–102.

43. For the evidence of Catholics voting with their feet, cf. Andrew M. Greeley, William C. McCready and Kathleen McCourt, *Catholic Schools in a Declining Church* (Kansas City, 1976), pp. 28–40.

44. Two appraisals of the strengths and weaknesses of the voluntary principle for Church organization can be found in "The Voluntary Church: A Moral Appraisal," in James M. Gustafson, *The Church as Moral Decision Maker* (Philadelphia, 1970), pp. 109–37, and "Freedom and Association," in James Luther Adams, *On Being Human Religiously* (Boston, 1976), pp. 57–89.

45. Bennett, *The Radical Imperative,* p. 73.

46. James Gustafson, *Theology and Christian Ethics* (Philadelphia, 1974), p. 95.

47. Vallier, *Catholicism, Social Control and Modernization in Latin America,* pp. 137–38.

48. Appalachian Pastoral, "This Land Is Home to Me—A Pastoral Letter on Powerlessness in Appalachia" (Washington, D.C.: Center of Concern, 1974).

49. For the best statement of the agenda of liberation theology, cf. Gustavo Gutiérrez, *A Theology of Liberation* (Maryknoll, 1973).

50. Argentina followed this progression but without the formation of a viable Christian Democratic Party; cf. "L'Eglise Catholique en Argentine: analyse d'un Argentin," in the bulletin published by the Centre Lebret in Paris, *Foi et Developpement* 32 (December 1975), p. 2. Thomas Bruneau *The Political Transformation of the Brazilian Church* (New York, 1974) notes a similar progression for Brazil, and Vallier, *op. cit.,* for Chile. Note that only Chile had a vigorous Christian Democratic Party capable of assuming government and providing an autonomous buffer between the Church and direct insertion into the political order. In neither Argentina nor Brazil did the Christian Democratic Party take deep roots.

51. Bruneau, *op. cit.,* p. 236.

52. *Ibid.,* p. 237.

53. Langdon Gilkey, *Catholicism Confronts Modernity* (New York, 1975), p. 204

54. Geno Baroni, "The Ethnic Factor/Ministry in Cities," in *Origins,* Vol. 5, No. 26 (Dec. 18, 1975), p. 409. I would not want to postpone the dialogue with theologies from other national churches until a later date as Baroni seems to indicate.

55. Ivan Vallier, *Catholicism in Three Contexts,* unpublished ms.

Part Three

THE AMERICAN CONTEXT

Chapter Seven

The Basic Crisis
in American Catholicism

I am going to add my voice to those who have spoken of a crisis state in American Catholicism.

I am using "crisis" in the classical sense to mean a decisive turning point in the life history of a people or an institution. One stage of development comes to a termination, history hangs in the balance, and it does not yet appear what shall be. David O'Brien captured this sense of the term when he stated: "The conflict and confusion within the Catholic Church in the United States . . . offers a promise of vitality and dedication that could have tremendous impact both on the Church and on American society, but it offers as well the possibility of failure, dissipation of energies and gradual erosion of institutional relevance and personal commitment."

The relative quietus in the American Church in the 1980's, compared to the "conflict and confusion" Mr. O'Brien cited, seems to me a possibly ominous sign of the darker potentialities latent in crisis. For the vitality and dedication that persisted as a residue of the collective élan in the last years of the Church of the immigrants was historically specific. If the ready commitment of the generation that rode the crest of the victory years of the pre-Vatican II immigrant Church with a highly salient Catholic self-identity is not tapped and channeled, there is no guarantee that succeeding generations will have the same energies and dedication. Much of it went untapped at the opportune moment. Thus, already there are those who refer to the Church most of us over thirty grew up in as "The *Last* Amen."

Nevertheless, nostalgic evocations of that collective élan will not serve us in diagnosing the crisis. We do not have to denigrate the genuine faith achievements of Catholics during the years 1930–1960 to recognize also the shadow side to that rich Roman Catholic life. The catalogue of its sins is numerous: clericalism; triumphalism; sexual prudery; ahistorical orthodoxy with its fear of open inquiry; a shallow interiority; a lack of serious commitment to civil liberties, the absence of symbolic foci to national Catholicism; institutional segmentation into uncoordinated and inefficient parochial units; the failure to generate critical alternative models either to the cold war or the smug American consumer and status-oriented society.

Even much that was lovely in that era of Catholicism—group solidarity; a texture of personal loyalties; a vision of high idealism coupled with a healthy dose of realism; a rich feeling for sacramental signs to accompany every season and stage of life; a solid sense of joy and good humor in the face of life's limits; a toughness in facing the tragic dimensions of existence; an absence of moralism; a high commitment to rationality and an unmistakable taste for continuity and tradition—can never again be retrieved in the forms and vessels in which it was then embodied. We neither want to nor could go home again.

DIAGNOSIS OF THE CRISIS

I do not think it will do to lump the American Catholic crisis in one bin with crisis elements in worldwide Catholicism. American Catholicism is both culturally and structurally different from other national churches. Its history has been extraordinary and unique. Nor is the Vatican Council to blame for the crisis because it came "too late" or "too soon and unprepared." While it is obvious that the council precipitated the crisis because of the abruptness with which American Catholics have been called to face modernity, it is clear that American Catholicism by the time of the council was ready for a crisis on its own terms.

For, with the accession of John F. Kennedy to the American presidency, the historic goals of American Catholicism had been achieved. Catholics had entered American history largely as a beleaguered minority of immigrants suffering cultural, religious and social-status deprivation. For one hundred and seventy-five years, the primary goals of American Catholics were survival and personal and collective achievement. Since the time of Bishop John Hughes, Catholics had vigorously battled against a self-definition of America as a Protestant land, preferring, even forcing, a secularization of the public school system rather than accept its Protestant character.

The faith of the immigrant, despite ethnic rhetoric to the contrary, was largely retained.[2] Indeed, the resources of the Church were so strained in accommodating the increase due to immigration and high birthrates that the American Church had little outward native missionary thrust. Moreover, deprivation in America was extremely relative when compared with other lands. The First Amendment guaranteed free exercise of religion and prohibited any political establishment of one Protestant church. The variety, number and diversity of American denominations and their mutual quarrels throughout the nineteenth century softened religious competition. Furthermore, America lacked any traditions of anti-clericalism or secular religion, such as the anti-church liberalism of Europe and Latin America in the nineteenth century or Marxist socialist movements in the twentieth century.

The American environment, despite the siege mentality of the ghetto church, was anything but vigorously hostile, religiously or socially. In fact, there is now some evidence that much of the ghetto mentality was self-generated by inter-ethnic Catholic conflicts. An expanding frontier and economy, as well as the open nature of the American political system, afforded ample opportunity for Catholics to gain their proportionate piece in the ever increasing American pie. As a result, Catholic leadership has always been relatively benign and, at times, inordinately enthusiastic toward the American political, social and economic ethos. In America, the Church adopted a low profile of criticism. Such criticism as there was tended to focus on permissive civil liberties, especially in the areas of censorship, family life or sexuality, or on issues of distributive justice for Catholics.

The strong and vigorous Catholic subculture, particularly as embodied in the parochial school, the urban neighborhood and the big-city political machine, served as an escalator of economic and social advancement for Catholics so that, by the 1960's, they were even more likely than Protestants to be achievement-oriented, in tune with the Puritan work ethic and firmly lodged in middle-class respectability.[3] Even before the council, then, the days of the ghetto church, battling for equal justice in a hostile environment, were over. Victory, however, brought with it the taste of ashes as it laid bare just how shallow much of the classic program of the American Church had been.

Upward mobility and acceptance by American culture constituted the core objectives of immigrant Catholics and their leaders. And yet, for all their achievements, American Catholics, as Richard Hofstadter has noted, have been influenced by the American environment to a far greater degree than they have influenced it. Recent historical work on American Catholicism, in forcing us to nuance Professor Hofstadter's judgment, recognizes the extent to which it mirrors a one-sided, Anglo-ethnic, assimilationist perspective. Thus, Michael Novak has referred to the ways in which Catholic ward politics softened the inhumane economic and political realities of a harsh urban life by a kind of participatory democracy—not participation in making the rules, but participation in a network of people who exchange services. Jay Dolan has documented the extent to which Catholic urban neighborhoods were the most diverse concentrations in terms of class and ethnicity within the American landscape. In its day-to-day living and institutions, Catholicism may well have been the best single embodiment of the often-flawed national ideal of unity amid pluralistic cultural diversity.[4]

By the time of the accession of Kennedy, Catholics had acquired their full share of that upward mobility, status and respectability they had so long and earnestly pursued. The immediate aftermath of their moment of success in the questioning climate of Vatican II was a Catholic explosion upon the national political life as Catholic names such as Eugene McCarthy, James Groppi, the brothers Berrigan and Sargent Shriver burst upon the public scene. At Selma, and in anti-Vietnam activities and the war on poverty, Catholics played a prominent role and set a tone to an era. Soon, however, this ever so brief Catholic renaissance exhausted its shallow roots as disillusionment, institutional setbacks measured in terms of a falling rate of Mass attendance, declining numbers of pupils in parochial schools, a drastic drop in vocations to the priesthood and religious life and a sapping of communal identity became the indices of the impact of *aggiornamento* on Americanization.[5]

POST-VATICAN DRIFT

Whatever the need from a historical perspective to nuance Professor Hofstadter's comments about Catholicism, it seems fair to conclude that, in the post-Vatican II period of drift, Catholics, with few exceptions, have indeed been more shaped by their American environment than they have reciprocally influenced it. For, in what can only be seen as delicious irony, many of those who argued vigorously for the substitution of a community/ people paradigm to replace the institutional model for the Church have largely forgotten the primitive sociological truism that a people prospers only when it lives out of richly textured communal symbols and achieves its own unique sense of history, heroes and collective story—what we can call, in code words, its tradition and peculiar language. Today, however, Catholic America, like the larger nation, is a land without adequate symbols.

I have argued thus far that American Catholics achieved middle-class respectability at a time when their own distinctive identity was called into question and without having any clear program that might either challenge or at least complement the ethos and institutions of the wider American society. Most of their leaders and intellectuals thereupon proceeded to disregard or jettison much of historic Catholic tradition and sensibilities upon which such a program might have been based. The responses to the Catholic identity-crisis have been varied.

Very few in the American Church have opted for what seems to me to be the only sensible and hopeful strategy for successfully weathering the crisis with some identity intact, namely, a profound and genuinely open-ended *resourcement,* which envisions creative engagement with the received Catholic symbols in a dialectical effort both to break them open to new purposes, experiences and questions and to allow these latter, in turn, to challenge the tradition.

Dialogue must have two partners if it is to exist at all. It cannot be entirely receptivity or entirely the imposing of one's own agenda. It implies for each partner a conversion to the process of growth and change. This is not the same, however, as the loss of family resemblances: a people's earlier story, myths and symbols. Openness is not the same as characterlessness. And yet, most American Catholics are near illiterates in their own history. American Catholic history is conspicuously absent from parochial schools, Church colleges and even seminaries.

It is helpful to consider some of the cultural paradoxes in contemporary American Catholicism. In a nation noted for its one-sided, if not pathological, emphasis on activism, instrumental rationality and optimistic pragmatism, Catholic intellectuals seem to have suffered a bout of amnesia about their classic wisdom concerning contemplation, mysticism, passivity and receptive acceptance of inevitable and unavoidable limits. The Church, which for Jung represented the strongest carrier of the feminine in Western Christianity, in its American incarnation has become almost exclusively masculine, with dominant concerns for action, success, building the new earth and results.

Some of its theologians seem to have reduced theology to ethics, thereby weakening both. Instead of creatively reformulating Marian devotion, which was, among other less noble things, freighted with a strong sense of one's passivity before God, it consigns it to benign neglect, without finding another substitute symbolic carrier for one's receptivity before God. In an age when environmental conditions are forcing a halt to endless industrial expansion and the compensatory cultivation of both sobriety and the limitation of superflouous learned needs, American Catholics seem curiously out of touch with an earlier Catholic rationale for ascesis, which could claim that the cultivation and expansion of needs is the antithesis of wisdom; it is also the antithesis of freedom and peace. Finally and most importantly, the Church seems to have suffered pastoral bankruptcy in dealing with a specifically *religious* agenda at a time when a kind of religious revival of interiority is occurring outside the Church.[6]

American Catholics have been bequeathed a centuries-old tradition of social Catholicism. Indeed, the American Church, in particular, had given renewed vigor to that tradition in the 1930's in the thought of Msgr. John A. Ryan and his associates, and in the 1950's through the work of John Courtney Murray. With all its defects, social Catholicism offered rich resources for finding a middle way between the excessive individualism, greed and disproportionate competition fostered by capitalism, on the one hand, and the unmediated collectivism of statism, on the other. Against the former, social Catholicism argued for the priority of the common good and the necessity to find criteria of ethical judgment beyond pragmatic purposes in the more ultimate this-worldly goals of human society. It refused to legitimate excessive economic concentration of power on the premise that every argument in favor of private property which is acceptable to the Christian conscience is also an argument for its greatest possible distribution.

Against unmediated state control of the economic order, social Catholicism proposed a doctrine of the state which stressed equally the duties and limits of state competence and the state's subservience to a more profound order of inherent and inalienable human rights and liberties. With a shrewd sociological wisdom, its principle of subsidiarity favored, by a presumptive rule, smaller, more manageable and natural units such as the family, primary networks of friends and work associates, the neighborhood and the region over larger, impersonal bureaucratic units.

Recalling Lord Acton's byword concerning the corruptive dangers of unchecked power, social Catholicism showed a decided bias toward decentralization and a balance of power in the economic and political orders. In this century, a new sense of evolving history detached social Catholicism from Scholastic cosmological premises concerning a static order to the universe or society. At least since the ground-breaking corpus of Emmanuel Mounier, who worked within the tradition, social Catholicism has included a much-needed commitment to personalism and human growth.[7]

Referring to this tradition, the Protestant social ethicist John C. Bennett has remarked: "Roman Catholicism, unlike Protestantism, has always kept some distance from capitalism."[8] The British economist E. F. Schumacher has written a contemporary underground classic, *Small Is Beautiful,* whose extraordinary ethical wisdom in great part relies upon Catholic notions of the common good, moral virtue and the principle of subsidiarity.[9] And yet, for most of the post-Vatican II American Church, it is as if that tradition never existed or were totally corrupt. Among Catholic social ethicists today perhaps only Ivan Illich continues to work within that tradition in new and exciting ways to give us some inkling of what a humane socialism or, as he perhaps more aptly terms it, a "convivial society" might look like.[10]

A STRATEGY FOR DECENTRALIZATION

In recent years the focus of concern of American Catholics, as of international Catholicism generally, has properly shifted to a global context. Imperialism, the armaments race, pollution, the inordinate and untamed power of the transnational corporations, the sad and steady decline of the third world nations, the exploitation of women, international racism, the population explosion—these topics appropriately loom large in contemporary Catholic ethical discussions.

On the other hand, there has been an almost total obliviousness to the fate of the soft and fragile institutions such as the family, the community and parochial school, and the neighborhood. And yet, the Church has had close intimate contact with and knowledge of these institutions. It has a doctrine of society that is biased toward them. Moreover, every sociological sensibility informs us that the neighborhood, the family, intimate networks of kin, friends and work colleagues and the ethnic and religious group are the primary loci for socialization to a sense of personhood, communal values, bonds of loyalty and—in hostile environments—resistance.

It seems hardly worth arguing the fact that these soft institutions—or some functional substitute for them—must be vigorous as an indispensable prerequisite for a convivial society.[11] Participation in them has been the source of what an earlier generation referred to as "common grace." They serve as workshops for apprenticeship in virtue, humane sensibility and practical wisdom.

These so-called institutions can also serve as key social turf to do battle against that unchecked economic and political bureaucratic centralization which makes life in contemporary America, with its exultant triumph of technical rationality, so often feel for some like Max Weber's image of the modern world as an "iron cage."

But where in the American Church are there signs that we are choosing to give strategic priority to sustaining the remaining strengths or enabling new directions of growth for the "buffer" institutions between the individual and impersonal, bureaucratic society?

Msgr. Geno Baroni has contended that "neighborhoods are the building blocks of the city. If neighborhoods are allowed to die, then cities also die with these neighborhoods."[12] He also argues that there is even yet an important potential role for the parish in the revitalization of our cities and neighborhoods. Baroni makes the case that the concrete struggle against the multinational corporation is better made at the level of the neighborhood and the city, where there are important shared values to mobilize a constituency, than at a grand global height, which few of us ever attain. At this global level, the only realistic resources which the Church can bring to bear are moral pronouncement and, as a symbolic gesture, the redeployment of Catholic investment portfolios. These things are already largely being done. However valuable, global analysis does not point to a strategy designed to mobilize the ready energies of the Catholic people. To paraphrase the Scriptures, if the people cannot be mobilized in the small wood of their neighborhood, they will not be mobilized in the large.

Baroni singles out the impact upon neighborhoods of the disinvestment and redlining practices of banks and savings and loan companies. He asserts that "no single issue has been more destructive of neighborhoods than the disinvestment and redlining practices of financial institutions. They not only exacerbate tensions between racial and ethnic groups, but they destroy the viability and stability of older communities."[13] In a similar way, many smaller towns and neighborhoods—even cities—in America are dependent for their futures upon one-sided corporate decisions to relocate either elsewhere in the United States or abroad. New England and Appalachia have long histories of the destruction of communities, even regions, by just such one-sided corporate decision-making power as shoe factories moved south and coal ceased to be king. One does not have to go to the third world to uncover the meaning of inordinate economic dependence.

In order to save the neighborhood or city, it seems, one may have to do battle with the regnant values of the corporate trusts. I am not contending that the Church as institution should directly substitute itself for other agencies in engaging that political and economic conflict. Indeed, I think it wiser and more responsible if it does not. Subsidiary functions would argue that the Church must not usurp the task of secular agencies unless it is the only possible substitute agency to do, in grave situations of need, what must imperiously be done. Theology would urge that the Church has no special wisdom at the level of concrete political action. Historical experience might suggest the perceptiveness of Ivan Vallier's contention that if the Church gets involved as an institution in controversial partisan programs, it either reenters or stays within the political realm and short-circuits its possible autonomy. The Church may have a more important function in legitimating change in its position of ethico-cultural leadership.[14]

The Church indeed can do battle at this level of values. By reaffirming its doctrine of subsidiary functions, it can underscore the importance of the neighborhood and small, voluntary associations of people. It might also have occasion to remind itself and others of the precept of social Catholicism that ownership is not a single, univocal right, but a bundle of separable rights and reciprocal duties; that the only legitimately Christian justifications for property rights are subordinate to the higher criterion of the common human welfare; that an increase in selective social control over decisions to build or relocate corporate sites—for that matter, over any corporate decision that impinges upon the general welfare—would not inherently constitute a violation of the Christian sense of a limited right to private property.

I would argue, then, that special-priority status should be given to pastoral strategies aimed at both nurturing present strength and enabling new directions of growth for the family unit, the functional work unit, the neighborhood and the region. Where territorial units have totally lost functional meaning, priority should be given to creating "base-communities" consisting of networks of families and work associates. Even within traditional and unwieldy American parishes, this strategic concentration on creating real grass-roots communities seems preferable to a neo-Christendom paradigm directed to the impossible task of total territorial inclusion.[15]

Where viable neighborhoods still exist, programs of community organizing may promise to do for the new, changed urban situations what the traditional neighborhood parish did for the old. There seems to be an elective affinity between the classic function of the Catholic parish as a neighborhood center and the goals of the community organization. Moreover, in black neighborhoods, the parochial school often serves a special neighborhood function. The American Church, never conspicuous for its concern for black Americans, should commit itself as a pastoral priority to maintaining, even at serious financial sacrifice, such parochial schools in the inner city.

A STRATEGY FOR PLURALISM

I am prepared to argue further that American society at large has never adequately implemented the national ideal of cultural diversity. It has stubbornly resisted language pluralism, only reluctantly achieved its genuine religious pluralism and looked askance at deviations from the dominant symbol for politics, morality and the family. But neither has American Catholicism, which was spun out of a web of extraordinary ethnic diversity, sufficiently allowed its internal cultural pluralism to surface. In revising the historical record, recent historians of American Catholicism have seen that, to some extent, the German immigrant Catholics of the nineteenth century, who lost their historic battle with the Irish Americanizers over the question of cultural diversity within the Church, represented a clearer ideal than that of the Irish—of Catholic unity amidst cultural pluralism. The Germans were also more likely than the Irish to be critical of the prevailing American ethos.[16]

A tendency toward factionalism among the Germans, Irish superiority in language, political organization, urban concentration and numbers, as well as the organizational imperatives of the American Church of that period, dictated that the Irish program should prevail. In the process, an enormous opportunity for a richer internal pluralism within American Catholicism was lost. Persisting resentments of Italians and, especially, Polish and Eastern European Catholics against the Irish style of dominance within the clergy and hierarchy is a witness to the Irish failure to do full justice to cultural diversity. And yet, providentially, the opportunity has not been entirely lost.

There are still strong residues of ethnic separateness among Italians, Poles and Eastern European Catholics and the more recent Hispanic immigrants from Puerto Rico, Cuba, Mexico and Central and South America, as well as the recently arrived Catholic refugees from Vietnam. Current statistics indicate that Hispanic Catholics in some dioceses constitute from a third to a half of the Catholic population. These ethnic groups are in touch with alternative cultural symbols which view authority, politics, morality, interpersonal loyalties, the structures of work and leisure, the rhythms of life and death, youth and old age and the dynamism of the human body in ways profoundly different from that of the dominant American symbolism.

These new Hispanic and Asian Catholic ethnic groups are mainly composed of the lower middle class and poor. I am enough of an economic determinist to think that the special American Catholic concern in the past for the cause of the working classes and poor, although perhaps prompted and given direction by the high intellectual tradition of social Catholicism, was largely rooted in the pastoral exigencies of working with a lower-class constituency. Because of its unique history and social-class basis, American Catholicism had much more impetus to become a champion of the encyclical tradition of international Catholicism than did many of the bourgeois-centered European churches. Hence, in America the Catholic working classes were not lost to the Church.

The persistence of a significant base of lower-middle-class and lower-class Catholics in its pastoral constituency may well be an indispensable link to keep the American Church alert to calls from the Roman international center for a more just economic order and the strategic choice by the Church to side with the cause of the least advantaged. America's new Catholic ethnic groups could be a necessary bridge to narrow the gap between the overly Americanized Church and its inescapable vocation to play a pivotal role for justice within international Catholicism. Those who are urging that American Catholic scholarship and pastoral strategies address themselves to the persisting phenomenon of ethnicity argue, persuasively it seems to me, that it is highly unlikely that the dominant American culture will be open to challenge and enrichment by other cultures across the globe if it is unable to respect cultural diversity in its own midst. If one wants to state it in the strongest possible terms, the new ethnic groups may be the primary provokers for us to heed what John C. Bennett has called "the radical imperative" of the Gospel toward justice and peace. Placing a strategic priority upon understanding and fostering ethnicity and Catholic pluralism would commit the American Church to a strategy that might not only challenge and complement the dominant American ethos but promise to nudge the American Church toward becoming as thoroughly Catholic as it is American. For, as James Joyce seemed to sense in *Finnegans Wake,* "Catholicism means, here comes everybody."

Finally, a serious confrontation with ethnicity bids fair to be for Catholicism a resource for dealing with its new sensibility to its denominational particularity and historical contextual relativism. With the effective collapse of neo-Scholasticism, Catholicism has lost all pretensions to have a secure, universal and static language. It is beginning to face squarely the particularity and limits of the Catholic tradition, generally, and that of the American Catholic experience. It knows that it is but one, finite symbol system, one language, one tradition among the many.

If the sectarian Catholic theology is dead, so is the Enlightenment. Truth, once again, only comes riding a donkey. For particularity, like history, is the human fate. In a sense, the recent puncturing of inflated Catholic pretensions to speak *the* universal language should make Catholics especially sensitive to the complaints of the various liberation movements among women and blacks that attack the imperial claims of male or upper-class white language or presumptive attempts to speak *for* those who have been robbed of active and passive voice.

If this sense of one's finite particularity requires extensive and multidirectional dialogue with a variety of other traditions, religious and secular, it no less demands a careful nurturing of one's own collective symbols. For if a people's collective symbols are allowed to wither and die, the people will die. Without a distinctive language and collective story, there simply is no vigorous sense of peoplehood. Just as the great collective symbols are ever so much more powerful than individual symbols, so the history and tradition of a people is of a richer texture than any individual life can fully absorb, embody or creatively shape. In dialogue, there is, of course, a place for a careful selective absorption of alien symbols from other traditions.

It is probably the case that only in dialogue with alien traditions can one even discover and retrieve lost echoes within one's own tradition. Selective absorption and transformation of alien symbols may be in order, although it is not always so easy a task as it sounds. In a pluralistic society, one resists, to be sure, inordinate claims that one's own symbolic is necessarily more universal or the exact counterpart to the other. One contents oneself with the satisfaction that the Catholic symbol, in all its particularity and finiteness, is one's own and offers the symbol to others who may find it useful or illuminative to help them understand the reality of their tradition, as Catholics, in turn, find alien symbols illuminative of theirs. One avoids sheer relativism, in turn, by adopting a twofold strategy of, on the one hand, epistemological humility and, on the other, the careful nurturing of one's own tradition, not simply because it is one's own but because one assumes it is in some sense a special vehicle of truth. It is only with the stance of epistemological humility that Catholic truth claims can ever be publicly tested. If this strategy of *resourcement* is a call for the American Church to become more deeply Catholic than it has perhaps even been, it should be clear that it is a call to become a very different kind of Catholic than prevailed in the pre-Vatican II Church. For what I am proposing as the most creative intellectual strategy for dealing with the crisis in American Catholicism is the kind of *resourcement* that Michael Novak has referred to as an "openness with roots": "To attempt to be open to all other cultures, without having roots of one's own, is almost certainly to misperceive the otherness of such culture. It is, perhaps, even to be incapable of culture. For culture is a kind of rootedness. The word itself suggests the patient cultivation of a living, growing plant. To have culture is to be shaped by a social tradition, shaped willingly and joyously, so that the shaping is appropriated as one's own, and so that the culture, as it were, becomes alive in oneself under one's own direction. One does not choose the culture into which one is born; but one may choose to go as deeply into it as one can, to realize every human potential it affords. Paradoxically, it is through the route of becoming particular that one finds, at the depths, genuine universality."[17]

NOTES

1. David O'Brien, *The Renewal of American Catholicism* (New York: Oxford University Press, 1972), p. 9.

2. Cf. Gerald Shaughnessy, *Has the Immigrant Kept the Faith?* (New York: Arno Press, 1969).

3. This is a major thesis in Andrew Greeley, *The American Catholic: A Social Portrait* (New York: Basic Books, 1977).

4. Jay Dolan, *The Immigrant Church* (Baltimore: Johns Hopkins Press, 1975).

5. For the evidence cf. Andrew Greeley, William McCready and Kathleen McCourt, *Catholic Schools in a Declining Church* (Kansas City: Sheed and Ward, 1976).

6. For evidence of the new religions cf. Jacob Needleman, *The New Religions* (Garden City: Doubleday, 1970) and Richard Anthony and Thomas Robbins, *In Gods We Trust* (New Brunswick: Transaction Books, 1980).

7. Cf. Emmanuel Mounier, *Personalism,* Philip Mairet, trans. (London: Routledge and Kegan Paul, 1952).

8. Cf. John C. Bennett, *The Radical Imperative* (Philadelphia: Westminster, 1975).

9. E. F. Schumacher, *Small Is Beautiful* (New York: Harper and Row, 1973).

10. Ivan Illich, *Tools for Conviviality* (New York: Harper and Row, 1973).

11. Peter Berger and Richard J. Neuhaus make the argument for "mediating structures" in *To Empower People* (Washington, D.C.: American Enterprise Institute, 1977).

12. Geno Baroni, "The Ethnic Factor/Ministry in Cities," in *Origins,* Vol. 5, No. 26 (Dec. 18, 1975), p. 407.

13. *Ibid.,* p. 409.

14. Cf. Ivan Vallier, *Catholicism, Social Control and Modernization in Latin America* (Englewood Cliffs: Prentice-Hall, 1970), pp. 69–71.

15. For some evidence about basic communities, especially in Latin America, cf. Sergio Torres and John Eagleson, eds., *The Challenge of Basic Christian Communities* (Maryknoll: Orbis, 1981).

16. Cf. Philip Gleeson, *The Conservative Reformers* (Notre Dame: University of Notre Dame Press, 1968).

17. Michael Novak, "The Social World of Individuals," in *The Hastings Center Studies,* Vol. 2, No. 3 (September 1974), p. 43.

Chapter Eight

The Fall from Innocence: Contemporary American Catholicism

A recently published and highly regarded work of intellectual history characterizes American Catholicism before the Second Vatican Council as *The Survival of American Innocence.*[1] William Halsey argues cogently in this book that while wider American society underwent an era of disillusionment in the post-World War I epoch, American Catholics continued—in their own house and under the protecting cover of the American revival of Thomist certainties—the qualities of nineteenth century American innocence: enthusiasm, cheerfulness, moralism, idealism and optimism. These persisted unabated in the Catholic community until the mid-1960's.

There are a number of different ways to describe the current period of American Catholicism: the definitive end of the immigrant Church, the rise of the communal Catholic, a third encounter with modernity. It is worth looking at each of these descriptions.

THE DEFINITIVE END OF THE IMMIGRANT CHURCH

It is a truism, of course, that American Catholicism is primarily a Church of immigrants and their descendants. At the time of the American Revolution, Catholics numbered around 35,000—less than one percent of the population. They were mainly of British and German extraction and centered in rural Maryland and Pennsylvania. Today they represent almost fifty-five million—twenty-eight percent of the population. As *The Yearbook of American and Canadian Churches 1980* makes clear, Catholics are found everywhere throughout the land.[2] Nevertheless, an inspection of a religious map of the United States shows that Catholics are particularly concentrated in large urban areas in the northeastern and the Great Lakes states. Catholics represent a majority of the population in many counties in the very lightly populated southwest (New Mexico) and in southern Texas where the Spanish-speaking Church is strong, in the delta country in Louisiana and in the heavily populated states of Massachusetts and Rhode Island. In the northeast and the Great Lakes states there are scores of counties where Catholics represent twenty-five to fifty percent of the population. In most large American cities in the northeast, midwest and southwest Catholics are the largest denomination—as they are in the nation as a whole. They are poorly represented in most of the south and in northern Wisconsin, northern Minnesota and the Dakotas as well as in the northwest. In all but two counties of California, on the other hand, they represent the largest single religious grouping.[3]

Catholic immigrants came in different waves of immigration and assimilated to the larger population in different rhythms. The earliest wave of immigrants, before the Civil War, included primarily German, French Canadian and Irish Catholics. These are, today, primarily third generation—or more—Americans. With the exception of the French Canadians, this first wave of immigrants has assimilated well into American society. As the research on Catholic ethnicity of Andrew M. Greeley and his associates at the National Opinion Research Center at the University of Chicago has shown, after Jews "Irish Catholics have the best education and the best income in the country and their educational and income mobility advantage over Protestants is substantial."[4] The Irish are the most financially successful of all the white Gentile ethnic groups in the United States. They are followed closely, among Catholic ethnic groups, by German Catholics.

The ethnic composition of American Catholics is as follows: Irish (8.3 million, 16%); Germans (7.6 million, 14%); Italians (10 million, 19%); Polish (5.3 million, 9%); French Canadians (5 million—8%); other Eastern European—Yugoslavian, Czechoslovakian, Hungarian, Austrian, etc. (3.6 million, 6%); English (1.5 million, 2%); Lithuanians (1.3 million, 3%); black and Asian American (1.4 million, 2%); Hispanic (20 million, 22%).[5] The last named ethnic group which has surged in numbers in the past twenty years is itself internally divided: Cubans in Florida, Puerto Ricans in New York, Mexicans in the southwest. Moreover, a significant proportion of the Hispanic speaking population originates from Central and South America. The Cubans in Florida have rapidly ascended to middle-class status (they were originally of middle-class origin) and political power largely through the Republican party. Other Hispanics are still lower class.

Italians, Poles, Lithuanians and other Eastern European Catholics came later than the Irish and Germans, mainly in the period 1880–1920. They have shown remarkable economic, educational and occupational mobility. While they lag behind Irish and German Catholics, they approach the current national average in education, income and occupational placement. Their generational rates of cohort mobility, however, far exceed the national average. In that sense, American Catholicism since World War II is overwhelmingly a middle-class Church.[6]

Throughout most of the nineteenth century and even into the twentieth, American Catholic energies were entirely spent on maintaining the allegiance of the immigrants. The classic study on this question proves that the Church, at least after 1820, showed remarkable ingenuity and resourcefulness in maintaining the immigrants within the fold. It is estimated that until 1920 only about 225,000 of these millions of immigrants lost the faith.[7] This effort to retain the allegiance of the immigrants and to provide helps toward assimilating into American life deeply taxed the resources, personnel and energy of the American Catholic Church in building parish churches, parochial schools, hospitals, welfare agencies, etc. to minister to the immigrants' needs. The Church and Church-affiliated institutions served as a way station and buffer as well as an agency of assimilation to wider American realities. The parochial school was especially successful as an educational avenue to upward mobility. Studies of its success show that it compares favorably to public school systems.[8]

Historian Jay Dolan has shown that the immigrants came to America with a very low level of Catholic practice and devotional life. More than mere sustenance was necessary. A genuine Catholic revival was needed. Unlike wider American revivalist movements, however, the Catholic revivals of the nineteenth and twentieth century lacked any specific social content, although they did reinforce the moralism, individualism and experiential bias of wider American religion. They led to unparalleled levels of religious practice and allegiance when compared to statistics for world Catholicism or to other American religious groups.[9]

Starting in the 1840's and recurring, at periodical intervals, until the 1940's, American Catholics had to engage in cultural defense against various American nativist groups such as the "Know Nothings," The American Protective Association, the Ku Klux Klan and Protestants and Other Americans United for Separation of Church and State. Catholics were accused of foreign allegiance and un-American mores and manners. The Church's stance was, simultaneously, to protect Catholic culture, life and institutions and to defend their integrity as a rightful expression of American life. As the largest and first "minority," Catholics had to break the exclusionary vision of a Protestant covenant with America and make room for what Will Herberg has referred to as the "triple melting pot" of an America legitimately Catholic, Protestant and Jewish.[10]

Debates within the Catholic community until the latter part of the nineteenth century were primarily over the tempo and desired amount of assimilation and Americanization and the extent to which an indigenous American Catholic culture and Church life was desirable. The general reaction of Catholic cultural elites toward American culture, institutions and reality was highly favorable. Before the end of the nineteenth century Catholic voices were generally silent or neutral on the major issues of social reform. There was no major Catholic involvement or coherent position on the Jacksonian reforms, the abolition of slavery, the Civil War or postwar reconstruction and the rise of an industrial America. Only the convert layman, Orestes Brownson, in his much neglected classic study of American institutions, *The American Republic,* joined an original voice to wider American discussions.[11]

The first signal of an achieved assimilation took place in the 1880's and 1890's in the so-called Americanist movement which also had repercussions among Catholics in France, especially those who supported Leo XIII's policy of *ralliement*. The "Americanist" bishops (Cardinal Gibbons, Archbishop Ireland, Bishops Keene, O'Connell and John Lancaster Spalding) desired full integration of American Catholics into the national life. They urged inter-faith discussion, participation by Catholics in the Chicago Parliament of World Religions, and the amalgamation of Catholic and public schools. All accepted as uniquely favorable the American institution of the separation of Church and state. The Americanists urged a vigorous Catholic participation in civic life, reform movements and the associational life of the nation.

The founder of the Paulist Fathers, Isaac Hecker, himself a convert from Unitarian transcendentalism and an alumnus of Brook Farm, called for an active, this-worldly experiential American Catholic spirituality. Cardinal Gibbons, an ardent champion of the incipient national labor movement (in which Catholics held disproportionate leadership positions), became a counselor to presidents. The tone of this Catholic approval of American life and institutions is caught in an address that Archbishop John Ireland delivered at a banquet in Chicago on October 7, 1899 honoring President McKinley:

> In America the general tone and trend of social life make for honor and honesty, for truth and morality. Public opinion metes out stern condemnation to wrongdoing, and unstinted approval to righteous conduct. The typical American home is the shrine of domestic virtues. . . . It matters little to me what the difficulties are that confront us, be they political, social or industrial. I have trust in the good sense of the people. . . . Perils have arisen and perils will rise; America has overcome those of the past; she will overcome those of the future.[12]

American Catholics seemed intent on preserving, at all costs, the survival of American innocence. If native American Protestant stock would betray that early innocent vision, Catholics would carry it on.

It is only after 1880 that Catholics began to enter fully into national political life as mayors of large cities such as New York, Boston, Chicago and San Francisco. They sided with the machine politics of ticket-balancing, pragmatic compromise and the beginnings of the welfare state against Tory WASP reformers in the progressive movement or the Protestant politics of cultural defense of a now receding rural America. In so doing, they entered an historic allegiance of Catholics with the Democratic Party. Catholics have long since found ample representation in national political institutions. While slightly underrepresented in the Senate, they represent the largest religious bloc in the House of Representatives (exceeding their percentage in the population). Their share of state governors (thirty of the fifty governors of states are Catholic) far exceeds their national percentage.[13]

Throughout the post-war period, the Catholic vote has consistently supported the Democratic Party and its presidential, gubernatorial and congressional candidates. Even those Catholics whose middle-class suburban location would indicate possible disaffiliation from the Democratic Party continue to vote disproportionately for Democratic Party candidates.[14] On indices of political and social attitudes measuring concern for civil liberties and support for social welfare, American Catholics consistently rank left of center.[15]

The voice which Catholics found in the national scene for the first time in the 1890's and thereafter is best exemplified by Archbishop John Ireland's crusade for a Catholic version of the kingdom of God in America. Largely uncritical of American institutions, culture and purposes, the Americanist program of Archbishop Ireland had several major planks. First, there was a complete—almost innocent—acceptance of American life and institutions. Second, there was an attempt to win Vatican acceptance for American arrangements not only for America (which, after all, was always forthcoming) but for export to Europe. This was finally achieved at Vatican Council II with the acceptance of the *Declaration on Religious Liberty*—largely the work of the American Jesuit John Courtney Murray. A third plank argued that American institutions and culture derived their strength from Catholic residues of medieval natural law still to be found in early Puritanism, Anglicanism and the thought of the founding fathers. Thereafter, however, Protestantism—it was argued—diluted this indispensable foundation for America. Only Catholics who maintained a steadfast belief in natural law could sustain the bedrock on which America rested. They were the last hope against the barbarian cynics who were undermining American institutions by their naturalism, positivism and utilitarian individualism. Protestants were seen as untrustworthy guardians of the American heritage.

Wilfred Parsons caught this natural affinity between Catholics and early American Puritans and affirmed his view of the untrustworthy character of Protestant guardianship of cultural origins:

> The modern intelligent Catholic finds himself drawing ever more closely to American cultural origins at the same time that his fellow non-Catholic Americans are disavowing those origins with almost indecent haste. A strange turn of history has brought it about that the very Catholics who were hated and persecuted by the old Puritans now find themselves looking back upon them with something approaching affection or at least with a sort of nostalgic and sympathetic understanding.[16]

In a last and important plank of the Americanist vision, Catholic Americans argued that they were the carriers of a special energy for the renewal of American life and institutions which would occur only when they entered in rightful numbers into elite positions in business, politics, the university—in short, the establishment. This Americanist program of Archbishop Ireland reappeared in different guise in the thought of Michael Williams, the founding editor of the lay Catholic *Commonweal* magazine, and George N. Shuster, president of Hunter College, in the 1920's. It was still being argued—in subtle forms—by John Courtney Murray in the early 1960's.[17] It was the basis of the position of men such as Michael Novak and Daniel Callahan in their vision of "The Generation of the Third Eye: American and Catholic" written at the time of the Vatican Council.[18]

As Andrew Greeley's studies of ethnic mobility show, American Catholics have now achieved their rightful places in the establishment. In that sense, by the 1960's the Americanist program of full Catholic assimilation was achieved, especially when the last bastion of cultural defense fell with the election of John Kennedy to the presidency. Yet, as the historian of American Catholicism David O'Brien argues in his *Renewal of American Catholicism,* the success of the "Americanist" program left bitter ashes in the mouths of those who rode the crest of the wave into the establishment. It became clear that Catholic Americans lacked any coherent perspective or program of their own. They experienced a fall from innocence when their enthusiastic "new frontier" became embroiled with harsher American realities, with war, corruption and imperialism.[19] Moreover, the cohesion of the Catholic force provided by the unitary umbrella of an immigrant Church, united in a politics of cultural defense against status deprivation and marginal discriminations, collapsed with the successful assimilation of immigrant Catholics. The momentum of old energies was lost. No clear vision to build a unified sense of an American Catholic bloc emerged. Catholics reflected the disunities, fragmentation and disillusionment of wider American society.

American Catholics had always showed up in survey research on American religiosity as the most orthodox, best practicing and most devout American religious group until the mid-1960's. Abruptly, the statistics began to show a marked shift. Catholic growth rates exceeded that of the national population through 1965. Although they have continued to grow into the 1980's, the rate of growth is slightly less than that of the total population. Moreover, when significant increases to the Catholic population due to the accretion of the new Hispanic speaking immigrants in the 1970's are taken into account, it is clear that many grandsons and granddaughters of the immigrants have indeed lost the faith.

Catholic rates of church attendance have always been considerably higher than those of Protestants or Jews. This remains the case. Still, they show a much greater rate of decline than that of Protestants. From a high of over seventy-five percent attending Catholic weekly Mass in 1957, Catholic weekly attendance has dropped to a low of fifty percent in 1980.[20] Precipitous declines have been registered for Catholic practices of daily prayer, monthly confession, occasional church visits, retreat attendance etc. The number of parochial schools and their student body have also declined yearly since the mid-1960's after decades of post-war growth.

American Catholics—as Americans generally—show high rates of orthodox responses to survey questions measuring acceptance of a personal belief in God, belief in life after death, and belief in the divinity of Christ. Very significant Catholic shifts, however, are apparent on beliefs in sexual orthodoxy (birth control, abortion, pre-marital sexuality, homosexuality). A majority of American Catholics dissent from official Church teaching on birth control. Sizable minorities accept the legitimacy of abortion and pre-marital sexuality. A Gallup poll survey shows American Catholics as the most tolerant religious group toward homosexuals.[21]

Especially revealing are American Catholic statistics on the authority of the Pope. In two national surveys of Catholics, respondents were asked if they believed that Jesus handed over the leadership of the Church to Peter and the Popes. In 1963, seventy percent thought it was "certainly true" that he had done so. Ten years later, only forty-two percent agreed. Moreover, in the 1973 survey, only thirty-two percent of the Catholics believed it was "certainly true" that the Pope is infallible when he speaks on faith and morals.[22] Andrew Greeley and his associates have argued that the impact of the papal teaching in *Humanae Vitae* and ineffective episcopal leadership on the part of the American bishops have led to a crisis in authority in American Catholicism that has eroded papal and episcopal authority. What is remarkable, however, is that while practicing Catholics differ sharply from Popes and bishops on issues of dogma, belief and morality, they remain within the Church. Very few effective sanctions exist to stifle this dissent. Despite enthusiastic turnouts to greet Pope John Paul II on the occasion of his visit to America in the fall of 1979 and Gallup poll data showing that he is the second most admired man in America (earlier Popes tended to rank sixth to eighth on the top ten of the most admired), surveys taken since the papal visit show that the Pope made no appreciable change in American Catholic attitudes toward birth control, priestly celibacy, the ordination of women, divorce, abortion and homosexuality.

Several significant shifts in the American Catholic population have taken place in the period after Vatican Council II. A large exodus of priests and nuns from religious life occurred (although the rate of this exodus is less than that for Europe and Latin America). There was a decrease in the American Catholic clergy of eighteen percent in the decade 1970–1980, due to death, retirement or resignation. The number of American nuns decreased by a third during the decade. Aspirants to the seminary or the postulant and novitiate houses of nuns have dramatically decreased in number during that same decade. On the other hand, a new program for ordained married deacons flourishes more in America than in any other country. Moreover, thousands of new lay ministers have been trained for catechesis, preaching, retreat work and spiritual counseling. The laity represent the overwhelming majority of teachers in parochial schools. A certain declericalization of the Church has become evident in the last decade.

Catholics (or ex-Catholics) were disproportionately represented in the new left movements such as Students for a Democratic Society and the anti-war movement. In 1968 at the height of the Vietnam War, one out of thirteen men granted conscientious objector status was a Catholic, a percentage larger than any other religious denomination and the greatest dissent by Catholics from any American war.[23] A significant Catholic pacifist movement remains as a legacy of the 1960's, symbolically centered in the Berrigan brothers. For the first time in American Catholic history, Catholics represent a significant proportion of the left. Catholics are also disproportionately represented among those who seek adherence to new religious movements in America—Zen Buddhist, yoga, Hare Krishna, Sufi and human potential groups.[24]

A third important shift involves the so-called "new immigrants" of the 1970's—Cubans, Mexicans, Central Americans, Haitians and others from the Caribbean area, Filipinos and Vietnamese. In a sense, it may be too soon to speak of a definitive end of the immigrant Church in America since these groups are overwhelmingly Catholic. Some indeed hope that this new wave of immigrants will allow for a re-emergence of a second, neglected, strand of American Catholic thought in the 1980's. Alongside the "Americanist" program—largely sponsored by the Irish Catholics—there was an alternative vision of what a Catholic contribution to American life might look like. Its historic carrier group in the nineteenth century was the German-speaking Catholics. Their disputes with the Irish in the 1890's were not entirely about adequate German representation in the episcopacy and other Catholic institutions. The Germans also criticized—at its core—the American assimilationist ideal. This German-Catholic vision for America was critical of American failures to respect genuine cultural pluralism. They also drew upon German Catholic social thought derived from Bishop Wilhelm Emmanuel von Ketteler to call in question American economic capitalism. More than the Americanists, these German Catholics embodied a genuine Catholic alternative to the dominant American life and culture. It is also clear that the major centers of innovation and pastoral renewal in America came historically from the so-called German Catholic triangle: Milwaukee, Cincinnati, Chicago and St. Louis.[25]

Some leading spokespersons for the Hispanic community continue this earlier concern for a Catholic protest against dominant American cultural imperialism and the failure to institutionalize genuine cultural pluralism. They insist on the validity of bi-lingualism, the right of ethnic Americans to maintain alternative ways of understanding work and leisure, politics and human values. They are sustained in this vision by institutions such as the Mexican-American Cultural Center in San Antonio and the Office for the Spanish Speaking of the United States Catholic Conference. Allegiance to their Spanish-speaking constituency has led the American bishops in recent years to some unwonted public stances such as championing the union organizing activities of Cesar Chavez and the farm-workers and sharply challenging the foreign policy for Central and Latin America of the Catholic secretary of state, Alexander Haig.

A related thrust toward an alternative vision of America is found in the new emphasis since the mid-1970's on ethnicity among American Catholics of Slavic and Italian background who represent, in Michael Novak's phrase, "the rise of the unmeltable ethnics."[26] Whether this ethnic consciousness will have much perduring impact on politics or the wider culture is subject to doubt. Much of the ethnic consciousness, at least among white groups, often has a quality of nostalgia and superficiality. Nevertheless, recent research shows that ethnic qualities perdure across generations—even in the absence of explicit ethnic consciousness—to create quite different symbolic worlds of the meaning of politics, family life, suffering, life in the world, work and leisure.[27]

The new concern for ethnicity has spawned in the last decade significant new historical reappraisals of the experience of American Catholic Italians, Slavs, Lithuanians and other ethnic groups. This turn toward "social history," viewing the immigrant experience in terms of family styles, inner experience and special ethnic values, has much enriched our sense of the varieties of ways that different American Catholic groups encountered the process of becoming an American.[28] Moreover, in the last decade a distinctively American Catholic new novel has emerged recounting specifically Catholic sensibilities of and within the American context. Most notable are Joseph Pintauro's *Cold Hands,* Mary Gordon's *Final Payments* and *The Company of Women,* Thomas McHale's *Principato* and John Kennedy Toole's *A Confederacy of Dunces.*

These novels exhibit the theme of a fall from innocence unacceptable to the Catholic community before the 1960's. As one literary critic has noted of these new novels of Catholic sensibility, they reflect the present Catholic condition as one of anguish—"between the gods."[29] Special sensibility to the Catholic ethnic experience is also available in the cinema of Martin Scorsese and Francis Ford Coppola and—in the theater—in the plays of Albert Inaurato. These films, novels and plays show that American Catholics no longer live in a paradise of certainty in America's goodness but in struggles—in F. Scott Fitzgerald's phrase—which take place this side of paradise.

Whatever the long-range importance of this emergence of a new Catholic novel and cinema and the proliferating historical studies of the Catholic ethnic experience, it seems clear that if there has been a definitive end to the ethnic immigrant Church, the immigrant experience has left interesting and perduring residues even into the 1980's. For the Church, however, the unquestioned loyalties generated by a merger of religion and ethnicity in the American context can no longer be taken for granted. A much more conscious effort at evangelization and strategies to bolster a vivid sense of Catholic identity and belonging seems called for. For too long the Church could simply rely on identities generated by an immigrant ghetto experience and the reaction to the exclusionary rejections of the American Protestant nativist culture to supply it with élan. It seems a reasonable guess, however, that future programs of Catholic identity will continue the now century-old quest for a distinctive contribution of Catholicism to American life and culture.

THE COMMUNAL CATHOLIC

A second way to characterize contemporary American Catholicism speaks of the rise of the communal Catholic. Andrew Greeley who has coined the term describes the phenomenon:

> They are loyal to the Catholic collectivity and at least sympathetic toward its heritage. At the same time they refuse to take seriously the teaching authority of the leadership of the institutional Church. Such communal Catholics are Catholics because they see nothing else in American society they want to be, out of loyalty to their past, and they are curious as to what the Catholic tradition might have that is special and unique in the contemporary world.[30]

Greeley sees this mode of allegiance particularly among younger well-educated Catholics who are selective and self-conscious in their style of being Catholic. They selectively dissent from Church dogma or moral injunctions. Still, they persist in sending their children to parochial schools. When asked, they identify themselves as Catholic. Religious affiliation remains but with less totalistic identification.[31]

It is clear that a sense of Catholicism as a distinctive American community of social networks, supports and interactions continues. Thus, Catholics still marry other Catholics in large proportions (88%). While American Catholics diverge widely in survey research testing issues such as "Is loyalty to the Church and other Catholics an important sign of a good Catholic?" (55% yes vs. 45% no) or "Is the Church the most important group membership for Catholics?" (54% yes vs. 46% no), seventy-eight percent of American Catholics claim that their closest friends are Catholic.[32] In most large American cities with a sizable Catholic population, informal networks link Catholics together as social partners in the worlds of leisure (golf partners and country club memberships) and work (professional informal networks of doctors, lawyers and other professions).

Moreover, American Catholics seem to be seeking experiences of Church which will build a sense of community beyond the large impersonal parishes. Sixty percent of all American Catholics express that they have had some contact with home liturgies, the Marriage Encounter movement or the charismatic prayer movement. The charismatic movement involves over a million American Catholics. In his study of the American Catholic charismatics, sociologist Joseph Fichter describes the charismatics as "personalized" Christians involved in a religious revival similar to earlier Protestant-sponsored evangelical revival movements. Fichter lists four unexpected qualities which characterize the Catholic charismatic movement in America:

> It was unexpected that a new and vigorous spiritual cult would (a) be inaugurated by lay Catholics; (b) attract adherents from the more advantaged middle class; (c) stimulate a preference for the emotional rather than the intellectual experience of faith; and (d) emerge in the midst of this scientistic, rational American culture.[33]

The American Catholic Church possesses a rich array of institutions for sustenance, evangelization, outreach and pastoral care. There are about one hundred and seventy-five dioceses and archdioceses, nearly three hundred bishops, hundreds of thousands of priests, nuns or professionally trained lay ministers, nearly ten thousand parochial elementary and high schools, a sprawling network of parishes, Catholic colleges and universities, diocesan newspapers, Catholic journals and professional organizations. Lobbying efforts are coordinated at the national level by the United States Catholic Conference and at the level of the states by separate statewide Catholic conferences. Catholic Charities represents the largest private relief service in the United States. Catholics maintain separate hospitals, orphanages, retirement homes, schools for the deaf and blind, etc.

Besides these "official" institutional agencies, an impressive array of unofficial organizations or movements exist to preserve Catholic interests or represent pastoral outreach. The most notable organization is the Right-to-Life Movement which takes an active educational and political stance on the question of abortion. It numbers millions of Catholics. The Marriage Encounter movement, mentioned earlier, has reached over a million Catholic families. There has been a proliferation of hundreds of Catholic "peace and justice" commissions in dioceses or religious congregations working against nuclear weapons. There is also a vigorous Catholic presence in the movement for community organizing in the tradition of Saul Alinsky. Perhaps the fastest growing lay movement in the Church in the past decade is the network of hundreds of thousands of divorced Catholics who associate together in committees, congresses and retreats. Dignity—an organization for Catholic homosexuals—has centers of worship or chapters in over a hundred American cities. As in the wider society, almost every Catholic special interest group has its appropriate organization.

One of the historic social functions of Protestant churches in America has been the sponsorship of non-denominational movements for social reform, voluntary associations in the public interest which are the outgrowth of church members but not official organs of the church. Alexis de Tocqueville, of course, noted such groups in his study of American society one hundred and fifty years ago. Typically, prior to Vatican Council II, voluntary associations founded by Catholics often catered rather uniquely to a Catholic constituency, e.g., the National Legion of Decency in film. One of the striking phenomena in post-conciliar American Catholicism is the leadership role of Catholics in founding, staffing or supporting various voluntary associations in the public interest such as Bread for the World (an organization to combat world hunger) or the Movement for Responsible Investment (organizations to pressure multi-national corporations about their investments or practices in South Africa and Latin America). The emergence of the communal Catholic in America, then, entails three different changes in the post-Vatican period:

1. a selective and self-conscious style of affiliation with institutional Catholicism which nevertheless keeps social and other ties with the Catholic community;

2. a desire for new religious forms, e.g., the charismatic movement, which provide personalized experiences of community among Catholics;

3. the emergence of Catholics into the wider community in spawning—as the Protestant churches did in the nineteenth century—voluntary, non-denominational associations of social reform.

A sympathetic non-Catholic observer of Catholicism, University of Chicago theologian Langdon Gilkey, has argued that Catholicism typically had five major strengths: (1) a high regard for rationality and the role of reason in public life, (2) a sense of mystic interiority and the legitimacy of mysticism in the spiritual life, (3) a deep sense of the symbolic, especially as mediated in liturgical and sacramental life, (4) the ability to generate loyalties to a transnational community, and (5) the sense of the role of moral norms and principles—as against situational intuitiveness—in public and personal life.[34]

American Catholicism since Vatican Council II has made notable strides on several of the factors enumerated by Gilkey. Several others remain problematical. American Catholic renewal of liturgical life is notable both in practice and in scholarship. Surveys show widespread support for the liturgical reforms mandated by the council. Important centers of experimental liturgy exist at the University of Notre Dame, at St. John's College in Minnesota, in Boston, New York, Washington, D.C. and Oakland and Berkeley, California. New songs, rites and experiments with liturgical gesture and dance have kept alive and renewed the Catholic sense for the symbolic. Similarly, Catholics have shown the most sensitivity—among American mainline religious groups—to the quest for mystic unity with God as experienced in the new religious movements—mainly of Oriental provenance—which have grown apace in the last decades.[35] American Catholic monasticism is once again on the increase. Catholic centers for meditation and teaching of Western mystic techniques and tradition have grown around the country. There is a revival of the tradition of the spiritual director to teach forms of prayer. The classics of Western mysticism—predominantly although not, of course, exclusively Catholic—have been made available recently in America by the Paulist Press.

In regard to the other three factors of Catholic "strength" noted by Gilkey, the evidence for a Catholic renewal is much more mixed. With the collapse of the Thomist synthesis, Catholics seem to lack a coherent way of defending reason in public life. The moral authority of the papacy and episcopacy has been severely compromised and, with it, a strong Catholic sense of the role of moral norms in public and personal life as opposed to a situation ethic.

In an earlier period, American Catholic feelings of inferiority about their cultural contributions to American life turned them to the "Catholic classics" from Europe or made them especially attentive to new literary or philosophic movements emanating from French Catholicism in the postwar period.[36] The papacy functioned as a transnational symbol. Extensive Catholic missionary activity in Asia, Latin America and Africa kept American Catholics aware, in John Courtney Murray's words, that "the Catholic may not, as others do, merge his religious and his patriotic faith, or submerge one in the other. The simplistic solution is not for him. He must reckon with his own tradition of thought which is wider and deeper than any that America has elaborated. He must also reckon with his own history which is longer than the brief centuries that America has lived."[37]

Finding some new ways to keep American Catholics deeply rooted in a sense of transnational loyalties which mediate a vivid consciousness of belonging to a world community of humankind is probably the biggest challenge to American Catholics in the 1980's. The embodiment of this sense of transnational loyalty and the other four factors of strength mentioned by Gilkey—rather than the "Americanist" program of showing that American Catholics are fully patriotic, more than one hundred percent American—would seem to offer the key, if there is any, to the long cherished American Catholic dream of making some unique contribution to the national life.

A THIRD ENCOUNTER WITH MODERNITY

In a recent essay, University of Notre Dame historian Jay Dolan has argued that contemporary Catholics are now undertaking their third encounter with modernity.[38] The first encounter took place from 1776 through 1800 under the impetus of British-American Catholics, especially the first American bishop, John Carroll. The British-American early Catholics were deeply influenced by the Enlightenment thought, as were the founding fathers. They encouraged the ideals of egalitarianism, ecumenism (Protestants and Catholics regularly visited each other's churches during this period), and democratization (the first three American bishops were elected by the lower clergy; parishes were controlled by boards of lay trustees). Carroll urged and clandestinely practiced, without Roman approval, a vernacular liturgy. He founded academies modeled on the Enlightenment ideal of science. Dolan cites a lay trustee of Charlestown who argued that "American Catholics should rear a national American Church with liberties consonant to the spirit of government under which they live."

This first experiment with modernity in American Catholicism was crushed in the early years of the nineteenth century. The anti-clerical bias in the French Revolution prompted a Vatican animus against the principles of reason, liberty and democratization which Bishop Carroll espoused. With the arrival of waves of immigrants, American Catholics—originally ethnically and culturally similar in all ways but religion with their Protestant British counterparts—increasingly began to seem foreign. Foreign-born clergy brought with them a conservative, traditionalist spirit inimical to the American Enlightenment which Carroll found so congenial. They distrusted the democratization of the Church and Carroll's insistence on the virtues of the republic within the life of the Church community itself.

The second experiment was that of the Americanists in the 1880's and 1890's to forge a marriage of American culture and Catholicism. Large national lay congresses were held to encourage a Catholic lay voice in the project. Four in all, the most important were the congresses held in Baltimore in 1889 and in Chicago in 1893 to seek points of contact between Catholicism and the leading cultural and intellectual movements of the day. At the University of Notre Dame, The Catholic University of America and Dunwoodie Seminary in New York, centers of Catholic scholarship addressed issues of science, technology, evolution and civilization. These Catholic scholars embraced the new historical scholarship abroad in the day. This second surge of Catholicism confronting modernity ebbed in the wake of Pius X's chilling anti-modernist encyclical, *Pascendi Dominici Gregis,* which condemned, in 1907, "modernism" and—by implication— modern scholarship. Scholars were dismissed at Catholic University and Dunwoodie. As Dolan sees it, "With the condemnation of modernism, the lights went out for American Catholic intellectuals." The suppression of this Americanist surge was all the easier to achieve since important elements of the American hierarchy—the German bishops, for example, and the conservative Irish bishops such as Corrigan of New York and McQuaid of Rochester—felt that the Americanizers were premature in their sounding of a death-knell to the immigrant Church.

Dolan argues that we are presently in a period of the third encounter of American Catholicism with the modern world. Catholic scholars fully endorse an historical and critical interpretation of the Bible and tradition. The traditions of Carroll and the Americanists are cherished as the best periods of Catholic history. Academic freedom in accord with general American university standards reigns on American Catholic university campuses. American scholars, long in tutelage to European trends in theological scholarship, have struck an independent voice. Catholic middle-class laity are no longer docile to traditionalist sanctions.

In many ways during the 1960's and 1970's Americans experienced an awakening to issues such as race, war and imperialism, women's rights, the environment, the government and misuse of power. William McLoughlin, the Brown University historian of American religion, has seen this period as another great awakening, "a transformation of our world view that may be the most drastic in our history as a nation." Because this cultural shift coincided with the religious awakening initiated by the Second Vatican Council, Catholics have been especially influenced by it.

Several factors make this third encounter with modernity different from the earlier two. First, it is, in a sense, a worldwide phenomenon in Catholicism. Second, American Catholics are no longer wedded to the immigrant traditional cultures. In the third place, the romance with modernity is not limited, as the earlier ones were, to the clergy and an elite group of lay intellectuals. It is a widespread phenomenon that finds support in the lay population which has opted for the style of the communal Catholic. This new class of professional, middle-class Catholics is asking different questions than their predecessors, questions of meaning and purpose in a modern, technological society.

Throughout their long history, American Catholics have sought a faith that would be distinctively American and distinctively Catholic. They wanted both to overcome their marginal, outsider's role and to incorporate that role in a phase of cultural creativity. With the definitive collapse of both nativism and the immigrant Church, the American credentials of Catholics have been assured. Whether in its third encounter with modernity American Catholics will succeed in their long dream to embody a distinctively Catholic vision in America or simply succumb to a subtle secularization of the faith will depend, in large part, on their success in finding new ways to embody the five factors of strength enumerated by Langdon Gilkey.

NOTES

1. William Halsey, *The Survival of American Innocence* (Notre Dame: University of Notre Dame Press, 1980).

2. For a list of American Catholic dioceses cf. Constant H. Jacquet, ed., *Yearbook of American and Canadian Churches 1980* (Nashville: Abingdon Press, 1980).

3. A map of Catholic population distribution can be found in Jackson Carroll, Douglas Johnson and Martin Marty, *Religion in America 1950 to the Present* (New York: Harper and Row, 1979), p. 64.

4. Andrew Greeley, *The American Catholic: A Social Portrait* (New York: Basic Books, 1977), p. 63.

5. As cited in T. William Bolts, *The Catholic Experience in America* (Encino: Glencoe Publishers, 1980), p. 17.

6. Greeley, *op. cit.,* p. 62.

7. Gerald Shaughnessy, *Has the Immigrant Kept the Faith?* (New York: Arno Press, 1969).

182 AN AMERICAN STRATEGIC THEOLOGY

8. Cf. Andrew Greeley and Peter Rossi, *The Education of Catholic Americans* (Chicago: Aldine, 1966); Andrew Greeley, William McCready and Kathleen McCourt, *Catholic Schools in a Declining Church* (Kansas City: Sheed and Ward, 1976) and the report of James Coleman to the Department of Education for the National Center for Educational Statistics which claims that parochial schools are not only educationally superior to public schools in America but that they practice less racial segregation, reported in the *Washington Post,* Friday, April 3, 1981, p. 1.

9. Jay Dolan, *Immigrant Church* (Baltimore: Johns Hopkins Press, 1975) and *Catholic Revivalism* (Notre Dame: University of Notre Dame Press, 1978).

10. Will Herberg, *Catholic, Protestant and Jew* (Garden City: Doubleday, 1955).

11. Cf. Orestes Brownson, *The American Republic* (New York: Shea, 1866) and Chapter 4 of this volume.

12. John Ireland, *Church and Modern Society* (New York: McBride, 1896), Vol. 2, pp. 116–118. The best history of the Americanist movement is Thomas McAvoy, *The Americanist Crisis* (Chicago: Henry Regnery, 1957).

13. As found in *Christianity Today,* Dec. 7, 1980, pp. 56–57.

14. Cf. Joan Fee, "Political Continuity and Change," in Greeley *et al., Catholic Schools in a Declining Church,* pp. 76–102.

15. For these indices of Catholic liberalism cf. Norman H. Nie, John Petrocik, and Sidney Verba, *The Changing American Voter* (Cambridge: Harvard University Press, 1976).

16. Wilfred Parsons, S.J., "Philosophical Factors in the Integration of American Culture," in Jesuit Philosophical Association, *Phases of American Culture* (Worcester, 1942). Halsey, *op. cit.,* pp. 61–83, shows that this position of Parsons was typical of the period 1920–1965.

17. John Courtney Murray, *We Hold These Truths* (New York: Sheed and Ward, 1960).

18. Michael Novak, ed., *A New Generation: American and Catholic* (New York: Herder and Herder, 1964).

19. David O'Brien, *The Renewal of American Catholicism* (New York: Oxford University Press, 1972).

20. Cited in Jackson Carroll, Douglas Johnson and Martin Marty, *Religion in America,* p. 20.

21. Cf. George Gallup, *Religion in America 1979–1980* (Princeton: Center for Religious Research, 1979), p. 37. Cf. this same work *passim* for Catholic attitudes on other sexual issues.

22. Greeley *et al., Catholic Schools in a Declining Church,* p. 33.

23. T. William Bolts, *The Catholic Experience in America,* p. 194.

24. This was confirmed for me in an oral communication with Jacob Needleman, director of the Center for the Study of New Religious Movements, Berkeley, California.

25. For the German vision of an alternative America cf. Philip Gleeson, *The Conservative Reformers: German-American Catholics and the Social Order* (Notre Dame: University of Notre Dame Press, 1968) and Coleman Barry, *The Catholic Church and German Americans* (Milwaukee: Bruce, 1953).

26. Michael Novak, *The Rise of the Unmeltable Ethnics* (New York: Macmillan, 1972). For a wider treatment of religion and ethnicity cf. Martin Marty, *A Nation of Believers* (Chicago: University of Chicago Press, 1976), pp. 158ff.

27. Andrew M. Greeley, *Ethnicity in the United States: A Preliminary Reconnaissance* (New York: John Wiley and Sons, 1974).

28. For a few, among many, of the titles of this proliferating literature on Catholic ethnic experience cf. Victor Greene, *For God and Country: The Rise of Polish and Lithuanian Consciousness in America* (Madison: The State Historical Society of Wisconsin, 1971), Humbert S. Nelli, *Italians in Chicago 1880-1930* (New York: Oxford University Press, 1970) and Paul Messbarger, *Varieties of Accommodation: Social Uses of American Catholic Literature 1884-1900* (Boston: Boston University Press, 1971).

29. Garry Wills, "Catholic Faith and Fiction," *The New York Times Book Review,* January 16, 1972, p. 3.

30. Greeley, *The American Catholic: A Social Portrait,* p. 272.

31. For a study of continued but marginal affiliation among Catholics cf. John Kotre, *View from the Border* (Chicago: Aldine, 1971).

32. Cited in Bolts, *op. cit.,* p. 16.

33. Joseph H. Fichter, *The Catholic Cult of the Paraclete* (New York: Sheed and Ward, 1975), p. 140.

34. Langdon Gilkey, *Catholicism Confronts Modernity* (New York: Seabury Press, 1975).

35. For several studies of the new religiosity cf. Charles Glock and Robert Bellah, eds., *The New Religious Consciousness* (Berkeley: University of California Press, 1976) and Robert Wuthnow, *The Consciousness Reformation* (Berkeley: University of California Press, 1976).

36. Cf. the evocation of the dependence of American Catholic liberals on French Catholic literature in the 1950's in Garry Wills, *Bare Ruined Choirs* (Garden City: Doubleday, 1971), Chapter One.

37. John Courtney Murray, *We Hold These Truths,* p. xi. This point is expanded in Chapter 12 of this volume.

38. Jay Dolan, "Catholicism in America," in a symposium on American religion in the *Wilson Quarterly* (Fall 1981).

Chapter Nine

American Culture and Religious Ethics

> It would seem as if the rulers of our time sought only to use men in order to make things great; I wish that they would try a little more to make great men; that they would set less value on the work and more on the workman; that they would never forget that a nation can not long remain strong when every man belonging to it is individually weak, and that no form or combination of social polity has been devised to make an energetic people out of . . . pusillanimous and enfeebled citizens.
>
> —Alexis de Tocqueville
> *Democracy in America*

In the middle of the summer of 1979 President Carter went into deep seclusion at Camp David to prepare himself to deliver a tough policy address to the nation on the issue of the energy crisis. As part of his briefing for this speech, the White House staff gathered together ten American religious leaders to discuss with the president the issue of our national spiritual malaise. One of the participants in that dialogue, Robert N. Bellah, has outlined the kind of speech he had wished that President Carter might have made to the nation:

Look, we have had a great history, we've satisfied a lot of needs, we've done a lot of terrible things too, but by and large we've been one of the more decent societies in human history . . . and *we've done it all by combining an ethic of deep concern for other human beings with an ethic of everybody looking out for number one.* And it's worked. But it is not going to work anymore. We're up against a new set of limits—ecological, political, economic— and we're not going to be able to afford the totally unlimited self-indulgence and the kind of economic system that feeds that self-indulgence any longer. Our choices are two: either we're going to solve it by authoritarianism, with a government that tells us what we can consume and what we're not going to be allowed to do, or we're going to solve it through a reorganization of our society along voluntaristic lines in accordance with our long tradition of democratic process. It's not going to be easy, because most of the basic interests of our society will have to be reoriented. . . . We're going to be working on this for the rest of the century at least. But what I'm saying is, it's not going to be like it was! And we'd better start thinking about what it's going to be. The best thing is to involve the whole nation in some kind of serious consideration of what the options are as we move into a different world.[1]

The president's speech on the energy crisis was not, of course, anything like Bellah's imagined address. Instead of an appeal to the deeply engrained, if also deeply eroded, American religious tradition of a Judaeo-Christian ethic (the root symbolic source in America for Bellah's postulated "ethic of deep concern for other human beings"), Carter lapsed into the language of productivity, the innate goodness of the people, material well-being and a technological advance which promised potential abundance of energy without any great concomitant social, moral or spiritual costs (Bellah's alternative ethic of "everybody looking out for number one").

By evoking our most potent—if deeply flawed—ethical tradition of liberal philosophy, Carter deserves the strictures of de Tocqueville with which this chapter begins. For he neglected, as the liberal tradition of public philosophy always has, any vision of the public order as an educational community, any strong sense of the inevitable—and sometimes tragic—limits in human life and politics, any recognition of the need for a deeply customary discipline and virtuous restraint in a people if a republic is to flourish, any attention to a direct address to the ends of communal life instead of the traditional liberal focus on means, procedures and utilities.

Perhaps, inspecting the political polls, Carter saw a pusillanimous and enfeebled citizenry instead of an energetic people ready to make sacrifices and build a community of equality and substantive justice. Perhaps he gambled that as liberal solutions based on a balancing of interests and sheer redistribution of the unquestioned good of material well-being and expansion had worked in the past—indeed, at least since the Civil War have dominated in American public philosophy—they would work their magic again. But as Bellah puts it in his projected alternative speech: it is not likely that it will work anymore!

I am going to discuss my capacious topic "American Culture and Religious Ethics" by taking a cue from Bellah's remarks about our curious American combination of an ethic of deep concern for other human beings and an ethic of everybody looking out for number one. Following the brilliant interpretive analysis of Wilson Carey McWilliams in his book *The*

Idea of Fraternity in America, I shall argue that the theories and ethic of traditional religion and those of the American Enlightenment liberal public philosophy are not easily compatible.[2] Indeed, the Enlightenment vision of human life and community and the political and, especially, economic institutions it has sustained have eroded, systematically, the very social bases on which these institutions have depended for their historic strength. As McWilliams states it, "Individualistic in law and theory, liberalism had depended in fact on local communities and on the common symbols provided by religion: the first gave men security and experience in common action, the second enabled them to articulate shared experience and communality."[3] But liberalism opposed and countervened both as parochial residues and barriers to the goal of some imagined thin universal community of reason.

Put succinctly, my argument in the first part of this chapter will be that Americans and American institutions live out of a moral substance few Americans believe in directly anymore and that they entertain, in public argument and philosophy, a vision of the human, of human community and the state which erodes that fragile substance even further.[4] If the liberal tradition of public philosophy will be painted as the enemy of the common good, it will not be because of its legacy of humane procedures of law and due process which I both deeply respect and support. Rather, my quarrel with the liberal public philosophy lies with its neglect and, in principle, retreat from addressing the issues of virtue, an adjudication of substantive goods for society and genuine fraternity in a populace, a neglect signaled by the de Tocqueville citation. McWilliams points to this very same neglect: "The great concern of American political philosophy has been the development of 'democratic theory.' That concern has focused on formal institutions and organizations, even when it rejected 'formalism.' In so doing, it has neglected the fact that democratic theory must always be primarily a theory about a *demos,* about the character and relation of citizens."[5]

Because I will be calling for a larger role for biblical religion in our public ethics, I will deal, in a second section of this chapter, with some characteristic obstacles or objections to a religiously based public ethics. Moreover, I will address the question how religion can essay a public theology without being sectarian. Finally, I will want to make some remarks about Catholic social ethics and the role it could or should play in public discourse.

THE UNEASY SYNTHESIS OF RELIGIOUS ETHICS AND LIBERAL PUBLIC PHILOSOPHY

I have argued elsewhere that three very different strands of tradition have contributed to America's public self-understanding: classical republican theory, biblical religion and the public philosophy of Enlightenment liberalism.[6] In this chapter I will omit discussion of the tradition of classical republican theory for several reasons. First, it has never, it seems to me, been a vigorous separately autonomous tradition when divorced from the Protestant covenant thought or Catholic natural law theory which subsumed it. At least since the mid-nineteenth century, it lapsed as a separately vigorous tradition of public philosophy. Second, as I have argued, the tradition of republican virtue is no longer a living part of the texture of American public discourse.[7]

The importance of classical republican theory is that it served to reinforce biblical religion in stressing love and sacrifice for the common good and the need to found the health of public life on virtue and a morally good citizenry. Moreover, with biblical religion, it stood in judgment of social theories which expect public virtue to arise from a healthy compromise balancing of private vices. Significantly, the major carrier of this republican tradition has always been American religious ethics. Indeed, contemporary voices who appeal to it against the grain of the dominant liberal philosophy all tend to take their orientation in public ethics from the religious tradition.[8] It is equally significant that there has never been an alliance between this tradition of republican theory and the public philosophy of Enlightenment liberalism. For our purposes, then, we can focus directly on a comparison of American religious ethics and liberal public philosophy as they have functioned in American culture.

Religious ethics, specifically Calvinist Puritan ideas of the multiple but inter-related covenants of grace, nature, visible Christians in the Church, and the political order, was first in possession of the public philosophy in American cultural life.[9] As de Tocqueville put it, "the principles of New England spread at first to the neighboring states; they then passed successively to the more distant ones. . . . They now extend their influence . . . over the whole American world."[10]

This early and culturally foundational Puritan religious ethics contained a strong sense of solidarity, a recognition of the mutual tissues and textures of interdependence in the body politic. John Winthrop, especially, outlined in his inaugural sermon a vision of a commonwealth of fraternity in which individual interest would remain subordinate to the common good and the dignity and responsibility of the individual would be nurtured and challenged within a collective context.[11]

The power of this tradition of religious ethics lay in its strong sense of inevitable frailty and tragedy as a consequence of human depravity and sin, its discouragement of a vain quest for an ideal state, its recognition of the need for limits to human possessions, wants and needs, and its conscious preference for obligation and constraining duty as the reciprocal, indeed prior, context for any self-assertion of rights. The state, in New England Puritan theory, while limited in its scope and distinguishable from society as such, was much more than a mere contractarian device or an instrument to balance competing interests whose substantive claims would lie forever beyond the bounds of societal capacity to adjudicate their competing value claims.

The Puritans, to be sure, championed procedural justice and the means and processes involved in English liberties. But they also thought it both proper and essential to raise within the political order issues of the substantive quality of communal life. Moreover, Puritan politics accorded a moral and educative role to the state and did not restrict its functioning to monitoring technical bargaining mechanisms between totally random ends. In these aspects, Puritan political theory remains continuous with the classical political thought in the West which ran from Plato and Aristotle down through medieval and early Reformation times until the decisive break inaugurated by Machiavelli, Hobbes and Locke.[12]

This second tradition within American culture found its voice in the American Enlightenment of the eighteenth century: Jefferson, Ben Franklin, Thomas Paine and James Wilson. McWilliams has extracted the view of the human and the human community inherent in this "irrational Lockeanism derived from rearing and culture in America."[13] Whereas John Winthrop and the Puritans feared the loss or erosion of natural community restraints, the Enlightenment sought to remove all constraints from the human imagination: " 'Natural right' was innate in the individual; he was born morally complete. Hence, the state did not exist to develop man as a moral personality; it could only be justified in terms of its utility to the individual, a doctrine expressed in the theory of the 'social contract.' Man's rights were negative and external to his personality, not bonds to his fellows."[14]

For the Enlightenment, the logic of interest and utility rather than that of the liberation of genuine liberty within the matrix of community held sway. Indeed, "interest—man's individual pursuit of power—was the motive power and safest guide for historical progress."[15] Few among the Enlightenment thinkers were inclined to doubt or question the integral benignity of ever-expanding material well-being and technological advance which remained the unchallenged, if superficial, goals of American politics. Politics ceased to be a moral and, indeed, in a proper sense, a political science and became a mechanical, i.e., purely technical, science judged principally by utilitarian considerations of consequence and technical notions of adjudication and balance.[16] Employed as a weapon to crush error and promote civil tolerance, Enlightenment political thought systematically undermined belief in the existence of any substantive truth. Seeking a universal fraternity, it remained hostile to all real communities. The latter were seen as parochial barriers to a "reasonable" fraternity.

The great central themes of the Enlightenment are patently antithetical to Puritan covenant theology: "the struggle against nature, the social contract, the superiority of individual decision and of science and contrivance over custom and natural law."[17] It would be hard to escape the judgment that the revised Augustinianism of the Puritan covenant thought should have seen the new political theory of Enlightenment liberalism as an enthronement of immoral *cupiditas* because of its preference for competitive ethics, privatism, political impersonality and concern for material power over and above other values.

That it did not do so is due to its own weakening sense of the priority of rooted religious affections over Scholasticism, its yielding to the temptation to believe, with other Americans, in an anti-Christian Adamic myth of innocence—a temptation hard to resist in the face of the sheer lure of a continent which seemed to contain infinite, unlimited possibility. Most important, however, is the reason alleged by McWilliams: "Concern for practice often led Americans to overlook differences in theory between the Enlightenment and their older heritage, a tendency magnified by the fact that both creeds employed a similar language, though radically different in substantive meaning."[18] For while the American Enlightenment fundamentally distorted the meaning of Christian symbols in its transformed use of them, it felt obliged to retain the older language as a vehicle of continuity and persuasive rhetoric. This muting of differences, while contributing to American unity, worked to undermine the earlier religious tradition.[19] It permitted Americans to pursue gain with an eased conscience in the conviction that their duties to their brothers and sisters and to their self-interested desire for affluence were one and the same.

> Both traditions, for example, spoke of the law of nature, but the older tradition implied by that term fixed ends which were "natural" to man, established by an Authority beyond mankind. The new philosophy denied the existence of fixed ends and affirmed infinite possibilities for men. The "laws of nature" were the laws of motion, and man's nature was determined by the desires by which he was "moved." Authority was dissolved by the inference that the individual might appeal to his desires and his conscience as a matter of "natural right." . . .
>
> Puritanism and the Enlightenment both spoke of equality, but where the former conceived of a democracy of the fall which yielded an aristocracy of redemption, the latter believed in an original equality modified by different degrees of science and understanding. For the religious tradition, a "natural aristocracy" was defined by personal moral character which belonged to the individual. The newer *aristoi* were defined by technical mastery, the ability to manipulate nature and history; the benefits of their knowledge, if not the knowledge itself, could be disseminated and perhaps established as the basis of a progressive historical movement.
>
> Similarly, the ancient idea of "balance" as a harmony within the individual or the polity was replaced by the conviction of the creative power of competition and balance in conflict. That doctrine reached what was perhaps its highest statement in *The Fed-*

eralist's thesis that competition between individuals and groups
on a scale wide enough to guarantee a "balance" between them is
almost a self-sufficient use of justice.[20]

Certainly by the time of the post-Civil War era, the liberal Enlightenment philosophy had become the overwhelmingly dominant force in
American culture, although there remained important minor voices, such
as that of Orestes Brownson, for example, which evoked the older religious
tradition of a political order rooted in a religious faith and the accumulat-
ed wisdom of republican theory.[21] The tenacious hold of the Enlightenment doctrines on American public philosophy is easy enough to explain.
Our governmental institutions have been founded on the liberal creed such
that deviation from it carries a suspect, alien quality. Public education, at
least until very recent times, has included that creed as part of its indoctri-
nation. Liberal philosophy has been the basis of modern science and reason
such that those who argue from different premises and motives are almost
forced to state their case in liberal terms in order to gain any wide hearing.[22]

It is also important to note that America lacked any vigorous social
movements which embodied what has been called "The Second Enlightenment." Whereas Marx, Nietzsche, Freud and Weber in Europe espoused a
dark, stoic and tragic view of human limits, thereby undercutting facile op-
timisms, their reception in America—particularly Freud and Weber—
transmuted their message. American Freudianism became focused on ego
psychology and neglected the darker side inherent in Freud's myth of a
death instinct. Weber was filtered through the functionalism of Talcott
Parsons and the "end of ideology" sociologists such as Daniel Bell and Edward Shils. Socialism—with its vivid counter-First Enlightenment symbols
of solidarity, struggle and fraternity—in America represented "the failure
of a dream." We cannot too much emphasize the cultural implications for
America of this failure of the Second Enlightenment, as a corrective on
easy myths of pragmatic progress and scientism, to reach beyond intellectuals and academia. The earlier Enlightenment myths were never effectively challenged in the popular media and culture. In this America differs
from Europe. It is harder, in our context, to speak of the emergence of a
post-bourgeois period.[23]

McWilliams has demonstrated how our seminal public philosophers
from Emerson through John Dewey, Horace Kallen and Walter Lippmann have echoed the individualist biases and substance-less formalities of
the liberal creed. In treating of Dewey's notion of a shared good, McWilliams contends that "the emotion in question is completely separate from
any judgment of the value of the shared good. . . . Anything shared will
satisfy it. And equally, it has no limitations. In other words, Dewey relied
on a potentially universal, morally indifferent 'fraternal instinct' as much
as the liberals of old had done."[24] William Sullivan has argued that more

recent revivals of a public philosophy in the work of Kohlberg, Nozick, Dworkin and Rawls never fully escape, despite their intentions in several cases, the utilitarian, individualistic and contractarian premises of the earlier Enlightenment.[25]

It would take us too far afield to document the various ways in which many of the liberal premises about human good and society have blended with romanticism, social Darwinism, nineteenth century utopian thought, the progressive movement and recent counter-cultural political and religious movements which seem, on the surface, so different from the liberal utilitarian creed.[26] None of these, even the nineteenth century utopian thought or more recent counter-cultural politics during the 1960's, ever really abandoned the essential postulate of eighteenth century political science, i.e., the belief that political problems are best solved by technology and instrumental means rather than by education to virtue, communal self-sacrifice and restrant and a love for the substantively good society.

McWilliams contends, further, that these tenacious liberal premises remain at the core of the various forms of the regnant pluralist school of political science:

> Within the pluralist school, individual theorists differ, but the old themes and premises are clear: a concern for individual liberty based on the belief that man is by nature a private, a-political being; the conviction that politics is the result of scarcity and conflict, and that the logical aim of politics lies in limiting conflict while pursuing the mastery of nature; the doctrine that the "checks and balances" of the competitive process are the best means of pursuing that aim. The "brotherhood of man," however, which was the ultimate goal of liberal planning and contrivance, has shrunk to the softest whisper (which is one of the reasons why the young, especially, see no "meaning" in the process).[27]

Throughout the nineteenth and into the twentieth century, the strange marriage Bellah referred to between the liberal philosophy's ethic of being number one and the biblical ethic of deep concern for care and community was able to work. In part, liberalism could rely on the substance of the religious heritage, which it continued to undermine, to soften its cruelest tenets. In part, religion, customary virtue and the residues of local or emigrant-based community provided fall-back defenses in times of crisis or against the harshest consequences of an ethic of exalted interest, unchecked competition and the erosion of strong symbols of solidarity. In part, it worked because of the unprecedented material wealth of the continent.

Moreover, a strange bargain was struck between liberalism and American religious forces to continue to employ the older religious rhetoric, but with this fundamental distortion of the older religious view—that religion was now prized uniquely for its utility to the common life rather than as a shaper and judge of the quality of political practice and a true good in its own right. Even the churches began to turn, after the Civil War, to an "interest morality" which stressed that righteous living paid off in success and evil-doing leads to material loss. Traditional religion suffered from this marriage of convenience. As McWilliams notes, in respect to the alliance between religion and the progressive movement: "God's city, located just around the corner, loses much of its glory, and fraternity lowered into compassion loses brotherhood; the desire for effectiveness threatens the authority as well as the wisdom of religion."[28]

It is not, of course, the case that the religious tradition of ethics in America has been uniformly beneficial. When it loses its mooring in a transcendent faith or when misinterpreted and twisted to serve selfish interests, religious ideas of community can and have, at various times in our history, fostered violent millennialism, exclusionary nativism, revivalist frenzy and political quietism. Nevertheless, religious ethics "have expressed a wisdom and truth which the Enlightenment did not possess, and they have always provided the emotional and symbolic bases for the appeal to fraternity in American politics as an immediate need rather than a distant goal."[29]

Indeed, the hold which the idea of a greater community based on mutual regard and self-sacrificing love has had on Americans, even continuing into our own times, flies in the face of that truncated vision of humanity and the public order rooted in pursuing self-gain and contractually balancing and negotiating interest which still remains our dominant cultural image and ethics for political life. A wiser truth has kept its hold in America to the extent that it has, and there has been less of what Robert Pranger has called "the eclipse of citizenship," because that truth found a home in the religious sentiments and in the sedimented custom which liberal philosophy has generally ignored, if not despised.[30]

It should by now be apparent why I am arguing here, as I have elsewhere, that the tradition of biblical religion is arguably the most powerful and pervasive symbolic resource for understanding America and for facing a new crisis of limits which forces us to recognize that the old amalgam of an ethic of deep concern and an ethic of looking out for number one will no longer work. In another context I have argued that our tradition of religious ethics seems, on the face of it, to enjoy a more obvious public vigor and availability as a resource for renewal in American culture than either the tradition of classic republican theory or the American tradition of public philosophy.[31] I am here contending that the American cultural tradition of public philosophy does not deserve retrieval without serious attention to its flaws as a vision of human life and community—without, that is, a serious revision of some of its most basic and substantive premises and biases in the light of the Judaeo-Christian ethic.

PUBLIC THEOLOGY AND PUBLIC PHILOSOPHY

In calling for a renewed public role for the symbolic imagery of the Judaeo-Christian ethic of fraternity, mutuality, conscience, human dignity and responsible participation in shaping the goals and choices of society, I am not necessarily arguing for a priority of public theology over public philosophy in all realms. Nor am I denying a perennial need for philosophy as ancillary to theological vision and reflective ethics.

It is my reading of the American record, however, that the strongest American voices for a compassionate just community always appealed in public to religious imagery and sentiments, from Winthrop and Sam Adams, Melville and the Lincoln of the second inaugural address, to Walter Rauschenbusch and Reinhold Niebuhr and Frederick Douglass and Martin Luther King. As McWilliams notes, in respect to these latter black voices: "Black America had far less interest than whites in achieving a 'synthesis' between Christianity and liberal secularism. Its claims could be met best by a victory of the first over the second. In the black churches, there was less talk of the contradictions between the 'real' and the 'ideal,' the 'rational' and matters of 'faith.' Rather there was a clearer understanding that what was involved was a conflict between competing definitions of the real and the rational, a choice between first principles."[32] They knew that you could not really put together an ethic of deep concern for other human beings with an ethic of everybody looking out for number one.

The American religious ethic and rhetoric contain rich, polyvalent symbolic power to command commitments of emotional depth, when compared to "secular" language, especially when the latter is governed by the Enlightenment ideals of conceptual clarity and analytic rigor. Secular Enlightenment language remains exceedingly "thin" as a symbol system. I do not think that, sociologically, a genuine sense of vivid *communitas,* in Victor Turner's sense of the term, is possible on the basis of a non-religious symbol system.[33] Yet, it is just such a renewed commitment to an ethic of solidarity in community that overrides individual interest which seems of paramount necessity in American culture and life today.

I am aware, of course, of the ambiguities in the American religious legacy. Not the least is the corruption of the biblical tradition by individualism and utilitarianism, "so that religion itself finally became for many a means for the maximization of self-interest with no effective link to virtue, charity, or community. A purely private pietism emphasizing only individual rewards that grew up in the nineteenth century and took many forms in the twentieth, from Norman Vincent Peale to Reverend Ike, was the expression of that corruption."[34]

Moreover, the "thicker," more powerfully evocative language of the Bible can become exclusive, divisive in public discourse and overly particularistic. It can rally hearts which share its history and nuances without providing an opening to those who stand as linguistic outsiders to its forms of discourse. This said, however, I do not find the mere "particularism" of the biblical heritage an overwhelming drawback. For I think that pretensions to a universal language and tradition are delusions. Every language is particular. Every language stands within a very particular tradition of interpretation. Every language is caught in the conflict of interpretations. To prefer a speciously "neutral" language of secular humanism to the biblical language seems to me either to be naive about the pretended neutrality and universality of the secular language or to give up on the claims of the Judaeo-Christian heritage to be illuminative of the human situation. I am further strongly convinced that the Enlightenment desire for an unmediated universal fraternity and language (resting as it did on unreflected allegiance to *very particular* communities and language, conditioned by time and culture) was destructive of the lesser, real "fraternities"—in McWilliams' sense—in American life.

Furthermore, when used as a public discourse, the language of biblical religion is beyond the control of any particular denominational theology. It represents a common American cultural patrimony. In that sense, as James Sellers has noted, "the locus of salvation has been displaced in America from its old setting in a specifically religious community and rebuilt upon a new center *that partakes of the religious* but is also public, civil and political in reality."[35] American public theology or religious ethics, then, cannot be purely sectarian. The biblical language belongs to no one church, denomination or sect.

In arguing for a priority for public philosophy over a public theology, Brian Hehir has distinguished between "the need for shaping 'the mind of the Church' (as a community and an institution) regarding social questions from the task of projecting the perspective of the Church into the societal debate about normative questions of social policy."[36] Hehir grants the usefulness of specifically theological argument for the first task but prefers exclusive philosophical language for the second.

My difficulties and disagreements with Hehir's position are several. First, I do not think that public theology as it has functioned in American political and social life is adequately described as "projecting the perspective of the Church into the societal debate about normative questions of social policy." This would be better described by some such phrase as "denominational theology in public." The genius of the public American theology, however, is that it has transcended denominations, been espoused by people as diverse as Abraham Lincoln and Robert Bellah who neither were professional theologians nor belonged to any specific church and, even in the work of specifically trained professional theologians, such as Reinhold Niebuhr, has appealed less to revelational warrant for its authority within public policy discussions than to the ability of biblical insights and symbols to convey a deeper human wisdom. In a strong sense, I would argue that the non-sectarian character of the sponsorship, appeal and style of this American religious mode of public address is precisely what characterizes this form of religious ethics as a *public* theology. Its task, in James

Sellers' sense of a public ethics, is to criticize American manners and morals (the operative, if unreflected, ethic) on the basis of American cultural ideals. Biblical imagery, I would argue, lies at the heart of the American self-understanding. It is neither parochial nor extrinsic.

Nor will it do to restrict ourselves to non-religious resources when addressing the societal debates about normative questions of public policy. This is true not simply because a philosophic ethic is very meager fare, although the latter is important as an issue if we consider that ethics relates as much to common vision and virtue as to carefully weighted arguments about norms, consequences and the relevance of situations. I am not, in fact, particularly interested in seeing that specifically formulated theological *arguments* enter societal debates about policy. I am concerned that these debates be informed by a religious vision and orienting value preference. If, as I have argued, the dominant philosophic tradition in American life presents a seriously flawed vision of human life and community, one that is, in part, a serious contributor to American cultural and spiritual malaise, the mere renewed cultivation of the public philosophy will not be sufficient nor, it would seem, desirable.

Moreover, I am convinced that since there are no purely neutral, universal languages, there is always the danger that a common use of a vocabulary referring to such code words as liberty, justice, human rights, authority, etc. will mean very different things to those who live within the American tradition of religious ethics and those who continue to think in Enlightenment liberal utilitarian categories. The danger remains today, as McWilliams claims it was in the past, that the specifically theological or religious vision will be undermined, betrayed or distorted by an unreflective use of a "common vocabulary" for shared discourse in a pluralistic society which is only, speciously, common. Robert Bellah has signaled this danger in some remarks about the current debates on human rights:

> It has been suggested that basic human needs and rights may provide criteria for evaluating a "New International Economic Order." Such a suggestion is a valuable one. However, "needs" and "rights" are key words in modern ideology. Needs in that context are grounded basically in biological appetites and rights derive essentially from the right of self-preservation as the highest of all rights. Placed in a religious context the terms take on entirely different meanings.
>
> "Needs," in this case, would include not only the individual appetites but the needs for community, meaning and spiritual aspiration. "Rights" would be grounded not merely in self-preservation of the individual but in divine justice, law or dharma.
>
> Above all, the use of "needs" and "rights" in a religious context would involve a critique of how these terms have been used precisely to justify the devotion to the endless accumulation of wealth and power that has done so much to create our prob-

lems. If the poor and powerless of the earth simply wish to join the presently privileged in their quest for wealth and power, the result will only increase the rate of our escalating crises. Only an assertion of needs and rights in the context of a general critique of modern ideology could contribute to the solution of our long-run problems.[37]

The only guarantee we can have that a common vocabulary for ethical discourse is not masking a deep distortion of the Judaeo-Christian heritage would be, of course, for religious ethics, as I am suggesting, to go public.

Complex issues about the relation of philosophy to theology are involved in my discussion with Hehir at this point. Suffice it to say that I do not think that a purely autonomous philosophical ethic is a Judaeo-Christian ideal either in the academy or in public discourse. As every philosophy contains an implicit anthropology and sociology, it contends, at crucial points, with theological visions of the human and social and vice versa. Elements and aspects of a "secular" philosophic view can, of course, be congenial with and correlate with the Judaeo-Christian vision of the human. Moreover, many elements and aspects of a religious ethic can be grounded on a non-religious warrant. Almost always they can be presented in public discussion in ways that do not presume assent to them on the specific premises of a faith grounded in revelation. Without being believing Hindus, many Westerners, after all, find in Gandhi's social thought a superior vision of the human than that of ordinary liberal premises.

With Hehir's second argument for philosophical resources for a public ethics I am in complete agreement. He signals "the need for mediating language that can move between the richness of biblical symbolism or theological affirmation and the empirical density of the complex technical issues that today make up the social question."[38] Hehir's remarks are especially to the point when the public policy discussion involves a choice between alternative means, e.g., competing health care schemes, rather than larger goals of the social enterprise.

Of course, religious ethics has, in fact, generally relied on a correlation with philosophic resources to provide it with modes of argument, analysis and insight. For no religious ethics is self-grounding at the normative as opposed to the value level of ethics. It requires philosophic resources. Both the classic Reformed theology of John Calvin and the American Puritans and traditional Catholic social thought have always assumed the existence of a legitimate appeal to some version of a natural law tradition and some dialogue with a "tradition of reason." It is very important to remember, however, that both were allied with pre-modern, non-utilitarian philosophic understandings of the human and society. Both subsumed the classical republican theory which the Enlightenment rejected. Their "traditions of reason" and natural laws, therefore, have been, at least since the mid-nineteenth century, culturally against the American grain. In that sense, their philosophies were never very publicly common.

At least in classic understandings the faith-vision played a normative role in any dialogue with a "secular" tradition of reason. (It should be noted, of course, that the tradition of reason to which Catholic social thought appealed was culled from pre-modern thought. It is not properly called "secular" or "non-religious." Only with the Enlightenment and the rise of modern ideology can we speak of an anti-religious or a-religious vision. Only it conceives of the world as "secular.") In the classic understanding of theology, the philosophic substratum was always informed, transformed and transmuted by the theological presuppositions and faith vision. This was sometimes absolutely necessary to avoid the contamination of the faith-vision. Indeed, philosophy and philosophical elements were Christianized.

I agree with Hehir that it would be a mistake for Catholic—or any religious—ethics to neglect this correlation with philosophy. It is especially important for the Catholic tradition since a respect for philosophy and the use of philosophic terms play such an important role in the theological arguments. But, again, clearly both Reformed and Catholic social thought have known all along that *agape* alone is not a sufficient principle on which to ground human relations and society. They have always rejected various millennial and perfectionist views of social life. Indeed, this very insight grounds part of their animus against the innocent perfectionism of parts of the liberal Enlightenment thought. The reflected wisdom of American religious ethics has understood that *agape,* in this world, requires the support and takes on some of the limits of both *eros* and *philia.* The hoped for yield from this commingling was a synthesis of love-in-spirit and love-in-the-body.[39]

If I understand Hehir's proposal correctly, he would not allow or, at the least, discourage a public appeal to the Judaeo-Christian or larger religious heritage in societal debates about normative questions of social policy. I would agree if the appeal violated respect for the specifically pluralistic faith-context of American public life or involved a cultural imposition through some form of force or coercion rather than persuasion in common debate and discussion. Moreover, it may be the case that the most important place for theological symbols in public debate is more as an ethical horizon and set of value preferences than in specific and concrete policy discussion.

But I think Hehir is mistaken inasmuch as he seems to neglect a patrimony which is already very much a *public* strand of our cultural heritage. I also suspect that he is more sanguine than I am about the possibility of escaping the "permanent hermeneutical predicament" of particular languages and community traditions in a conflict of interpretive schemes through the emergence of a common, universal language. I fear that his proposal could court the risk of a continuation of the pernicious intertwining of an ethics of deep concern with an ethic of looking out for number one. But finally, and most persuasive for me, I simply do not know anywhere else to look in American culture besides to our religious ethical resources to find the social wisdom and ethical orientation we would seem to need if we are to face as Americans our new context of increasing interdependence at the national and international level. As McWilliams sums up that wisdom, the tradition of religious ethics knows that "the best life is bound up with its limitations, even with its agonies. Dependence is often torture, involving fears of loss, misuse, or betrayal; but men are dependent, and without the strength of others' support are worse than lost. Life is, in the old idiom, a good which is inadequate for man's spirit, one which fraternity helps men love without being enslaved to."[40]

NOTES

1. Robert N. Bellah, "A Night at Camp David," *The San Francisco East Bay Express,* July 27, 1979, p. 4.

2. Wilson Carey McWilliams, *The Idea of Fraternity in America* (Berkeley: University of California Press, 1973).

3. *Ibid.,* p. 526.

4. For some empirical evidence of the erosion of American belief in the social and ethical consequences of traditional religion cf. Charles Y. Glock and Rodney Stark, *Religion and Society in Tension* (Chicago: Rand-McNally and Company, 1965) and Jeffrey Hadden, *The Gathering Storm in the Churches* (Garden City: Doubleday, 1969).

5. McWilliams, p. 96.

6. "Theology and Philosophy in Public: John Courtney Murray's Unfinished Agenda," *Theological Studies,* Vol. 40, No. 4 (December 1979), pp. 701–06.

7. *Ibid.,* p. 705.

8. Two major appeals in the last decade from a base in religious ethics to this earlier tradition of republican theory are James Sellers, *Public Ethics: American Morals and Manners* (New York: Harper and Row, 1970) and Robert N. Bellah, *The Broken Covenant* (New York: Seabury, 1975).

9. For treatments of Puritan covenant thought, cf. McWilliams, *op. cit.,* pp. 112–169; Sheldon Wolin, *Politics and Vision* (Boston: Little, Brown, 1960), pp. 165–194; Perry Miller, *The New England Mind* (2 vols.) (Boston: Beacon, 1961); Michael Walzer, *The Revolution of the Saints* (Cambridge: Harvard University Press, 1965).

10. Alexis de Tocqueville, *Democracy in America* (abridged edition) (New York: New American Library, 1956), p. 46.

11. For an exegesis and discussion of Winthrop's sermon cf. Robert N. Bellah, *The Broken Covenant,* pp. 13–18.

12. Cf. Wolin, *op. cit.,* pp. 195–286.

13. McWilliams, *op. cit.,* p. 557.

14. *Ibid.,* p. 172.

15. *Ibid.,* p. 183.

16. Wolin, *op. cit.,* pp. 286ff, argues that liberalism led inevitably to the eclipse of the properly political and yielded to government by experts in the bureaucratic state.

17. McWilliams, *op. cit.,* p. 97.

18. *Ibid.,* p. 171.

19. For the absence of major conflicts between Enlightenment thought and religion in America as compared to Europe, cf. Henry May, *The Enlightenment in America* (New York: Oxford University Press, 1976).

20. McWilliams, *op. cit.,* pp. 172–73.

21. For the supremacy of Enlightenment thought on American life and institutions, cf. Louis Hartz, *The Liberal Tradition in America* (New York: Harcourt Brace, 1955). Brownson's political thought is set out in *The American Republic* (New York, 1866).

22. I argue that John Courtney Murray did not entirely escape this tendency and that there are some infections of his thought by liberal distortions in "Theology and Philosophy in Public," *loc. cit.,* p. 705.

23. Cf. Seymour Lipset and John Lazlitt, eds., *The Failure of a Dream* (Garden City: Doubleday Anchor, 1974) for the failure of socialism in America. Johannes Metz speaks of a post-bourgeois epoch in his *The Emergent Church* (New York: Crossroad Books, 1981).

24. McWilliams, *op. cit.,* p. 534.

25. William Sullivan, *Reconstructing Public Philosophy* (forthcoming) (Berkeley: University of California Press).

26. Robert Bellah has argued that many of the counter-cultural movements of the 1960's were mirror images of the utilitarian vision; cf. his "New Religious Consciousness and the Crisis of Modernity," in Paul Rabinow and William M. Sullivan, eds., *Interpretive Social Science* (Berkeley: University of California Press, 1979), p. 347.

27. McWilliams, *op. cit.,* p. 558.

28. *Ibid.,* p. 482.

29. *Ibid.,* p. 99.

30. Robert Pranger, *The Eclipse of Citizenship* (New York: Holt, Rinehart and Winston, 1968).

31. "Theology and Philosophy in Public," *loc. cit.,* p. 703.

32. McWilliams, *op. cit.,* p. 581. I expand this point in Chapter 5 of this volume, "Civil Religion and Liberation Theology."

33. Victor Turner, *The Ritual Process* (Chicago: Aldine, 1969). Turner restates Durkheim's classic contention that *communitas* depends upon a shared religious consciousness; cf. Emile Durkheim, *The Elementary Forms of Religious Life* (New York: The Free Press, 1965).

34. Robert Bellah, "New Religious Consciousness and the Crisis of Modernity," p. 344.

35. James Sellers, *Public Ethics,* pp. 227–28.

36. J. Brian Hehir, "Theology and Philosophy in Public," in *loc. cit.,* p. 711.

37. Robert N. Bellah, "Faith Communities Challenge—And Are Challenged By—The Changing World Order," in Joseph Gremillion and William Ryan, eds., *World Faiths and the New World Order* (Washington: The Inter-Religious Peace Colloquium, 1978), pp. 165–66.

38. J. Brian Hehir, *op. cit.,* p. 712.

39. McWilliams criticizes the social thought of Martin Luther King for placing too much weight on an unmediated *agape* as the ground for social community in *op. cit.,* p. 585. But see the following chapter for the positive role of *agape* in social ethics.

40. McWilliams, *op. cit.,* p. 616.

Chapter Ten

Charity and the Nature of American Society

American Catholic social thought in recent years has taken a rather dim view of the primacy of charity. Indeed, the very word "charity" has come to have a decidedly pejorative ring. It smacks of a kind of paternalism—the movement to help those who are weak or needy out of our excess as a work of supererogation. Charity has been trivialized such that it conjures up thoughts of tax deductions or phrases like "I already gave at the office." In this view, charity is voluntary—perhaps optional, even though praiseworthy—rather than of deeply felt obligation. It is largely individualistic, interpersonal in a strictly I-Thou relation, one-on-one, rather than structural.

Against this sickly pale, justice, by contrast, seems virile, vigorous and specific. In its basest forms as caricature, charity has become a vague and waffly word eliciting what the major character in Saul Bellow's novel *Herzog* refers to as "potato sentimentality." Justice, on the other hand, seems capable of providing us with a concrete and practical program. No wonder, therefore, that American Catholic social thought in recent years has followed the lead of wider secular thinking in stressing the primacy of justice over charity and focusing almost exclusively on the just society.

One is taken up short, then, to read the following description as the first meaning of charity in Webster's dictionary: "Christian love, specifically the act of loving men because they are sons of God." Somehow, a noble concept has been terribly debased!

It is not my purpose in this chapter to provide a history of the process by which the classical Catholic view of charity as the first and most formative of the virtues in the personal and social order—the virtue which transfuses and transforms all the others so that they who aim higher than they can reach actually reach higher than they could alone—came to fall into such bad repute. That story can be recounted in a shorthand way by recalling how a degenerated Catholic Counter-Reformation theology separated nature from grace by such an unbridgeable chasm that later Scholastic theologians could no longer make any sense of Aquinas' dictum about grace transforming and fulfilling rather than destroying nature. In the classical Catholic view there was a certain proportion of analogical likeness between the two. Indeed, grace presupposed nature just as charity presupposed justice as a necessary, if not sufficient, condition. On the other hand, in a world of tragic sinfulness, both nature and justice *had need* of transformation by grace and charity respectively. And yet, because nature and grace and justice and charity possessed a certain affinity toward each other, they were never fully strange or foreign to each other. They needed their opposite number as Adam needed Eve to achieve the full stature of humanity and social community.

The false opposition between nature and grace led to a parallel and fundamentally misleading separation of charity and justice. As we saw in the previous chapter this has meant an absence of strong symbols of solidarity and a truncated, utilitarian individualistic view of justice in American public ethics. Moreover, by a strange and illogical inversion, the fact that the ability to love in a Christian way is an unmerited gift bestowed by God was often translated to mean that the exercise of charity toward others, especially the weak or needy, was itself gratuitous, a question of mere benevolence rather than duty. And so the doctrine of the primacy of charity in personal and social life was misread as if a concern for justice or structural reform was purely discretionary, at least secondary, if not unimportant. The result of this corruption of the best tradition was a turn toward a concern for justice in Catholic social thought and a concomitant placing of charity on the back-burners of discussion as if it had little or no relevance for the understanding of the public order or the nature of the good and humane society.

If the striking recent turn toward justice by American Catholic social thought merely redressed the false opposition between charity and justice by reminding us, in the words of Gene Outka, that "charity exceeds but never abrogates what justice requires," it would have meant a simple gain for those concerned with the good society. For justice is the hallmark and prerequisite of any humane society. As Outka trenchantly puts it, "Love has justice as its pre-condition; love can never neglect justice and loving actions are never performed at the expense of justice but only 'beyond and through' it."[1]

Stated in its clearest terms, justice is the order which love absolutely requires as its pre-condition. For charity without regard for the terms of justice invariably degenerates into sentimentality. Love without or against justice is unspecific, vague and dangerous. It provides no criteria except intuitive sentiment for determining with any ethical substance which political movements, programs or persons to support and which to oppose. It gives little guidance about which societal structures are more fair, humane and liberating. Love without justice leads to mushy ethics. The Nazis, after all, were fond of citing the passage from John's Gospel: "Greater love than this no man has, than that he lay down his life for his friends."

It should be clear, then, that charity is never an alternative to continuous involvement in the struggle for a more perfect justice, however rough, in this world. Nor can charity be divorced from movements for

structural reform and, in some instances, revolution in society. Daniel Day
Williams has well stated the connections between charity and structural
reform:

> Since love is the Spirit at work in the community of reconcili-
> ation, the work which love prompts is to be in actual history,
> where the neighbor is met. If, however, the neighbor's life is
> bound up with community, then he can be served only in relation
> to the social structure which shapes his life. Therefore, the secur-
> ing of a social order in which men can be neighbors to one an-
> other is a necessary expression of loving concern.[2]

A deeper understanding of the best tradition would lead us, then, to
lay to rest all views, Catholic or Protestant, which simply oppose charity
and justice to one another. It is my contention, however, that in turning its
attention almost exclusively toward justice as the defining characteristic of
the good society as a corrective to vague or downright misleading appeals
to charity, contemporary American social ethics has seriously impoverished the discussion about and the search for a more humane society. The
balance has been lost. Contemporary society needs once again to take a
long look at charity as a social ideal and its role in American society. For
the truth is dialectic. If charity without justice is impotent, a mockery of
love, justice without charity is harsh, sometimes narrowly calculating and
inhumane. Without a vision of an earthly city informed by charity, justice
all too easily disintegrates into the solitary question of who gets what from
whom under what form of coercive organization and society is seen as the
arena wherein individuals, groups, classes or sections are locked in battle
in cruel Hobbesian terms, *Homo homini lupus,* primarily to vindicate their
own claimed interests and rights.

Justice and charity must not be opposed since they most often overlap
and always correlate. On the one hand, as Outka reminds us, "charity may
require more but never less than justice does." From the other side of the
dialectic, in Paul Tillich's fine and almost medieval Catholic phrase, charity is ecstatic justice since "love *alone* shows what is just in the concrete
situation."[3] This is so because love introduces into the ethical equation nuances about persons, situations and concrete possibilities and also calls for
fitting human responses which, because they extend beyond the range of
obligation, elude a more impersonal calculation of justice. It follows also
from a theory of knowledge in ethics which refuses to separate knowledge
and love such that only the good person, the one who loves the good in
sustained virtue, can even know what justice requires in the concrete situation. In Gerard Manley Hopkins' lovely line, in a profound sense only "the
just man justices." Charity is necessary if justice is to be creative.

But correlation is not the same as simple-minded equation or identification. Charity and justice must be distinguished if we are not to lose clarity of vision about the nature of the good society and meaningful, publicly

defensible, discriminating judgments in ethics. The burden of my complaint in this chapter is about the almost complete eclipse in contemporary discussions of the classic concern for societal charity—what we might call, following Maritain, "civic friendship" in loving community—as part of the definition of the good society, indeed its highest flowering. The absence of attention to charity as a social ideal has debased not only ethical vision or discourse but the very nature of contemporary society. It has also eviscerated justice itself of its deepest meaning, for, following Tillich again, charity gives to justice its dimension of depth. That depth will not be plumbed by a single-minded fixation on justice and, even at that, an often impoverished concept of justice as identical with distributive justice, i.e., who gets what from whom as their due.

The collapse of a creative tension between charity and justice has meant that certain powerful and evocative symbols of the good society have been almost totally disregarded or dismissed as pious frauds because they are not spontaneously elicited by a solitary vision of justice. Recent social ethics and political theology, on the one hand, and public policy discussions, on the other, have registered a noticeable recoil and, indeed, silence about speaking of consensus, reconciliation, community, healing, forgiveness, mercy or a comprehensive ideal of social cooperation based on the organic model of society as a body—politic and civil—somehow seen as the body of Christ in the world. In place of symbols of social charity or civic friendship, discussion has been focused—it is claimed, "more realistically"—on conflict, dependence, domination, struggle, judgment and prophetic protest. Moreover, the symbolic ideal of the good society suggested by charity has come to be viewed as illusory or as an ideological cloak which masks naked self-interest or cruel domination. That charity is sometimes used this way justifies a certain healthy cautionary suspicion of symbols of the loving society to forestall cheap reconciliation, false forgiveness or unjust consensus. On the other hand, if all there is in the social arena is the matched wrestling of competing and selfish interest groups (or, more blatantly, if our cause is naively assumed to be noble and the other's to be debased), there can be no other terms to the debate about the good society besides those dictated by a narrow conception of justice—justice defined as the relatively defensible balance of competing wills and interests.

Johannes B. Metz captures this same sense of an impoverishment in current ethical debate—an impoverishment, it should be noted, that flows from sociological causes and is related to the privatization of religion in our society:

> The bourgeois virtues of stability, competitive struggle, and achievement obscure and overlay the merely believed-in messianic virtues of conversion, selfless and unconditional love for the "least of the brethren," and active compassion—virtues which cannot be practiced within relationships of exchange and barter; virtues for which one gets literally nothing in return, like the love

which does not insist on recompense; virtues like loyalty, gratitude, friendliness and grief. The presence of these virtues is diminishing; at most, they are allocated, under the prevailing division of labor, to the family, which, however, is coming in its turn more and more under the anonymous pressure of the exchange processes permeating society.[4]

A truncated notion of justice will not honor—even recognize—these virtues.

Let me be very clear on one point. Justice remains the unfailing remedy against ideological uses of charity as a social ideal which suppresses the rights in justice of oppressed individuals and groups. But justice itself can be used as an ideological symbol to warrant narrow and selfish purposes. For without mercy and charity's face, justice can easily turn into a harsh, self-seeking, tough and calculating attitude and practice. As Reinhold Niebuhr once put it, "even the most perfectly balanced system of justice in history is a balance of competing wills and interests and must therefore worst those who do not participate in the balance,"[5] because they lack either numbers or resources to organize as an effective interest group in a justice-game called "getting one's rightful piece of the pie!"

Classic Catholic social thought certainly gave its due—most Reformation theologians always claimed that it was more than its due—to the order of justice. Whatever the weight and burden of collective sin and self-blinding egoism, social Catholicism argued that the human spirit could still at least glimpse essential truth and justice in history. Neither human nature nor society is inherently depraved or totally infected by sin. Indeed, even in the midst of a sinful and tragic history, Catholic social thought sustains a cautious optimism. At root and on balance, the human person and society are more good than evil, although always a precarious balance of both. In fact, even fallen nature and Niebuhr's "rough justice" still remain oriented by a profound existential thirst toward a reality greater than themselves. Emmanuel Mounier captures this Catholic sense of both the integrity and autonomy of justice and its essential orientation beyond itself in charity in a splendid aphorism in his book *Personalism:* "Justice aims higher than it can reach."[5]

On the other hand, Catholic social thought tried to give to sin its proper weight in the ethical question. Its stance toward the possibilities of a human life or society embodied what Mounier calls "a tragic optimism." It maintained that without grace, without, that is, sacrificial and self-spending love, even just social conditions tend to degenerate into something less than themselves. Catholics opposed, in hard-headed realism, romantic notions about a whole new species of humanity emerging in history or society whether this new species was claimed for the French or Russian Revolution or, more recently, China, Cuba and Tanzania. Yet, they never despaired of the human project or the possibility of attaining some new creative possibilities in history. To ground this trust, they turned

to the power of charity and the hope in the emergence of ethical heroes—
we used to call them saints—whose lives might model new creative possibilities to the dreary equations of rough political justice and the balance of
power. Ever ethical democrats, Catholic social thinkers held that charity
could elicit a kind of everyday heroism—we used to call it virtue—in the
lives of ordinary Christians which could make a difference to society by
opposing that drift toward disintegration and chaos—what the French
moralist Pascal calls the lure toward dissipation and the Catholic theological tradition called concupiscence—that seems to characterize human lives
and societies. Finally, social Catholicism's varied efforts at achieving a society of Christian inspiration, to use Maritain's phrase, all point to a second aphorism about the good society amidst the reality of sin: Justice
needs charity over the long pull even to be itself.

The vision of a just society infused by charity is not without its secular
analogues. Emile Durkheim, who once said that justice was the only cement which could hold together modern society and instill into it a common conscience and unity, harkens back to the more classic notion of
charity in his book *The Division of Labor in Society:*

> It is customary to distinguish justice from charity: that is, simple
> respect for the rights of another from every act which goes be-
> yond this purely negative virtue. We see in the two sorts of activ-
> ity two independent layers of morality: justice, in itself, would
> only consist of fundamental postulates; charity would be the per-
> fection of justice. The distinction is so radical that, according to
> partisans of a certain type of morality, justice alone would serve
> to make the functioning of social life good; generous self-denial
> would be a private virtue worthy of pursuit by a particular indi-
> vidual but dispensable to society. Many even look askance at its
> intrusion into public life. . . . In reality, for men to recognize and
> mutually guarantee rights, they must, first of all, love one an-
> other; they must, for some reason, depend upon each other and
> on the same society of which they are a part. Justice is full of
> charity, or, to employ our expressions, negative solidarity is only
> an emanation from some other solidarity whose nature is posi-
> tive.[7]

The profound sense of a just society informed by charity strikes me as
essentially identical with the biblical notion of justice where the words we
would translate as justice (*sedek* in Hebrew and *dikaiosyne* in New Testament *koine* Greek) imply a kind of faithfulness in love to God and each
other in community which is itself a gift of God. Biblical justice is modeled
on Yahweh's justice which transcends ours because his justice is so much
more than "justice as fairness" since it includes merciful forgiveness, special compassion for the outcast even beyond the call of obligation as well
as fair and equal regard for all. Justice in the Bible always includes some-

thing profoundly more than distributive, retributive or commutative justice. As applied to us, biblical justice is a human justice informed by loving kindness which stands ready to give to others what is their due as the image of God and to regard others in the light we attribute to God's regard for them.

Andrew Greeley in his book *The Communal Catholic* asserts that the most important issues on the agenda of American culture and society today are precisely the value issues of the nature of the human person and society. He goes on to lament the flabbiness of American Catholic thought in recognizing its unique opportunity to take part in this serious deliberation and to address these value questions with intellectual rigor and honesty.[8]

The burden of my concluding remarks is essentially simple. Catholic social thought has turned quite properly in recent years to concern for justice and structural reform. It has taken other people's definitions of justice as its own as it joined other men and women of good will in the struggle for a more just society and world order. Justice has helped to provide us with a program of some ethical rigor. In this sense, we have let, as we should, the world write our agenda of justice, since there is no uniquely peculiar Catholic or Christian conception of justice as such. We will be bankrupt, however, in the dialogue about the good society if we let the world provide our horizon or perspective on justice as well. For charity is related to justice as transforming and illuminative symbols (what some theologians call eschatology) are related to ethics. An insistence on justice as a characteristic note of the good society will tend to force us to careful and definable programs of social action against vague appeals to love and community.

On the other hand, in those situations where interests are being pressed insistently in a locked struggle for justice, self-sacrificing charity can act as a restraint—perhaps an indispensable restraint if justice is not to degenerate into inordinate self-seeking. "Achieving one's due" all too easily slips into the cruel and naked "getting one's own." Again, justice can define for us the indispensable minimum for a tolerable society. Charity can remind us that much more than justice is needed for that society we would ever call humane. For charity warrants sacrifice, if need be, where the self's interests are at stake (obviously we cannot decree sacrifices for others!) in ways which justice does not. It is true that charity as a kind of eschatological symbol of the good society does not provide us with a definable program or give us additional information about the concrete shape of just laws, acts and structures. It supplies instead an attitude, a perspective, a horizon which is both corrective and fulfilling of justice, although, as Outka reminds us, always "through and beyond" it.

It is time that the Christian perspective of charity, taken in its largest societal sense and not just in terms of voluntary efforts to help the needy, be placed squarely on the docket for discussion about the nature of American society. American society will be poorer if it is not. Moreover, this perspective of charity could make a profound difference in helping us to delineate the kind of society we thirst to live in. I conclude with a quote from Jacques Maritain's *Christianity and Democracy* which suggests what that difference might be:

> Not only is there civic friendship, as the ancient philosophers knew it, i.e., the soul and the constitutive link of the social community (for, if justice is first of all an essential requirement, it is as a necessary condition that makes friendship possible), but this very friendship between citizens cannot prevail in actual fact within the social group unless a stronger and more universal love, brotherly love, is instilled in it, and civic friendship, itself becoming brotherhood, overflows the bounds of the social group to extend to the entire human race. Once the heart of man has felt the freshness of that terrible hope, it is troubled for all time. If it fails to recognize its supra-human origins and exigencies, this hope risks becoming perverted and changing into violence to impose upon all "brotherhood or death."
>
> [But if secular society is infused by Christian love] what has been gained for the secular conscience, if it does not veer to barbarism, is faith in the brotherhood of man, a sense of the social duty of compassion for mankind in the person of the weak and the suffering, the conviction that the political task par excellence is to render common life better and more brotherly, and to work to make the structure of laws, institutions and customs of this common life a house for brothers to live in.[9]

Making a "fundamental option for the poor," central to any strategic *Christian* theology, will take us beyond the categories of justice to those of solidarity, community in suffering and *agape.* American social ethics, as I argued in the previous chapter, needs this addition.

NOTES

1. Gene Outka, *Agape: An Ethical Analysis* (New Haven: Yale University Press, 1972), p. 81.
2. Daniel Day Williams, *The Spirit and the Forms of Love* (New York: Harper and Row, 1968), p. 249.
3. Paul Tillich, *Love, Power and Justice* (New York: Oxford University Press, 1954), p. 80.
4. Johannes B. Metz, *The Emergent Church* (New York: Crossroad Books, 1981), p. 6.
5. Reinhold Niebuhr, *Moral Man and Immoral Society* (New York: Charles Scribner's Sons, 1960), p. 78.

6. Emmanuel Mounier, *Personalism* (London: Routledge and Kegan Paul, 1950), p. 31.

7. Emile Durkheim, *The Division of Labor in Society* (New York: The Free Press, 1964), p. 227.

8. Cf. Andrew Greeley, *The Communal Catholic* (New York: Seabury, 1976).

9. Jacques Maritain, *Christianity and Democracy* (New York: Charles Scribner's Sons, 1944), pp. 50–51.

Chapter Eleven

Religious Liberty in America and Mediating Structures

John C. Bennett has claimed that "there is no one Protestant doctrine concerning Church-state relations."[1] The best single historical-theological survey of varying Protestant theologies of Church and state distinguishes five sharply divergent ideal-typical sets of doctrine. These range from the classic Lutheran two kingdom concept with its stern, perhaps unbridgeable, division between law and Gospel through the Anabaptist disdain toward the state as an agency at best sub-Christian or the Quaker perfectionist expectations for a pacifist liberal state to the strict separationists for whom the guiding metaphor is "the wall" as opposed to the transformationists who argue that "God has an intention for society as well as the Church which the churches must mediate and make effective."[2]

A rounded theology of Church-state relations would demand close attention to a series of questions such as: (1) What is the nature of the Church or the religious people? Is it a purely voluntary association of persons united for religious purposes or does it represent an institution ordained by God? Who speaks for the Church on public issues and what authority and style is appropriate to this address?[3] (2) What is the nature of the state? To what degree is it the result of sin, to what degree ordained by God? Are there permanent or accidental aspects of the state (war-making, coercion, office-holding, oath-taking) inconsistent with Judaism or Christianity? How does the Church handle such religious conflict? To what extent can the state be perfected to serve the purposes of the kingdom of God? What is the relationship between society and the state? (3) To what degree must the Church or people be independent of the state? Is there a gradation in forms of Church-state relationship, some more in accord with Jewish or Christian concerns than others? (4) Does the independence of Church and state deny all relationship between the two? Is God sovereign over both? If so, in what forms does the sovereignty of God over the state manifest itself? (5) What obligations toward the state have the Church and Christians and Jews as citizens with dual loyalties? To what extent should the Church support the aims of government? Is patriotism a Judaeo-Christian virtue? (6) With what means and under what conditions may Christians or Jews oppose a tyrannical or unjust government? What obligations, if any, does the state or society have toward the churches and the care of religion? Under what circumstances can a state restrain claims to religious freedom? Can the Church legitimately demand concessions from the state? Under what circumstances can the Church try to influence the state? (7) How virtuous can a government be? How does Christianity or Judaism enhance this virtue? What is the role of order, peace, justice, welfare and the care for societal freedom in God's intentions? (8) What is the theological ground for asserting religious liberty or defending the non-establishment clause of the First Amendment of the U.S. constitution?[4]

Thomas Sanders contends that very few of these questions have attracted the sustained attention of Protestant-wide bodies with the exception of religious liberty, the nature of the Church and the religious base for social and political responsibility. He also claims that "the most minimal objective studies now taking place in the denominations reveal the obvious, that Protestants have functioned in this key area through misinformed anti-Catholicism and *legal* rather than *religious* norms."[5]

As this thorny thicket of theological, ethical, political and juridical issues involved in Church-state thinking might suggest, one would not normally expect to find a definitive Protestant, Catholic, Jewish or secularist position on Church-state.[6] The very complexity of the issues and the wide range of questions connected with determining a coherent Church-state position lend themselves to plural outcomes. As the range of questions makes clear, it is difficult to conceive of separation as an *absolute* category.

It is clear, at any rate, that there is still no *one* Catholic position on all aspects of Church-state. Writing at the time of the Vatican Council II debates on the Declaration on Religious Liberty *(Dignitatis Humanae),* John Courtney Murray could distinguish five positions in the Council aula.[7] One was the older Catholic view that error had no rights, that only the one who is in the truth, therefore only a Catholic, has an intrinsic and natural right to religious freedom. Moreover, this stance claimed for the Church a pre-eminent juridical position in civil societies as something demanded by theology and reason. As the vote on the Declaration at the council showed, this position was held by a decided, even miniscule, minority. And yet, as Msgr. Pietro Pavan—who with Murray was the principal architect and draftsman of *Dignitatis Humanae*—has argued, this understanding has emerged again in some sections of the post-conciliar Church.[8] It lacks, however, articulate spokesmen or suasive argument.

Among those who supported a declaration on religious freedom at the council, some pleaded for a merely practical document, a declaration of pastoral policy rather than a statement of theological principle. They were countered by the argument that this might seem to be the work of opportunists, a dubious—you will excuse my embarrassment at the consecrated term—jesuitical act of mental reservation. Still others wanted to ground the declaration upon the indubitable Catholic principle of the freedom of conscience. Proponents of the final declaration argued that this tack would not eventuate in a rationally justified stance in favor of religious expression in the public order. The subjective rights of conscience could still be countered by objective claims to truth.

The final two, still seriously competing, Catholic theological positions on religious liberty are Murray's, and they carried the day at the council by contending that the case for religious liberty should rest on a complex religio-political-moral-juridical structure of argument which appealed simultaneously to the exigencies of human dignity and the learning experiences of history. Murray demanded that the document include a statement about the juridical need to enshrine religious liberty as a *civil* right in a constitutional government of limited powers. A second position, largely that of French theologians, tried to radicate religious freedom *entirely* on theological grounds. This understanding runs the risk of triumphalism and the patently false assertion that religious liberty is primarily a Christian invention. As George Linbeck has remarked about similar Protestant moves to substantiate religious liberty purely on particularist Christian theological premises, there is no way one can show, on these grounds alone, why reasonable persons who are not Christian should grant religious liberty to all.[9] Moreover, a purely theological argument for religious liberty does not lend itself to civil discussion in a broader secular context.

There has been very little Roman Catholic theological writing or discussion on religious liberty or separation of Church and state since the adoption of *Dignitatis Humanae* and Murray's death, although there has been some new thought in the area of understanding the constitutional provisions of the First Amendment and on policy related to American governmental aid to religiously sponsored activities such as schools or welfare organizations. In part this paucity of discussion is attributable to a prevailing sense that Murray's position has carried the day. The problem is solved and the question closed. In part it reflects the fact that in Catholic thought the more limited constitutional issue of Church-state separation is subordinated to broader questions of Church-society relationships, the proper mission of the Church to modern society and what "the signs of the times" tell the Church about its role and appropriate evangelical style of ministry. These issues are raised in the council document *Gaudium et Spes* and since the council by political theology in Europe and liberation theology in Latin America.[10]

Murray saw *Dignitatis Humanae* as the forerunner of *Gaudium et Spes*. Religious liberty set the Church free to pursue social ministry in modern society. As he noted, *"Gaudium et Spes* is clear that the Church's ministry is religious, not political in nature; yet the animating religious vision of the Gospel has substantial political potential."[11] The general thrust of post-conciliar Catholic thought has been to fight vigorously against narrow "churchy" conceptions of the religious task and the pervasive privatization of religion. Thus, for example, the 1971 Synod of World Bishops could assert, "Action on behalf of justice and participation in the transformation of the world fully appear to us as *a constitutive dimension of the preaching of the Gospel,* or, in other words, of the Church's mission for the redemption of the human race and its liberation from every oppressive situation."[12] This position contains a strong animus against any attempts to segregate the Church from participation in the formulation of the moral aspects of political questions or relegate it to the sacristy. It places social service and social action, even that directed toward non-Catholics and non-believers, on an equal *religious* footing with preaching the Gospel and pastoral care for the people of the Church. We find in it a twentieth-century Catholic version of the earlier Calvinist keen sense of a worldly-calling. It is appropriate to note that this self-understanding of the Church spills over to the claims the Church makes for that freedom of the Church in the public order the Church seeks as necessary to fulfill its proper mission. Such a self-understanding will chafe at narrowly construed definitions of the public scope for the Church in some interpretations of Church-state separation.

Despite the fact that the issue of the role and style of Church response to the problems of modern society or to issues of liberation and development in the third world, rather than the narrower questions of religious liberty or Church-state separation, is the dominant issue in Catholic theological social thought since the council, it remains true, as James Rausch contends, that "the nature of the Church-state relationship in a given political culture directly and significantly shapes the field within which the Church can exercise prophetic witness in society" such that "the classical issue of Church-state is an essential factor in determining how the contemporary issue of Church-society takes concrete historical shape."[13] The key issue here, it seems to me, is the extent to which an understanding of the separation of Church and state promotes or restricts the Church's role as a mediating structure in society. What scope, beyond worship and catechesis, is allowed to the Church for action in education, welfare, health, the media and the world of work and economics? The strategy and style for Church influence upon the tenor of culture and societal life has changed dramatically in the post-Vatican II era with the Church's adoption of a new posture of dialogue and pluralist participation. There is no evidence, however, that its ambitions toward influencing the morality and quality of public life have in any way diminished.

In our American context, new questions about Church-state separation related to abortion laws, indirect aid to religious schools through vouchers and the threat by the IRS to determine what constitutes "authentically religious" action not only raise anew legal or constitutional questions about the interpretation of the First Amendment but demand some clarity on the range of theological and ethical presuppositions of that amendment in a pluralistic society.

It is as true today, as it was two decades ago, that one has to draw from the well of the works of Murray, Jacques Maritain, Yves Simon and H. A. Rommen to articulate the Catholic case for disestablishment, religious liberty, the nature of the state and its distinction from society, and subsidiarity.[14] There have been no recent Catholic theoretical breakthroughs on these issues. However, with the adoption of *Dignitatis Humanae*, the theses of these writers came into ascendancy in Catholic theology.[15] Theirs is, indisputably, the reigning paradigm among Catholic intellectuals and theologians.

I am going to draw upon the work of these authors, especially Murray, to rehearse briefly in this chapter the dominant theological-ethical-juridical case for religious liberty, separation of Church and state and subsidiarity. I will note throughout how this case depends simultaneously on theological underpinnings and a secular warrant. Much of the Catholic brief for religious liberty is well known. I want to highlight, however, a little noted aspect of the brief, namely the way Murray's structuring of the argument is dependent on a strong corollary case for mediating structures. At crucial points, Murray's argument for religious liberty subsumes a case for subsidiarity as the critical middle term of argument. It will be my contention that the freedom of the Church flourishes best in societies with a vigorous structure of mediating associations. Moreover, in totalitarian societies, those churches with their own network of mediating structures are best able to withstand the state and assert effective freedom of the Church. I will add my voice at various points to the policy debate on the role of mediating structures raised by Berger and Neuhaus' *To Empower People* and Dean Kelley's "Confronting the Danger of the Moment."[16]

THE IMPORT OF SECULAR WARRANT IN THEOLOGICAL ARGUMENT

It would be a mistake to see the "Catholic" case as an exclusive Catholic preserve. Of course, more than it has pretended in the past with its claims to speak for the "natural law," the Catholic way of structuring the argument on Church-state relations is often infected with particularist theological bias. It is eminently clear that not all persons of intelligence and good will see the same secular truths that Catholics claim as self-evident.

Catholic theories of the state have always relied upon reason—what the tradition called natural law but I prefer to call "secular warrant"—as well as revelation. Protestant, Jewish and secularist disclaimers from the theory of natural law, basically three critiques, are well known. First, it is argued, largely by Protestants, that the Catholic appeal to "secular warrant" is not justified theologically because of the pervasiveness of sin which both distorts human desires and reason. Only a basic certainty given in revelation, Protestants argue, can overcome the distortions of reason by sin. Second, not all persons of intelligence and good will in fact agree upon the neutral secular warrants alleged as integral to the Catholic case. Finally, the substantive norms and principles developed by Catholic social thought often reflect the social and cultural conditions of the medieval period in which the theory developed.[17]

It would take us too far afield to entertain extensive discussion about renewed Catholic understandings of the usage of secular warrant in the theological argument. In a summary way, I merely want to allude to three theological shifts in recent Catholic theology which have tried to meet the three objections to natural law head-on. The importance of raising the issue is that critical elements of the Catholic position on Church-state rest on secular warrant. The first shift is an explicitly theological understanding of the "natural" or "secular" as transformed in grace. As the Protestant ethicist James Gustafson states this new theological understanding of nature, "Persons know grace who do not know grace *as* grace; those who are acting in conformity with their true natures are acting in grace. Those who act morally are Christian; they are not to be thought of only as autonomous rational beings governing their conduct in accord with principles derived from the moral order of 'nature' (in the sense of something distinguished from grace). Though anonymously so, they are Christian. Those who act morally are not only preserving the created moral order in the face of threats to it; they are participating in the order of redemption."[18] As Gustafson further notes, this is a new Christian theological warrant for the possibility and necessity of dialogue between Christians, non-Christians and non-believers. Its appeal is not so much to a putative residual order of autonomous "nature" untouched by sin (objectionable to classic Reformation thought as a species of Pelagianism) as to the universal ontological transformation of all persons by grace, whether they are Christian or not, whether they are conscious of the transformation or not. This understanding of natural law and the secular agrees fully with the classical Protestant insistence on the absolute necessity of the grace of Christ to overcome the pervasiveness of sin. It assumes, however, that the grace of Christ is available even to those who do not consciously accept the Christian revelation. The sacred claims for Christian grace are extended to include at least some secular experiences and warrants. The Reformation theologians asserted that all was either grace or sin. Catholics agree. Yet some grace is not consciously known as such. My purpose in dredging up this intermural Christian theological discussion is to show the possibility, on these grounds, for Christians to seek non-particularist warrants for their moral stances. They can base parts of their theological reasoning not only on special revelation but on a general revelation available to all. Their appeal, in short, is also based on secular warrant.

The second shift is the growing assumption that only when the claimed secular warrants in Catholic moral and social theory in fact gain a wide ecumenical consensus among other Christian groups, Jews and secularists is there any clear indication, even for Catholics, that the alleged secular warrants are not unique conclusions surreptitiously derived from the Catholic tradition. This is not per se a consensual view of truth or an argument that rests on majority vote. Many will continue to disagree with claims made by Catholics on secular warrant. The point is that if all or most non-Catholics disagree with a Catholic claim on secular warrant, Catholic assumptions about its general availability to persons of intelligence and good will must become suspect, even to Catholics. I take it that this was the purport of Murray's persistent appeal to "the public consensus" as a code word for determining in concrete historical circumstances what Catholics traditionally referred to as "natural law."

The third shift is a new Catholic insistence upon seeing natural law as a dynamic process, a reality capable of evolution, advance and regress, moderation and dramatic restatement under the impact of new historical circumstances. A new and strong sense of historical consciousness no longer allows the social structure of the medieval period to function for Catholics as an a-historical ideal.

Elements of the Catholic argument for disestablishment, religious liberty and subsidiarity cross-cut other theological and secular positions. The Catholic understandings of the nature and mission of the Church are very close to those Protestant positions Sanders calls transformationist. In general, Calvinist theories of Church-state will be closer than other Protestant options to Thomistic Catholic positions. In particular, I find John C. Bennett and John Courtney Murray in agreement on almost every substantive ethical and theological warrant for Church-state relations.[19]

As regards governmental competence in religion, Catholics may be closest to the strict separationists. The following words are those of the early Baptist, Thomas Helwys. Although they assert an individualist notion of religion mostly foreign to Catholics—what Baptists call "soul competency"—they conclude in terms which parallel Murray's assertions, on other grounds, of governmental incompetence to adjudicate in religious matters. "For men's religion to God is betwixt God and themselves: the king shall not anser for it, neither may the king judg betwene God and man. Let them be heretikes, Turcks, Jewes, or whatsoever, it apperteynes not to the earthly power to punish them in the least measure."[20]

The genius of Murray's theological argument, it seems to me, lies in his ability to appeal, simultaneously, to both a theological source and a correlative secular warrant. Particularist theological symbols anchor Christian or Jewish policy statements on human rights, religious liberty and the state firmly in the particularist identity of the respective traditions. They serve to motivate believers in their political orientations and public moral stances. They affirm the ways in which faith has public policy implications. In this way believers are moved to engage in what Martin Marty calls public theology. They must articulate the public policy implications of their particularist symbols. On the other hand, the secular warrant has a validity independent of its connection with a particularist Catholic, Protestant or Jewish theological symbol. The secular warrant opens up possibilities of dialogue with others who do not share the faith vision connected with it. Thus, public theology becomes truly public when it becomes also civil discourse.[21]

A THEOLOGICAL UNDERSTANDING
OF THE FIRST AMENDMENT

Just as there are two separable parts of the First Amendment provisions on religion—the no-establishment and free exercise clauses—so the Catholic case for the two First Amendment provisions rests on two very different kinds of arguments.

Disestablishment

Murray contended that no *theological* brief could be mounted either to vindicate or reject the non-establishment clause. That part of the First Amendment was good law, suited to the circumstances of the American situation and the temperament of the people. It had rightly proven itself through testing in a long historical experience to be useful to the people, the American state and the churches. It serves as the first of our national prejudices, as, in another context, Edmund Burke insisted that establishment was the first of English prejudices.

In the American case, the no-establishment clause is best seen as an article of peace rather than an article of faith. The First Amendment does not assert or imply a particular sectarian or secularist concept of the Church or say anything about the ontological nature of truth and freedom or the manner in which the spiritual order of man's life is to be organized or not organized. For if any particular sectarian theses enter into the content or implications of the First Amendment, "the very article that bars any establishment would somehow establish one."[22]

If American Catholics in unbroken succession since the beginning of the Republic have insisted—almost in dreary monotony—on their support of the First Amendment, it is because they stand in what Winthrop Hudson calls "The Great Tradition of the American Churches."[23] As Hudson argues, the voluntary Church in America has given birth to numerous voluntary societies active in the public interest. These, in turn, spawned secular voluntarism. The Church best flourishes as a free Church in an ambience where such voluntarism is strong. As de Tocqueville early noted, such voluntarism *in the public sector* of the national life early set a characteristic stamp of vitality, creativity and pluralism on American public affairs. The Church is strongest both as a Church and as a mediating structure in a climate where other, non-Church, mediating structures also thrive. Public recognition for and the public impact and power of Church voluntarism stand and fall with them. The briefest inspection of the comparative position of churches in Brazil, Malawi or South Korea where the churches are struggling valiantly to assert the freedom of the Church will substantiate my point.

Moreover, as my former colleague Brian Smith argues, it is precisely those churches with a strong infrastructure of Church-sponsored mediating organizations that possess the greatest capability of withstanding state tyranny by asserting the claims of religious liberty.[24] They contain the space for free discussion and corporate planning. They also generate motivation in a large clientele. Comparative evidence to validate this contention could be drawn from the examples of Poland vs. Czechoslovakia and Cuba and Uruguay vs. Chile and Brazil. As I will show further on, there is a logical link in the argument for religious liberty and the case for mediating structures. They are also clearly linked empirically. On the basis of the felicitious connection between Church-voluntarism and the hitherto voluntary character of American society which has been the fruit of the no-establishment clause, it deserves to be the first of our American prejudices.

With a tutored sense for historical and constitutional variation, however, Murray could discover no theological warrant to oppose the very notion of establishment in other countries or historical contexts. So long as there is no confusion of the religious and the political, no infringement of the freedom of the Church or the freedom of personal conscience to express itself in the private and public arena, so long, further, as the orderly relation between Church and state does not result in the alienation of the people from the Church, a case for a kind of establishment might, in principle, be made. The clincher for this contention of Murray's is his assertion that it is nonsense to speak of an a-historical constitutional idea. Murray preferred Aristotle's *The Politics* to Plato's *The Laws*. The litmus test for constitutions and juridical systems is their usefulness, their suitability to the mores, history and peculiar circumstances of a people.

No kind of establishment makes any sense in the American circumstance. Elsewhere, an establishment such as one finds in England or Sweden or a "multiple establishment" which it is sometimes alleged—mistakenly I think—characterizes The Netherlands might be defensible.[25] Under no circumstances, Murray alleges, can "an argument be made today that would validate the legal institution of religious intolerance."[26]

Murray never contended that America's disestablishment should serve as the constitutional ideal of other countries. The concept of one constitutional ideal valid cross-nationally is a contradiction in terms. But if America is not a constitutional ideal for Catholics, neither is Colombia nor was Franco's Spain. As John Murray Cuddihy has stated it, in his dealing with the issues of the First Amendment, "civil religion was knocking at the door. Murray refused to open it."[27] Instead, he opted for the conditions of civility, an interpretation of the no-establishment clause as an article of peace. The First Amendment clauses are a statement of policy. They are not deontological principles which represent moral absolutes. Moreover, they are not self-interpreting. Various interpretations of them clash in law. None is established as doctrine. Catholics give to these articles of law absolutely no *religious* assent. They obey, support and uphold them on *moral* grounds, because they are good law. Catholic "commitment is limited in the sense that it is not to the truth and sanctity of a dogma but only to the rationality and goodness of a law." For Murray, "this is all that need be shown; it is likewise all that can be shown."[28]

"The Constitution," Murray insisted, "is not a theological but a political document, defining the concept of the state, not of a Church."[29] The concept of the state defined by the no-establishment clause is that of a limited constitutional state which acknowledges its own incompetency to judge in areas spiritual or religious. The clause is simply silent about the competencies of the Church. The state's proper competency is the temporal common good, the arena of peace, public order, the public welfare, distributive justice and the protection and enhancement of the people's freedoms.

The only circumstances under which the state might act to restrict claims to public religious expression is on its warrant as a guardian of the temporal common good when religious expression represents a serious, clear and present danger to public order and peace. Murray was stringent in placing conditions on any state intervention in religious matters touching the public order: the violation must be really serious; state intervention must be really necessary and a sort of last resort; regard must be had for the privileged character of religious freedom; the rule of jurisprudence of a free society must be stringently followed.[30] As an article of peace, the First Amendment permits state intervention in areas touching religion only when the public peace urgently commands it. The presumption always lies against such intervention until sufficient proof warrants the contrary. For, in Elizabeth I's exquisite phrase, "No government may make windows to men's souls." As Murray put it, "The public powers are not competent to make theological judgments. . . . The public powers are not competent to inquire into the norms whereby conscience is formed and to judge their truth or falsity."[31]

A major element in Murray's historical reconstruction of Catholic Church-state doctrine depended on his historical judgment that the American disestablishment differed radically from the European secularist or laicist state condemned by the Popes where separation of Church and state represented state claims that religious authority depended on the good graces of the state. In France, Germany, Mexico and elsewhere serious efforts were undertaken to restrict religious activity to the sanctuary and the sacristy. Significantly, the Church's capability of generating its own mediating structures—schools, hospitals, charity organizations—was severely curtailed. In the American case, Murray claimed, "it is contrary to the American tradition to view separation of Church and state as a categorical absolute, to be rigidly enforced, no matter what may be the effects on free exercise of religion. [For] the whole intent of the First Amendment was to protect, not to injure, the interests of religion in American society."[32] The two clauses of the First Amendment exist in dialectical tension. They comment on each other.

Murray could feel secure in his interpretation of the First Amendment because it is widely shared by non-Catholics. Thus, John Bennett asserts that "our nation or state is not in principle secular or even neutral as between religion and the rejection of it."[33] In his characteristic wisdom,

Bennett goes on to assert that "we have to weigh the negative religious freedom of a small minority over against the positive religious freedom of the vast majority. In doing so, we should protect this negative religious freedom to the extent that it involves freedom to express opposition to religion. We should not, in protecting it, deny to most people opportunities for positive religious expression in the context of their national life."[34] The Quaker, Wilmer Cooper, concurs: "It was certainly not the intention of our founding fathers, who made provisions for the separation of Church and state in our Constitution, to divorce religion from politics. What they were concerned about was that there should be no particular establishment of religion or preferential treatment of one religion as opposed to another, but this is not to say that religion should have no influence upon government and political decisions."[35]

Finally, the Supreme Court itself had declared, "The First Amendment . . . does not say that in every and all respects there shall be a separation of Church and state . . . otherwise, the state and religion would be aliens to each other—hostile, suspicious, and even unfriendly. . . . We are a religious people, whose institutions presuppose a Supreme Being."

The unrestricted moral consent of American Catholics to the First Amendment flows from this kind of interpretation. America differed from the laicist France of the Third Republic precisely because, as John Bennett states it, "the American system of Church-state separation was not the result of hostility to Christianity or of the desire to put the churches at a disadvantage."[36] Indeed, the First Amendment, in this view, constitutes a species of governmental care for religion. America represents the classic example of governmental care for religion by its scrupulous care for the freedom of religion. This care for the freedom of religion is precisely what Catholic theology demands of the state. As *Dignitatis Humanae* puts it, "In turn, where the principle of religious freedom is not only proclaimed in words or simply incorporated in law but also given sincere and practical · application, there the Church succeeds in achieving a stable situation of right as well as of fact and the independence which is necessary for the fulfillment of her divine mission. This independence is precisely what the authorities of the Church claim in society."[37]

Because the Catholic case for American disestablishment is moral rather than religious, an adherence to good law instead of to religious dogma, American Catholics contend that they enjoy the right, no less than others, to press for the adoption of disputed interpretations of the First Amendment as yet unresolved in the courts. They do not feel bound to obey, in advance, interpretations of the First Amendment which are not yet law. Their case for religious freedom rests on religious as well as legal norms.

Thus, Catholics champion the so-called Kurland rule that it is not unconstitutional if a law having proper secular objectives incidentally benefits religion. They do so because this rule strikes them as sane public policy. They do so because only something like this rule protects their claim on theological grounds for the effective freedom of the Church. Of course, they also support it because it is in their self-interest. Unless something like the Kurland rule obtains, the First Amendment becomes a serious penalty for religion and puts religious activity in an unfair competitive position vis-à-vis secularism. For, if the state effectively stakes out a monopoly in the public sector, this carries the danger of totalitarian democracy. Or if the state subsidizes only non-religious voluntary organizations to the exclusion of auxiliary groups of the churches, the state is exercising a preferential establishment of a kind of religious position.

In effect, the social situation which relegates religious activity more and more to the sanctuary could only be acceptable to those who follow Dean Kelley in drawing sharp distinctions between religious meaning and social service, education and public activity. For many religious believers this sharp distinction betrays the very caritative mission of the Church, its call to combat and transform sinful social structures as part of its obedient hearing of the word of God. For many, the effective absence of religious voice from key areas of the public sector is a kind of false statement about the role and function of religion in society. It is important to note that many of Kelley's policy proposals depend on his particular view of the Church, his ecclesiology, rather than on secular warrant. It was just the danger of further privatization of religion by restricting its activity to the sanctuary and its own parochial grounds that led James Rausch to observe, "What must be constantly watched is any attempt in the practical or theoretical order, coming from within the Church or without, to translate the separation of Church and state into a prevailing doctrine of separating the Church from society."[38]

It is important to note that the public Catholic case for the Kurland interpretation of the First Amendment, touching a disputed issue in law, rests entirely on secular warrant. No one is asked to ascribe to the Catholic self-understanding of the mission of the Church or the particularist grounds for asserting the fact and scope of the freedom of the Church. Civil as opposed to theological discourse appeals to norms of distributive justice, the public good, the value of pluralism for the social order and the wisdom of structuring society in ways which encourage, promote and utilize mediating structures. While the theological case depends on civil warrants as an integral part of the structure of its argument, in no sense does the civil warrant necessarily rest on any appeal to particularist theological creed.

In a similar way, Catholic pleas that the state recognize the double financial burden of parents who send their children to private or parochial schools rely on the norm of distributive justice in adjudicating burdens and benefits within society. They also ask for *effective* state recognition of the fundamental right of parents to determine the style of education for their children. At present, this parental right represents a special burden which penalizes parents who choose to exercise it. Catholics also claim that the state should acknowledge the public services rendered to society by the various parochial and private school systems. Finally, they cite the societal good derived from competition and pluralism in alternative school systems. Catholics do not claim that they have any *religious* right to federal or state aid. Nor do they ask for a special privilege which would be withheld from other parents—Jews, Episcopalians, Seventh-Day Adventists, Missouri Synod Lutherans, secularists—in the same category of parents suffering double taxation.

I know of very few Catholics who are not persuaded of the justice of state aid to parents or students in parochial and private schools. They argue that in areas such as education and welfare where the state rightly claims an interest the state should also allow some choice and pluralism. I know of even fewer Catholics who can divine any cogent differences between permissible aid to sectarian colleges and universities and non-permissible aid to primary and secondary schools. The interests lobbying for the former, of course, include powerful private universities with political influence and clout. The justice of the two cases seems to Catholics roughly parallel.

Some Catholics argue that it is preferable to forego their rights to relief from double education costs either in the interest of ecumenical peace or, following Dean Kelley, to forestall the situation by which "the 'Queen's shilling' will sooner or later be followed by the Queen." I will not enter here into discussion of the numerous ways in which it is perfectly possible to build into public policy itself protections against the Queen following the Queen's shilling when it is in the public interest to separate financial subsidy from outright control. The British government-sponsored British Broadcasting Company is the classic example of that possibility.

My point here is that choosing to forego the pressing of a right or fatalism about it being accepted as a right in a pluralistic context is something else than a denial of a just basis for the claim. It might, of course, be possible to make a suasive case that even indirect aid to Church-sponsored and private schools would necessarily and seriously undermine support for quality public schools or lead to fragmented and antagonistic sub-cultures within society. In that case, the argument against aid to parents and students in parochial and private schools should be properly couched in terms of the good of public order or the common weal. It is simply wrong to assert that such aid is per se an issue of the First Amendment. For the Catholic case for aid for parents and students in parochial schools is not raised in terms of claims of true religion or preferential treatment for Catholic or even religious schools. The question is phrased, as Murray raised it, in secular moral terms: "Is it justice?"

Religious Liberty

Liberty of conscience and public freedom of personal and ecclesial religious expression rests on a firmer Catholic theological basis than does disestablishment. The normative conciliar document *Dignitatis Humanae* looks both to the revealed word of God and reason itself to ground the base point for religious liberty: the dignity of the human person. It is a category mistake in the use of language to assert that either truth or error has any rights. If a right is defined as an urgent moral claim on another to respect an immunity or deliver a good that it is in the other's power to grant, it may even be a category mistake in language to assert rights of God. He is beyond the realm of claims. Only persons enjoy rights.

Dignitatis Humanae asserts that every human person enjoys the right to religious liberty because, in Catholic theology, the act of faith, to be truly human, must eventuate from a free response to the initiative of God. A second theological argument for religious liberty insists that the authority of the Church is in no way derivative from the state. The authority of the Church flows directly from its obedience to God, while the authority of the state derives from God indirectly through the people in whom sovereign authority ultimately rests. The state exists to serve the needs and interests of the people. Its authority is instrumental, not substantive. Murray refers to these two kinds of authority as a dyarchy, citing the Gelasian maxim: "Two there are, August Emperor, by which this world is ruled on title of original and sovereign right—the consecrated authority of the priesthood and the royal power." Hence, as he further asserts, "By divine authority this world is to be ruled by a dyarchy of authorities, within which the temporal is subordinate to the spiritual, not instrumentally but in dignity."[39] The sign of that subordination is the state's recognition of its incompetency in matters religious. It follows from this sense of dyarchy that, as *Dignitatis Humanae* puts it, "The freedom of the Church is the fundamental principle in what concerns the relations between the Church and governments and the whole civil order."[40] As James Rausch puts it, "the Church ... seeks neither privilege nor special protection from the state, only the freedom to fulfill its religious mission and ministry to society."[41]

Dignitatis Humanae also structures a moral argument for religious liberty. It appeals to human dignity, the *res sacra homo*. Every person "has the right and duty to seek the truth in matters religious."[42] Persons are endowed with dignity by reason of their freedom and intelligence. They are privileged to bear responsibility toward the truth and for their own self-chosen identity as moral agents. Each person has inescapable personal responsibility to fix his or her own relationship to God. People cannot rely on another—family, Church, state or other groups or persons—to replace them in establishing their unique relationship to transcendent values, the order of meaning in the universe, God. Nor may any other agency coerce their choice in such matters.

Human dignity is in no way conditional on personal merit or subjective character. It is ontologically grounded in the very fact of personhood. Thus, *Dignitatis Humanae* asserts that "the right to religious freedom has its foundation, not in the subjective disposition of the person but in his very nature."[43] This moral argument, based on secular warrant, should find resonance and accord among all those who, with Emile Durkheim, see that in modern societies under conditions of religious pluralism only justice and the sacred character of the individual person—*res sacra homo*—and his groups can function as the indispensable collective conscience and civil religion.[44]

Religious liberty in the council document involves a twofold immunity. No one "is to be forced to act in a manner contrary to his conscience. Nor, on the other hand, is he to be restrained from acting in accordance with his conscience, especially in matters religious."[45] The second immunity was denied in pre-conciliar Catholic teaching, at least in regard to the public expression of religion, because of a traditional Catholic insistence that societies, as well as individuals, have obligations toward God and truth. This insistence is the characteristic Catholic way of holding to the indispensable concept of the sovereignty of God over society and nations and fending off excessive individualism and the privatization of religion. It is a matter of Catholic belief that every nation exists under the judgment of God.

This more traditional Catholic understanding which denied freedom to the *public* expression of non-Catholic religions was undercut by two crucial distinctions. The first is the acknowledgement of a necessary connection between private belief and public expression. The connecting link is the social nature of man: "The social nature of man itself requires that he should give external expression to his internal acts of religion, that he should participate with others in matters religious, that he should profess his religion in community. Injury, therefore, is done to the human person and to the very order established by God for human life, if the free exercise of religion is denied in society when the requirements of public order do not so require."[46]

The second distinction, essential to the shift away from the traditional prohibition of the *public* expression of non-Catholic religion, is that between society and the state. I want to develop this distinction because it bears out my contention that the Catholic structure of the argument for religious liberty is simultaneously a strong case for mediating structures. The text which needs explaining at least to non-Catholic ears reads in *Dignitatis Humanae*: "The truth cannot impose itself except by virtue of its own truth, as it makes its entrance into the mind at once quietly and with power. Religious freedom, in turn, which men demand as necessary to fulfill their duty to worship God has to do with immunity from coercion in civil society. Therefore, *it leaves untouched the moral duty of men and societies toward the true religion. . . .*"[47]

The italicized phrase indicates that Catholics have not abandoned their belief that God is sovereign over society and that it is incumbent upon society to recognize its dependence on God. One indication of this sovereignty is the state's recognition of the Church's claim for immunity in the juridical order in matters touching religion. By appealing to the distinction between society and the state, Murray shifted the burden of public acknowledgement of the sovereignty of God from the state—which is, in any event, incompetent in religious matters—to the wider society, the people acting through their voluntary mediating structures and corporate groups. For the freedom asserted in *Dignitatis Humanae* as a limit on state power is more than the freedom of the Church or individual religious consciences. The document signals as well the rightful freedom of mediating corporate groups. Indeed, it envisions as normative neither the confessional state nor the laicist secular state but the limited constitutional state. There is a juridical as well as a moral and theological premise to *Dignitatis Humanae*: "The demand is also made that constitutional limits should be set to the powers of government in order that there may be no encroachment on the rightful freedom of the person *and of associations*."[48]

The state's care for true religion is restricted to its care for the freedom of religion. Society's obligation to care for religion is more extensive. The fulfillment of its religious duty depends on an interpretation of the First Amendment which would allow some controlled contact and cooperation between the autonomous state and the several independent churches. For it is the free people, organized through their own mediating structures, not the state as such, which expresses and acknowledges the sovereignty of God over the society and nation. As Murray put it, he held "in common with all Catholics that an obligation to profess faith in God and to worship him is incumbent on society—on the people as such as well as on individuals; this obligation, however, is not fulfilled by a legislative or executive action by the public power. It is fulfilled by occasional public acts of worship on so-called state occasions. These acts of worship are organized by the Church, not the government, which has no competence in liturgical matters. Moreover, they are voluntary acts, since they are formally acts of religion."[49] While no one should be coerced into religious behavior, neither should others be restrained from a public expression of religion in the context of the national life.

STATE VS. SOCIETY

In its distinction between state and society, Catholic social thought contains a strong animus against the view that the public sphere is synonymous with the government or the formal polity of the society. It does not assume that everything public must *ipso facto* be governmental. In distinguishing between state and society it also distinguishes between the public order entrusted to the state—an order of unity, coercion and necessity and the common good which is entrusted to the whole society, a zone of comparative freedom and pluralism. As the abnormal instance of societies under foreign occupation makes evident, this distinction between state and society makes eminent empirical sense.

Even in the normal case, however, there is a proper distinction between state and society. Catholic social thought is pluralistic in its insistence on the limited, service character of the state. The state exists as an instrument to promote justice and liberty. The ends of the public order entrusted uniquely to the state are fourfold: public peace, public morality, welfare and justice, and the freedom of the people. As Murray puts it, "the democratic state serves both the ends of the human person (in itself and its natural forms of social life) and also the ends of justice. As the servant of these ends, it has only relative value."[50] If the state is both subject to and the servant of the common good, it "is not the sole judge of what is or is not the common good." Moreover, "in consequence of the distinction between society and state, not every element of the common good is instantly committed to the state to be protected and promoted." On the contrary, "government submits itself to judgment by the truth of society; it is not itself a judge of the truth in society."[51]

Perhaps the clearest and most developed statement of the distinction between society and the state is found in Maritain's now classic book, *Man and the State*, on which Murray relied. Maritain ascribes to the state an instrumental, service character which is a part—the topmost part and agency—of the whole society which he calls "the body politic." The state is the part which specializes in the interest of the whole. Its authority is derivative. It exists not by its own right and for its own sake but only in virtue and to the extent of the requirements of the common good. At least two corporate units in society, the family and the Church, have rights and freedoms anterior to the state. Other corporate units—voluntary associations such as universities, unions, agencies in the public interest—stake out a zone of free sociality in society. The right to voluntary association is based on the social nature of man whose sociality is not exhausted by citizenship in the state. Maritain asserts that "the state is inferior to the body politic as a whole and is at the service of the body politic as a whole."[52] He denies that the state is a moral personality, the subject of rights or, in any sense, the head of the body politic. It serves a purely instrumental role in the service of the people, the proper subject of rights.

Maritain argues that mediating structures should be as autonomous as possible because family, economic, cultural, educational and religious life matter as much as does political life to the very existence and prosperity of the body politic. Normally, the principle of subsidiarity should govern the relation between the state and mediating structures "since in political society authority comes from below through the people. It is normal that the whole dynamism of authority in the body politic should be made up of particular and partial authorities rising in tiers above one another up to the top authority of the state."[53]

Subsidiarity is an esoteric Catholic term, first coined in 1931 by Pius XI in his encyclical *Quadragesimo Anno*, although the principle to which it points has long existed in democratic pluralist theory. It is a derivative rule of the state-society distinction. Its purpose is to delineate both the moral right and the moral limitations of state intervention in cultural, social and economic affairs. Its formulation reads: "It is a fundamental principle of social philosophy . . . that one should not withdraw from individuals and commit to the community what they can accomplish by their own enterprise and industry. So, too, it is an injustice and at the same time a grave evil and a disturbance of right order to transfer to the larger and higher collectivity functions which can be performed and provided by the lesser and subordinate bodies. Inasmuch as every social activity should, by its very nature, prove a help to members of the body social, it should never destroy or absorb them."[54]

While the term is esoteric, because Catholic, the concept is not. Subsidiarity is in no sense a religious maxim. It rests entirely on secular warrant. It grew out of reflection on social experience, not revelation. Catholic social thought looks to it as a congealment of historic wisdom about the arrangement of social orders. It is a presumptive rule about where real vitality exists in society. Clearly, as *Quadragesimo Anno* realized and *Mater et Magistra* made very clear, the state can and must intervene for public welfare when intermediate associations are deficient. But the presumption is that such intervention, while justified, should never "destroy or absorb" the lesser or subordinate bodies. In point of fact, the principle of subsidiarity is simply a version of the theory of democratic pluralism to be found, in more secular guise, in de Tocqueville, Durkheim and more recently E. F. Schumacher and Michael Walzer.[55]

The case for subsidiarity can be made on different theological and social grounds. Thus, Anabaptists argue that "the real dynamic of society does not lie in the state; state action is obviated when subordinate groups, like the Church, effectively deal with education, health, relief and social security. Christians should not rely too much on the state and thus become completely obligated to it."[56] Some Protestant thinkers appeal to the concept—not the term—in their insistence on the sinful corruption of power and the need for countervailing power to check the all-powerful state. One Dutch Calvinist group, the *Gereformeerden*, has concluded to something like it in their translation of the sovereignty of God to mean "sovereignty in our own circle." *Gereformeerden* church control over their own mediating structures serves as a crucial check on idolatrous claims of state sovereignty, even when the state provides subsidy. If The Netherlands is, perhaps, the paradise for mediating structures and the principle of subsidiarity, it is clear to anyone who knows its history that it was a Calvinist, Abraham Kuyper, who was the principal architect of the Dutch subsidiarity state.

The secular warrants for subsidiarity are many. Thus, E. F. Schumacher contends that the principle is a rule for efficiency, the best way to increase both productivity and participant satisfaction. Berger and Neuhaus argue that a society governed by subsidiarity is more humane since "human beings understand their own needs better than anyone else—in, say, ninety-nine percent of all cases."[57] H. A. Rommen insists on intermediate structures as a fountain of creativity and experiment: "The state is not creative, but individual persons in their free associations and their group life are creative."[58]

Maritain's argument for subsidiarity is redolent of Emile Durkheim's communication theory of government in *Professional Morals and Civic Ethics* where Durkheim pleads for intermediate associations because the state is too abstract and distant.[59] As Maritain puts it, "To become a boss or a manager in business or industry or a patron of art or a leading spirit in the affairs of culture, science and philosophy is against the nature of such an impersonal topmost agency, abstract so to speak, and separated from the moving peculiarities, mutual tensions, risks, and dynamism of concrete social existence."[60] Andrew Greeley appeals to subsidiarity as a bulwark for freedom: "The principle of subsidiarity—no bigger than necessary—is fundamental precisely because it is a guarantee of personal freedom.... Freedom is ultimately facilitated by having roots, by having a place to call home, by having a group to which one belongs. . . . You can't be free without belonging, you can't be autonomous without being committed, you can't be independent without being secure, you can't go somewhere else unless you can go home again."[61] Nor are Catholics the only religious body to espouse this wisdom. The World Council of Churches asserted in its Evanston meeting that "forms of association within society which have their own foundation and principles should be respected and not controlled in their inner life by the state. Churches, families and universities are dissimilar examples of this non-political type of association."[62]

The principle of subsidiarity is not writ large on the fabric of the universe because it is distilled wisdom, an empirical generalization from experience and a maxim for ordering a sane society rather than an ontological principle or a phenomenological description of how states always or actually operate. The principle is of renewed interest today precisely because of two new threats to the voluntary society. The first is the extensive growth of welfare organized by the state which will not be dismantled for romantic visions of a simpler agrarian society. The modern state, by reason of its duty to enforce and promote social justice, has inevitably and properly moved into a vacuum to make up for deficiencies of a society whose basic mediating structures are not sufficient to provide universal welfare and justice. The second danger stems from the fact that increased governmental intervention in the name of welfare is coupled with what Ivan Illich refers to as "professional monopoly." Detailed regulations, certification and preconditions imposed upon the service sector of society are pricing voluntary agencies out of the market. The voluntary society is in a new danger, and, with it, human freedom, humane scale and local corporate wisdom and creativity.

I take it that Berger and Neuhaus' three policy propositions on mediating structures are a fair capsule of the biases of Catholic social theory and the principle of subsidiarity: (1) Mediating structures are essential for a vital democratic society. (2) Public policy should protect and foster mediating structures. (3) Wherever possible, public policy should utilize mediating structures for the realization of social purposes.[63] Maritain makes a similar claim: "Civil legislation should adapt itself to the variety of moral creeds of the diverse spiritual lineages which essentially bear on the common good of the social body—not by endorsing them or approving them but rather by giving allowance to them."[64]

The principle of subsidiarity is a sub-set rule of the larger distinction between state and society. The sign that this distinction is not just an abstraction consists in the presence of multiple, vigorous voluntary associations active in the public sphere cooperating and competing with the government in defining the common good. It is not the case that the lower authority envisioned by the principle of subsidiarity is exclusively or primarily the Church or local communities served by the Church. The literature on subsidiarity cites primarily universities, trade and credit unions, cooperatives, neighborhoods and regional associations. Indeed, in neither *Quadragesimo Anno* nor *Mater et Magistra* is the principle even directly applied to the Church, although such application is not excluded. The Church and its agencies (the latter often only tenuously connected to the Church juridically when they represent what Maritain refers to as associations of Christian inspiration as opposed to units of the Church) seek neither preferential treatment nor protection. They merely desire that they not be excluded from protections and benefits granted to all intermediate associations, secular or religious. They can argue that such exclusion is tantamount to the denial to them of freedom of religious expression.

It is also not true that the principle of subsidiarity asserts that the government should subsidize without any monitoring of how its money is spent. As the principle is stated in *Mater et Magistra* both the competency of government (it "encourages, stimulates, regulates, supplements and complements") and its limitations (it does not destroy or absorb mediating structures) are clearly set forth.[65]

The key link between the Catholic case for religious liberty and the case for subsidiarity is dependent on an understanding of religious activity and expression as something more than "providing meaning in the sanctuary." As *Dignitatis Humanae* states it: "In addition, it comes within the meaning of religious freedom that religious bodies should not be prohibited from freely undertaking to show the special value of their doctrine in what concerns the organization of society and the inspiration of the whole of human activity. Finally, the social nature of man and the very nature of religion afford the foundation of the right of men freely to hold meetings and to establish educational, cultural, charitable and social organizations, under the impulse of their own religious sense."[66]

The connection between Church-state theory and Church-society relations is clear. The freedom of the Church guaranteed by the First Amendment must be such as not to impede or penalize its freedom to pursue its mission as it understands it in society. But the Church's self-understanding in terms of its mission to society rests on particularist theological warrant. We cannot expect that self-understanding to become public property enshrined in law. The Church can garner public support for the freedom it demands for itself in fidelity to Gospel warrant only if it states its case simultaneously on secular warrant. The secular warrant is the argument for mediating structures as a key element in public policy. For, as Murray clearly saw, the freedom of the Church is linked inextricably to other civil freedoms: "The personal and corporate free exercise of religion as a human and civil right is evidently cognate with other more general human and civil rights—with the freedom of corporate bodies and institutions within society, based on the principle of subsidiary functions; with the general freedom of association for peaceful purposes, based on the social nature of man; with the general freedom of speech and of the press based on the nature of political society."[67]

The long lessons of history and the recent struggles of the Church in Latin America and East Africa make clear that the voluntary Church only flourishes in climates where voluntarism is generally prized in the wider society. Churches which understand their mission in society beyond the narrow confines of the sanctuary depend upon an interpretation of Church-state separation that would encourage intermediate associations generally. The secular warrant which mediates the Church's theological understanding of its mission to society as constitutive of its very essence as Church is a social philosophy which insists on the distinction between society and the state and the concomitant obligation of the state to protect, nurture and promote mediating structures as essential to the vital life of the society. Catholics will grant a theological valance to mediating structures beyond their secular warrant since a climate which nourishes them is essential to the kind of freedom and scope of religious activity called for by *Gaudium et Spes* and the synod document on *Justice in the World*.

Churches are not just "mediating structures." They have other functions, especially that of providing meaning, identity, belonging and commitment to transcendent truth. I do not, however, on theological grounds, think that these other functions are intrinsically more important or that "mediation" is necessarily a "distraction" for the Church. As I understand the thrust of post-conciliar Catholic theology, the Church exists precisely for mission and ministry to the world. Service to the world is not something the Church does after being fully constituted. It is not a luxury. The Church's very in-gathering as community is constituted by its being sent in mission. Its mission, moreover, depends on its ability to function as a mediating structure. Therefore, its freedom to be itself is threatened whenever the general climate for mediating structures is endangered. In championing the rights of other non-religious mediating structures in society the Church is protecting its own interests and its own freedom. For, as Murray saw, when insisting on a juridical component in the final version of *Dignitatis Humanae*, a claim in society under the rubric of civil discourse for freedom for the Church is simultaneously a plea for similar liberty for other religious and human intermediate associations: "Constitutional government, limited in its powers, dedicated to the defense of the rights of man and to the promotion of the freedom of the people, is the correlate of religious freedom as a juridical notion, a civil and human right, personal and corporate."[68] It was in this sense that he could state that "in the present moment of history the freedom of the people of God is inseparably linked to the freedom of the people."[69]

I do not expect any non-Catholics to agree with my theology of the Church and its mission to society. Neither do I assume that they will necessarily concur with the Catholic way of construing a theology of Church and state. I have rehearsed it here as an exercise in public theology to show the public policy implications of a particular theological position. It may be of interest to others, as it was to me, to discover that the Catholic case for religious liberty depends—at a crucial point—on the distinction between state and society and the principle of subsidiarity to reach its term in concluding on theological grounds to the public religious liberty of non-Catholic churches. It may be also of interest to note that the only way to make the Catholic case for religious liberty in *civil* discourse and on *secular* warrant is by making a simultaneous case for the freedom and vigor of other, non-religious, mediating structures. The Catholic understanding of the mission of the Church will be diminished or frustrated in societies which construe separation of Church and state so narrowly that voluntarism as a vigorous aspect of public life begins to wane.

But apart from the particularist Catholic theological case for the freedom of the Church and religious liberty, there are sufficient secular warrants to consider the wisdom and usefulness of subsidiarity and mediating structures as public policies on their own merits. As an exercise in civil discourse I propose that we do so. The obstacle to this discourse will be narrow notions of the intent of separation of Church and state which might sacrifice voluntarism to shore up some imaginative wall. I suggest that we might listen again to the plea Jacques Maritain made to Americans concerning the interpretation of the First Amendment in his *Man and the State*: "Sharp distinction *and* actual cooperation, that is an historical treasure the value of which a European is perhaps more prepared to appreciate because of his own bitter experiences. Please to God that you keep it carefully, and do not let your concept of separation veer round to the European one."[70]

NOTES

1. John C. Bennett, *Christians and the State* (New York: Charles Scribner's and Sons, 1958), p. 205.

2. Thomas G. Sanders, *Protestant Concepts of Church and State* (New York: Holt, Rinehart and Winston, 1964), p. 257.

3. This question is raised in Paul Ramsey, *Who Speaks for the Church?* (Nashville: Abingdon, 1967) and James Gustafson, *Christian Ethics and Community* (Philadelphia: Pilgrim Press, 1971).

4. For these questions cf. Sanders, *op. cit.,* pp. 288–99.

5. *Ibid.,* p. 279.

6. For a theocratic position with strong assertions about the rights of Judaism vis-à-vis the state cf. Manfred Vogel, "Critical Reflection," in Walter Burghardt, ed., *Religious Freedom: 1965–1975* (New York: Paulist Press, 1977), pp. 54–69.

7. John C. Murray, "Religious Freedom," in John Courtney Murray, ed., *Freedom and Man* (New York: P. J. Kenedy and Sons, 1965).

8. Msgr. Pietro Pavan, "Ecumenism and Vatican II's Declaration on Religious Freedom," in Burghardt, *op. cit.,* pp. 32–33.

9. George Linbeck, "Critical Reflections," in Burghardt, *op. cit.,,* p. 54.

10. The failure of this new theology to address the issue of the limited constitutional state is part of my criticism of liberation theology in Chapter 4 of this volume.

11. John Courtney Murray. "The Issue of Church and State at Vatican Council II," *Theological Studies* 27 (March 1966), pp. 599–600. Cf. Chapter 1 of this book for theological warrants for Church involvement in politics.

12. Cited in David O'Brien and Thomas Shannon, eds., *Renewing the Earth: Catholic Documents on Peace, Justice and Liberation* (Garden City: Doubleday, 1977), p. 391.

13. James Rausch, "Dignitatis Humanae: The Unfinished Agenda," in Burghardt, *op. cit.,* pp. 40–41. Church-state relations set the tone for any strategic theology.

14. Cf. John Courtney Murray, *We Hold These Truths* (hereafter *WHTT*) (New York: Sheed and Ward, 1960); *The Problem of Religious Freedom* (hereafter *PRF*) (Westminster: Newman Press, 1965); Jacques Maritain, *Man and the State* (Chicago: University of Chicago Press, 1951); Yves Simon, *The Philosophy of Democratic Government* (Chicago: University of Chicago Press, 1951); H. A. Rommen, *The State in Catholic Thought* (St. Louis: B. Herder and Co., 1945).

15. The text of *Dignitatis Humanae* in O'Brien and Shannon, *op. cit.,* pp. 291–306.

16. Cf. Peter Berger and R. J. Neuhaus, *To Empower People* (Washington, D.C.: American Enterprise Institute, 1977) and Dean Kelley, "Confronting the Danger of the Moment," in Jay Mechling, ed., *Church, State and Public Policy* (Washington, D.C.: American Enterprise Institute, 1978), pp. 9–21.

17. For these objections, cf. James Gustafson, *Protestant and Roman Catholic Ethics* (Chicago: University of Chicago Press, 1978), p. 62.

18. *Ibid.,* p. 118.

19. Cf. Gustafson's remarks about family resemblances between Calvinism and Thomism in *ibid.,* p. 119.

20. Cited in Sanders, *op. cit.,* p. 172. In a very illuminating remark Sanders claims that the strict separationist theological position, based as it is on individualism (soul competency) and a contract view of the origin of the state, does not do justice to mediating structures: "One finds little or no recognition [in contemporary separationist thought] of the significant pluralistic social philosophy by which the rights of corporate groups are guaranteed and which many interpreters regard as one of the chief characteristics of Anglo-Saxon democracy" (cf. p. 202).

21. I do not want to enter here into the discussion of how much the civil discourse ideal is ultimately of peculiarly Protestant provenance or the further question of how this civil discourse can emasculate, tame and denude theological

identity. Cf. John Murray Cuddihy, *No Offense: Civil Religion and Protestant Taste* (New York: Seabury, 1978).

22. Murray, *WHTT*, p. 63.

23. Winthrop Hudson, *The Great Tradition of the American Churches* (New York: Harper and Row, 1953).

24. Cf. Brian Smith, "Pastoral Strategy in the Third World," *America* (May 18, 1974), pp. 389–92, and *The Chilean Church and Political Change: 1925–1975*, unpublished dissertation, Department of Political Science, Yale University, 1978.

25. For the nature of Dutch subsidy politics cf. Arend Lijphart, *The Politics of Accommodation* (Berkeley: University of California Press, 1968) and my *The Evolution of Dutch Catholicism* (Berkeley: University of California Press, 1978), pp. 58–87.

26. Murray, *PRF*, p. 203.

27. Cuddihy, *op. cit.*, p. 72.

28. Murray, *WHTT*, p. 85.

29. Cuddihy, *op. cit.*, p. 74.

30. Murray, *PRF*, p. 45.

31. *Ibid.*, p. 42.

32. Murray, *WHTT*, p. 150.

33. Bennett, *op. cit.*, p. 5.

34. *Ibid.*, p. 10.

35. Cited in Sanders, *op. cit.*, p. 145.

36. Bennett, *op. cit.*, p. 209.

37. In O'Brien and Shannon, *op. cit.*, p. 302.

38. Rausch, *op. cit.*, p. 43.

39. Murray, *WHTT*, p. 32.

40. In O'Brien and Shannon, *op. cit.*, p. 302.

41. Rausch, *op. cit.*, p. 41.

42. In O'Brien and Shannon, *op. cit.*, p. 293.

43. *Ibid.*

44. Emile Durkheim, "Individualism and the Intellectuals," in Robert N. Bellah, ed., *Emile Durkheim on Morality and Society* (Chicago: University of Chicago Press, 1973), pp. 43–58. Durkheim's point here is the reason for a need for a civil religion. Cf. Chapter 5 in this volume.

45. In O'Brien and Shannon, *op. cit.*, p. 293.

46. *Ibid.*, p. 294.

47. *Ibid.*, p. 292.

48. *Ibid.*, p. 297.

49. Murray, *PRF*, p. 93.

50. Murray, *WHTT*, p. 308.

51. Murray, *PRF*, p. 42.

52. *Man and the State*, p. 13.

53. *Ibid.*, p. 11.

54. Cited in O'Brien and Shannon, *op. cit.*, p. 62.

55. Cf. Michael Walzer, "The Problem of Citizenship," in *Obligations: Essays on Disobedience, War and Citizenship* (Cambridge: Harvard University Press, 1970), pp. 203–28.

56. Cited in Sanders, *op. cit.*, p. 107.

57. Peter Berger and Richard J. Neuhaus, *To Empower People* (Washington, D.C.: American Enterprise Institute, 1977), p. 7.

58. Rommen, *op. cit.,* p. 253.

59. Emile Durkheim, *Professional Ethics and Civic Morals* (London: Routledge and Kegan Paul, 1957), pp. 73ff.

60. *Man and the State,* p. 21.

61. Andrew Greeley, *Neighborhood* (New York: Seabury, 1977) p. 68.

62. Cited in Bennett, *op. cit.,* p. 77.

63. Berger and Neuhaus, *op. cit.,* p. 6.

64. *Man and the State,* p. 169.

65. In O'Brien and Shannon, *op. cit.,* pp. 62–63.

66. *Ibid.,* p. 295.

67. Murray, *PRF,* pp. 26–27.

68. *Ibid.,* p. 67.

69. *Ibid.,* p. 70.

70. *Man and the State,* p. 183.

Chapter Twelve

American Catholics and the International Life

> Nothing is more foreign to us than the state
> *(res publica),* for there is only one state that we rec-
> ognize and that consists of the entire world.
> —Tertullian
> *The Apology*

I am going to take a retrospective look at an essay which the sociologist Thomas O'Dea wrote twenty years ago on "American Catholicism and the International Life." I chose to look at it again because I am fascinated by its title and topic. From one point of view, O'Dea's essay is still instructive as a piece of social history and as a sociological analysis of American Catholicism. From another vantage point, it is a curiosity piece.[1]

O'Dea stood in the long line of "Americanizers," Catholic liberals who, from the time of Brownson and Hecker in the period before the Civil War, were preoccupied with the possibility of an indigenous American Catholicism, with finding a strategic fit between Catholic organizational and cultural life and the wider concerns and structures of America.[2] The Americanizers all held a relatively benign—in some instances uncritical— view of American culture and society. Their program was aimed at successful Catholic social mobility and a concomitant Catholic influence on society. They were preoccupied with the issues of "how to make it" in America and how to have influence on America.

In his treatment of the question of American Catholics and the international life, O'Dea notes that Catholic attitudes toward foreign affairs were often askew from mainstream American liberal values. O'Dea laments this fact. He notes that in the nineteenth century, scientism, liberalism and the emergence of socialism dominated world affairs. Catholicism felt uncomfortable with each of these realities. As O'Dea puts it, "While Americans tended to become sympathetic to European revolutionary movements, Catholic thought, traumatically affected by 1789 and 1848, tended to align itself with conservatism. The American public looked with sympathy on the Greek revolt against Turkey, the Hungarian uprising against the Hapsburgs and the seizure of Rome by the Italian army. When Kossuth (the Hungarian hero) visited Washington in the early 1850's, he was welcomed by Daniel Webster, then Secretary of State, by the President and by both Houses of Congress. The American populace generally received him with applause. To leading Catholics like Bishop Hughes, Orestes A. Brownson and the editor of *The Freeman's Journal,* he was a fraud, a demagogue and a foe of Christianity."[3] In his essay, O'Dea set himself the problem of explaining, sociologically, why American Catholic attitudes diverged markedly from those of mainstream America.

O'Dea explains the discrepancy by rehearsing the now familiar factors of the immigrant status of the Church, the low socio-economic position of the laity which led to a clerical dominance unchecked by a lay intelligentsia, and, finally, the tendency of clerical leaders to take their cues rather directly from Rome. O'Dea notes that while Catholics were prominent in domestic politics, they were notoriously absent from the foreign policy establishment in the Department of State and in elite groups which influence foreign policy such as the Council on World Affairs. The question O'Dea sets himself in his essay is very similar to the questions being asked in the 1950's by the Americanizers about American Catholic intellectual life when they wondered aloud—in the words of John Cavanaugh—"Where are the Catholic Oppenheimers and Einsteins?"[4] O'Dea's transposed question was directed to international life: "Where are the Catholic Dean Achesons and Catholic members of the foreign policy establishment?"

This is a curious and, perhaps, ultimately wrong-headed question. The question is wrong-headed on several counts. First, by restricting his attention to the so-called "attentive publics" of the nation (i.e., that small, elite group in any nation—rarely larger than five to ten percent of the population—which takes an active interest in foreign policy issues), O'Dea was bound to miss the arena where Roman Catholicism can and does make its greatest impact on international life.

Moreover, O'Dea focused his attention on an area which depends on "thin conceptual rhetoric" and neglected "thick symbolics." As I will argue in a moment, it is more at the level of symbolic community than in appeals to intellectual norms that the churches can contribute most to international life.[5] The question was misplaced because it overlooks the greatest strength of Roman Catholicism for political thought and social ethics. I will argue, in this chapter, that that strength does not consist primarily in a body of doctrine, even as wonderful a body of doctrine as the papal encyclical tradition or the "high theory" of social Catholicism. Most Catholics do not live out of this high doctrine. Few American Catholics have read and assimilated the encyclical tradition. Fewer still have taken their cues on international issues from this tradition.

Again, the implicit assumption of O'Dea's question was that Catholic thought would have some special vision to supply in the foreign policy arena, presumably from its social ethical tradition. I do not think, however, that the most important potential Catholic contribution to social ethics and the international life lies in any particular ethical norm or theory such as, for example, the principle of subsidiarity or theories about the just war or about integral development.[6] No, the greatest possible strength of Catholicism in social ethics consists in its potential for generating primordial loyalties to a community which transcends the nation, to weave into Catholic life a texture of deep symbols which could evoke for Catholics a sense that they are citizens and members of a community of worldwide dimensions. In that sense, the Catholic task is to generate, following Tertullian, a recognition of that state which consists of the entire world. That, after all, is the very root meaning of the term "Catholic."

O'Dea looked in the wrong places. Had he looked elsewhere he might have come up with a very different picture of American Catholicism and the international life. I am going to rehearse some themes from history concerning the "Americanizers" in American Catholicism and also concerning "popular religion" in the nineteenth and early twentieth century to make a point about a potential contribution of American Catholicism to the international life.

The Americanizers—I am using this term to refer to a distinctively liberal Catholic position which runs from Brownson through John Courtney Murray—asked two questions about American Catholicism. The first question was, "What is the role of American Catholicism for American life?" The second was, "What is the role of American Catholicism for the world Church?"

Americanizing Catholics tended to answer the first question by contending that Catholicism was the only safe bulwark for American values and institutions. As early as the mid-nineteenth century, Orestes Brownson was arguing that Americans are a providential people, a people with a great manifest destiny. In his view it is only through Catholicism that the country can fulfill its mission to the world. "Catholicity is the future hope of our country."[7] As late as 1960, in his book *We Hold These Truths,* John Courtney Murray was re-echoing this same fundamental theme. In Murray's view, the American proposition of separation of Church and state as well as the American virtues of liberty and republican participation depended on a firm adherence to the natural law foundations of our founding fathers. Since only Catholics still adhered to the natural law, in Murray's contention, Catholics had become the indispensable bulwark of America.[8] This curious yet persistent theme of Catholics as the "best Americans" dies hard. Thus, Michael Novak plays a variation on the same theme when he argues in his book, *The Rise of the Unmeltable Ethnics,* that only Catholic ethnics can really appreciate and embody genuine American pluralism. In this view, not only are Catholics not foreign, they are the best representatives of what is most American.[9]

The Catholic Americanizers took over the American notion of a special religious significance to the nation but gave it a new twist. They were less likely than Protestants to be expectant of a whole new revelation from the American experience. Notoriously, Jews and Catholics in America have used a generally more "secular" rather than an overtly religious rhetoric to refer to the nation. Their religions include references to loyalties beyond the nation. In John Courtney Murray's terms, the Catholic Americanizers saw the nation itself as of moral rather than of religious significance. Instead of seeing the nation as itself religious, the Catholic Americanizers tended to focus on the question about the special role of the American Catholic Church in the world Church.

As they saw it, the contribution of American Catholicism to the world Church consisted in its demonstration that democracy and Catholicism could exist side by side, that religious liberty was a blessing for the Church. America, the Americanizers argued, could contribute through American Catholics a worldwide blessing to the Church. The Americanizers could have easily made their own the words of José Comblin in his book *The Meaning of Mission:* "It is the new centers of Church life, not the old established centers of the Church that give rise to a new stage in Church life."[10] The Americanizers tended to see America as the future hope of the world Church.

By the turn of the century, Catholicism's dynamic confidence led the American Church to an outward thrust. The Catholic Extension Society undertook missions to Protestants. Only a few years after the American Church ceased to be a missionary territory in 1908, American Catholics began to send missionaries to all parts of the globe. Maryknoll was founded and religious congregations in America began to send missionaries abroad. In this, American Catholics followed the lead of American Protestants who made of the late nineteenth century a unique epoch of Christian missionary expansion in Asia and Africa. American Catholics included their own version of American Protestant optimism which proclaimed that the whole world would become Christian in a generation.

Recent studies have shown how American Catholic missionaries, like their Protestant counterparts, brought to China and Latin America their own version of Christianity combined with American national interests and their own way of furthering the mission of America abroad.[11] I am not, in this chapter, interested in pursuing the way in which missionaries exported American ideals abroad. My main concern is with the key question of the Americanizers, i.e., "What is the role of American Catholicism in the world Church?" It remains a good question for us to press today. The activity of American Catholic missionaries abroad provided American Catholics with living symbols of the reality that they belonged to a community larger than the nation and had responsibilities and community with non-Americans.

It may have been paternalistic and a bit imperialistic but "buying pagan babies" provided a generation of American Catholic school children with a vivid concrete symbol of their membership in an international organization and culture, world Catholicism. Rather than memberships in elite foreign policy establishments or a generation of Catholic Dean Achesons, I would argue, American Catholicism's major contribution to international life consisted in providing some vivid symbols of belonging to and having bonds with an international community. This was partially achieved by the Americanizers' outward thrust to mission. American missionaries abroad and on home leave and missionary societies through fund-raising and mission magazines brought to ordinary people in the pews some sense—however distorted or idealized—of China, Latin America and Africa as part of the same human community with America.

Coupled with the United States Relief Services' outreach to the international community, this outward missionary thrust touched more than attentive publics. Then, as now, it generated an American Catholic concern for international life. Msgr. Joseph Gremillion has contended that United States Catholic Relief Services—which reach more than seventy nations—animated social ministry in local churches. It is no secret that American missionaries in Latin America in the 1950's pioneered in several new social ministries such as radio schools and credit unions which set the stage for a greater political turn on the part of the Latin American Church several decades later.[12]

Gremillion recounts how Bishop Edward Swanstrom and James Norris of the United States Catholic Conference took the lead in authoring the international chapter in the Vatican II document. *Pastoral Constitution on the Church in the Modern World.* He also notes that the Office for International Justice and Peace of the United States Catholic Conference deals with almost every country to which American economic and political power reaches.[13] It would be my contention that these efforts—rather than placement in foreign policy elites—is the proper place to look for the assessment of American Catholicism and the international life.

O'Dea might have also looked to popular religion in the nineteenth and early twentieth century to gain an alternative view of American Catholics and the international life. Professor Jay Dolan of the University of Notre Dame has written a book which tries to recapture the popular religion of American Catholicism of the period 1865–1900. In his book *Catholic Revivalism* Dolan argues that a "devotional revolution" occurred in American Catholicism in the latter half of the nineteenth century.[14]

Dolan reminds us that a devotional revival was necessary since, contrary to certain popular stereotypes, the Irish, German and Italian immigrants who came to America were not "practicing" Catholics. The immigrants were, to a large extent, nominal Catholics. Dolan sees the Catholic parish missions with their itinerant mission-band preachers, the call for instant conversion, the focus on vivid symbols of hell, damnation, the cross, sin and conversion and the appeal to "heart religion" as parallel to Protestant revivalism. He mentions instances of sobbing, moans, groans, tears, etc. in connection with the parish mission. Like Protestant revival religion, popular religion among Catholics tended to be moralistic and individualistic. It focused its attacks on intemperance, dance halls, immoral books, etc.

Despite this overtly individualistic content of the preached morality, however, American Catholic popular religion fed into a communal sense. First, parish missions were used to help organize new parish congregations. Second, they spawned innumerable parish devotional confraternities and sodalities. Most importantly for the issue of this chapter—a point Dolan only alludes to in passing—popular religion in the nineteenth century also fed into internationalism. For the devotional revolution of the nineteenth century wove into ritual, symbol and the "heart religion" of conversion a rich, thick set of primordial symbols of identity—symbols of ultramontanism and universality. Rome, the papacy, Roman discipline, even Latin came to symbolize for American Catholics—a cultural minority feeling inferiority in a Protestant and often overtly anti-Catholic culture—their membership in an international community which transcended American time and space.

It was out of such experiences that ordinary Catholics could claim against Protestant pretensions—even if defensively—what John Courtney Murray remarked: "The Catholic may not, as others do, merge his religious and his patriotic faith or submerge one in the other.... He must reckon with his own tradition of thought which is wider and deeper than any that America has elaborated. He must also reckon with his own history which is longer than the brief centuries that America has lived."[15]

In the post-World War I period, with the rise of a new educated Catholic laity, some of this same sense of universalism and internationalism was mediated through symbols which came to the fore in efforts to inculcate a distinctively American Catholic literature and culture. As William Halsey has shown, these efforts ultimately failed to bear cultural fruit. In the process, however, American Catholics turned to Dante, Newman, Péguy, Bernanos, Sigrid Undset, Waugh and Greene and other representatives of international Catholic literature as properly their own.[16]

I know as well as anyone that there were enormous flaws in these earlier Catholic symbols of internationalism. The universalism they proclaimed was often triumphant rather than in a posture of service. Much of this earlier internationalism was defensive. Much was unecumenical. The primordial symbols which carried this earlier internationalism (Rome, the papacy, Latin) were static rather than dynamic. They lacked any referent to specific mission or social justice content. They focused much too much on the Church as the privileged international community and, even at that, on the images of *the institutional Church* rather than on the Church as a community making up the body of Christ.

My purpose in evoking these earlier symbols is not an exercise in nostalgia. I do not pretend that we could ever symbolically recreate that world. Neither would we want to. My point is to claim that the existence of these vivid, lived symbols of internationalism, a sense of belonging concretely to Catholicism as an international community, was the most important contribution of Catholicism to social ethics and international life. These earlier symbols of papal ultramontanism, "buying pagan babies" and looking upon foreign Catholic literature as one's own patrimony were each ways of inculcating in American Catholics a sense of loyalty to an international people.

Some of the askewness that O'Dea noted in American Catholic attitudes on foreign policy grew out of this lived, vivid sense of belonging to an international community. Notoriously, few sociological variables are more powerful than nationalism. World War I showed that nationalism overruled social class solidarity across national borders, much to the dismay of European socialists. It also showed the power of nationalism to overrule ethnicity—witness the almost complete collapse of German American ethnic groups during and after World War I. O'Dea notes two occasions in the 1930's—the Spanish Civil War and American involvement with Mexico—where American Catholics markedly diverged from the general American public in foreign policy positions. He deplored the particular stands American Catholics took in each instance.[17]

Because O'Dea focuses on the content of the policy issues in the Spanish Civil War and American involvement with Mexico he misses the more striking fact. That religion should ever be as strong a variable as nationalism is always startling. While O'Dea may have been correct in lamenting the content of Catholic askewness from mainstream American foreign policy stances on these two occasions he neglects to note that this askewness came from a strong primordial identification with Catholicism as an international community, culture and entity. This identification led American Catholics to diverge from their compatriots on foreign policy issues where they perceived a threat to the international Church.

It is over twenty years since O'Dea wrote his essay on international life. Yet I still often hear his older question being asked about American Catholics and the international life. In its new form it tends to be phrased as: "Where are the Catholic voices in debates about the new international economic order? Where are Catholics in debates about development, liberation and structural change? Where are Catholics as members of Amnesty International, the League of Human Rights or other non-governmental organizations working in human rights?"

It is noteworthy that the question is still focused on the narrow perspective of the attentive publics, the elite few who are preoccupied with international issues. It is still focused on issues at a remove from the more basic concern of generating primordial international identities. While I do not want to suggest that elites are not important, I have been contending in this chapter that the most important potential Catholic contribution to social ethics is not in its elites or in some norm or a body of social teaching. American Catholicism's main contribution to international life consists in a fact and a challenge. The fact is that the Church can sometimes generate primordial symbols—symbols which deeply touch self-identity and are woven into the texture of ordinary family life and community existence— that can, on some occasions, produce competing loyalties to the state. Few other organizations or groups—e.g., social classes, ethnic groups—can do so.

This chapter began with a citation from Tertullian: "Nothing is more foreign to us than the state *(res publica),* for there is only one state that we recognize and that consists of the entire world." It is my contention that there are two basic contributions of the Church to the political order. First, within the national state, a dynamic and independent Church, as a lived community of interaction and belonging, is one of the few institutions capable of generating a primordial identity strong enough to compete against loyalty to the state. Compared to ethnicity or class solidarity—two other candidates for generating dual loyalties—religious belonging has been more successful in challenging the state. One of the reasons for the importance of religion to national self-identity is precisely this ability to link the nation to a larger world community which both relativizes and stands in judgment on the nation.[18]

Long ago, Ernst Troeltsch argued that the major ethical achievement of the first three centuries of Christianity was not a special doctrine of the state, justice or community nor even any direct special concern for transforming the social order as such. In Troeltsch's view, the major political achievement of the early Church was its ability to maintain a sense of the Church as a place and a community which did not derive from the state and, further, demanded its own freedom and independence in the space organized by the state.[19] Eisenstadt has also shown, in his study of the political role of religion in centralized empires, that "the extent to which the religious institutions were organizationally autonomous greatly influenced the degree to which they could participate in the central political struggle of a given society."[20] Achieving genuine autonomy from the state—regardless of the particular content of its social ethical program—is already a political achievement of the Church, an act of political pluralism and limitation to national sovereignty.

Institutional and cultural autonomy is the major political achievement of the Church in national politics. It represents the pre-condition for any possible critical counter-loyalty to nationalism. So, also, the Church's main contribution in the international arena is the establishment of a vivid sense of belonging to a real community which consists in some genuine way in the entire world. At the Call to Action convocation of the American bishops held in Detroit in 1976, Philip Scharper called for the establishment of a "committee on humankind." My reaction, when I heard about this resolution, was to ask: What *real* group could presume to be a carrier-group of the aspirations of humankind? There are, indeed, very few vivid carriers of the reality of transnational community. As Ivan Vallier has noted, there is only *one* transnational actor in the world which can be said, in some real sense, to be one organization, one culture and genuinely mass-based. World Catholicism would not be a bad candidate to serve as a "committee on humankind."[21] An important task of each national Church is to keep alive this reality of transnational community.

Gustavo Gutiérrez has remarked that one genuine act of liberation and solidarity with the poor is worth all the volumes of liberation theology.[22] I take it that it is not an unfair translation of this sentiment to state that the creation of one viable base community which could root primordial loyalties and identity as a resource of dual loyalty resistant to the national security ideology of Brazil, Chile and Argentina is more important than all the formal teachings of liberation theology on social ethics. I am trying in this chapter to make an analogous point. The generation of a genuine sense of international community is worth more than any norm, principle or social doctrine in assessing American Catholicism's contribution to the international life. Similarly, Segundo Galilea and others have argued for the need to move beyond preoccupation with elites and attentive publics to popular religion which could provide rich, vivid symbols of lived religion. I am arguing in a similar way. We need to ask about the way Catholicism can create real communities embodying transnational loyalties and how this sense of internationalism can be translated into popular religion.

Professor Dolan ends his book on the popular devotional revolution of the nineteenth century with a comparison of nineteenth century Catholic revivalism through the parish mission with the new devotional forms of Catholic pentecostalism.[23] Dolan notes some of the differences between the two forms of popular devotion, especially the lay character of leadership within pentecostalism and its very different symbols of community when compared to the symbols of the nineteenth century Church. Dolan passes over completely the way in which the symbols of universalism, transnational belonging and international life embedded in the nineteenth century's ultramontism and the expansive missionary outreach of the American Church in the first half of the twentieth century have died a seemingly irretrievable death. Papal symbols, a sense of properly "belonging" to a worldwide Catholic literary culture, and the purchase of "pagan babies" are all remnants of the past. Unfortunately, their demise has left a lacuna in the church. Nothing analogous has been found to take their place.

At the level of popular religion, the old carriers of internationalism have been lost. American Catholic piety has become very American indeed. I have, personally, no special wisdom about what symbolic resources are necessary to retrieve this lost earlier sense of Catholicism as entailing "international belonging." Some important and obvious resources would seem to be the exchange of people—Americans going abroad to communicate with the Church in Latin America, Africa and Asia and similarly inviting representatives of the Church in Latin America, the Philippines and Africa to share with us their struggles and hopes. Perhaps, as I suggest in the following chapter, an exchange of episcopal letters such as Chile's Cardinal Henrique Silva's letter to European Catholics in 1972 could evoke a specific international sense. Themes in liturgy and song—the celebration of contemporary Catholic martyrs in Latin America, for example—might also help to focus on the international character of Catholicism.

While I lack any special wisdom about the best resources to revive a waned international consciousness, I think the old question of the nineteenth century Americanizers remains germane today: "What is the role of American Catholicism in the world Church?" Our answer to the question will be very different from theirs in their day. The gist of the contemporary answer would consist in something like the following. If America has an important role in world history—as a superpower, an economic, cultural and ideological *imperium,* and as the world center for a worldwide capitalist economic order—then, I would argue, the role of American Catholicism in the world Church will be to reach wherever that American power reaches and to ask, in ecclesial solidarity, what that American power is doing to people in other countries. In this respect, the opposition of the American bishops to Secretary of State Haig's military policy in El Salvador represents an instance of this crucial Church role. The main role of American Christianity in the world Church, in this view, is to keep vividly alive—in rich symbols of popular religion—the sense of Tertullian that we belong to a community that embraces the world. There are very few sociological resources to challenge the enormous power of nationalism. Religion is one of those few.

It will be helpful, in concluding, to take some cues from José Comblin's excellent little book *The Meaning of Mission.* Comblin signals a characteristic Catholic proclivity to stress *communio* over *missio,* to emphasize the Church over its Gospel mission to the world. Comblin correctly reminds us that "the Church comes after Gospel mission, not before it."[24] He further notes that characteristically "most Church activities and structures, even in so-called mission lands, are designed to abet the administration, consolidation and expansion of what is already in existence."[25] In Comblin's view, the community is gathered only in terms of its being sent in mission. He notes: "Christians exist in order to speak to other people."[26]

Comblin signals the dangers of becoming overly preoccupied—as the Americanizers often were and are—with adaptation, acculturation, and indigenization. As he puts it, "the danger is that the Gospel message and the activity of the Church will be reduced to the role of helping to integrate people into a given society and culture." He adds: "The potential danger is that the Church will become too integral a part of a given society, that it will renounce the Gospel mission and accept a subordinate role in the prevailing culture."[27] These dangers which Comblin cites are real enough. As important as acculturation and indigenization are, they must not be allowed a monopoly. They need to be balanced by a keen sense of internationalism. Comblin contends that "the task we face right now is the formation of a missionary Church. We must create it out of a non-missionary Church so that we can initiate a new stage in Christ's mission to the world."[28]

We have undoubtedly seen, in the American Church, the heyday of a dynamic élan which assumed that America as a new center of Church life had a definite mission to the world Church. In that sense, we American Catholics are today someplace very different from the optimistic world of the nineteenth century Americanizers. Again, it is probably unlikely that we will see an outpouring of American missionaries to Africa, Asia or Latin America to match the exodus of American Catholic missionaries in the period 1920–1960. Surely, however, some continuation of this outward thrust will be essential for the American Church to keep its international sense alive.

The new sense of mission since Vatican II assumes that the young churches can also teach, evangelize, indeed revitalize, the "established" churches of Europe and North America.[29] Becoming a genuinely missionary Church will mean, for American Catholicism, a specific openness to the realities—religious, social and political—and aspirations of the young churches. The burden of my argument in this chapter has been that in an earlier period American Catholicism in popular religious life generated symbols of transnational belonging. These earlier symbols have largely collapsed without new substitute forms. I also have been arguing that the ways in which popular religion sustains a genuine sense of internationalism is more important than the size of the Catholic population in the cohort of foreign policy elites. Finally, I would agree with Johannes B. Metz' assessment that the Church's work of reconciliation must take as its main task "the reconciliation between the poor and rich churches as a whole, and by so doing make a contribution to our agonizingly riven world."[30]

Achieving dual loyalty (to America and to world Catholicism and through it to the world) will not be easy. To the extent it is achieved, American Catholics may not be able fully to acculturate to American life or gauge American successes or failures in terms of the nation alone. Achieving dual loyalty may be the pre-condition—following Pope Paul VI—of seeing the social question as worldwide. The greatest contribution of American Catholics to the international life would consist in being able to boast—in some paraphrased sense—with Tertullian: "Nothing is more foreign to us than the state *(res publica),* for there is only one state that we recognize and that consists of the entire world."

NOTES

1. In Thomas O'Dea, *Sociology and the Study of Religion* (New York: Basic Books, 1970), pp. 39–68.

2. One of the best treatments of the Americanists can be found in Robert Cross, *The Emergence of Liberal Catholicism in America* (Cambridge: Harvard University Press, 1958).

3. O'Dea, *op. cit.,* p. 51.

4. In response to the famous essay by Msgr. John Tracy Ellis, this became a dominant question among Catholics in the late 1950's, ironically just as Catholic cohorts of intellectuals were arriving on the scene. For one account cf. Thomas

O'Dea, *The American Catholic Dilemma* (New York: Sheed and Ward, 1958). For counter-evidence about the failure of American Catholics in the intellectual life cf. Andrew M. Greeley, *American Catholics: A Social Portrait* (New York: Basic Books, 1977).

5. Cf. Chapter 9 in this volume for another treatment of "thick symbols" in social ethics.

6. For Catholic social theory cf., *inter alia,* David Hollenbach, *Claims in Conflict* (New York: Paulist Press, 1979). For Catholic just-war theory and its recent applications cf. Thomas Shannon, ed., *War or Peace* (Maryknoll: Orbis, 1980). For a Catholic view of integral development cf. Denis Goulet, *A New Moral Order* (Maryknoll: Orbis, 1974). I am indebted to a personal exchange with Professor Stanley Hauerwas of the University of Notre Dame for the insight being developed in this chapter.

7. Orestes Brownson, *The American Republic* (New York, 1866), p. 371.

8. John Courtney Murray, *We Hold These Truths* (New York: Sheed and Ward, 1960), p. 43.

9. Michael Novak, *The Rise of the Unmeltable Ethnics* (New York: Macmillan, 1972).

10. José Comblin, *The Meaning of Mission* (Maryknoll: Orbis, 1977), p. 126.

11. Cf. Eric O. Hanson, *Catholic Politics in China and Korea* (Maryknoll: Orbis, 1980) and Thomas A. Breslin, "American Catholic China Missionaries 1918–1941," unpublished Ph.D. dissertation, University of Virginia, 1972.

12. Cf. Dan C. McCurry, "U. S. Church-Financed Missions in Peru," in Daniel Sharp, ed., *U.S. Foreign Policy and Peru* (Austin: University of Texas Press, 1972), pp. 379–415 and Gerald M. Costello, *Mission to Latin America: The Successes and Failures of a Twentieth Century Crusade* (Maryknoll: Orbis, 1979) for an assessment of some of the negative impact of U.S. missionaries abroad.

13. Msgr. Joseph Gremillion, "American Economic Power and Pluralism," in *Toward a North American Theology: Working Papers* (Chicago: Loyola University Press, 1981), privately circulated but available in some libraries, e.g., The Woodstock Library at Georgetown University.

14. Jay Dolan, *Catholic Revivalism* (Notre Dame: University of Notre Dame Press, 1977).

15. Murray, *op. cit.,* p. 11.

16. Cf. William Halsey, *The Survival of American Innocence* (Notre Dame: University of Notre Dame Press, 1980), p. 96 which speaks of an American Catholic "supranational universalism" in literary taste.

17. O'Dea, *Sociology and the Study of Religion,* pp. 61–62.

18. This point is dealt with at greater length in Chapter 5 of this volume.

19. Cf. Ernst Troeltsch, *The Social Teachings of the Christian Churches,* Olive Wyon, trans. (New York: Harper and Row, 1960), Volume 1.

20. S. N. Eisenstadt, "Religious Organizations and Political Process in Centralized Empires," *Journal of Asian Studies* 21 (May 1962), p. 292.

21. Cf. Ivan Vallier, "The Roman Catholic Church," in Robert O. Keohane and Joseph Nye, Jr., eds., *Transnational Relations and World Politics* (Cambridge: Harvard University Press, 1972).

22. Gustavo Gutiérrez, *A Theology of Liberation* (Maryknoll: Orbis, 1973), p. 308.

23. Dolan, *op. cit.*

24. Comblin, *op. cit.,* p. 11.

25. *Ibid.,* p. 17.
26. *Ibid.,* p. 38.
27. *Ibid.,* p. 76.
28. *Ibid.,* p. 132.
29. Cf. Walbert Buhlmann, *The Coming of the Third Church* (Maryknoll: Orbis, 1977).
30. Johannes B. Metz, *The Emergent Church* (New York: Crossroad Books, 1981), p. 11.

Chapter Thirteen

The American Social Gospel
of Justice and Peace

In the fascinating journal of his journeys to England and Ireland, Alexis de Tocqueville recounts conversations he held on the very same day in Cork, Ireland with a Roman Catholic cleric and the rector of the Anglican Church of Ireland. The priest spoke about the inequality of land holdings, the sovereignty of the people and its political capacity to discern its true interests. He championed the separation of Church and state. De Tocqueville's laconic remark was, "If he were to say these things in France, he would be taken for a Protestant minister!" On his part, the Anglican minister defended the institutions of an aristocracy, a national established church and a clergy salaried by the state. He disparaged the people's capacity for self-government. In his marginal note, De Tocqueville wrote, "Were he to say the same thing in France, he would be mistaken for a Catholic priest!"[1]

The Roman Catholic Church, as this anecdote illustrates, is not now and never has been an organizational or cultural monolith. The key problematic for Church-society relations varied and continues to vary from country to country and even within a given country. The variation depends on such factors as the size and class location of the Catholic population, the extent of the national Church's autonomy from governmental patronage or control, the economic and political forms of government, the historical alliances between sectors of the Catholic population and secular political forces, and the extensiveness of Church infrastructure, beyond parish and diocese, to generate secular impact, i.e., schools, hospitals, newspapers, voluntary societies, mobilization groups of Catholic Action, etc.[2]

It is very difficult to speak of *the* problematic of Church-society relations or of the Gospel strategic imperatives for justice and peace as if there was only one problematic or blueprint for action or strategy cross-nationally. The secular political task of the Church in Poland or Lithuania face to face with totalitarian secularist governments is very different from the task for the Church in Zambia or Tanzania where the Church enjoys excellent ecumenical relations, good informal contacts with the government, a visibly Christian head of state and the loyal support of the indigenous population. Even within Latin America where a relatively homogeneous Church-society strategy has been emerging in recent years in liberation theology, the political role of the church in Cuba, Nicaragua, Chile and Colombia will markedly differ.[3]

In an earlier period of Catholic social thinking, the Vatican envisioned a unitary worldwide Church-society strategy. Pius XI in the encyclical *Quadragesimo Anno*, for example, could speak of *the* papal model of social reconstruction in corporative, vocational groups. In the post-Vatican II period, Catholic social thought has undergone several extensive shifts. It is now more rooted in religious biblical imagery than in the philosophy of natural law. It recognizes, as Paul VI put it, that the social question is now worldwide. Catholic social thought has shifted from a strategic support for welfare capitalism to new openness toward socialism and the greater insistence on the social nature of property.[4]

Recognizing this vast diversity of contexts and social situations, Pope Paul VI wisely noted in his 1971 apostolic letter *Octogesima Adveniens*:

> There is of course a wide diversity among the situations in which Christians—willingly or unwillingly—find themselves according to regions, socio-political systems and cultures. In some places they are reduced to silence, regarded with suspicion and, as it were, kept on the fringe of society, enclosed without freedom in a totalitarian system. In other places, they are a weak minority whose voice makes itself heard with difficulty. In some other nations, where the Church sees her place recognized, sometimes officially so, she too finds herself subjected to the repercussions of the crisis which is unsettling society; some of her members are tempted by radical and violent solutions from which they believe that they expect a happier outcome. While some people, unaware of present injustices, strive to prolong the existing situation, others allow themselves to be beguiled by revolutionary ideologies which promise them, not without delusion, a definitively better world.
>
> In the face of such widely varying situations, it is difficult for us to utter a unified message and to put forward a solution which has universal validity. Such is not our ambition, nor is it our mission. It is up to the Christian communities to analyze with objectivity the situation which is proper to their own country, to shed on it the light of the Gospel's unalterable words and to draw principles of reflection, norms of judgment and directives for action from the social teaching of the Church.[5]

These words of Paul VI constitute a charter for the emergence of regional strategic theologies directed, respectively, to Eastern Europe, Western Europe, Latin America, North America, Africa, and Asia. It has been a major thesis of this book that it is impossible, without serious translation, to transplant European political theology or Latin American liberation theology to the United States. In that sense, we need to develop a regional strategic theology of justice and peace appropriate to our own context. Thus, for example, religion in America is neither as "privatized" nor is the society as secularized as in Europe.[6] The Enlightenment—so central to the political theology of J. B. Metz—had a very different reception in America than in Europe. It was not anti-religious. As mentioned in Chapter 9, America has never had popular movements embodying the second, anti-positivistic, Enlightenment associated with the masters of suspicion, Marx, Nietzsche and Freud. These have been restricted to the academy. American separation of Church and state did not mean a separation of Church from society. America lacked anti-clericalist laicist thought so important in the European context. It also never knew an established Church. I will later develop the point that this means that, in America, a peculiarly non-denominational ecumenical style of voluntarism is essential for any Church impact on the secular order.

Similarly, the class structure in the United States—lacking an established aristocracy—differs from the class structure in Latin America. While America knows, to be sure, specific forms of oppression, its government has, by and large, guaranteed some access to disenfranchised groups and protected civil liberties. Our middle class is too large and variegated to speak, in any simple terms, of a cleavage between oppressed and oppressor as in Latin America. Finally, much of the Latin American liberation thought assumes a deeply engrained Catholic cultural matrix foreign to America.

THE PROBLEM OF INTERNAL CHURCH PLURALISM

Before treating of some specific strategies of mobilizing for justice and peace proper to our own country, I want to make two preliminary remarks and a set of four sociological generalizations about Church-society relations. First, one of the sociological obstacles to concerted Catholic action for justice and peace is the very pluralism of the Church. Not only does the situation of the Church in Poland differ vastly from the situation for the Church in Uganda or the Republic of South Africa in terms of the demands and possibilities of justice and peace. It is also the case that the Church is often extraordinarily diverse within any country. To take one example, Catholics, by reason of their size and the number of institutions with secular import such as large universities and a settled place in the professions and politics, *can* have an impact in the dioceses of Chicago, Boston or San Antonio—which is not to say, of course, that they will— that Catholics would be simply unable to achieve in the dioceses of Oklahoma City or Atlanta.[7]

Moreover, as the sociologist Joseph Fichter reminds us in his ground-breaking studies of urban parishes, Church membership includes adherents with widely different degrees of commitment, socialization into Gospel values and identification with the Church. They exhibit a range from marginal to nominal through passive regular participants and nuclear, active Catholics.[8]

TARGETING POPULATIONS

An issue of strategy for the Church, then, entails targeting strategic regional and demographic sub-populations for campaigns of intense evangelization and mobilization for action for justice. Catholic Action strategies in France, for example, focused on workers, intellectuals and the youth. Latin American liberation theology has directed especial attention to the poor, long alienated from Church programs. It is impossible to speak about a strategic theology in the absence of some such targeting. For a strategy involves setting priorities, and setting priorities means favoring some groups or attainable goals over others. French Catholic Action targeted its chosen groups because such groups were those most apt to lapse from the Church and those considered, in its context, as carrier groups for wider societal transformation. These criteria were mainly sociological, although based on the perception that France was a "mission country." Latin America includes theological alongside sociological warrants for its strategic choice of the poor. The poor represent the largest—and marginalized—class in most Latin American countries. They are also the privileged *anawim* of the Gospel.

There seems little evidence, however, that American Catholics have made any such choices on either sociological or theological grounds. An American strategic theology remains to be forged. American Catholics have traditionally followed an inclusive Church rather than an exclusive sectarian self-understanding. American Catholicism represents a main-line "public Church."[9] This past history will continue to condition American Catholic strategies for justice and peace. These strategies must speak to middle- and professional-class Catholics since these are now the main constituency of the Church. An important strategic task, as Johannes B. Metz has put it, will be to find ways to protect this middle-class Church from degenerating into a "bourgeois" Church, devoid of any sense of the promise of a "messianic future" in tension with the status quo.[10] Even at its best, however, the internal pluralism of the Church will limit the sociological possibility of a unitary, prophetic stance.

Especially in the United States, where the Catholic population almost perfectly mirrors the social class stratification of the nation, many, if not most, of the Catholic population will be influenced as much by class interests, social location and social class perspectives as by the religious factor. This seems unavoidable. Since any strategic theology must be a "critical theology," the way to protect against inevitable class bias is for the Church to accept, as a fundamental priority, the Gospel option for the poor, to work to further the interests of the poor in our own country and abroad, to strive to give the poor voice and access as full participants in the institutions of society, and to attempt to see American achievements also from the vantage point of the victims of "social progress."

Much of the significant secular impact from the Church and much of the stirring up of energies within the Church will be the work of small cadres of committed social Catholics.[11] How to identify this minority, minister to its needs and allow it voice and access to the pluralistic Church at large becomes a chief strategic problem in organizing a national Church for justice and peace. We simply lack, at this time, an adequate inventory of American Catholic justice groups, popular and progressive communities working for justice.

A SUGGESTED PROGRAM FOR A
NORTH AMERICAN POLITICAL THEOLOGY

In an article about communities of justice in Canada, Tony Clarke suggests a fivefold program for a North American political theology.[12]

1. Develop an historical analysis of indigenous communities for justice.

This historical task would look at the historic role of the Church and various Christian social movements and their impact upon and alliance with secular movements for justice. In the United States, we would need to study, among others, the Catholic Worker Movement, the Catholic Rural Life Movement of the 1940's, Catholic labor schools of the 1930's and 1940's, the Catholic Cooperative Movement of the 1940's, Cesar Chavez' Farm Worker Movement, civil rights activism in the 1960's, the Catholic Committee on Urban Ministry, and the peace movement, e.g., Clergy and Laity United, Pax Christi U.S.A., etc. As this, very partial, listing makes evident, American Catholicism has already had a history of efforts toward peace and justice. Re-entering that history to assess its successes and failures will constitute an indispensable step toward forging our contemporary story of action for justice.

Gregory Baum, in a recent book, takes a look at Canadian Catholic social movements of the 1930's and 1940's. He asserts that "while there was a radical tradition in the United States, Catholics tended to stay away from it. It appeared un-American to them."[13] Part of Baum's research aim in this book on *Canadian Catholics and Socialism* is to uncover Canadian Catholic non-conformists who espoused radicalism. We would need to find out about similar American Catholic non-conformists from Edward McGlynn onward.

An obviously important historical project would relate to the question of the American Catholic contribution to the American labor movement. What were the causes of the historic American Catholic alliance with American labor and with the New Deal? What is the significance of a more recent apparent cleavage between Catholics and American labor? What alternative vision of society—if any—animated the Catholic labor schools of the 1930's and 1940's, the cooperative movement, spawned by Canada's Antigonish movement, and other Catholic movements of the past? I suspect we will be led to conclude that the Catholic Church in America espoused no clear concrete historical ideal toward which it directed its social mission. Perhaps we will discover that its historic project was *ad hoc* adhesion to political movements which promised greater inclusion and a wider distributive justice but that American Catholics lacked any critical cultural, economic and political ideal against which American realities were to be tested.

2. Study the current role of popular and progressive grass roots groups in the Church.

As a second step toward a North American strategic theology, Clarke suggests that we conduct an inventory and assess popular and progressive groups in the contemporary Church. Clarke distinguishes between "popular" groups of the indigenous poor and "progressive" groups of the middle class who take sides with the poor, the marginalized, and the oppressed. These will be important groups to locate in developing any national strategy for justice and peace. In America, the first will include, especially, Hispanic, black and native American groups for whom the experience of oppression is real. There can be no substitute for a careful listening to their experience of American realities—even if we feel the need to complement their viewpoint with others. Seeing America from their vantage point will be a corrective to our own inevitable class biases.

Study of progressive groups which have made an option for the poor should uncover some of the obstacles to gaining a hearing for a Gospel of justice and peace, obstacles which arise either from the wider American environment or from the narrow rhetoric of such progressive groups, their exclusion from mainstream reality and politics which could lead to a mere prophetic posturing, utopian religiosity or ineffectiveness in dealing with the actualities of cultural, social, political and economic life. The Catholic Committee on Urban Ministry which, until recently, represented a national network and clearing house for many such groups has, unfortunately, fallen into some disarray. Valuable as such groups are, I suspect we will find that our inventory of popular and progressive groups will not add up to an American strategic theology because of the failure of such groups to continue in the direction of Clarke's next three steps, especially the move toward a holistic social analysis.

3. Develop a common social analysis.

I am less sanguine than Clarke about the probability of achieving his third step, a *common* social analysis. I will treat this topic of social analysis further in the next chapter. I would propose that any strategic theology will agree with liberation theology in its assertion that we must begin our theology with some social science evaluation of our national context. It will seek, in the words of the Jesuit 32nd General Congregation, "the identification and analysis of the problems involved in the service of faith and the promotion of justice and the review and renewal of our apostolic commitments. Where do we live? Where do we work? How? With whom? What really is our involvement with, our dependence on, our commitment to ideologies and power centers? Is it only to the converted that we know how to preach Jesus Christ?"

I was recently involved with a team of five others in a year-long study of "The Context of Our Ministries," commissioned by the ten American Jesuit provincials. Our mandate was to develop "a description and assessment of the social, religious and cultural context of the United States, evaluated in the light of the Gospel and Catholic social teaching."[14] As a team, with the help of consultants, we looked at American demographics, the American economic and political system, family life, the criminal justice system, the American educational system, the media, social issues and American religion and Church life.

In the next chapter I will describe the method we followed in this study. Briefly, we tied social analysis to a discernment of moments of light and darkness in American culture, life and society when viewed from the vantage point of the Gospel. We explicitly sought a critical method which would acknowledge both American strengths and weaknesses. One citation from our collective "Discerning Statement" will illustrate our common judgment:

> The very values and realities for which we give thanks are not—
> if we subject ourselves to any degree of objectivity—in the ascendancy in our culture. If anything, they are endangered by counterforce ideologies of a hardened neo-conservatism informed by an economic system which, as C. S. Lewis has observed, can only be described as anti-evangelical (a sad reality, sadly intensified by the paradoxical fact that a mercantile Christianity unfortunately claiming both "morality" and "majority" is its main support) and an effete, highly relativistic liberalism that has neither fire nor consistency in its programmatic for social justice.
>
> The nuclear family, communitarian life, egalitarian sharing of wealth and a compassion for the disenfranchised are all under siege. The accumulation of money, the unchecked exercise of power and the pride of life which are in so many ways endemic

to capitalism take a massive toll on Gospel sensitivities. So much is this so as to reduce the truly transforming and revolutionary revelation of Jesus to an unreal and inapplicable mysticism. Pride, lust, envy, covetousness and the other capital sins seem no longer such; they have become culturally and economically legitimated virtues, necessary for the survival of our system.[15]

While I am making no special brief here for our own analysis of American realities in this study, I am convinced, with Clarke, that any regional political theology will need to begin with a careful social analysis of its own context and situation. In this respect I was struck by the comment of a leading American social justice activist, Msgr. John Egan of Notre Dame, who said of this Jesuit project, "What you are doing is what the American bishops should be doing for the whole American Church."[16] Like Latin America, we need our own Medellín and Puebla, our own attempt to assess the Church in the contemporary American world. In the absence of this exercise of strategic planning by the American bishops—or the American Church at large—it is difficult to speak yet of an American strategic theology. Not only do we lack a *common* social analysis—in any event very difficult to achieve—we have not as a Church even begun the task of attempting any sort of social analysis as a first step toward an indigenous regional theology.[17] As I will note in the following chapter, there are ambiguities in the American pragmatic temperament which tends to eschew holistic analysis for *ad hoc* pragmatic solving of problems. These ambiguities make the attempt at structural social analysis all the more important for an American regional theology.

4. Develop common theological reflections on the prior social analysis.

In this fourth step, Clarke suggests that we follow *the method* of Latin American liberation theology, even if our tools of social analysis or the content or strategies eventuating from it will differ. Liberation theology has at times been criticized for the crude nature of its theological reflections on social analysis. It has also been faulted for the vagueness of the social analysis it uses or its questionable adoption of exclusively Marxist categories of social analysis. What is more difficult to contest, in my judgment, is the methodological insight that theological reflection—for a strategic contextual theology—must be tied to prior social analysis of the situation for faith. In the absence of step three, this fourth step will remain impossible. We already have, in North America, three partial, yet indigenous, American liberation theologies in black theology, native American theology and women's liberation theology. They are a logical place to start, especially as they are already in dialogue with Latin American liberation theology.[18]

5. Explore the available political options for the Church.

Clarke's final step involves an exploration of the available political options for the Church. I leave this comment unexplored here since I return to this point later in the chapter when I treat of "elective affinity" between the Church and secular movements for justice. It seems a fair historical judgment that in the absence of any concrete historical ideal of its own, American Catholicism in the 1930's and 1940's "tilted" toward the New Deal. It also seems clear that a political theology will remain wholly abstract unless it backs (or, at the least, tilts toward) some existing political movements which represent an available political option in context.

With the collapse of an American consensus on the liberal welfare state in the 1980's and the rise of what Joe Holland and Peter Henriot refer to as "national security industrial capitalism," American Catholicism will probably need to look elsewhere than to the historic program of the New Deal in exploring currently available political options. The situation which made the liberal New Deal creative for its time has passed, giving rise to a new era of limits and interdependence.[19]

THE AMBIGUITY OF THE IDEAL OF PLURALISM

My second preliminary remark is directed toward the ambiguities in the American ideal of pluralism. While any American political theology will respect pluralism, a merely formal "pluralism" will not suffice. It is part of the problem. There is a clear directionality entailed in Gospel values and authentic Church social teaching. That directionality will include a Gospel bias toward the poor, those who have least voice in the courts of justice and least lobbying power in city halls, statehouses and the national capital. Catholic social teaching insists that any government or economy exists to serve human needs. Any exercise of power must be limited by the necessity of respecting basic human rights which include both civil and social-economic rights. A magisterial summing list of such rights can be found in Pope John XXIII's encyclical letter, *Pacem in Terris.*[20]

Moreover, Catholic social thinking which is *personalist* in the sense that it insists that the state and economy exist to serve the needs of persons and not vice versa is also *solidarist*. It contends that human rights are not absolute but exist in the context of solidarity, include duties as well as rights and lie always under the judgment of the common good of the community. Catholic views of the common good, in their turn, intend much more than an additive summation of individual utilities. Rather, the common good is seen as a *structure* of opportunities, allocations and participatory access, the set of social conditions which facilitate the realization of personal good by individuals. The common good is primarily structural.

In cases of a conflict among rights, as David Hollenbach has argued:

1. the needs of the poor take priority over the wants of the rich;
2. the freedom of the dominated takes priority over the liberty of the powerful;
3. the participation of marginalized groups takes priority over the preservation of an order which excludes them.[21]

Notoriously, Catholic social thought does not accept that private property is an absolute right. As Pope John Paul II has remarked, property always exists under "a social mortgage."[22]

Finally, Catholic social teaching is *pluralist* in its claim for the right to existence and nurturance of small groups of human scale to counteract the authority of the state and the massive power of economic conglomerates. Subsidiarity was the code word in earlier days to express this conviction that the state must not do for other groups what they can do for themselves or, when intervening to supplement what intermediary groups, such as the family, neighborhood, voluntary associations or the churches cannot achieve, it must not do so in ways which eclipse or bypass their participation. More recent social teachings such as the encyclical *Populorum Progressio* of Pope Paul VI and the 1971 World Synod of Bishops' document *Justice in the World* underscore a fundamental right to participation not only in the political but also in the economic order.

In an essay attempting a critical retrieval of Catholic social thought on the economic order, Philip Land argues to nine basic principles for a just economic order:

1. The economy is for people.
2. Economics is for being, not having.
3. The economic system ought to be needs-based.
4. The economy is the stewardship of world resources.
5. The economy must be a participatory society.
6. There must be fair sharing.
7. The system must permit self-reliance.
8. The economy must be sustainable.
9. The economy must be productive.

Land reminds us that Catholic social thought contains a bias against rule by the experts and the exclusion of workers from co-ownership and co-determination of the productive resources of a society.[23]

It is not my purpose in this chapter to review the details of international Catholic social teaching. Rather, I want to recall that it contains a definite and unmistakable bias toward decentralization, neighborhood organization, the rights of labor, and democratic participation in both the political *and* the economic orders. Drawing on Gospel values, it exhibits a preferential, although not exclusive, option for the poor. Catholic social teaching insists on the need to balance political-civil rights with economic rights to a living wage and a minimum floor for standards of health, housing and material well-being. It grounds both sets of rights in the meaning of human dignity, in seeing human persons as the images of God.[24]

Finally, against every "tactical provincialism" which would attempt to judge a given political or economic system in isolation from its worldwide impact, Catholic social teaching envisions a universal common good which recognizes that the social question is worldwide and linked.[25] Put bluntly, the moral worth of the American economic and political system cannot be truly assessed by looking to America alone. As Holland and Henriot assert:

> The root of the problems facing the poor countries can be found in the international economic order and *in the national economic orders linked to it*. No amount of "tinkering" with the current global order will remedy the situation. The rich/poor relationships need to be transformed through the creative efforts to restructure the global social system. The call for a "New International Economic Order" (NIEO) is an instance of the structuralist response, though a more thorough response *requires new national social orders as well*.[26]

While Paul VI in *Octogesima Adveniens* acknowledged a legitimate pluralism in various strategic theologies, he also hastened to add that each should "draw principles of reflection, norms of judgment and directives for action from the social teaching of the Church." Pluralism cannot have the final word.

Catholic social teaching is difficult to type as either pro-capitalist or pro-socialist. A case can perhaps be made for either from the teaching. But in almost any country we know, Catholic social teaching stands in judgment of current economic and political arrangements. It offers little to sustain consumerism, multi-national monopolies of power, a vast disparity in the distribution of wealth which allows significant portions of the population to fall beneath the poverty level of basic human needs or the prevalent utilitarian rationalism and centralizing bureaucracies which characterize much of American and Western European life and thought.[27] It is simply bizarre and out of touch with this social teaching to suggest—as Michael Novak recently has been doing—that Catholicism should endorse existing American capitalism.[28]

Luckily, American Catholic social thought—embodied in the writings of John A. Ryan, John Courtney Murray, Msgr. George Higgins and others and in the corporate letters of the American bishops from their 1919 statement on *The Social Reconstruction of the Economy* through their more recent statements, *The Economy: Human Dimensions* (1975), *The Eucharist and Hungers of the Human Family* (1976) and *American Indians*

(1977) never succumbed to Andrew Carnegie's near blasphemous American gospel of wealth which exhorted congregations to fulfill their duty to get rich. Far from an uncritical endorsement of American capitalism, the American bishops assert in *The Economy: Human Dimensions:* "It is not enough to point up issues in our economy and to propose solutions to our own national problems while accepting uncritically the presupposition of an economic system based in large part upon unlimited and unrestrained profit."[29]

It may indeed be a tactical mistake to begin reflection upon an American strategic theology with a focus on the issue of pluralism since this could lead to an uncritical celebration of the American economy and politics.[30] Whatever the pluralism in world Catholicism, Catholic strategic theology in any national setting will necessarily be linked to worldwide Catholic social premises of a just, communal and free society tilted toward basic human needs, the prior claims of the poor, a participatory society and the endorsement of simplicity in the use of material goods and luxuries. This is hardly an apt description of current American arrangements.

One does not have to be a Marxist to see how the American economy excludes or discriminates against blacks, women, native Americans, and the aged. Neither does it demand a Marxist analysis to see the ways in which the American consumeristic mania trivializes our lives or how large segments of the American populace experience alienation in their working life.[31]

No celebration of pluralism can let us forget that a genuinely Christian strategic theology will envision an order of greater justice and peace. This will necessarily include—especially if we take seriously the preferential Gospel option for the poor—elements of what Johannes B. Metz has referred to as "class treason."[32] Every Christian strategic theology worthy of the name will entail controversy. It will be rejected by segments of the population.

FOUR DILEMMAS OF CHURCH-SOCIETY RELATIONS

My set of sociological generalizations about the possible impact of the Church on secular society are four. They deal with the problem of achieving a delicate balance between the Church's unmistakable role as a public agency in society and its vocation to be faithful to its own identity as a free community of those who proclaim Jesus as Lord and live according to the standards of the Gospel. I am stating these four generalizations as dilemmas which will not allow choices between the various poles of the dilemma.[33] Hence, the need for a balancing act between competing values. Note that these four generalizations are sociological in character. They will be uncongenial to several theologies.

Dilemma #1: The Political Role of the Church: The Dilemma of Political Relevance Without Partisanship

Latin American liberation theologians have correctly noted that the Church always, willy-nilly, plays some political role in society. It can neither escape history nor the pressing claims and counter-claims of divergent political groups or economic interests. Even the pretense of being above the fray or Church silence on secular issues is a kind of political stance. Silence is generally a way of baptizing the status quo. Silence is a kind of tacit consent. The problem for the Church is not whether it will be political or not but how to find the appropriate arena, style and stance where it can handle the political role it is most suited to play in society, a political role which is most consonant with its character as Church.

I would suggest that the political role which the corporate or institutional Church in its official voices, episcopal or synodal, can best play in society is one of moral leadership as an ethico-cultural force to articulate and monitor the values of social justice, human rights and community based on human dignity and participation. The Church can only play this role if it eschews too great structural connection or bondage to highly partisan political movements. It can only play this role as a voluntary society, autonomous from the state and political parties.[34]

Too great separation from the issues of the political order can lead to irrelevance and an inward-turning other-worldly piety. This first delicate balance consists of simultaneously specifying and implementing Catholic social values in the social order and keeping the institutional Church free of too close identification with any one partisan group or political party. The normative teaching of the Church must be specific enough to make a difference.

Normative pronouncements can and sometimes should be very concrete in condemning certain abuses of power or violations of human rights such as torture, unjust tax laws, the escalating armaments race, and racism. But the Church should not suggest in its normative teaching that it has some concrete political wisdom of its own which robs secular political or economic movements of their rightful autonomy. Nor should the Church lay burdens of conscience upon its membership which cannot be unmistakably grounded in Gospel warrant or principles of justice.

The power of the Church, sociologically, is its ability to lend sacred legitimation, the aura of its charism, to secular orders of society or to counter-movements which embody new secular orders of society. The Church can only achieve this if it controls that charismatic power—which depends on its own autonomy, its separation from control or subtle sell-out to the secular apparatus of the state or its total enmeshment in concrete partisan groupings of left or right. Thus, for example, new strategies of extrication of the Church from state cooptation in Latin America have enabled Latin American bishops, theologians and laity to challenge the religious claims of national security state ideologies.[35] Where the Church in Latin America has achieved less autonomy from these political entanglements, e.g., Argentina and Colombia, its voice has remained more muted. Clearly, ideology critique of Church actions which are entangled with secular enmeshments constitutes a part of any strategic theology.

Just as the Supreme Court of the United States plays an indispensable moral political role as guardian of the values of the Constitution of America precisely by eschewing direct partisan involvement, so the Church as a corporate body, articulating the moral values of justice, human rights and community which flow from the Gospel, can effectively "tilt" or nudge society in new directions only if it avoids, in the main, overly partisan stances. The very pluralism of the Church's constituency means that in most cases the Church will, indeed, be able only to tilt or nudge society in a given direction. We should avoid unrealistic expectations about the political impact of the Church as if it were a "state within the state." A certain appropriate humility in our sociological expectations of Church impact on society is in order. As Brian Smith has noted in his assessment of Latin American Church influence, Catholic political action there is basically a reactive strategy. It also tends to have much greater impact on the churches than on society as such. As he puts it, "In no case . . . have churches been able, by themselves, to effect major changes in the political and economic structures underlying or causing the violations of civil, social and economic rights."[36]

Whenever the Church has become overly partisan in its moral pronouncements and actions, it has introduced secular political divisions into its own midst, thus paralyzing its own ability to act as a corporate body at all, because it has itself become hopelessly divided or it has led to a loss of credibility in the Church's claim to speak in the role of a transpartisan moral authority articulating Gospel values. On the other hand, when its normative messages have been overly general, diffuse and vague and filled with mixed signals, with something for everybody, the institutional Church has also been ineffective politically as a moral voice which could make a difference in secular issues of justice.

There is enough bite and concreteness in the orienting principles of the Gospel and the tradition of social Catholicism that if the Church courageously articulates them in season and out it will be *wrongly* accused of being partisan, as Pope Paul VI was accused of warmed-over Marxism by the *Wall Street Journal* for his encyclical letter *Populorum Progressio* and the American bishops were indicted for socialism in response to their 1919 statement on *Social Reconstruction*. A careful reading of the corpus of the papal social encyclicals and of selected episcopal letters such as the 1974 letter of the Dutch bishops on *Consumerism and Simplicity of Life*, the 1973 letter of the French bishops on nuclear policy for France, the letter of the Appalachian bishops, *This Land Is Home for Me*, and the recent letters of the episcopacy in Brazil, Paraguay and Chile will show abundant examples of this genre of non-partisan concreteness in normative teaching.[37]

It is important to note whether the import of normative social teaching indicates the need for serious structural reform in society or restricts itself to suggestions of mere piecemeal legislation and ameliorist schemes. In this respect, as Daniel Levine argues in a recent book, post-Vatican II social thought has shifted from a "moralist" to a "structuralist" analysis of social problems. The first approach sees the solution of social problems primarily in the reform of heart of individuals. The second recognizes the reality of structural social sin and calls for both social analysis and structural change. Levine notes the greater social impact in normative statements and actions which involve a structural form of reasoning. He also notes that this way of construing social analysis more and more leads the Church to recognize that politics is as much a problem for religion as fanatical religion which lacks respect for the rightful autonomy of politics the necessity of public *civil* discourse can be a serious problem for politics.[38]

Achieving a delicate balance between its political role as a moral authority and political revelance will be a permanent task for the Church in every national setting. By the inspection of its history, it is clear that the American Church has never felt the lure of enmeshment into partisan politics as has the Church in Europe and Latin America. Has it also always been concrete enough in preaching the fullness of the social gospel as a judgment on American economic and political affairs? The great danger in America is less the encapsulation of Catholicism by one or other political party or movement. The great danger is its becoming enmeshed in certain cultural pre-suppositions shared by almost all of the parties such as, for example, tactical provincialism or an unexamined commitment to increased GNP and an increase in consumption patterns or, alternately, aquiescence in "a widespread tendency toward privateness, a diminishment of belief in the possibility of authentic civic discussion in the community, and, finally, the tendency to discourage . . . any significant role in the realm of the polity for those whose principal home is the realm of culture."[39]

It is important to distinguish, as Daniel Levine does, between programs of Church political *activism* and programs of *activation*. The first, as he defines it, envisions a direct insertion of the corporate Church into the partisan political order. It is almost always a mistake. The second, more respectful of pluralism, points to "consciousness raising," educational programs in relation to politics and social justice, programs to activate the laity which then takes its own principled stand within the social order, Christians in action.[40] Clearly, without a serious program of lay *activation*, it is mere rhetoric to speak about an American strategic theology. To this point, we now turn in our second dilemma.

Dilemma #2: Structural Carriers of Christian Motivation for Political Engagement: The Dilemma of Religious Identification and the Worldly Calling

I do not think that American Catholics have ever achieved the articulation of a concrete historical ideal. They lack any manifesto or vision of the just society—what Paul VI refers to in *Octogesima Adveniens* as a rebirth of utopias. These do not, of themselves, however, provide the ready population with motivation and commitment to implement the vision. One key variable for religious impact on secular society, as Max Weber argued in his classic study *The Protestant Ethic and the Spirit of Capitalism,* is the ability of the churches to create structural carriers of motivation for political engagement to change the world. Mere pietism or socio-emotional groups of revivalism (whether the revival movement in American Protestantism or the Cursillo, charismatic and Marriage Encounter movements in Catholicism) are not enough.

As Weber saw, the delicate and, indeed, precarious balance was to generate motivation for social action that was seen to be a worldly *calling,* that is, a positive *religious* vocation to transform the world. Too great stress on the religious identity might lead to inward-turning pietism. Too ready emphasis on political engagement could lead to a loss of a distinctively Christian vision and input into the secular order, a sell-out to the prevailing winds of culture or the abandonment of the Christian nurturing cell for political involvement. It is ancient sociological wisdom that what begins in religion as the sociological "starting mechanism"—political movements, universities, science—often ends up not only rightly autonomous but even totally secular and irreligious. Thus, many of those trained in Catholic Action movements in France, for example, simply went over to the secular left without any further attention to the initial religious inspiration of their action in the world. In the process, it became questionable that their political action had any Christian inspiration.

There have been no cases of significant and widespread religious impact on modern culture without the combination, simultaneously, of a disciplined group life of prayer, discussion and Gospel reading and a clear "compulsion"—to use Winthrop Hudson's term—"to fulfill a distinctive vocation in society."[41] Intense disciplined pietism and, simultaneously, an equally intense sense of mission to transform society must be kept in delicate balance. As Weber saw, the balance was inherently unstable. It can never be taken for granted.

It seems clear to me that something other than the open, often large and unwieldy parish structure, with few demands on commitment other than attendance at Mass and financial support, on the one hand, or the intensely activist *ad hoc* lobby or ginger group, on the other, is necessary to engender large numbers (albeit a minority leaven in the mass) of lay Christians with a vivid sense of occupational and political life as a *religious* calling. And yet, the early American Puritan disciplined congregations,

John Wesley's Methodists in England and, in their own way, Catholic Action groups with their imperative to see, judge, and act, with also, at least in the French workers' Catholic Action, the demand for simultaneous involvement in a group of religious formation and as part of a secular organization—all these examples show that sometimes a delicate balance of combining an intense religious identity with a secular calling can be achieved and have secular impact.

The third world theologians and bishops have discovered a functional equivalent to the Catholic Action strategy—without its clericalism or dated ecclesiology—in the *communidades de base* which are devoted, in principle, to *religious* praxis which combines politics and mysticism, a this-worldly asceticism.[42] No functional equivalents to such groups—with the exception of some *communidades de base* among Hispanics—seem available in the American Church. As I argued in Chapter 2, attention to this lacuna is a pre-condition for an American strategic theology.

Dilemma #3: The Pastoral Needs of the Church: The Dilemma of Social Action and Wider Pastoral Care

As the brief flourishing of the social gospel among American Protestants shows, the identity of the Church can be such that the this-worldly can at times be linked to transcendent symbols such as "the kingdom of God" to produce what Weber called "this-worldly asceticism," the confluence of pietism and a compulsion to fulfill a distinctive vocation in society. Most of the post-Vatican II theology makes this kind of confluence normative for Church self-understanding. The appropriate theology for a worldly asceticism, I would argue, is in place for a renewal of Church and society. The vehicles to translate that theology into action and mobilization for action are not.

Individuals are religious for various reasons. In all authentically religious conversions the conscious life-turn is rooted in some experience of transcendence at a limit-situation of life. For some few, social action for justice or the cry of the neighbor in need represents the privileged locus for this experience of transcendence and the taste of the reality of God. They seem, however, to constitute a distinct sociological minority.

Most people turn to the churches for comfort, meaning and a sense of vivid identity and belonging. They seek in a religious tradition a place of loyalty where they can take a stand when faced with the near chaos of the almost unmanageable pluralism which constitutes the situation of modernity. Such people seek answers to personal hurts and ecstasies, tragedies, failures and travail. They look for the ultimate meaning of their lives and deaths and the strength to carry on their daily tasks. For most people, social justice issues ride "piggy back" on these other personal religious issues.

Survey evidence suggests that such people are not necessarily adverse to issues of social justice or totally inward-turning.[43] They show specific openness to the social justice implications of a Christian life, even though this is not the privileged or primary locus for their specific experience of religiousness, quest and transcendence. Most people, I would argue, turn to religion for personal reasons. The challenge will be to link their personal hurts, wonders or quests with larger structural issues. This will require, as C. Wright Mills once put it, a specifically "sociological imagination" which can demonstrate the connections between structural analysis and personal biography.[44]

This third delicate balance for the Church's action for justice and peace consists in the necessity to combine and connect pastoral care for deeply felt personal religious needs with programs directed to social action. To neglect intense pastoral care for interpersonal and personal needs is to run the risk of losing the Church constituency. Dean Kelly has argued that the conservative evangelical churches are growing apace precisely because they succeed in providing personal pastoral care and vivid religious identity.[45] Social-action programs which neglect this pastoral dimension run the risk, as Jeffrey Hadden puts it, "of a gathering storm in the churches."[46]

We can learn a lesson from the decline of the social gospel among an earlier generation of American Protestants. Winthrop Hudson has remarked, in discussing this decline of the social gospel:

> During the early years when the evangelistic concern remained central, the institutional churches enjoyed amazing success, multiplying their membership with astonishing rapidity, but when they began to fall in line with the new theological temper, discarding the evangelistic features of their program and devoting themselves almost exclusively to social service, their membership dwindled as rapidly as it had increased. Social work alone attracted few recruits. "The minister who engages in social work in order to build up his own church," Edward Judson acknowledged with some dismay, "is doomed to disappointment."[47]

While action on behalf of justice is a constitutive part of the very preaching of the Gospel, it is not the only part. The American Church will forget this truth at its peril.

Dilemma #4: Elective Affinity: The Dilemma of Church Influence and Collaboration with Wider Secular Groups

My final generalization about Church impact on secular society is related to Max Weber's point about certain moments of "elective affinity" between religious and secular movements. As I read it, Weber's assertion is that the churches alone never generate social change. Religious and social renewal seem always to co-vary. Indeed, it seems that Church reform itself can only be successful if it is carried forward by important socio-political trends in society.

The churches, to be sure, sometimes make a positive, unique contribution to society but always in alliance with secular movements articulating alternative visions of the social order. In this Weberian view, religion's contribution to social change is never simply the work of the Church but involves a tactical alliance or elective affinity between religious groups and wider movements of social and cultural change. Religious social creativity, Weber argues, is never, in any simple sense, merely against the world. It always involves a conjoining of Church and world. In such situations, religion makes an independent contribution—it is not simply a dependent variable—but it does so in alliance with other social forces.

Together with other groups, the Church can give a distinctive stamp to the social order. Yet the best historical examples of social creativity of the Church point to alliances of elective affinity as in the combination of the social gospel movement in American Protestantism with the progressive movement or that of the Catholic Action movement and Christian Democracy in post-war Europe in alliance with other forces of resistance or the support of American Catholicism in an earlier era for trade unionism.[48] Latin American liberation theologians see this Weberian point about elective affinity when they argue, in their context, for a collaborative merger of their Christian vision of a radically transformed social order with movements of the secularist, sometimes Marxist, left.

Many churchmen, I find, resist this Weberian point. They hold exaggerated views of what the Church alone might achieve. They resist "contamination" by any alliance of "elective affinity." In so doing, I would argue, they also resist the pre-condition for religious social creativity. I would also contend that Weber's point holds true even in ostensibly Catholic countries. It is remarkable, for example, that in Poland and Lithuania increased Church impact on the social order has coincided with a new openness to collaboration with "secular" dissident groups of workers, intellectuals or nationalists.[49] The need for such alliances is all the more obvious in a religiously pluralistic country such as America. No American Catholic strategy for social change will be effective unless in tactical alliance with wider ecumenical and secular movements for change.

In fact, Gregory Baum has criticized classic Catholic social teaching because "it did not correspond to any actual historical movement. Catholic social teaching was "idealistic" in the pejorative Marxist sense, inasmuch as it was a pure creation of the mind, outlining what ought to happen according to an abstract ideal of justice, and not a social theory based on the actual historical experience of people struggling for emancipation."[50] If I read him correctly, Baum is suggesting that in the absence of serious programs of activation of Catholics and real political choices by Catholics (if not the corporate Church as such), Catholic social teaching—however splendid and wise as a theory—runs the risk of being an ideology.

It is not entirely clear, in the present American scene, what groups constitute a likely strategic ally for social Christians. In the absence of any clearly formulated symbolic vision of a concrete historical ideal it is very difficult to decide. I have personally found Joe Holland and Peter Henriot's analysis of the American situation extremely helpful. They distinguish between an earlier liberal pastoral strategy appropriate to a former historical stage of social welfare industrial capitalism and a radical strategy more appropriate—if their analysis of the situation is credible—for national security industrial capitalism. They chart strategic pastoral responses of the traditional Church (a reaction to modernity), the liberal Church (adaptive to modernity) and a more prophetic Church which envisions an imaginative transformation of modern society.[51]

Those who follow Holland and Henriot's analysis will look to different strategic allies in America than the older ethnically balanced ticket of the Democratic Party. They will look to movements which display imagination toward a transformation of American society to a more ecologically responsible, just and communal society. My own personal choice has been to join the Democratic Socialist Organizing Committee of Michael Harrington and other ecological and peace movements of the secular left within—and alongside—the Democratic Party and the American Labor movement as a way of exploring available political options in our present American context. Others will choose differently. What seems incontrovertible, however, are the following three theses:

1. Any strategic choice to join one or another political movement will flow from a prior moment of interpretation and social analysis: What authentically American or human values are under threat? Who is articulating a genuine alternative of a more communal society in tune with Catholic social teaching and Gospel values?

2. Without a strategic choice the constituency of the churches (what I call, in Chapter 1, the dynamic, charismatic as opposed to the institutional Church) will in no way "tilt" toward any really available political options.

3. Without such a tilt of "elective affinity" between America's religious groupings and secular movements of change we will not see, in America, a Weberian creative moment of religious impact for social justice.

CONCLUSION: AMERICAN VOLUNTARISM

The American Church differs greatly from other national churches because it stands firmly in what Winthrop Hudson calls "the great tradition of the American churches," voluntarism. Here, separation of Church and state has meant that the Church must generate its own resources of the concerned and committed to have an impact on the larger society. A great part of the secret of the influence of religion in American life, as de Tocqueville observed, is to be found in the undisputed hold which the churches have, as *disciplined* communities, upon their members. A large part of this influence is also due to the fact that in America Church members could and did inaugurate or join non-Church voluntary associations of reform and social movements to shape American life, mores and culture in accord with some definite and specific vision of the good society which they imbibed in the churches.

What might be some of the mechanisms by which the American Church, corporately and in its members, can transform the shape of American life around a vision of justice and peace? I am going to end this chapter with a select list of some possible mechanisms or strategies to increase the sense of a worldly calling to transform society. I make no brief that this list is exhaustive or even that it includes the most important strategies for social action. My treatment of each strategy will be very short and merely suggestive. My main hope is that the list will make clear that there are ways to move the voluntary Church toward more concerted action, to tilt it in the direction of greater justice. I hope also that the examples suggest that fragmentation and the suburban captivity of the Church in the lure to comfort instead of challenging, while real pitfalls of any voluntary Church in a situation of acute pluralism, are neither inevitable nor necessary.

SOME MODELS OF MOBILIZING CHRISTIAN SOCIAL ACTION IN A VOLUNTARY CHURCH

1. Normative statements by individual bishops, synodal groups such as the Call to Action Convocation and collective episcopal statements are one obvious way to specify Christian values for the social order. They could be useful as guideposts for strategy and action, reminders that the Christian life has social import and responsibilities, elements of discernment toward a concrete historical ideal. Especially if they grow out of genuine grass-roots consultation, as I have argued in Chapter 2, they can represent distillations of the Church's discernment of the signs of the times.

Although I list these first, they are not the most powerful nor the most important contributions to a strategic theology. Their import should not be over-stated. Few read such episcopal statements. Fewer still are converted or changed by them. Most often they remain mere words, not followed up by action. Still, the corporate social teaching of the Canadian and U.S. bishops has been progressive and constructive. Their teaching shows a bias toward the poor. A recent study of U.S. Catholic moral teaching in the past decade argues that the credibility of episcopal teaching on social issues has been undermined by the inconsistency of the bishops' ethical reasoning when applied to social as opposed to personal or sexual ethics.[52] It seems clear that the American bishops' social teaching—"an extraordinarily rich corpus of social teaching as responsible and progressive as that of any group in the country"—has not gained a hearing.[53] Kenneth Overberg suggests that this might be remedied if such statements grew out of a wider consultative process.[54]

2. Sermons are localized normative statements. They can show how the Christian Gospel relates to local issues of social life—criminal justice, racism, consumerism, a sense of powerlessness. Like encyclicals, sermons need to be both specific enough as normative proclamation to provide genuine orientation for action or judgment of community situations yet not so specific as to violate Christian freedom and a rightful pluralism of political implementation of values. Yet what sociological evidence we have suggests that very few priests or ministers *ever* preach sermons touching social questions. A study by Harold Quigley of California clergy found that less than three percent of the clergy have ever preached on a social issue.[55] A sociological study of the role of the churches during the racial integration crisis in Little Rock, Alabama uncovered very few pastors who—*in any way*—broached the issue during the whole time federal troops were in Little Rock. Those who did lost their jobs! If concern for action on behalf of justice and the transformation of the structures of society is a constitutive part of the Gospel, it would seem that the Gospel is not at all being preached, at least from pulpits.[56]

3. A less controversial way to evoke a Christian response to social issues than direct preaching is to use the entire liturgy to highlight global hunger, unemployment, the north-south development question, the armaments race and other social issues. Here the emphasis is less on specific solutions than attention to urgent social problems which are not being satisfactorily addressed. I was struck several years ago when I lived in The Netherlands by the way the Dutch bishops commissioned the writing of special liturgies to focus on the meetings of the United Nations Trade and Development Commission (UNCTAD) and the question of the necessity of a new international economic order. Some European groups have followed Dorothee Sölle's example of political prayer meetings in Germany to give symbolic stress to the political dimension of the Gospel. It would be a mistake to make the social justice theme the only one at parish liturgies. Surely, however, by any count of the times it is referred to in parish liturgies, it seems *not* to be a regular part of the Gospel in ordinary parishes.[57]

4. Churches have often served as sanctuaries for political groups to meet and for planning groups in the community. Providing hospitality for such groups does not necessarily constitute an endorsement of their specific actions. Hospitality for social activists shows the public responsibility of parishes and their commitment to the "place" in which the parish is located. Canon law, of course, has always assumed that pastors of a parish are to be responsible to *all* the people and groups which lie within the territorial boundary of the parish, Catholic or not. One obvious way to fulfill this pastoral responsibility is to provide meeting space and hospitality for action groups. Another would be the sponsorship of town meetings where

important community issues can be discussed. Many parishes already do this. Every parish and diocese needs to ask about the extent to which it genuinely provides facilities to the community of its neighborhood and cities. If it fails to do so, it has misplaced its emphasis away from the foundational Gospel mission.

5. The oldest liturgical practice we know is the collection. A liturgical scholar once waggishly noted that we know at least one early canon of the Mass which seems to have left out an explicit formula of eucharistic institution. We know of few early liturgies which neglected the collection plate! As St. Paul reminds us, in his appeal for a collection for the poor in Jerusalem, the collection is fundamentally linked in Christian history to amassing alms for the poor. Collecting money to further social justice programs—for example, the annual American bishops' collection for the Campaign for Human Development to fund programs of self-help for the poor—is one simple strategy to activate social awareness. Such collections work best when they provide direct links of identification with specific groups at home and abroad. Generic giving runs the risk, as Johannes B. Metz implies, of "salving our conscience" without also raising our consciousness. Referring to Church aid organizations, he suggests: "Ought they not, precisely because they are aware that money is in no way innocent, play a powerful role in raising the consciousness not only of the recipient nations but also, and especially, of the benefactors?"[58]

6. Christian journals of current commentary and opinion on the ongoing political and social events of the nation are key vehicles for translating Christian social principles into specific forms where they can give shape to the social life and national priorities. Journals such as *America, Christian Century, Commonweal, Sojourners, New Catholic World,* and *Worldview* deserve financial support as indispensable aids to the Christian community in its reading of the signs of the times. Unfortunately, with a few exceptions, most diocesan newspapers are mere house organs which skirt controversial issues and tend to be overly churchy and inward-turning in their focus.

7. Bishops or church members from developing countries can be invited to write pastorals to dioceses or the whole national Church. Cardinal Enrique Silva of Santiago, for example, wrote such a letter to European Catholics at the time of the UNCTAD meeting in Santiago in 1972 specifying what third world Christians expect from their brothers and sisters in the developed world. Such a practice recalls early practices of exchange between local and regional churches in the early Church.

8. At the local level, programs of community organizers have done much to enlighten parishioners about the locus of power in their communities and issues such as redlining practices of banks and inadequate sanitation and services. I know of no local church programs so effective in making a first start toward achieving what the Latin Americans call "conscientization" as community organizing programs in neighborhoods. I also know of no other strategy in the American Catholic Church so cre-

ative for social justice. If ever there was an instance of what Weber called "elective affinity," it is that between community organization and the issues of the neighborhood and a parish. For parishes and neighborhoods— at least in inner cities—stand or fall together. The danger is that this splendid vehicle for empowerment at local levels is capable of its own version of "tactical provincialism" which fails to join the issues where people are hurting to a wider social analysis of national and international structures of injustice.

9. American religious congregations, especially of women, and the National Federation of Priests' Councils have been in the forefront in the movement to demand corporate responsibility by multi-nationals in investment.[59] Perhaps because American Catholics run so many separate institutions, such as schools, hospitals, etc., with investment portfolios, they can play a commanding role in attempting to force American-based multi-national corporations to face up to the human dimensions of an economy mainly based on profit motive and growth. They have also helped to educate the public to the power of the corporate conglomerates. Joe Holland has suggested, besides responsible investment strategies, that churches and religious congregations might think about setting up a development bank to loan money for alternative forms of housing and community-controlled enterprises.[60]

10. Some Protestant groups such as the American Friends and certain Baptist congregations view the local church congregation itself as a community of moral discourse and decision, a place of moral discernment about the political and social issues of our time. The Protestant moralist James Gustafson insisted that this function of corporate moral discernment stands along with the sacraments and the preaching of the Gospel as an indispensable mark of the Church.[61] The American Friends' pre-eminence in social Christianity stems from their brilliant marriage of intense and disciplined formation in piety and simultaneous concern for social service and action. They exemplify very well the delicate balance of piety and worldly address needed to achieve Christian impact in the world. While most Catholic parishes are too large to function as such communities of moral discourse and discernment, smaller units in the parish, house churches or base communities or groups formed for justice could constitute the cell units for formation and reflection on social justice issues. It should be clear by now that I think that thought and action in this area of activation for social justice is the deepest need at present for an American strategic theology.

11. The key instrument of the voluntary Church in affecting the social order in America has never been a political party or even the whole corporate Church as such. It has always been voluntary associations of Christians who form lobby groups to effect social policy. From the abolitionist movement, through the temperance and early women's suffrage movements, to the civil rights, anti-war and ecological movements, such

groups have always been the main American Church vehicle to effect justice and peace. Winthrop Hudson remarks about these groups:

> Such voluntary societies, organized by individuals within the churches but without any definite structural relationship to the denominational bodies, had several advantages. For one thing, they could be formed as need arose and they provided a channel for concentrated and concerted effort. More important, action did not need to be delayed until a corporate decision could be reached by a church or a denomination. A few interested friends could take the initiative and, then, through the society they created, could proceed to enlist broader support for their cause. Not only this, but such societies provided the necessary statewide and nationwide organization so essential to effective strategy and successful action.[62]

These groups were ecumenical and inter-denominational.

I have a strong impression that one of the major shifts in American Catholic social action with the demise of the immigrant church has been the decline of distinctively denominational Catholic groupings (such as earlier Catholic Action groups) and the rise of voluntary groups in the public interest with Catholic sponsorship or vigorous membership. Such groups have proliferated in the post-Vatican Church. Unofficial, and not denominationally sponsored, such groups, e.g., Bread for the World, represent a new form and style for Catholics to work for justice and peace. As I mentioned earlier, the key issue is to sustain the sense of inner piety and Christian identity in such groups that they do not go the way of earlier Christian-inspired movements such as the YMCA which eventually moved away into complete secularism. At the moment, the proliferation of voluntary groups in the public interest in American society could give hope for the Church and social justice, for as James Luther Adams has remarked about earlier voluntary associations of Protestant inspiration, "By their groups you shall know them!"

I want to end this chapter with the simple but wise remark I heard E. F. Schumacher make a few years ago in California at a Conference on intermediate and appropriate technology. Schumacher was confronted by a student questioner who asked anxiously what could be done to tame the growth of worldwide bureaucracy and the decline in a participatory society. Schumacher responded, "Look, if you see something that needs doing, start a group to do it and link up with other groups working for similar causes. If you can't start your own group, join one of those already existing. If enough people do that, the movement will be on its way." It may sound naive or simplistic, but it has been out of such voluntarism that every important American movement of social reform and change for justice has ever been born. It will only be through such voluntarism that we will achieve justice and peace American style. But while voluntarism is an essential American style, it will not alone suffice unless it is joined to a wider social analysis and a move to articulate, for our present moment in history, a genuine concrete historical ideal. Voluntarism abounds in the American community. The social analysis and vision to inform it does not.

NOTES

1. Alexis de Tocqueville, *Journeys to England and Ireland,* George Lawrence and K. P. Meyer, trans. (New Haven: Yale University Press, 1958), pp. 160–73.

2. Cf. Ivan Vallier, "Comparative Studies of Roman Catholicism: Dioceses as Strategic Units," *Social Compass,* Vol. VI, 2, 1969 for these variables, pp. 148–84.

3. For Cuba, cf. Meg Crehan, "Salvation Through Marx or Christ: Religion in Revolutionary Cuba," in Daniel Levine, ed., *Churches and Politics in Latin America* (Beverly Hills: Sage Publications, 1979); for Chile cf. Brian Smith's chapter, "Churches and Human Rights in Latin America," in the same volume. For Colombia cf. Daniel Levine, *Religion and Politics in Latin America* (Princeton: Princeton University Press, 1981). I am surprised that few American theologians who write about liberation theology seem familiar with the social science studies about particular churches in Latin America. They tend to substitute the rhetoric of theology for empirical analysis.

4. For these changes cf. Charles E. Curran, "The Changing Anthropological Bases of Catholic Social Ethics," in *The Thomist,* Vol. 45, 2 (April 1981), pp. 284–318.

5. *Octogesima Adveniens* in David O'Brien and Thomas Shannon, eds., *Renewing the Earth* (Garden City: Doubleday Image, 1977), pp. 353–54.

6. For a careful sociological assessment of contrasting states of "secularization" in Europe, North America and Latin America cf. David Martin, *A General Theory of Secularization* (New York: Harper and Row, 1978).

7. Cf. Vallier, *op. cit.,* for the relevant indices of comparison among dioceses.

8. Cf. Joseph Fichter, *Southern Parish* (Chicago: University of Chicago Press, 1951) and *Social Relations in the Urban Parish* (Chicago: University of Chicago Press, 1954).

9. Cf. Martin Marty, *The Public Church* (New York: Crossroad Books, 1981).

10. Chapter 1, "Messianic or Bourgeois Religion?" in Johannes B. Metz, *The Emergent Church* (New York: Crossroad Books, 1981).

11. Cf. Chapter 2 of this volume for a fuller treatment of this theme.

12. Tony Clarke, "Communities for Justice," *The Ecumenist,* Vol. 19, No. 2 (Jan.–Feb. 1981), pp. 17–25.

13. Gregory Baum, *Catholics and Canadian Socialism* (New York: Paulist Press, 1981), p. 152.

14. Cf. *The Context of Our Ministries: Working Papers* (Washington, D.C.: The Jesuit Conference, 1981), p. 3.

15. *Ibid.,* p. 23.

16. Personal communication to the author.

17. An important beginning for an American social analysis is found in Joe Holland and Peter Henriot, *Social Analyis: Linking Faith and Justice* (Washington, D.C.: Center of Concern, 1980).

18. For some examples of black theology cf. J. Deotis Roberts, *Liberation and Reconciliation: A Black Theology* (Philadelphia: Westminster, 1971) and James Cone, *A Black Theology of Liberation* (Philadelphia: Lippincott, 1970); for one example, among many, of women's liberation theology, cf. Letty Russell, *Human Liberation in a Feminist Perspective* (Philadelphia: Westminster, 1974), and for one example of native American theology, cf. Vine Delorio, *God Is Red* (New York: Grosset and Dunlap, 1973).

19. Holland and Henriot, *op. cit.,* p. 29.

20. *Pacem in Terris* and the list of rights in O'Brien and Shannon, *op. cit.,* pp. 126–35.

21. David Hollenbach, *Claims in Conflict* (New York: Paulist Press, 1979), p. 204.

22. For the phrase "social mortgage" cf. John Paul II's opening address at the Puebla Conference in John Eagleson and Philip Scharper, eds., *Puebla and Beyond* (Maryknoll: Orbis Books, 1979), p. 67.

23. Cf. Philip Land, "The Earth Is the Lord's: Thoughts on the Economic Order," in Thomas E. Clarke, ed., *Above Every Name: The Lordship of Christ and Social Systems* (New York: Paulist Press, 1980).

24. For an excellent overview of Catholic social teaching cf. David Hollenbach, *op. cit.*

25. The phrase "tactical provincialism" is from Johannes B. Metz in his *The Emergent Church,* p. 71.

26. Holland and Henriot, *op. cit.,* p. 17. Italics mine.

27. This tradition of social Catholicism is restated in John Paul II's *Addresses and Homilies in Brazil* (Washington, D.C.: U.S. Catholic Conference, 1980).

28. Cf. Michael Novak, *Capitalism and Socialism: A Theological Inquiry* (Washington, D.C.: American Enterprise Institute, 1979).

29. *The Economy: Human Dimensions* (Washington, D.C.: U.S. Catholic Conference, 1975), p. 7.

30. For one very uncritical celebration of American economics in the context of a discussion on pluralism cf. Joseph Gremillion, "American Economic Power and Pluralism," in Daniel Flaherty, ed., *Toward a North American Theology: Working Papers* (Chicago: Loyola University Press, 1981), limited edition. For a critical understanding of pluralism cf. David Tracy's magisterial *The Analogical Imagination: Christian Theology and the Culture of Pluralism* (New York: Crossroad Books, 1981).

31. For a non-Marxist indictment of consumerism cf. Delwood Brown, *To Set at Liberty: Christian Faith and Human Freedom* (Maryknoll: Orbis, 1981), p. 78; for American workers' accounts of alienation at work cf. Studs Terkel, *Working* (New York: Avon, 1972).

32. Cf. Metz, *op. cit.,* pp. 14–16.

33. For a similar understanding of dilemmas cf. Thomas O'Dea, *The Sociology of Religion* (Englewood Cliffs: Prentice-Hall, 1966), pp. 94ff.

34. Cf. Chapter 1 of this volume. Note that I refer here to the institutional Church. I will balance the institutional Church model against a model of the Church as sacrament to the world in Dilemma 4 which deals with the issue of "elective affinity."

35. Cf. Jose Comblin, *The Church and the National Security State* (Maryknoll: Orbis, 1979).

36. Brian Smith, *op. cit.,* p. 183.

37. For recent Latin American bishops' normative pronouncements cf. Robert Mitchell, "Recent Developments in Latin American Bishops' Statements," Working Paper, The Woodstock Center, 1979.

38. Cf. Daniel Levine, *Religion and Politics in Latin America* p. 78.

39. The citation is from David Tracy, *op. cit.,* pp. 11–12.

40. Daniel Levine, *Religion and Politics in Latin America*, pp. 179–80.

41. Winthrop Hudson, *The Great Tradition of the American Churches* (New York: Harper and Row, 1953), p. 10.

42. For some background (not empirical) on base communities cf. Sergio Torres and John Eagleson, eds., *The Challenge of Basic Christian Communities* (Maryknoll: Orbis, 1981).

43. For Catholic attitudes on welfare and civil liberties cf. Mary Hanna, *American Catholics and Politics* (Cambridge: Harvard University Press, 1979), pp. 101–117. Note also the openness to social justice issues in the sample employed in Joseph Fichter, *The Catholic Cult of the Paraclete* (New York: Sheed and Ward, 1975).

44. Cf. C. Wright Mills, *The Sociological Imagination* (New York: Oxford University Press, 1959).

45. Dean Kelley, *Why the Conservative Churches Are Growing* (New York: Harper and Row, 1977).

46. Jeffrey Hadden, *The Gathering Storm in the Churches* (Garden City: Doubleday, 1969).

47. Winthrop Hudson, *op. cit.,* pp. 207–08.

48. For the social gospel and the progressive movement cf. Henry May, *Protestant Churches and Industrial America* (New York: Octagon Books, 1963); for Catholic Action and Christian democracy cf. Michael P. Fogarty, *Christian Democracy in Western Europe* (London: Routledge and Kegan Paul, 1957).

49. The case for new alliances in Lithuania is presented in V. Stanley Vardys, *The Catholic Church, Dissent and Nationality in Soviet Lithuania* (New York: Columbia University Press, 1978). The case for a shift in Poland is presented in Leszek Kolakowski, "The Church and Democracy in Poland," *Dissent,* Vol. 57 (Summer 1980), pp. 316–20.

50. Baum, *op. cit.,* p. 80.

51. Cf. Holland and Henriot, *op. cit.,* pp. 28–38.

52. Cf. Kenneth Overberg, *An Inconsistent Ethic?: Teachings of the American Catholic Bishops* (Lanham, Md.; University Press of America, 1980).

53. Citation from Francis Meeghan, "The Bishops' Moral Teaching," *The Priest,* Vol. 32, No. 2, 1978, p. 15.

54. Overberg, *op. cit.,* p. 175.

55. Reported in Charles Glock, Rodney Stark and Harold Quigley, *Wayward Shepherds* (New York: Harper and Row, 1975), p. 93.

56. Cf. Will Campbell, *Race and the Renewal of the Church* (Philadelphia: Westminster Press, 1962), pp. 73ff.

57. For sample liturgies in Latin America and India cf. Sergio Torres and John Eagleson, eds., *The Challenge of Basic Communities,* pp. 217–27.

58. J. B. Metz, *op. cit.,* p. 13.

59. For the role of the National Federation of Priests' Councils in founding

The National Catholic Coalition for Responsible Investment cf. James H. Steward, *American Catholic Leadership: A Decade of Turmoil* (New York: Mouton, 1978), p. 112.

60. Cf. Holland and Henriot, *op. cit.,* pp. 26–27.

61. James Gustafson, "The Church and Moral Discernment," in *Theology and Christian Ethics* (Philadelphia: Westminster, 1974).

62. Hudson, *op. cit.,* p. 61.

Chapter Fourteen

Reflections on a Political Theology for America

In this final chapter I am going to make some concluding remarks about a political theology for America. First, I want to present, briefly, an appropriate method for an American strategic theology, the method of "the pastoral circle."

THE PASTORAL CIRCLE

Joe Holland and Peter Henriot in their booklet *Social Analysis: Linking Faith and Justice* coin the phrase "the pastoral circle" to indicate a method for an American political theology.[1] It was the method we followed in our year-long study of American realities for the ten Jesuit provincials, *The Context of Our Ministries*.[2] This pastoral circle method of theological reflection for a practical theology includes four elements: (a) the statement of experience; (b) social analysis; (c) theological reflection; (d) pastoral planning.

THE STATEMENT OF EXPERIENCE

The return to experience has been a lively American theme since the time of Emerson onward. It is key in such American philosophers as William James, John Dewey and George Santayana and an important perspective in the American Protestant reflections on social issues in the works of Rauschenbusch, H. Richard and Reinhold Niebuhr.[3] America has always seemed, to European observers, to constitute the place of the experiential and experimental. Here, experience—rather than theory—praxis and the pragmatic predominate.[4] As Sidney Mead once termed American religious history, America represents "a lively experiment."

The statement of experience in the pastoral circle method of theological reflection looks not only to the *empirical* (which, often, is a social science abstraction, a statistical "map" of experience) but to the the *experiential*. Beyond gathering data for social analysis, the statement of experience will point to lived encounters with other persons, with the world and with God.[5] The experience being stated will be both individual and corporate. The narratives recounted will include the American stories of both persons and groups. It will be important to note whose experience is being recounted and what groups are included or excluded from the collective narrative of American experience, for not every group's experience of America will be the same. The Irish in San Francisco, for example, will find it difficult to relate to the Boston Irish experience of a feisty supplanting of a hostile Puritan establishment with vivid memories of signs of "No Irish need apply." In San Francisco Irish Catholic names such as Flood and Phelan were part of the city's founding epoch. It will be also important to note whether the experience of America's poor is included—indeed, preferentially weighted—in the American narrative.

Any recounting of American experience will most likely uncover some common traits. Key themes might include pluralism, pragmatism, personalism, voluntarism, localism and loyalism to sub-groups such as religious denominations or ethnic groups.[6] These retrieved traits will set a tone for the project of an American strategic theology. But, as with any narrative, there will be continuities as well as discontinuities in the story-line. For example, voluntarism—as I argued in Chapters 6 and 13—has been an essential element in American political life. Is it, however, today under a new threat? Does voluntarism mean the same thing in the 1980's in an America dominated by corporate conglomerates and the world of computerized information retrieval as it did in an earlier America of small farms and family firms? Can voluntarism today attain results similar to the political achievements of the past?[7]

Beginning our method for a strategic theology with explicit attention to experience has several advantages. It helps us to avoid the dangers of rationalism and idealism, the substitution of mere abstraction for concreteness. It roots theological reflection in vivid personal and group memory. It starts the reflection with the question, "What is happening to people?" Moreover, it is, in intention, an inclusive method. Experts do not have the first—or last—word. We begin with the experience of ordinary people.

Alongside our own personal experience, our sense of the American story will be enriched by our readiness to listen to the many other American stories of experience, some of them painful narratives of injustice, racism, poverty, fear of crime and a sense of powerlessness. It is also possible to expand our experience notably by programs of "insertion" into various kinds of milieus where the experience of the poor or the oppressive character of some American economic and political structures can be tasted and touched first-hand. Finally, as Thomas E. Clarke notes, the experience drawn upon in this first step, while "many-faceted, touching every dimension of our human involvement in the world," will be at its core a *faith*-experience, "the encounter with God manifesting himself and his call to us in all dimensions of our life and in the signs of the times."[8] Already, this first step includes a faith component. It involves an initial essay at a correlation between lived experience and our experience of faith. For, ultimately, the praxis which constitutes the starting point for the theological reflection is our praxis of faithfulness to the Gospel.

SOCIAL ANALYSIS

The first step in the pastoral circle, the statement of experience, takes place in the narrative mode. It involves a distillation of personal and collective memory and experience. It is possible, however, to "jog" memory by suggesting some questions and categories for the experiential narrative to guarantee a multi-faceted coverage of cultural, social, economic, political and ecclesial experiences.[9] When this is done, the second step of the pastoral circle is anchored in vivid symbols and anecdote. It will then be possible to move from the anecdotal to the analytic in the second step, social analysis.

Social analysis moves beyond the narrative mode to identify social issues, policies, structures and systems. Holland and Henriot define the term: "Social analysis examines causes, probes consequences, delineates linkages and identifies actors. It helps make sense of experiences by putting them into a broader picture and drawing the connections between them."[10]

A recent news report helps to illustrate the meaning of social analysis. When the nation's governors opposed plans to shift the responsibility for welfare funding from the federal to state governments, they responded to an initiative of the Reagan administration to make such a shift by asserting: "The overwhelming majority of governors are violently opposed to a shift of welfare to the states. The governors view welfare as a national, a federal, responsibility *because national economic policy largely determines how many people need welfare* and what level of assistance should be provided."[11] Whereas the first step in the pastoral circle will look, for example, to the experience of welfare mothers, the second step of social analysis will ask about national economic and social policies which largely determine how many jobs will exist, differential structures of opportunity for education, housing, jobs etc., the economic climate in the northeast vs. the southwest, even inner migration patterns within the nation and the city. Social analysis turns from the "victims" to the policies and structures which tolerate—even sometimes create—them.

Social analysis is an indispensable and integral component for any strategic theological reflection. Nevertheless, it is a difficult step in the pastoral circle for several reasons. First, the human mind finds the narrative mode congenial. It typically thinks in terms of persons rather than structures. Indeed, even many social scientists—including Max Weber, ultimately—reduce the structural to the typologically personal in what has been called "methodological individualism."[12] Structures, causes (especially when, as normal in social science analysis, causal thinking is tied to arguments from statistical probability) and linkages involve abstractions.

Much social analysis, therefore, focuses uniquely on the process of "identifying actors"—inner vs. other-directed types, the lazy vs. the ambitious, oppressors vs. the oppressed—rather than on full-scale attention to structures of opportunity, allocation and oppression. Social structures have a *sui generis* reality, whatever the personality or personal virtues of the actors who fill roles in the structure.

Moreover, social reality—especially the American complex social reality—is extraordinarily dense, complex and changing. Because of this, too, social analysis is difficult. Indeed, social reality is always so much more complex than any abstraction—whatever the empirical or statistical fit between the "map" and reality—can fully capture that it is difficult to speak of invariant laws or findings in the social sciences. As reality changes, so must the social science study of any phenomenon. Social analysis is a never ending and constantly changing process.

It is important to recognize several of the difficulties involved in achieving a common social analysis. First, there are diverse—sometimes complementary but sometimes contradictory—traditions of social analysis: Marxist, functionalist, behaviorist, symbolic-interactionist, Durkheimian, Weberian etc. Notoriously, the questions we ask determine what we look for and see. How we see a problem, in its turn, determines how we respond to it. To the best of my knowledge, no one in the social sciences has yet constructed a unified theory which would relate the divergent traditions of sociology or economics in ways which eliminate this conflict of interpretations. Moreover, no tradition of social science analysis, even positivism or behaviorism, is theory-free. It would be naive and misleading, therefore, for theologians who urge the use of social analysis to suggest that there exists an already unified field called "social analysis." There are, instead, conflicting traditions of social analysis which yield divergent definitions of the situation, differing assessments of "facts," "data" and "reality." Conservatives and liberals, Marxists and Weberians each claim to be truer to the "facts." One initial task for the theologian, then, will be to become sensitive to the presuppositions which lie behind different social science traditions, theories and methodologies.

Secondly, as a corollary of the above conflict of interpretative traditions of social analysis, no social science analysis is, in any simple sense, value-free or neutral. The social world being analyzed is a human construct, built up by human actors and groups to protect their interests and values, ward off threats and fears, and further special goals. Values and interests are built into any social system which exists. Every institution is, in some sense, an institutionalization of values. It is impossible, therefore, to "read" that social reality divorced from the value components which underpin it. When faced with value questions, the human mind rather naturally evaluates.

Because social analysis is not value-free, the dialogue between social science and theology is a two-way street. Every sociology involves, at least implicitly, a correlative theology and vice versa.[13] In dealing with social analysis, one's own or another's, the ethical and philosophical assumptions underlying the analysis, often very implicit and unstated, must be explicitated. One of the difficulties in undertaking social analysis as part of the pastoral circle method for strategic theology is linked to this value-laden character of social science. Every social analysis will be controversial, contested, part of the human situation of the conflict of interpretations. Holland and Henriot state this point trenchantly:

> We always choose an analysis that is implicitly linked to some ideological tradition. The claim to have no ideology is itself an ideological position! Locating ourselves within some vision of society—whether it be one of the many interpretations of capitalism, socialism, feudalism, tribalism etc.—we interact with various social and political movements, many of them fiercely antagonistic toward each other. The reluctance to move toward social analysis can be explained, in part, by this element of controversy. Behind our protests that social analysis is too difficult or irrelevant may be a fear that it is really too "radical." If we were to examine the institutions and processes of our society and of our Church, would we not become continual questioners and doubters, driven to "radical" responses?[14]

The "fact" vs. "value" distinction is not as iron-clad as positivists have suggested. Nevertheless, something of the tradition of value-neutrality deserves support.[15] Social analysis has its own logic, tools and methodological exigencies. It contains its appropriate canons for evidence, warrant and explanation in adjudicating conflicting claims about reality. Social analysis cannot be reduced to *a priori* theological or ethical positions. Nor is it a mere projection of human ideals. There are such things as "stubborn facts," although their meaning is never disclosed in isolation from other "facts" as part of a larger explanatory or interpretative theory. At some level, also, social science subjects itself to testing by data which can disprove and disqualify theories.

Catholic thought has always accorded an autonomy to the secular as a reality in its own right. There is an important tension between Christian faith and human reason—whether scientific or philosophic—by which the faith seeks to understand and transform the world. The fruitful relation between theology and social analysis cannot afford an imperialistic use (or, better, misuse) of social analysis, controlled by theology. Social science has its own autonomy.

I have argued elsewhere, following Bernard Lonergan's notion of eight functional specializations, that there are areas—establishing the "text" or data to be analyzed and interpreted, the phenomenological description achieved by passing-over to the situation of actors and *their,* not our, definition of the situation for action—where the ideal of value-neutrality, at least as a heuristic device, is essential to social science methodology. We need to hold our own valuations temporarily in check in order to discover and understand social worlds and values foreign, even repugnant, to our own. In other functional specializations of an empirical and historical science—what Lonergan calls "history" and "dialectics"—strict value-neutrality is neither possible nor desirable.[16]

Given the plurality of conflicting traditions of social analysis, theologians who utilize social analysis as part of the pastoral circle are compelled to adjudicate between competing social science interpretations to justify their choice of one rather than the other. They should do this on inner sociological or social science grounds. Mere intuitive preference for one or another social science tradition will not suffice. Nor is it adequate simply to adopt the culturally prevailing social science models, whether functionalist or Marxist, merely because they are in possession in a given national setting.

One of my criticisms of the use of social science analysis by many Latin American liberation theologians is their failure to justify the choice of Marxism as a social science tool on inner sociological warrants. They leave unclear and unjustified why just this social science tradition is chosen in preference to Weberian, Durkheimian, functionalist or symbolic-interactionist perspectives. Some of Marx's hypotheses have been verified by social science. Some have been found wanting.[17] I am also wary of the Latin American phrase *la realidad,* as if the "factual" reality being pointed to or its interpretation is beyond legitimate dispute. The rhetorical annunciation of *la realidad* could betray a certain naiveté about the inevitable conflict of interpretations in social science.

Perhaps, much like the social gospelers in an earlier period of American history who turned to positivistic understandings of "science" as a way to deliver the "facts," beyond theological disputes, the liberationists are trying to finesse the hermeneutical circle with its inevitable conflict of interpretations by appealing to a putatively solid and unassailable *la realidad.* Their sensitivity to hermeneutics in theology is often wedded to a non-hermeneutical, even positivist, understanding of science as capable of delivering an uncontested *la realidad,* now dated in European and North American views of social science.[18]

We lack, at the present time, any study of the use of social science analysis by the liberation theologians.[19] Often, to this reader, that use seems selective and even rhetorical at times. We remain, however, in debt to them for their methodological insistence on social analysis as an integral component of theological reflection.

In economics, social analysis will focus on descriptions and explanations of: (1) the kinds of productive processes (state-controlled, market-controlled, worker co-determination, mixed; monopoly or oligopoly vs. true competition); (2) the kinds of goods and services produced (whether geared to basic human needs or not?); (3) the paths of distribution of goods and services and (4) patterns of consumption. In politics, analysis will ask questions about where and by whom key decisions are made, how much popular participation is involved in setting social policies and the realistic prospects for the successful implementation of decided-upon policies or goals. Key questions will include: "Who has power? For whom is it used? Guided by what values? With what vision of the future?"[20]

In their treatment of the social analysis step in the pastoral circle, Holland and Henriot note the limits of social analysis as a tool for theological reflection. First, social analysis discovers causes, consequences, linkages, structures and principal actors. It can never provide a blueprint for action. Analysis tells us what *is* and why, some of the limits and possibilities for action and the probable consequences of choosing one rather than another course of action. It does not dictate, among several, which actions to choose. Action itself depends on creative choice, risk, the values we espouse. The construction of alternative economic and political structures will ultimately flow from creative cultural vision rather than analysis. In that sense, analysis is a negative instrument.

A second limitation involves the danger of leaving social analysis to the intellectuals, the technocrats and the experts. "The best and the brightest," too often the victims of a narrow technical rationality, have no corner on creative vision. Leaving social analysis to the experts runs the risk of undermining older American ideals of a participatory, democratic society premised on a trust in the native wisdom of common people.

Still, social analysis remains a major component in the pastoral circle method for a strategic theology. As Thomas Clarke states it, "the value and role of sound social analysis is partly in its helping us to move beyond personal experience of the milieu and to provide us with the empirical and analytical basis for the evaluative judgments and the pragmatic decisions that will represent our response of faith to the needs of our times. Without sound social analysis, our apostolic choices run the risk of being visionary, romantic or simply misguided and irrelevant."[21]

THEOLOGICAL REFLECTION AND PASTORAL PLANNING

The third and fourth steps in the pastoral circle involve theological reflection and pastoral planning. Theological reflection looks to a Christian evaluation of the context of our ministry. It will find in the doctrines of creation, sin, redemption, resurrection and eschatology further guideposts for understanding and evaluating the American experiential narrative and the realities inferred by social analysis. Our American experience will be viewed in the light of living faith, the Scriptures, Catholic social teaching and the retrieved memory of Catholic tradition. The word of God, addressed to our situation, raises new questions to it, offers fresh horizons, new criteria for evaluating the meaning of America.

Finally, after seeing and judging, we will be moved to act. Pastoral planning, the fourth step in the pastoral circle, asks about the appropriate responses of individuals and Church communities to the analyzed situation. What target groups should be emphasized for programs of ministry and evangelization? What strategic secular allies suggest themselves as apt candidates for a coalition in elective affinity for social action? Given Church resources, how can the limited money and personnel of the Church be best utilized for action on behalf of justice? Who takes part in the process of pastoral planning? Only bureaucrats, the clergy, hierarchs?

All four steps in the pastoral circle are necessary components for the method of a strategic theology. None can be dispensed with. The method is called a pastoral *circle* for several reasons. First, the divisions between the four steps are not as rigid as the analysis suggests. Faith questions and theological themes will be operative from the beginning in directing our attention to experience and raising certain questions for social analysis. The Gospel bias toward the privileged character of the poor, for example, will incline us to certain types of social analysis that concentrate on issues of distributive justice and stress equality. Second, the action responses of pastoral planning change our situation and bring, in their wake, new experiences. These, in their turn, call for further analysis, theological reflection and planning. The pastoral circle comes round, again, full circle.

THESES FOR AN AMERICAN STRATEGIC THEOLOGY

In this second part of the chapter I will state seven theses for an American strategic theology. Since this chapter subsumes the arguments and contentions in previous chapters, these theses are not meant to be all-inclusive. Nor are they intended as a summary of this book. Rather I am stating them by way of supplementing earlier contentions, e.g., an American strategic theology will be in dialogue with European political and Latin American liberation theology; an American theology will address ways in which the social question is worldwide; American theology will keep alive the Catholic sense of internationalism; American theology will be linked to voluntarism etc.

Thesis One: An American strategic theology will grow out of *essential* socio-political functions of the Church.

It has been a major contention of this book that strategic theology is not a luxury for the Church. The Church exists for mission, and its Gospel mission is shaped, in part, in response to its milieu. The Church is not authentically Church except in mission. Its mission determines the kind of community it must be. *Communio* and *missio* are inextricably linked. The Church is sacrament both of Christ and of the world.[22]

I would contend that there are six *essential* socio-political functions of the Church in its mission for justice: (1) consciousness raising through education for justice, (2) advocacy for programs of justice for the poor, (3) providing direct services to those in need, (4) stewardship in justice of its own resources, (5) community-building, and (6) activation of the laity for action for justice.

The Church will educate for justice. Such education will include programs to elucidate the Gospel horizons for justice, Church social teaching and the global and national situations for justice. It will pursue education for justice through many means (preaching, curriculum in Catholic school systems, the media, symposia, town meetings, the sponsorship of insertion programs). It will also extend education for justice at every level of the Church: parish, diocese, region and nation. Programs of education for justice probably are the Church's major tool in seeing that action on behalf of justice and the transformation of unjust structures become a constitutive part of the preaching of the Gospel.

The Church will also be *an advocate* for efforts for the poor. It does so by direct-lobbying efforts for specific programs and legislation. The United States Catholic Conference and the various state Catholic conferences in state capitals are a logical outgrowth of the Church's moral role as a public advocate for the poor. As is well known, these conferences testify before congress or state legislatures and take stands on proposed legislation and lobby, not only for legitimate Church interests, but for wider social issues consonant with Church social teaching. Advocacy adds to programs of education a specificity of response. Besides these institutionally sponsored agencies the American church includes other advocacy groups such as The Center of Concern, Network and various peace and justice commissions of religious congregations.

But the Church cannot effectively advocate unless it also is organically in contact with the poor, their needs, frustrations and resources. Providing direct services to the poor is a permanent and essential mission of the Church. The Church should never allow the state to preempt all programs of service to the poor or become so entangled with the state as to lose its own autonomy for initiative in providing services to the poor. Society needs watchdogs who monitor the kind and quality of services to the aged, sick, retarded and the poor. The Church cannot speak realistically *for* the poor unless it speaks continuously *with* them through its own programs of service. Direct experience with the poor, through services, will move the Church to become an advocate to give the poor their own direct voice in society. The empowerment of people is the final goal. Providing services to the needy is a duty in charity. I am also here arguing that it is a pre-condition for the Church becoming an effective advocate for the poor. The United States Conference of Catholic Charities, as the largest private American welfare organization providing direct services to the poor, will be an integral partner in American Catholic strategies for justice.

A fourth socio-political function of the Church involves the Church's own commitment to justice as steward of Church resources. The Church which advocates a living wage must pay one to its own employees. The Church which preaches the right to unions must not undermine the union movement in the institutions it runs. The Church which espouses, in its social teaching, a participatory society must find ways to further genuine co-participation of employees in Church-run parish plants, school systems, hospitals etc. As the bishops' synodal document *Justice in the World* reminds us, the principles for a just, communal society found in the Church's social teaching apply to the Church's inner life as well.[23]

I have dealt in earlier chapters with rationales for Church concern for building community through, for example, community-organizing and with the issue of activation of the laity for a worldly vocation. I list these six functions here to indicate that already the Church is entrusted with essential and constitutive socio-political functions. It need not create new ones. A strategic theology need not move beyond what is already part of the Church's mission. It will reflect on Church praxis of education for justice, advocacy for the poor, services to the needy, stewardship, community-building and activation of the laity for direct action in the world. Are all six functions actually operative and effective? What is the relationship in providing services between those who "serve" and those who are served? Do services respect human dignity and point toward empowerment? Do the agencies for advocacy base their claims on the actual experiences of the needy? Does advocacy flow from social analysis and an articulated concrete historical ideal? Probing these and similar questions about essential socio-political functions of the Church constitutes a good place to start the process of the pastoral circle.

Thesis Two: An American strategic theology involves a call to relinquishment.

A series of social analyses have pointed to a new sense of inter-dependence of the world economy and a need for a global limit to unchecked growth.[24] An American strategic theology, in the face of new limits to the carrying capacity of the planet, will necessarily involve a relinquishment. Americans already consume unjust shares of the world's energy. However disputed in points, there is truth in analyses which accept a "dependency" theory in economics by arguing that the wealth of rich nations has been achieved, in part, at the expense of the poor nations. Past colonialism and neo-colonial terms of trade and the transfer of technology and capital in the world market create and sustain dependent under-developed economies in the third world. The luxuries of the rich, become internalized necessities, preempt fulfilling basic human needs for the poor majority of the world.

The United States is not itself a poor country. Nor—despite its tolerance of higher levels of poverty than most other advanced industrial nations—are the overwhelming majority of its citizens poor. Liberation theology is a theology for and of the poor. It speaks of the power of the exodus narrative and Jesus the liberator as a dangerous memory of the

Exodus promise of "good news for the poor." Liberation theology cannot directly address America since most Americans do not feel fundamentally oppressed. What might be good news for the rich?

Marie Augusta Neal, in her book of essays *A Socio-Theology of Letting Go,* argues that "what is called for on the part of the non-poor is relinquishment. Relinquishment has always been called for by the Gospel but it has frequently been resisted or else cast in individualistic terms because we have no theology of relinquishment."[25] John Langan, in an essay on "Liberation Theology in a Northern Context," has suggested that the preferred scriptural text for a North American strategic theology will be less the Exodus passages favored by Latin American liberation theologians than 2 Samuel 11:12 where Nathan confronts the unjust King David with the admonition, "Thou art the man!"[26]

Relinquishment need not entail penury, hardship or a new poverty. Relinquishment looks to that simplicity of life which has always been a Gospel ideal. Simplicity was also the foundation for republican virtue, the ideal of America's founding fathers. A theology of relinquishment should not and need not be couched entirely or primarily in negative terms. What we relinquish is an addictive bondage to luxury and consumerism in a conversion to solidarity, community and the full enjoyment, in measure, of the earth's good resources. Relinquishment points to greater freedom to enjoy and celebrate.

No one, of course, is ever authentically converted by negative guilt trips. Approaches to a theology of relinquishment which stress, with Ivan Illich, the search for a convivial society of simplicity and solidarity stand a better chance of gaining resonant response than moralistic appeals simply to "let go."[27] As in any behavior modification, success depends on positive motivation and reinforcement. We relinquish in order to *be*—if not *have*—more. Already movements exist in America which emphasize quality and durability in goods, simple yet convivial modes of solidarity and enjoyment. Church communities, especially Catholic congregations of men and women religious with their tradition of poverty for the sake of the Gospel and the community of goods, can model the positive rewards of a simple, yet joyful and enjoying community.

Thesis Three: An American strategic theology will stress, more than has been usual in American political thought, messianic and eschatological elements in the Scriptures.

In its beginnings, America was born out of messianic expectations that God would do some new mighty act on this new continent. Over time, the promise turned into a celebration of achieved prosperity and power. Much of the early messianism was self-righteous, the rhetoric of ideology rather than reality. Some of it was terribly destructive. Yet, as I argued in

Chapter 5, American civil religion also contains prophetic strands which foresee a promised worldwide order of justice, freedom and equality.

Most recent American political theology has placed less emphasis on messianic and eschatological elements in Scripture than its European and Latin American counterparts. American political theologians grow out of a tradition of pragmatic realism. The doctrines of the orders of creation, sin, and redemption take precedence over eschatology, the sense of a "not-yet" but promised future. Daniel Berrigan and William Stringfellow, following the lead of Jacques Ellul, stand out among American contemporaries writing on politics with their stress on apocalyptic and eschatological imagery.[28]

There are dangers, of course, in an over-emphasis on eschatology. The "not-yet" can fail to find correlation with the "already-always" fulfillment of promises in Jesus, the Christ. Eschatology can eventuate in a sterile "eschatological proviso" which becomes, in principle, impatient with every status quo. This could militate against concrete utopias which envision "making the hope for history's fulfillment truly historical."[29] It could also pervert the Gospel into pure denunciation without its corresponding annunciation.

Ultimately, symbols of eschatology need to be seen alongside the other primal Christian symbols: God, Christ, grace, creation, redemption, Church-world, nature-grace, grace-sin, revelation, faith, hope, love, word-sacrament, cross-resurrection-incarnation.[30] There is a legitimate sense, for example, despite its possible ideological misuse, to the doctrine of orders of creation—fragile structures of civility, community, relatively undistorted communication, solidarity—which deserve nurturance, preservation and support rather than rejection or denouncement.

On the other hand, the eschatological modes of thought ingredient in political and liberation theology remind us that the messianic promises still lie in the future. They balance the Christian already-always fulfillment in Christ with the equally Christian not-yet. They can help to jog our imaginations into the construction of alternative scenarios, concrete utopias and new visions of what American life, culture and society could be. They force us to be honest by going through a methodological suspicion of the status quo.

I suggested in Chapter 4 that eschatology will need to be balanced by a sense of providence by which we discern the concretely possible and demanded appropriate response to our particular time and situation. Nevertheless, very few American political theologians do justice to eschatology. Few experiment with that utopian imagination which is more "the creation of the artist than the engineer."[31] Is there not a place, also in American theology, for the dangerous, even subversive, memory of Jesus the crucified and liberated one? Is there not also room for rehearsing the memory of suffering—the suffering of native Americans, blacks and countless working-class people on whose labor—and backs—this land has been built? It is possible to translate these eschatological themes of Metz's political theology into an American idiom without falling prey to the politically sterile "negative dialectics" of the Frankfurt School on which Metz bases much of his theology.[32]

In a profound sense, all of politics is about hope. An American retrieval of a sense of hope premised on the messianic and eschatological promises of the Gospel will remind us of the fundamental source of hope in the political arena. Ultimately, American failures flow from the narrowness of our cultural vision, the exclusivity of our concerns, a failure of hope. Religion is the substance of every culture. It will be key, as I argued in Chapter 9, for a rebirth of a hopeful vision for America, once again but in a transformed way, the original vision of America as a beacon of freedom.

Thesis Four: In America a strategic theology will concentrate on the twin symbols of freedom and fairness.

Liberty and fairness are resonant and deeply rooted American symbols of self-understanding. No political program will be successful which does not appeal to them. America has always boasted of itself, often self-righteously, as "the land of the free." One reason that concern for civil liberties is so keen in America is this deeply engrained sense of America as a place and protector of freedom. Like every symbol, freedom is ambiguous. Liberty can become synonymous with license. Liberty, as Anatole France once put it, can mean the sovereign but cynical "equality" under the law which allows the rich and the poor to sleep at night on a park bench (the one can do no other!). Liberty can—as so often in American usage—become the enemy of solidarity and the promoter of an alienating atomistic individualism.

Nevertheless, as Delwin Brown argues in a recent book which weds the American philosophic resources of process thought with liberation theology, a liberated environment constitutes an absolutely necessary prerequisite of a liberated life. Brown points to two poles of freedom, creativity and contextuality. Sin is the refusal of freedom. It takes two forms, pride and sensuality. "In a theology of freedom where freedom is viewed as contextual creativity, pride is the denial of freedom's contextual side."[33] The denial of limits is destructive. American refusal to accept a new context of global inter-dependence is, quite simply, the sin of pride. American efforts at one-sided autonomy is a sign of the denial of genuine human freedom.

Sensuality is the denial of responsibility, "the self's denial of its unique powers, its claim to be, like the animals, without responsibility."[34] Brown asserts:

> In a factual sense, we are the enemies of freedom. We wish that we had never settled into these comfortable structures of inhumanity, although they grew out of our own wills, but now that

we are here we do not move beyond them to a new form of social and economic organization where freedom and justice are more nearly one. St. Augustine said that we willingly enter the bondage wherein we unwillingly find ourselves. It is also true that we *willingly remain* in the bondage wherein we unwillingly find ourselves. We wish we were not here, but we choose to stay.[35]

A theology of freedom impels us to see how freedom is of a piece. For the universally loving God of Judaism and Christianity, the source of freedom, wills and lures toward the extension of freedom. "The experience of freedom implies the extension of freedom everywhere, in whatever form it is lacking. That is the obligation of the kingdom of freedom. The free community is free*ing.*"[36] As the Scriptures remind us, the one who has been liberated will remember that liberation and thus will be liberat*ing.*

A theology of freedom will help us to see that in relinquishment what we are letting go of is our bondage to consumerism, cruel individualism and modes of economic and social life which stifle community, a personal sense of effective initiative, participation and equal justice. There is no sure way to keep the primordial American symbol of freedom from being abused for idelogical purposes. Such is the fate of every symbol. We can, however, probe that symbol deeply, as Delwin Brown does, to find an authentic sense of America as the land of the free. John Courtney Murray, Catholicism's most American theologian, sensed the centrality of the symbol of freedom when he chose to focus his thought on liberty. He also expanded, beyond tactical provincialism, the sense of freedom to a worldwide dimension by insisting that, "in the present moment of history, the freedom of the people of God is inseparably linked with the freedom of the peoples of the world."[37]

The second symbol central to an American strategic theology will be justice as fairness. In his widely influential book *A Theory of Justice,* philosopher John Rawls claims that he is primarily making explicit, at the level of philosophical principle and argument, the intuitive sense of justice by which Americans make ethical judgments. They understand justice to involve procedural fairness.[38] Rawls' theory of justice, it will be remembered, contains two basic principles of justice. In the first, Rawls asserts a principle of basic equal liberties for all. His second principle, an equality principle, stipulates that fairness provides that "social and economic inequalities are to be arranged so that they are both (a) to the greatest benefit of the least advantaged and (b) attached to positions open to all under conditions of fair equality of opportunity."[39]

Rawls' theory of justice has been much reviewed, debated and contested. Some see in it a continuation of atomistic individualism. Some claim it to be a WASP rather than an inclusive American ethic. Still others feel that his lexical ordering of the two principles of justice exalts liberty to the detriment of equality. Be it noted, however, that Rawls restricts his principle of liberty to *basic* liberties which are enumerated as the equal right to vote, eligibility for public office, freedom of speech and assembly, liberty of conscience, freedom of thought, the right to hold personal property, and freedom from arbitrary arrest and seizure. Rather pointedly, Rawls excludes economic freedoms such as the freedom to own productive property, freedom of contract, freedom to appropriate what one has produced, and freedom to inherit or to leave one's possessions to persons of one's choice. These latter do not constitute, for Rawls, instances of basic liberty.

Rawls has been accused of providing a set of bourgeois principles to justify capitalism. He denies this strongly in an essay, "Fairness to Goodness," in which he contends that there are arguments which, if true, would lead to the conclusion that capitalism and justice are incompatible.[40] Building on Rawlsian theory, Robert Amdur has formulated three such arguments:

1. The Rawlsian principles of justice would require some sort of socialism if the stability of a well-ordered society could be achieved in no other way.

2. The principles of justice would require some sort of socialism if the self-respect of the worst-off could be maintained in no other way, or if the fair value of liberty could be protected in no other way, or if fair equality of opportunity could be achieved in no other way.

3. Assuming that capitalism and socialism are equally acceptable in terms of their effects on self-respect, liberty and equal opportunity, then the principles of justice would require socialism if a socialist economy were capable of providing the worst-off with a higher level of wealth and income than could be provided under any other system.[41]

It is not my purpose in this book to make a case for or against capitalism or socialism. As such both terms are hopeless abstractions. It would be my contention that Catholic social thinking is capable of either a democratic socialist or a restructured capitalist interpretation. It will be important, whatever the principles of justice we adopt, that our theory of justice not preclude, in advance, openness to new imaginative structures to the American economy. Amdur contends that the deep principles of justice which Rawls has formulated, far from being bourgeois ideology, can be satisfied only in a democratic socialist economy. While that conclusion could be legitimately contested, he is on the right track in asserting that Rawls' principles of justice do not simply describe nor prescribe current American economic or political arrangements.

If Rawls is correct in his empirical contention that this formulation of justice as fairness is a distillation of an American intuitive sense of justice as fairness, then Americans intuit that a fair society would take them beyond current economic and political arrangements. In Chapter 4 I argued, in criticizing liberation theology, that the move from eschatology to politics needs to be mediated by a resort to ethics. An American strategic theology will need to link up with some theory of justice, such as Rawls', if the adjudication of conflicting claims is not to remain wholly abstract or rhetorical. Rawls' theory has thus far withstood most of the complaints raised against it. Its virtue is that it is radicated, he claims, in the American intuition of justice as fairness. It is also tied to the American penchant to see justice as procedural as well as substantive justice, following legal metaphors. It is capable of application beyond the nation-state to issues of world order.[42] No theory of justice derived from countries which do not share the common law tradition of equity, impartiality and procedural fairness will resonate with Americans.

My main contention in this thesis is that an American strategic theology, utilizing primordial American symbols of freedom and fairness, can go beyond the justification of the status quo to pursue alternative political, economic and social policies, structures and systems. The twin, strong symbols of freedom and fairness will play a central role in making that argument.

Thesis Five: An American strategic theology will assess both American strengths and weaknesses. It will look to the shadow side of American realities.

In the preceding chapter, I indicated that American pragmatism includes crucial ambiguities. It can encourage tactical provincialism by taking on problems piecemeal. It makes a holistic social analysis more difficult to attain. On the other hand, as I argued in Chapter 4, the peculiar genius of the social-ethical tradition in America has been its ability to make particular social proposals and to suggest among genuinely optional courses of moral action those which might be judged morally approvable. It has also paid attention to the historical character of ethical issues—why certain things are judged to be bad in context and what concrete proposals are necessary to make them better.[43] It would be a mistake, despite the ambiguities in the American tradition of pragmatism and with legitimate efforts to correct for its bias, to lose sight of the advantages in the American pragmatic temperament. Tackling issues piecemeal and *ad hoc* allows for greater tentativeness and readiness for experiment. It remains agnostic and humble about claims to see the whole. It avoids what Martin Luther King decried as "the paralysis of analysis."

In Chapter 9 I appealed to Wilson Carey McWilliams' study, *The Idea of Fraternity in America.*[44] McWilliams claims that Americans have been much better in preserving the First Enlightenment ideals of liberty, justice and equality than in furthering fraternity or solidarity. In that chapter, I argued that American religious resources constitute our most potent cultural source for redressing American individualism, the eclipse of community and American isolationist tendencies toward self-sufficiency. An American strategic theology will attempt both a creative retrieval of elements of the American tradition as well as a healthy suspicion about the shadow side of that tradition.

Thesis Six: An American strategic theology will recognize that you cannot do all of your politics from political theology.

Catholic theology affords a rightful autonomy to the secular. It knows, in its doctrine of political prudence, that much of political wisdom is the distillation of concrete experience, custom and practice. The achievements of "secular" community and civility are goods in their own right, not mere utilities as favorable environments for the Church. Without falling into a mindless "law and order" mentality, Catholic thought respects the function of law in building a stable community of trust and undistorted communication.

Much of American politics simply grew up out of tested procedures, styles of communication, channels of influence. Corruption there has been, a-plenty and in the highest places. At its best, however, the success of the American political system has depended on a certain amount of ticket-balancing, trade-off of interests and, even, patronage for friends and supporters. Much of politics depends on established routine ways of aggregating demands and supplying responsive remedies to demands and in trusted paths of insuring communication ("off the record"). Without political compromise and a measure of bi-partisanship, the American political system will not work.

It is perhaps not necessary to articulate what should be obvious. It is impossible to do all of our politics from political theology alone. Political prudence, not theology, stumbled upon a two-party system, Robert's Rules of Order, the common law, the judicial system of precedent and review. Politics, in classic Catholic views, is less a science than a wisdom, the art of the possible, of compromise as well as ideal justice, a creative artistry achieving community out of often stark plurality. An American strategic theology will recognize and respect distilled political wisdom, even customary procedures, and work through and with them to seek greater equality and justice. The genuine achievement of American procedural justice is that it can be used to pursue substantive aims.[45] American theology will also recognize the genuine pluralism of American society and the dazzling achievement of political consensus and community despite that pluralism. It will know and proclaim the rightful province of the political and the limits of theology. Ultimately, no theology can supplant political prudence forged in experience as the highest virtue of the political society in its own sphere. An American political theology will avoid Platonic temptations to construct ideal political orders unsuited to a nation's limited political genius, mores and customs. Eschatology challenges a putative "prudence" to move beyond conservative ideologies which defend an unfair status quo when genuine and more just alternatives are available. Authentic political prudence, in its turn, resists the language of eschatology when it is a romantic and unrealistic rhetoric. It knows how the best can be the enemy of the good. It celebrates the homely achievement of an improved "rough justice." It knows too its rightful claim that, at its most authentic, politics is a generator of hope and justice in a community, an instrument for the kingdom of God.

Thesis Seven: An American strategic theology will contain about it a note of tentativeness and reformability.

In the last analysis, no revolutionary pattern from other countries—not the French, Russian, Chinese, Cuban or Nicaraguan revolutions—will fit America. We are the product of a unique revolution of liberty—an ambiguously conservative revolution respectful of inherited law, customs and civil procedures which nevertheless extended the revolution to include liberties for all. That revolution eventuated in a political system that has withstood the tests of time longer than any other regime, with the exception of Britain, in history. Moreover, we do not have any historic precedents for the substantial transformation of advanced industrial capitalist societies. Our task is not to copy other models, especially models devised for third world countries which are not advanced industrial capitalist societies. Although development and modernity often seem to us like an "iron cage," we do not know foolproof ways to unlock that cage and unleash our creative imaginations to reconceive an American sense of solidarity and inter-dependence with the world community and a more deep-reaching liberty, justice, equality and solidarity at home. Yet, that remains our task.

I want to conclude this chapter and this book with the thoughtful remarks of John Langan about the contours of a North American political theology:

> American Christians need a theology that hears the call of Christ in the cry of the world's poor and sees the face of those of other races and cultures. But in the American context, this will have to be a theology of the cross, of burdens patiently shared, of limitations graciously borne and of goods justly distributed. It will have to be a theology that stresses the criticism of earthly power and the service that human institutions owe to human need. It will have to be a theology of self-criticism and self-giving, not of self-assertion and self-defense. But it will also have to be based on self-esteem and not on self-hatred. It must be a universal theology that moves beyond dialectical tensions and social conflicts to reconciliation and charity; but it must also be authentically American, acknowledging both the grandeur of American accomplishment and the misery of American racism and social blindness. It will have to be a theology that is willing to listen to the cry of the world's oppressed and needy and that is also willing to speak out on the uses and abuses of American affluence and power. It will have to be a theology of response and responsi-

bility. It will be a theology that responds to the various forms of liberation theology rather than a form of liberation theology itself.[46]

NOTES

1. Cf. Joe Holland and Peter Henriot, *Social Analysis: Linking Faith and Justice* (Washington, D.C.: Center of Concern, 1980), pp. 3–12.

2. *The Context of our Ministries: Working Papers* (Washington, D.C.: Jesuit Conference, 1981).

3. Walter Rauschenbusch, *Christianity and the Social Crisis* (New York: Macmillan, 1907); H. Richard Niebuhr, *The Kingdom of God in America* (New York: Harper, 1959); Reinhold Neibuhr *et al.*, *The Irony of American History* (New York Scribner's, 1952).

4. Note David Tracy's remarks, "What was once considered a major 'failure' of American theology by European commentators and their American followers— viz., its practical character—is now largely ignored rather than reclaimed by many recent American 'political' and 'liberation' theologians in favor of denouncing the 'academic' and 'theoretical' character of American theology," in *The Analogical Imagination* (New York: Crossroad, 1981), pp. 93–94.

5. I am following here the account of Thomas E. Clarke S.J., "Methodology," in *The Context of Our Ministries*, pp. 6–9.

6. For these six traits cf. Andrew Greeley, "Is a North American Theology Possible?" in Daniel Flaherty, ed., *Toward a North American Theology: Working Papers* (Chicago: Loyola University Press, 1981), limited edition.

7. Greeley, *op cit.*, does not deal, in his short chapter, with any issues of discontinuity. He and his fellow contributors to the Flaherty collection tell a story of American experience that Hispanics, blacks, I. F. Stone, Dorothy Day or Robert Coles might find unrecognizable. The failure of this collection, besides the fact that it does not relate American realities to a wider world order, is its exclusion of too many authentic voices from the narrative. The indigenous American radical tradition in American labor or the various American populist traditions nowhere gains a hearing.

8. Thomas E. Clarke, *op cit.*, p. 7.

9. For some examples of questions to guide the recounting of experiences cf. Holland and Henriot, *op cit.*, pp. 42–43, and Edmundo Rodriguez, "Practical Methodology," in *Context of Our Ministries*, pp. 85–86.

10. Holland and Henriot, *op. cit.*, p. 3.

11. *The New York Times*, Aug. 14, 1981, p. A8. Italics mine.

12. For the claim that Weber was a methodological individualist cf. the chapter on methodological individualism in Stephen Lukes, *Individualism* (New York: Oxford University Press, 1973).

13. For one attempt to show the correlation between particular styles of social science and corresponding styles in theology cf. William W. Everett and T. J. Bachmeyer, *Disciplines in Transformation: A Guide to Theology and the Behavioral Sciences* (Washington, D.C.: University Press of America, 1979).

14. Holland and Henriot, *op cit.*, p. 7.

15. A classic case for value-neutrality in social science is Max Weber's "Science as a Vocation," in Hans Gerth and C. Wright Mills, eds., *From Max Weber* (New York: Oxford University Press, 1958).

16. For the functional specializations in Lonergan cf. *Method in Theology* (New York: Seabury, 1972). The sense of culture and society as a "text" is found in Clifford Geertz, *The Interpretation of Culture* (New York: Basic Books, 1973). My longer treatment about ways in which social science is or is not value-neutral can be found in "Theology and Sociology," *Proceedings of the Catholic Theological Society of America,* 1977, pp. 52–72.

17. For an analysis of the ways in which Marx's hypotheses represent genuine social science conclusions cf. Lewis Coser, "In Praise of Marx," *Dissent,* Vol. 27, No. 3 (Summer 1980), pp. 335–340.

18. I am indebted to Michael Lacey, director of the American Studies program at the Woodrow Wilson Center, Washington, D.C., for the suggestion that the social gospelers turned to a relatively unhermeneutical notion of science as a way to finesse any conflict of interpretations. Albion Small and Richard Ely, founders, respectively, of The American Sociological Association and The American Association of Economics, were both very close to the social gospelers.

19. Professor James Steward of St. Olav's College is currently conducting a study of the use of social science in the works of liberation theologians.

20. Holland and Henriot, *op. cit.,* p. 12.

21. Clarke, *op. cit.,* p. 7.

22. For an argument that the symbol, "the Church as sacrament of Christ *and* of the world" subsumes the notion of the Church as mission, cf. David Tracy, *op. cit.,* p. 442.

23. Cf. *Justice in the World* in Joseph Gremillion, ed., *The Gospel of Justice and Peace* (Maryknoll: Orbis, 1976), p. 518.

24. Cf. *inter alia,* Ronald Müller, "Poverty Is the Product," *Foreign Policy,* 13 (Winter 1973–74), pp. 71–103, and the report, *Global 2000* commissioned by President Carter to the Council on Environment and the Department of State (Washington, D.C.: Government Printing Office, 1980).

25. Marie Augusta Neal, *A Socio-Theology of Letting Go* (New York: Paulist Press, 1977), p. 104.

26. John Langan, "Liberation Theology in a Northern Context," *America,* Vol. 140, No. 3 (Jan. 27, 1979), pp. 46–49.

27. Cf. Ivan Illich, *Tools for Conviviality* (New York: Harper and Row, 1973).

28. Cf. Daniel Berrigan, *Uncommon Prayer: A Book of Psalms* (New York: Seabury, 1978); Jacques Ellul, *The Politics of God and the Politics of Man* (Grand Rapids: Eerdmans, 1972); William Stringfellow, *An Ethic for Christians and Other Aliens in a Strange Land* (Waco: Word, 1973).

29. Citation from Delwin Brown, *To Set at Liberty: Christian Faith and Human Freedom* (Maryknoll: Orbis, 1981), p. 123.

30. For this listing cf. Tracy, *op. cit.,* p. 373.

31. Delwin Brown, *op. cit.,* p. 129.

32. For Metz' use of eschatology cf. *Faith, History and Society* (New York: Crossroad, 1980). For negative dialectics cf. Theodor Adorno and Max Horkheimer, *Dialectic of the Enlightenment* (New York: Herder and Herder, 1979). I judge the Frankfurt school to have been culturally fecund but politically sterile especially because negative dialectics made it difficult ever to affirm any concrete political course of action.

33. Delwin Brown, *op. cit.*, p. 67.

34. *Ibid.*, p. 70.

35. *Ibid.*, p. 81.

36. *Ibid.*, p. 94.

37. John Courtney Murray, *The Problem of Religious Freedom* (Westminster: Newman Press, 1965), p. 70.

38. John Rawls, *A Theory of Justice* (Cambridge: Harvard University Press, 1971).

39. *Ibid.*, p. 81.

40. John Rawls, "Fairness to Goodness," *Philosophical Review* 84 (October 1975), p. 546.

41. Robert Amdur, "Rawls and His Radical Critics: The Problem of Equality," in *Dissent,* Vol. 27, No. 3 (Summer 1980), p. 333.

42. For an argument that Rawls' difference principle which states that social and economic inequalities should be arranged so that they are to the greatest benefit of the least advantaged should be applied globally cf. Charles R. Beitz, *Political Theory and International Relations* (Princeton: Princeton University Press, 1980).

43. Cf. James Gustafson, *Theology and Christian Ethics* (Philadelphia: Westminster Press, 1974), p. 188.

44. Cf. Wilson Carey McWilliams, *The Idea of Fraternity in America* (Berkeley: University of California Press, 1973).

45. The case for using the law to subvert unjust structures is strongly made in Illich, *op. cit.,* pp. 104–05.

46. Langan, *op. cit.,* p. 48.